ArtScroll History Series®

Rabbi Nosson Scherman / Rabbi Meir Zlotowitz

General Editors

Published by
Mesorah Publications, ltd

Voice of Truth

The life and eloquence of
RABBI SHOLOM SCHWADRON
the unforgettable Maggid of Jerusalem

Adapted from the Hebrew Kol Chotzeiv by
Libby Lazewnik

FIRST EDITION
First Impression ... March 2000
Second Impression ... April 2000

Published and Distributed by
MESORAH PUBLICATIONS, LTD.
4401 Second Avenue / Brooklyn, N.Y 11232

Distributed in Europe by
J. LEHMANN HEBREW BOOKSELLERS
20 Cambridge Terrace
Gateshead, Tyne and Wear
England NE8 1RP

Distributed in Israel by
SIFRIATI / A. GITLER
10 Hashomer Street
Bnei Brak 51361

Distributed in Australia and New Zealand by
GOLDS BOOK & GIFT SHOP
36 William Street
Balaclava 3183, Vic., Australia

Distributed in South Africa by
KOLLEL BOOKSHOP
Shop 8A Norwood Hypermarket
Norwood 2196, Johannesburg, South Africa

ARTSCROLL HISTORY SERIES®
VOICE OF TRUTH
© Copyright 2000, by MESORAH PUBLICATIONS, Ltd.
4401 Second Avenue / Brooklyn, N.Y. 11232 / (718) 921-9000 / www.artscroll.com

---

ISBN:
1-57819-500-4 (hard cover)
1-57819-501-2 (paperback)

Typography by CompuScribe at ArtScroll Studios, Ltd.
Printed in the United States of America by Noble Book Press Corp.
Bound by Sefercraft, Quality Bookbinders, Ltd., Brooklyn N.Y. 11232

Table of Contents

Acknowledgements   7

1   **The Difficulties of Life**   11
Tears by the Well / The Bitterness of Orphanhood / Scoring a Goal/
A Carton of Leben

2   **At the In-Laws**   28
A Match Is Made / Guidelines of the Marriage / The Good Days / The
Last Spoon / The Books / Toras Chaim / Hidden Practices / A Whole
Egg? / "May Your Desire Be …" / Clothed in Glory / *Chametz!* / And
She Will Laugh on the Last Day / R' Chaim Leib Tells a Story / The
Essence of a Man

3   **At Home**   56
Night Watch / A Special Kiss / Letting Go / Epidemic / Open House /
One Seder Night / Cats, Cats, Everywhere / A Different Kind of Guest
/ Switching Gears / Home Talk / Around the Table / Minute by Minute
/ Joy of Life / Without Words / A Personal Conversation / More
Eloquent than Words / The Rebbetzin: Native Wisdom / His Mother

4   **The Maggid's World**   96
Parting / The *Shtreimel* / In Europe and America / R' Sholom on
Sunday / Always Scrupulous / A Lighthouse / Lettuce and Water /
Yichud / The "pushka" from Jerusalem / Danger? I Won't Eat! / Sweet
Symbols / Fall — and Rise!

5   **The Voice of Truth**   128
Let's Dance! / Searching / Torn Shirts / A Burning Flame / Diligence /
I Learned It from You! / A Breadth of Knowledge / *Magen Avraham* /
Your Mother's Teaching / *Mishnayos* and R' Elyah Lopian / Labor of a
Lifetime / *Bitul Torah* / "I Want to Serve" / They Learned Torah! /
Around the Maharsham's Table: R' Sholom on His Grandfather / Three
Tractates / He Didn't Feel a Thing / Saying Good-bye

6   **Of Good Character**   162
To the Last Ounce of Strength / Forgive Me! / "I'm Sorry" / Who Was
Right? / The Mission / A Pocketful of Seeds / The Steipler / Humility /
Mixed Messages / I Was Mistaken / *Ahavas Yisrael* / Love of *Chesed* /
The Midnight Feast / First and Last / To Build the *Beis HaMikdash* /
Pollution / Fifty Pairs of Slippers / Like Old Friends / The Broken Bottle
/ Never Enough! / Kosher Tears / Up the Hill / A Night Among Nights
/ Magnificent *Middos* — Neither In nor Out / Carrying the Burden /
Your Brother

7   Refined Silver   200
All for the Public / Payment / I Never Asked / A Potent Parable /
Making an Effort at Making a Living / It's Not Mine / Charity / One
Holiday Eve / The Many Faces of *Tzedakah* / Kosher Money / I.O.U. /
He Couldn't Sleep / Dollars and Sense / Standoff

8   Small Stories About a Great Man   225
In a Dream / I Am Ready / The Scent of Spirituality / Honoring the
Torah / Reverence / "I'm Getting Out!" / *Emunas Chachamim* /
Changed Plans / A Widow's Pleas / Two Dances / Words of Wisdom /
Don't Make Me Rich / "Not a Chance!" / Halachah and *"Frumkeit"* /
Those Who Fear Him / Scrupulous in Every Detail / Questions / What
to Do? Just Stop! / The Sure Route / Strong as a Lion / To Stand and to
Serve

9   A Penetrating Voice   269
Into the Lion's Den / Explosion / One Newspaper Reporter / Heart to
Heart / "My Meyer'ke" / The Fire

10 Chevron Yeshivah   295
The Meeting / In the Chevron Furnace / Before the Shofar Blew / R'
Sholom's *Mussaf* / The First Time / Emotion / Absence / The Crown of
Kingship / For Our Sins / *Tashlich* / Music / I Should Be / A Chevron
Simchas Torah / Intoxicated with Torah / *Vus Vet Zein Mit Mir?* / En
Route to Brisk / The Rosh Yeshivah's Last Dance / The Voice of Mussar

11 Stormy Times   328
Where is Yossele? / Storm Signals / Drawn Guns in Ein Shemer / A
Rav's Tears / Journey of Fear / Disruptions and Threats / A Public
Outcry / Bullets / First Blood / Rescue / Government Crisis / The
Government Falls / Spokesman / The Chazon Ish and Pe'ilim

12 Summary of a Life   377
Beloved Above and Below / Strong Roots / Early Influences / Petach
Tikvah / On to Chevron / Marriage / Learning and Teaching / A New
Role / A Special Desire / The Rosh Yeshivah / Extracurricular Activities
/ Bending to His Will / Person to Person / A Word to the Wise / R'
Sholom Asks a Question / After the Fact / A Steadfast Goal / Fear of
Falling / Until the Last Minute / *Mein Benkel* / No Change / Know
Him from Afar / Acknowledgments

Acknowledgments

I N THE YEAR FOLLOWING R' SHOLOM'S PASSING, THE MEMbers of his family welcomed us into their homes and their hearts.

While they cautioned us time and again that it would be impossible to present the many facets of R' Sholom in a single book, and though they would not themselves undertake the daunting task of portraying this great man, they did speak with us.

They reminisced. They shared their recollections and impressions. And they conveyed many of the lessons they had learned from R' Sholom. They reflected his *lev tov* – his goodheartedness – in their desire to enable the broader public to appreciate and get to know him.

We gratefully acknowledge the support and assistance of R' Sholom's esteemed son, R' Sholom's daughters and sons-in-law, each of whom is a noted talmid chacham, and to R' Sholom's many grandchildren, all of whom played a role in this endeavor.

In addition to working with R' Sholom's family, we were also privileged to come into contact with many of those closest to him. Some of them described what it was like to interact with him. Others shared first-hand stories. Many shed tears that spoke volumes about R' Sholom and his influence. They are listed at the end of the volume, in the order in which we spoke to them.

In order to avoid offense, we have avoided the use of honorific titles in the book.

We express particular thanks to those of R' Sholom's grandchildren who assisted in collecting and editing the material in this book, and who offered advice and encouragement. We make particular note of R' Yisrael Katzenelenbogen; R' Yaakov Aryeh Ariel, who wrote the entire Hebrew work; R' Sholom's oldest grandson, R' Eliezer Reichman; and R' Meir Stern. May Hashem repay them for their efforts.

We have unbounded appreciation to the noted journalist R' Yisrael Friedman, editor of *Yated Ne'eman's Erev Shabbos* supplement whose advice served as an invaluable guide, and whose incisive mind and good heart played an important role in a good portion of this work.

We extend our best wishes to R' Sholom's son-in-law R' Simcha Nosson Segal, who bears the burden of directing Kollel Daas Torah and Machon Daas Torah. May he blessed with all the best.

Heartfelt thanks are due R' Aryeh Krohn, who offered insightful suggestions based on his close relationship with R' Sholom. This was a relationship that began with R' Sholom being the guest of R' Aryeh's father, R' Avraham Zelig Krohn, during his visits to the United States, and it continued and was nurtured as R' Sholom stayed in R' Aryeh's home in later years.

Above all, we express our unbounded gratitude to He Who is the Source of all. It is only through His gracious kindness that we have merited to publish this work. May it be His will that we are granted the ability to study and teach Torah for many years.

Machon Daas Torah

Adar II 5760

We ask that anyone who has recordings of, knows stories about, or remembers Torah thoughts from R' Sholom kindly forward them to us at:

Machon Daas Torah
P.O. Box 5286
Jerusalem

Voice of Truth

Chapter 1

The Difficulties of Life

I N THE 1920'S, A LACK OF TOYS AND OTHER FORMS OF entertainment forced Jerusalem's youngsters to expend their energy at the local water well. Their mischievous faces held a carefree charm as they ran around the well playing "tag," *peyos* flying in the wind.

Tears by the Well

Sholom, an orphan, spent many long hours by the well. He had no father to summon him home, nor was there any great motivation to hurry home to an empty dinner table. In place of food, he sated himself with play. Like many precocious young boys, he loved to jump and run wild — to give vent to his ebullient, youthful spirit.

But the picture changed for Sholom when the month of Elul came around. Early in the day, his mother would come out to the open square near the well. From that vantage point she would watch her son, a troubled look covering her face.

"Sholom'ke!" she would call. "It's Elul! Even the fish in the sea tremble in fear of Heavenly judgment — and you are just running around?"

Sometimes his mother would stand at the window casting anxious glances at her son, engrossed in his play. "Elul!" she thought. "What will become of the child when he grows up, if he continues with these childish antics? Master of the Universe … !" And a tear would fall from her eye as she pleaded for guidance … and another tear … and yet another tear …

Anyone who has ever heard R' Sholom, many years later, roar out his famous "*ELUL!*" might discern within that mighty cry a trace of his mother's call: "Sholom'ke — Elul!" At the age of 70, R' Sholom remembered that call clearly. Standing before the large crowds assembled to hear him speak, he would tell the story of his mother and the tears she shed for him — and he, too, would weep, his tears mirroring hers.

The forlorn widow's Elul prayer was eventually answered in full measure. The years, with G-d's help, did their job. "Sholom'ke," a gifted child, gradually began to ascend the stairway that leads to the House of Hashem. He moved slowly, step by step, with great labor and a tremendous investment of effort. His spirit and strength of character were astonishing, especially to those who remembered the scenes at the well just a few years earlier. All that youthful physical energy had apparently hidden an incredibly deep wellspring of spiritual energy. Those who knew him began to anticipate the moment when these immense inner resources would join forces with the boy's exceptional diligence in study and his purity of heart.

They were not disappointed.

From the moment that change overtook him, R' Sholom toiled endlessly in Torah. Night became as day for him — a fresh opportunity for him to submerge himself in his studies. His teachers inspired and encouraged him, and they were careful to nurture his unusual talents. Among these teachers were some of the generation's great Torah scholars: R' Yaakov Katzenelenbogen, R' Eliyahu Dushnitzer, and R' Sholom's best-known mentor, the great R' Leib Chasman.

When the time came for R' Sholom to marry, he already possessed an impressive array of spiritual assets. His mother had been following his spiritual growth with tremendous pride and joy. The unstinting labor he invested, and the unrestrained effort he expended, reminded her of her late husband's extraordinary diligence. The Talmud, after all, tells us that "a son is like an appendage of his father." But even his mother did not recognize the true extent to which her son had risen … until an incident took place by the well.

R' Sholom had been married for several months. He did not spend much time at home, learning Torah from morning till evening at the Ohel Torah *kollel*. At night he studied with his illustrious brother-in-law, R' Shlomo Zalman Auerbach, until 3 in the morning. This arrangement lasted for many months.

One morning, R' Sholom's wife glimpsed a troubled look on her husband's face. "My dear," he said when she questioned him, "you have been hauling buckets to the well morning after morning for several months now. Drawing water is not easy. You have to bend over far and pull up pail after pail. Enough! I will not stand for it any longer. From now on, *I* will draw the water and carry it home. Leave the buckets by the well in the morning; on my way home from shul I will take care of it." Decisively, he ended, "No more drawing water for you. From now on, it's *my* job!"

The young Rebbetzin was stunned. Her mind raced, weighing the issues. On the one hand, she had tried hard until that day never to interfere with her husband's learning or to take any of his precious time away from Torah. On the other hand, perhaps it was wrong for a wife to refuse her husband's wishes. And it *was* very hard work. She gazed at her hands, painfully swollen from the arduous daily task, and was inclined to accept the offer.

Then, suddenly, she knew what her answer must be.

"It is forbidden to let mere physical difficulty on my part interfere in even the slightest way with the growth of a great scholar whose soul thirsts for Torah," she resolved.

R' Sholom, with his keen intuition, divined her thoughts. With uncompromising authority, he declared, "Tomorrow, after *davening*, I will be at the well — and that's that!"

The next morning the Rebbetzin adhered to the plan and left the buckets near the well for R' Sholom to fill. Back home, she waited for her husband to return with the day's supply of water. She waited … and waited. He was surely finished *davening* by this time! Where could he be? Why was it taking him so long to draw water? She made her way to the window which overlooked the street. Her husband was nowhere to be seen.

Then her eyes strayed to the well where she beheld a curious sight. There stood R' Sholom, pen and paper in hand, engrossed in writing. Wondering, she left the house and walked to the well.

"What happened?" she asked her husband, who was still lost in his thoughts and his writing.

Her voice startled R' Sholom. Quickly regaining his composure, he returned the pen to his pocket.

"I forgot to draw the water!" he apologized. "A *chiddush* suddenly occurred to me — the answer to a difficult question I was grappling with last night. I was afraid I'd forget my train of thought, so I decided to write it down immediately."

"Where is the drawing pail?" the Rebbetzin asked curiously.

"Oh!" Slowly, R' Sholom was beginning to focus on something other than his Torah thoughts. "The pail must have slipped from my hand as I was taking out my pen to write. I must have let go of the rope for a second and lost it."

Tears began to stream down the Rebbetzin's face. They were not tears of sorrow over the loss of a costly bucket, forever gone in the depths of the well. They were tears of joy over the knowledge that she had merited marrying such a magnificent scholar, a man who could not stop thinking about Torah even while drawing water.

R' Sholom in a common pose — standing, pen and paper in hand, writing a Torah thought

R' Sholom also wiped away a tear — of regret and pain for causing his wife anguish.

There by the well, their tears mingled.

R' Sholom was to remember that moment all his life. Sometimes, when he wished to demonstrate what it means to study with persistence and diligence, he would say, "Once we used to *really* learn! A Torah thought once occurred to me while I was drawing water, and I simply forgot where I was."

When R' Sholom's mother heard of the incident, she stood up and lifted her eyes heavenward. This was the moment she had striven for all her life. Her hands covered her eyes as the joyous tears flowed. She recalled how she had wept by the well over her little boy's wild antics so many years before.

Ecstatically, she thought, "This is the child I prayed for!" (*I Shmuel* 1:27). And once again, old tears mingled with the new.

The Bitterness of Orphanhood

THE AUTUMN SUN WAS SHINING WARMLY AS YOUNG SHOLOM'KE made his way home from *cheder*. Not far from his home in Jerusalem's Beis Yisrael neighborhood, several men unexpectedly stopped him in the street. Sholom'ke did not understand why they were blocking his way.

"Come with us," they said. "It is better for you not to go home right now."

They led him off to a side street and began to pat his head compassionately. One of them slipped a large candy into the boy's pocket. They had not taken more than a few steps when another man suddenly interrupted their progress, declaring unceremoniously, "Don't take him too far. The father is dead. He will have to say *Kaddish*, you know!"

"Dead?" a bewildered Sholom'ke shouted, trying to break free of the strangers' hold. "Who's dead? Where is my father? Take me to my father!"

"Why did he have to say that out loud?" the men muttered angrily to each other. "He could have whispered quietly to us!"

Desperate to get the situation under control, they turned to the thrashing boy. "Don't worry. There's another big candy waiting for you!"

But Sholom'ke did not hear a word they said. He had won his freedom and was running home as fast as his legs could carry him.

The house was already filled with rabbis and scholars who had gathered to recite *Psalms* near the shrouded body of R' Yitzchak Schwadron.

"Tatty! Tatty!" Sholom sobbed. One of those assembled picked him up and patted his head. The voices mingled in mournful cacophony. Sholom jumped up and ran from room to room until he found his mother. He fell into her arms, crying, "Tatty! Tatty!"

"He understands very well," one of the neighbors murmured, her eyes swollen with weeping. "He understands *too* well!"

"Tatty!" The little boy stamped his foot in frustration. "I love you so much!"

During the funeral, the echo of his *Kaddish* reverberated throughout the neighborhood. Sholom was about to embark on a new course in life.

The date was 19 Marcheshvan, 5680 (1919). Sholom was 7 years old.

⌒⌒

The candy Sholom'ke had received that bitter afternoon was the last he ever tasted in his life. From that day on, the bereaved Schwadron household became a place of grinding poverty. The years of Sholom's youth were very difficult ones.

During the long winter nights, young Sholom Mordechai could not make up his mind whether to think about his father or about his stomach aching with hunger. The pain and deprivation of orphanhood affected him greatly and left a lasting impression upon his soul — an impression that stayed with him till the end of his days. But it did not embitter him or give rise to a troubled spirit.

His was a youth filled with struggle and inner turmoil. There were the trials of hunger to contend with on the one hand, and on the other a new world full of difficult challenges. Sholom felt bereft and alone. Still, despite all the pain, his soul found the enormous inspiration to grow and develop.

Rare were the moments, years later, when R' Sholom chose to reveal to others the inner feelings of his youth. The following incident took place approximately 30 years later, when R' Sholom was serving on the staff of Yeshivah Tiferes Tzvi. The story is retold by the subject of the story himself:

R' Sholom as a young boy, wearing the suit and hat provided by the Diskin Orphan Home

While I was studying in Tiferes Tzvi, my father passed away. I found myself orphaned at the tender age of 15. My mother was left a penniless widow who, in addition to the worry of supporting her family, had the additional burden of marrying off several of her older children who had become engaged before my father's untimely death. The sadness in the family was intense, the sense of bereavement overwhelming. A perpetual darkness seemed to settle over our household. We had no one from whom to seek guidance or financial support.

It was only natural that the weight of the family's expectations should eventually fall upon me. When I turned 16, I was fit and able-bodied, capable of going out and earning a few extra lira to bring home. I found a job in a Jerusalem printing shop, assisting the workers on the second shift from 5 in the afternoon until 9 at night. Since this schedule required a two-hour absence from my study schedule in yeshivah, I brought the matter to the attention of the *Rosh Yeshivah*, R' Michel Shlapovarsky who, understanding the lack of alternatives, reluctantly gave his approval. I became a print-shop worker.

It is difficult to describe the feelings of a young boy, raised and nurtured in the yeshivah study hall in an atmosphere of purity and fear of Heaven, suddenly finding himself in the company of boorish workers who have never set foot in a *beis midrash*. Irresistibly, he finds himself picking up their mannerisms and becoming influenced by them in subtle ways. Still, I stuck with the job for an entire winter. My friends at yeshivah often asked me about my absence during certain hours, and wondered why I always had ink stains on my hands. Embarrassed, I dodged the questions and kept my secret.

One day at the end of Adar, R' Sholom, the *mashgiach*, called me over. He asked me to accompany him home at the end of the morning learning session, which concluded after *Minchah*.

At age 16

We walked together along Yellin, Yechezkel, and Strauss Streets, to the corner of HaNevi'im Street. There we paused near the wall of Bikur Cholim Hospital. Our conversation continued on that corner for some time.

R' Sholom revealed some of his innermost feelings about his youth. He described being orphaned at the age of 7, his suffering through hunger and deprivation, and his years of homelessness, some of them spent in an orphanage. He told of his feelings of crisis as a maturing youth and his sense of being victimized in whichever framework he found himself. As he spoke, the smile gradually left his face and was replaced by an expression of anguish. His story transported him back to those days of pain and misery. He was carried back to the years when he was forced to struggle alone against the temptations of the street. They were days of dramatic ups and downs, of conflict and tribulations, of personal failure and triumphs — days when, through great effort and perseverance, he found the strength to push past the various temptations and remain firmly implanted on the path of Torah.

When he finished his story, R' Sholom said, "By leaving yeshivah and going out to work, I could have improved my financial situation tenfold. But how would I have turned out in that environment? I would have developed into a worker or an artisan, and perhaps even counted myself among the ranks of the community's prestigious and prosperous families.

"But is this really where our duty lies? Is this the ideal for which we are meant to strive? Is this our goal in life? Thank G-d," he concluded, "that I remained in the world of Torah, and have become what I am."

At that point, R' Sholom fell into a lengthy silence. I gazed at him with admiration, lifting my youthful eyes toward this giant of Torah and master of inspiration who had managed to beat a path to the summit of Torah knowledge through unstinting toil and effort. Anxiety about my own path in life seized me.

Suddenly, he roused me from my thoughts. With a penetrating glance directly into my eyes, he said, "Do you really want to grow up to be a laborer or craftsman? You should know, my dear boy, that many people have suffered the pain of orphanhood and still managed to succeed beyond anyone's wildest dreams. That is why I decided to speak with you and advise you to separate yourself from the new path on which you have embarked."

In the Slobodka Yeshivah, Chevron, 1932

R' Sholom did not wait to hear my opinion or to see my reaction to his words. With his vigorous parting handshake, he turned around and continued on his way toward his home in Sha'arei Chesed.

I returned home full of reflections and doubts. I had actually begun to enjoy my time in the print shop, with its professional work and creative atmosphere. But R' Sholom's description of his own childhood experiences had a powerful effect on me. I could almost see his penetrating eyes glaring at me over the printing press, and hear his voice saying, "Young man, this is no place for you!"

Several months passed before I took leave of the course that had been charted for my future, and returned to full-time Torah study.

When I look back and think of those people who helped shape my life and develop my invincible love for Torah, I consider R' Sholom to be the number one influence in my life. I feel an extraordinary debt of gratitude toward him!

THERE ARE MANY WHO OWE THEIR THANKS TO R' SHOLOM FOR his guidance. With his keen insight and wisdom, R' Sholom fre-

Scoring a Goal

quently helped others in their personal lives. One particular story comes to mind:

The period of time following the establishment of the State of

Israel was spiritually trying. Hundreds of souls were swept away in a powerful tide by the new spirit of openness, which offered so many alluring — but ultimately empty — alternatives. Together with a group of other Torah scholars, R' Sholom organized gatherings for young men and established a framework of Torah study for them.

One of the boys who had been regularly attending the night classes missed several sessions. R' Sholom decided it was his duty to try to locate the boy and restore his love for Torah.

He knocked on the boy's door, and the young man appeared in the doorway. Before long, the two were engaged in a riveting conversation.

"Hello, my dear friend!" R' Sholom began. "We've been missing you lately. We thought you might be ill, or that something might be troubling you."

"No, Rebbi, thank G-d, I'm fine. I still love to study the Talmud — I really enjoy it. It's just that I'm not able to attend classes this week. Next week I'll be back into the swing of things."

"What has happened?" R' Sholom asked curiously. "Is there someone in the family who is not well?"

"No, Heaven forbid. I have a certain personal reason that's keeping me from class this week. But, as I said, I plan to return — with enthusiasm — next week."

"I am just curious. What is the disturbance that has managed to occupy you at exactly the same hour of the evening when our class is held?"

"It's — it's hard for me to say. It's embarrassing."

"Don't be embarrassed. You can tell me; I won't be angry. Tell me at least the gist of the problem, if it's not too personal. What is it that's so important for you, that lasts exactly one week and will be over by next week?"

Yielding to R' Sholom's coaxing, the young man decided to confide in him. "I will tell you the truth. The soccer championship is on this week. Game time conflicts with the hour of the evening *shiur*. I must watch the soccer games! I love following the game and its players."

R' Sholom considered this for a few moments. Then he lifted his eyes, and they were sympathetic, filled with wisdom and an uncanny grasp of human nature. "My dear friend, I hear what you are saying, and I understand it completely. But I am interested in knowing the secret of this game that you find so captivating. Please explain how the game works."

Hesitantly at first, the young man said, "If the Rebbi really wants to know, I'll explain." The talk began to take on a friendly, intimate tone as R' Sholom sat down. He listened to the young man, now quite comfortable, begin to describe his favorite pastime. "You see, the players are divided into two teams. There is a large, netted goal at either end of the playing field. If you had to put the whole idea of the game into a nutshell, you could say that whoever manages to score a point, by kicking the ball into the goal, feels immense satisfaction over his accomplishment. The moment that ball flies through the goal is the most exciting part of the game!"

Never in his wildest dreams would that young man have imagined himself sitting and talking about soccer with R' Sholom. He sat back, smiling. R' Sholom continued asking questions, pretending to have difficulty grasping the game.

"What is the great skill involved in kicking the ball into a goal?" he asked. "Come with me now — I'll show you how I can kick 20 balls into that net without any effort at all!"

The young man laughed. "Oh, I forgot to explain that part. "There is a goalie standing next to the goal, whose job is to prevent anyone from kicking the ball in."

"If there's a guard by the goal, how does anyone ever score a point?"

"That's it! That's the whole skill of the game! Seeing a player manage to outsmart or outmaneuver the goalie and get the ball in — that's the great thrill!"

"I want to understand this," R' Sholom said. "The goalie never goes home to sleep? He stands by the goal 24 hours a day? He eats there and sleeps there?"

"No, of course he goes to sleep," the other answered, beginning to find R' Sholom's naivete boring. "He stands there only while the game is being played! After that, he goes back to living a normal life, like anyone else."

"So what's the problem?" R' Sholom asked eagerly. "Let's go out to the field now, while the goalie is away, and score some goals!"

"But that's pointless!" the young man exclaimed, exasperated. "When the goalie's not there, there's no challenge and no skill involved. How do you expect to gain points just by getting the ball into the goal? The whole idea is to score a goal when the opposition is present — when everyone is trying to prevent you from doing it!"

R' Sholom stood up and gazed deeply into the youth's eyes. "Why don't you listen to what you yourself are saying?" he asked. "Real accomplishment can only be meaningful when achieved in the face of a challenge. You want to wait until next week to resume your learning, when your distraction has disappeared. That's no accomplishment! The trick is to overcome this obstacle, to pursue your Torah study specifically when there's something trying to prevent you from doing so! *That* is when you have to try to get the ball in the goal."

"Y-yes, you're right. 'The reward is commensurate with the effort,' as the saying goes. But …"

"Don't break the rules of the game," R' Sholom urged. "Set your goal in the *beis midrash* now, and feel the thrill of overcoming the opposing forces!"

With a hearty handshake, R' Sholom went on his way.

The next evening, the youth was back at the *shiur*. When he entered the room, R' Sholom rose to his feet in recognition of this impressive personal accomplishment.

☙

On another occasion, R' Sholom spoke about a particular difficulty he experienced as a child.

"There was a big, spacious playing field near Beis Yisrael, where I grew up. As I left my mother's house, I would hear the roar of the spectators as they cheered the players in the game. As a child, I longed for a taste of the excitement that gripped all those people — to take part in the youthful pastime that others enjoyed so much. I wanted to take a closer look, to learn the players' names, to watch their moves. Once, I even stood behind the fence and stole a glance at the field. But, thank G-d, I managed to escape this temptation. G-d protected me from it."

R' Sholom often reminisced: "Football (it was by this English name that he always referred to soccer) was an activity that brought together boys from different backgrounds and created a strong camaraderie among them. When a boy played football with a team, he became personally involved with the others on the team, walking along a common path with them — and following, too, when they began to stray off the path. Apart from the game itself and its attendant hero-worship — and apart from the constant temptation to waste more and more time in play — the main danger was the negative social environment that went along with the game."

R' Sholom, who escaped the "football bug" along with numerous other similar obstacles to his spiritual growth, nevertheless understood how to learn as well as teach an important lesson from the popular game. It is a lesson that has relevance for every person, every day of his life: "Scoring a goal when it's most difficult — that is the most satisfying feeling a person can have!"

※

"Temptations? Who in this world does not face temptations?" R' Sholom once asked with a smile. "Didn't our people's greatest religious leaders experience temptations, and pride themselves on successfully conquering them? Nevertheless, we pray to G-d: 'Do not bring us into contact with temptation or shame.' A temptation is, Heaven forbid, an opportunity for failure and the shame that comes with it. And if a person does stumble in the face of temptation, he is obligated to strive again and again until he triumphs.

"Today's yeshivah boys think, 'It's so hard today. Once, life's challenges were much simpler.' This is nonsense. Many years ago, the oppressive poverty we lived with in Jerusalem, together with the sudden development of democratic freedoms and the spread of liberal ideas, created a tremendous inner turmoil within every youngster's soul. The temptations we faced in those days — the appeal and excitement of joining the underground Irgun or Lehi — were every bit as challenging, if not more so, than those we face today. In fact, it was even more difficult in those days to isolate oneself from the allure of the street than it is today."

R' Sholom, who confronted — and overcame — the temptations of his own generation, who stepped unscathed through the blazing embers of youthful enticements, knew how to laugh in the face of trials, past and future.

"To score a goal when it's difficult! That's what life is all about." R' Sholom was to return to this theme again and again, in a variety of applications and on many different occasions.

IN HIS OWN LIFE, R' SHOLOM EXPERIENCED MANY STRUGGLES and challenges. Even as a boy, he observed certain stringencies

A Carton of Leben

with regard to the laws of Shabbos. He felt a tremendous personal apprehension about desecrating the Shabbos — an attitude which preceded his public militancy on behalf of that holy day.

As a youth, R' Sholom and one of his yeshivah friends decided that, as a stringency, they would not eat products made by a certain firm in which Shabbos was not observed. This was in the year 5692, when "Tenuvah" (the largest distributor of dairy products in Israel) had begun to market leben and cheese, and it was public knowledge that this company transgressed the Shabbos. So the two youths decided not to eat any "Tenuvah" products. They supported one another in this resolution and undertook not to waver in it.

Upon returning home from Yeshivah after making this commitment, R' Sholom saw that his widowed mother had prepared him a meal containing a "Tenuvah" product: On the table stood half a container of leben bearing the "Tenuvah" label.

Here was a quandary: They were living at a time of great poverty, and it was often difficult to obtain even a piece of bread, let alone a full meal. Before him, on the table, were bread, coffee, and leben for his supper. A meal fit for a king!

Should he give up such a meal? He had bound himself to do so. And yet, his mother had prepared it; she was likely to be distressed if he did not eat. She was not only his mother, but also a widow. Who could estimate the exertions this poor widow had made in order to acquire a container of leben?

Which way would the scales tip?

The leben seemed to glisten in front of his eyes. His internal battle raged on.

A resolution was a resolution! It was the *yetzer hara* that was coming up with all these reasons to eat the leben. And yet, wasn't it true that eating gave one the strength to learn Torah?

Sholom Mordechai sat at the table, gripping his hands together lest they pick up the spoon lying there. To eat or not to eat? All along, his insides shouted with the hunger that came after a full day's learning. This did nothing to make his decision easier.

Years later, R' Sholom would vividly recall this episode. "I must have dipped that spoon into the leben 10 times. Ten times I put in the spoon and was about to eat. Then I would overcome the desire and take the spoon out. In and out, 10 times ..." At last, he became firm in his resolve: No! I made a resolution, and I must stick to it!

R' Sholom stood up, picked up the container of leben, and placed it in the cooling box (where, in the absence of a refrigerator, food was kept for cooling). Then he returned to the table to eat the bread.

"How did I know that it was my *yetzer hara* speaking?" R' Sholom would ask long afterwards. "After all, there were genuine arguments for eating that leben. The best proof was the fact that my mother did not say a word, the next morning, about the leftover leben. She was not offended at all.

"It was all a test. For that is the *yetzer hara's* way — to confuse the issue, to magnify everything and imbue it with an aura of holiness."

As was often the case, R' Sholom found the most interesting point of the story in its aftermath.

"The next morning, I went to my friend's house — the one who had formed the resolution with me [R' Avraham Roth of the Eidah HaChareidis]. I decided to knock on his door and tell him the whole story.

"I had just reached his building when my friend came out and began to relate virtually the same story: 'Last night, my mother served me a carton of Tenuvah cheese.'

"I was very moved," R' Sholom continued, "by the way the *yetzer hara* had seized upon two yeshivah *bachurim* who were trying to strengthen themselves in the area of honoring the Shabbos. He [the *yetzer hara*] ran after us, to put us to the test over a container of leben. He made such a great effort. And it all came from a resolution to honor the Shabbos.

"As is well known, a person is never given a test that he is unable to withstand. *Baruch Hashem*, we passed it."

(Right to left): Avraham Roth, Aharon Levi, and Sholom Mordechai Schwadron in 1931

Chapter One: The Difficulties of Life | 27

Chapter 2

At the In-Laws

THE EARLY PART OF THE 20TH CENTURY BEGAN TO SEE the luxuries and conveniences of the modern world make **A Match** their way into the Holy Land. **Is Made** Economically and socially, the *yishuv* (the Jewish community living in *Eretz Yisrael*) was changing at a dizzying pace.

Prosperity came hand in hand with social upheaval. In Jerusalem's venerable Jewish community, there was a precipitous decline in the number and predominance of the type of Jew prepared to sacrifice everything in favor of a total commitment to matters sacred — the type of Jew who, until recently, had been the hallmark of that community. Despite this shift in emphasis, however, several illustrious families remained staunch, and it is to these families that tens of thousands of Orthodox Jews who thrive in Israel today owe their spiritual existence.

One such household belonged to R' Chaim Yehudah Leib Auerbach. The family breathed Torah, ate Torah (there wasn't much else to eat!), went to sleep and woke with a love of Torah. They knew of no other value in life besides learning Torah.

When the time came for "R' Chaim Leib'ke," as he was known to his acquaintances, to search for suitable husbands for his daughters, he made it clear that he was not interested in young men of fame or reputation. He had no desire for sons-in-law with impressive family pedigrees or financial security. There was only one thing that concerned him:

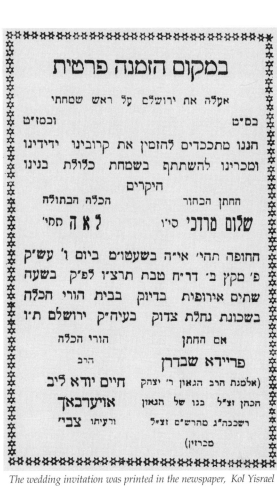

במקום הזמנה פרטית

אעלה את ירושלם על ראש שמחתי

בס"ט   וכסז"ט

הננו מתכבדים להזמין את קרובינו ידידינו ומכירינו להשתתף בשמחת כלולת בנינו היקרים

החתן הבחור   הכלה הבתולה

שלום מרדכי סי"ו   ל א ה תחי'

החופה תהי' אי"ה בשעטומ"צ ביום ו' עש"ק פ' מקץ ב' דר"ח טבת תרצ"ו לפ"ק בשעה שתים אירופית בדיוק בבית הורי הכלה בשכונת נחלת צדוק בעיה"ק ירושלם ת"ו

אם החתן   הורי הכלה

פריידא שבדרן   הרב
(אלמנת הרב הגאון ר' יצחק   חיים יודא ליב
כהן זצ"ל בנו של הגאון   אויערבאך
רשכבה"ג מהרש"ם זצ"ל   ורעיתו צבי'
(סכריזין)

The wedding invitation was printed in the newspaper, Kol Yisrael

that the young man be a serious Torah scholar, however humble.

His first son-in-law was to be R' Sholom Schwadron.

THE LAST TIME R' SHOLOM EVER SPOKE DURING THE MONTH of Elul was during the interval between his engagement and his

Guidelines of the Marriage wedding. One of the things he and his bride-to-be agreed on was the "Great Silence" that R' Sholom would observe after the wedding. Sunrise to dusk on Mondays and Thursdays were to be times of complete silence. For 40 days, from the first of Elul until after Yom Kippur, R' Sholom also abstained from any kind of speech.

"In the case of something very urgent, I will speak in *lashon hakodesh*, and only briefly," the groom declared. He said it, and he meant it; this was a vow he kept for the rest of his life.

His daughter tells of two other policy decisions the young couple made concerning their joint aspirations in life. The first was that the study of Torah was to be their only activity; no other objective would ever be pursued. And the second declared that indulgence in physical luxuries and amenities — the gilding of this world — would not be tolerated in their home.

Though she had agreed to refrain from indulging in "*olam hazeh*" — in the luxuries of this world — the bride did express a desire to store her articles of clothing in a closet, instead of (as R' Sholom preferred) hanging them on nails in the wall. The groom understood her need and consented to this exception.

"When we had three children, we were still sleeping on mattresses on the floor," R' Sholom once told his friend, R' Paysach Krohn. "Beds were bought some time after that."

But even in such poverty, it was hard to imagine a man more overflowing with the joy of living than R' Sholom Schwadron!

At the start of their life together, the couple lived in a small apartment, one room of which was already rented out to a Polish woman. When she left and her room became available, the couple bought it. Now they owned two rooms and a hallway.

The house and the well

The kitchen was in the courtyard — without even a door upon which to affix a *mezuzah*! Until the end of R' Sholom's life, there was no bathtub in the house. Running water did not exist in the apartment; the water they used was drawn from a well near the window. Milk was kept in the closet, as there was no refrigerator. "It stayed much fresher than milk does today!" R' Sholom used to quip.

Managing with the bare minimum was a permanent way of life for the Schwadron family, yet their lives proceeded with joy and contentment. It is interesting to note the saintly Rebbetzin's feelings about her modest way of life, and especially about the closet they had installed in their home. After her death, when her will was read aloud, her children broke down when they heard the following:

"Father used to sit with *tallis* and *tefillin* well into the morning, but he did not always manage to remain that way from morning to evening. Sometimes he had to be disturbed with various household matters. If only I would have agreed to hang the clothes on the wall and to sleep on benches, the way he wanted, perhaps it would have been better for me, both in this world and the next. After all, whatever is predetermined for a man's life — that, and no more, is what he is destined to live, both in terms of the quality and the longevity of his life."

R' Sholom fulfilled the lesson of the *mishnah* in *Pirkei Avos* to the letter: "This is the way of Torah: Eat [only] bread with salt; drink a small measure of water; sleep on the ground, and lead a life of self-deprivation." Together with his Rebbetzin, his eager and indispensable partner, he faithfully observed this recipe for attaining the "way of Torah." Together, they fulfilled the *mishnah's* concluding words: "Fortunate will you be in this world, and it will be good for you in the World to Come."

ORPHANED AS A YOUNG BOY, R' SHOLOM NEVER HAD A FATHER figure or family role model as he was growing up.

The Good Days "I did not know how a household was supposed to be conducted," he remarked once, later in life. When he was a boy, his hard-working mother was forced to leave the house early each morning to procure sustenance for her children. Coming home from school, young Sholom Mordechai would find a plate of food waiting for him on a shelf, left there by his thoughtful mother. He would wash and sit

The day after sheva berachos

down to eat — all by himself. He never knew what it meant to eat together with other family members. Never, that is, until the "good days" of his life began, when he joined the Auerbach family.

Copious tears flowed from R' Sholom's eyes as he stood under the wedding canopy. They were tears of sorrow for his past life, and tears of joy for the promise that his new life held for him.

R' Sholom loved to reminisce about his first days as an honorary member of the Auerbach family, immediately following the week of *sheva berachos*.

"I came home from *davening* and was received with a warm smile. My father- and mother-in-law showed me to a table that had been set for my breakfast. I sat down and began to eat. They had promised me '*kest*' (support) for the first three years of our marriage, and this was the first meal in fulfillment of that obligation.

"What was on the table? Some black bread, a little cream, a cup of coffee, and a piece of halvah. That was all they had and, thank G-d, it was a fine breakfast. I did not notice anything out of the ordinary. I ate, recited *Bircas HaMazon*, and immediately set out for the *kollel* Ohel Torah to learn. It did not dawn on me until breakfast the next morning that there might be something unusual about the fact that, for the second day in a row, I was eating breakfast by myself.

"At first I hadn't paid attention, because eating alone was something I was used to. An orphan remains an orphan! But that second day, before I left the house, I stepped into the next room and asked my saintly mother-in-law where my wife was? 'Why is it that both yesterday and today she did not come to breakfast?'

"'Oh, she had to go somewhere,' my mother-in-law replied casually.

"When my wife did not come to breakfast on the third morning either, I became troubled. 'What's going on?' I demanded. 'Three days in a row she has such urgent business so early in the morning?'

"Rebbetzin Auerbach's face turned red with embarrassment, and tears welled up in her eyes. Finally, shamefaced, she provided an explanation for her daughter's absence from the breakfast table.

"'R' Sholom,' she said sadly, 'for *you* we promised *kest* — but we just don't have enough to give her also! For her we have only bread and water. That's why she eats by herself, later on in the morning.'

"*Rabbosai*," R' Sholom would conclude with great emotion when recounting this story, "this is how they raised children to a life of Torah! This is how they merited having a son like R' Shlomo Zalman Auerbach!"

And he continued, "My mother-in-law became ill. As her life drew to an end, she had one thing on her mind just before she slipped into unconsciousness. '*Kinderlach*, I ask you to forgive me if I ever caused you to spend some of your time away from the study of Torah — especially Shlomo Zalman'ke.'

"This is how these remarkable people lived their lives. And this is how they ended their lives!"

THIRTY YEARS IS CONSIDERED THE AGE WHEN A MAN ATTAINS his full strength. In R' Sholom's case, 30 was the age at which he at-

The Last Spoon   tained his full strength in Torah. In the throes of creative labor, he was just days away from presenting his new book, a compendium of his original Torah thoughts. R' Chaim Leib and Rebbetzin Tzivia appreciated their son-in-law's awesome gifts. They knew him to be brilliant in Torah, the possessor of a great mind, well-versed in all of the Talmud, and a deeply original thinker. They observed in wonder the way he never rested on his laurels, but always strove to labor harder and harder in the fields of Torah. How, R' Chaim Leib wondered, could he and his wife express their love for their son-in-law and daughter?

There was no money. Simply none. Their last piece of silver had been handed over as security for Yeshivas Sha'ar HaShamayim! But a burden of debt in the support of Torah did not deter R' Chaim Leib from wishing to show his appreciation to R' Sholom and his wife. Troubled, he considered the matter long and hard, but could find no solution.

A week passed. R' Sholom's book was published, complete with endorsements from the generation's Torah lights. One of these, naturally, had been penned by his father-in-law, R' Chaim Leib Auerbach himself — an emotional outpouring: "A man whose spirit contains a double measure of Torah and *yiras Shamayim*, who expounds beautifully and practices beautifully, who lights up the land and all who dwell in it ... who uproots mountains ... My son-in-law, as dear to me as a son, the honored Rav *HaGaon* Sholom Mordechai HaKohen."

And still, R' Chaim Leib was caught in the toils of the question that plagued him: How? In what way could he express his appreciation and admiration?

Suddenly, R' Chaim Leib came to a halt in the doorway. Grasping the lintel, he broke into a broad smile. "Tzivia! Tzivia!" he called. "*The spoons!* We haven't pledged the spoons as security. The Yom Tov spoons ..."

The couple had received two silver spoons as a personal gift on their wedding day. Every Pesach, the two shining spoons were used to adorn the Seder table. Even more than their monetary worth was their sentimental value.

"What could be more personal than these two spoons that we have left — engraved with our names?" asked R' Chaim Leib. "We'll give him one of the spoons today, and save the other for the next time he publishes a book. I have nothing better with which to show him how we feel."

Rebbetzin Tzivia did not hesitate an instant. She climbed the stepladder to the high cupboard where the precious spoons were kept, reached in, and took one of them down.

"One spoon filled with fragrant spices for *talmidei chachomim*," R' Chaim Leib murmured to himself.

He took the spoon from his wife, held it a moment, then handed it back to her. The Rebbetzin pressed it to her heart, as though in parting. As the minutes passed, memories rose up in her mind: their

The spoons with the engraving

wedding day, their first Yomim Tovim together, the sight of those gleaming spoons on the snowy white tablecloth … With each memory, the value of the spoon rose in her eyes. Only then, as she felt the full strength of the spoon's connection to her life, did Rebbetzin Tzivia feel that the gift was perfect. It would be a gift in honor of the Torah … Pure silver, from a pair of pure hearts.

Once again, R' Chaim Leib took the spoon. He gazed at the engraved letters, "C. Auerbach." Then, with a joyous smile, he left the house. His wife stood in the doorway and looked happily after him as R' Chaim all but danced down the street.

R' Sholom was presented with the spoon. He noticed the engraving. Understanding the nature of this precious gift, his feelings overwhelmed him. But before he could say a word, his father-in-law whispered in his ear, "The second spoon is waiting for your next book."

Sure enough, with the publication of the *Da'as Torah Maharsham*, R' Sholom received the second spoon — with the name "T. Auerbach" etched in the silver.

R' Sholom ate from his spoon every Shabbos, to his last day on earth. With his death, the spoons passed on to his son, as a keepsake from a generation past: the last drops of blood that R' Chaim Leib and his Rebbetzin squeezed out in the Torah's honor.

R' CHAIM LEIB AUERBACH, HEAD OF THE FAMILY, WAS A GAON of the "hidden" — one of the luminaries of his time in the secrets

The Books of Torah. He was also a leading light in terms of his modest bearing. The only thing he made no attempt to play down was his burning love for Torah. Jerusalem stood astounded at this towering man of Torah who supported hundreds of outstanding young men in Yeshivas Sha'ar Hashamayim — at the cost of great personal sacrifice. He and his household often stood in danger of starvation, and yet he continued to give.

Another special craving that he was unable to conceal was a powerful hankering after *sefarim*. Eighty years ago, it was no easy matter to pick up a *sefer* and study it. The prices were sky-high, and often an edition was not in print. Still, one by one, R' Chaim Leib acquired a library of holy books. "A horse without reins will never pull the wagon," he was fond of saying. "The *sefarim* will do the pulling." His knowledge of the material contained in these works was extraordinary, and he could locate any volume in the room — even in the dark — as though he had bought it just that day.

Most of his acquisitions were made during a specific period in his life. During the years between the two World Wars, *Eretz Yisrael* was held in the grip of famine. Desperate for extra cash with which to buy food, people were selling off their *sefarim* — sometimes rare old volumes — for the price of bread. R' Chaim Leib, on the other hand, sold his bread in return for *sefarim*. R' Chaim Leib's collection was enriched, and his heart was filled to overflowing.

One day, Rebbetzin Tzivia sent her husband to the market to buy some dried dates. He returned an hour later, leading a donkey loaded down with holy books.

"A man sold me these books by the meter," he exclaimed. "I found a bargain!"

"And what about the dates?" inquired his wife.

"*Oy*, I completely forgot about them!" he exclaimed. "I jumped to take advantage of this tremendous bargain, and forgot why I had come." (as told by their son, R' Avraham Dov, *shlita*)

During that period, the price of land dropped dramatically. There were those who snapped up property for next to nothing, and later sold it again at a huge profit. R' Leib once remarked with a smile, "They bought *misparim* (numbers — referring to the numbered lots for sale), while I bought *sefarim*."

A riveting tale, related by Rebbetzin Reichman, who heard it from Rebbetzin Tzivia herself, took place in their youth. Famine ruled in Jerusalem. People pawed desperately through the trash cans for scraps of leftover food. In the Auerbach home, no one knew what a full piece of bread looked like ... And then the Rebbetzin noticed that her husband had acquired a new *sefer* for his library. It had cost them money they did not have. "Little Shlomo Zalman'ke's eyes are longing for a piece of bread. Who knows if this is not already a case of *pikuach nefesh*?" she thought in anguish.

Distressed, she decided to discuss the matter with her mother.

"How will my husband survive without food?" she asked her

R' Chaim Leib in his study with his brother-in-law, R' Eliyahu Porush

mother. "And the children ..." A tear coursed down her cheek. Her own hunger pangs were tripled by the suffering of her precious family.

"My young daughter," her mother said, "we are living through very hard times, economically. Imagine if your husband were a tailor, and found a new sewing machine — a really special machine that would help him sew five garments a day instead of one. Surely, if that were the case, you would be happy. And if your husband were a shoemaker, and bought himself a machine to fix shoes in half the time, you would rejoice with him.

"The Torah is your husband's profession," the mother ended forcefully.

And so, her daughter — Rebbetzin Tzivia — wiped away her tears and hid them away in the depths of her heart, to be saved for *erev* Yom Kippur.

There were moments when tears fell onto the pages of R' Chaim Leib's *sefarim*. The scene at the Auerbach home as R' Chaim Leib blessed his children with the traditional *erev* Yom Kippur blessing was one of its kind. The parents' sobs spoke volumes to their sons and daughters.

Before he began, R' Chaim Leib would walk over to his bookcases and pass a loving hand over the *sefarim* there, occasionally pausing to plant a kiss on one of them. This ritual lasted several minutes. It was as though he wished to arouse his fullest love of Torah before blessing his children with that same love. With a final kiss, he left his *sefarim* and walked over to one side of the room. One by one, his children came forward to be blessed.

Walking into R' Sholom Schwadron's household in later years, one would see a similar sight. In the large, book-lined room, R' Sholom and his wife — R' Chaim Leib's daughter — would stand, he wearing his *tallis* and she holding a small *siddur*, as the children stepped up one by one to be blessed. From time to time, sobs would erupt from beneath the *tallis*. Soon, both mother and father were soaked in tears, and the rest of the family were drawn in after them.

A friend of the family who chanced one year to walk in and

witness the scene, says solemnly, "I will never, ever forget those moments."

ABOUT 30 YEARS AGO, R' SHLOMO ZALMAN AUERBACH UNDER-

Toras Chaim

went brain surgery. Both he and his family understood that his chances were "50-50." Sha'arei Chesed erupted in prayer. In every Jewish community, the sky was figuratively darkened with pleas for the *gaon's* recovery. His own family *davened* day and night, visiting the graves of their forefathers to pour out their love and admiration for the man and his Torah.

One *tefillah* was especially remarkable. It came from the Schwadron household — from behind the curtain. It was Rebbetzin Schwadron, R' Shlomo Zalman's sister, who *davened*.

R' Sholom himself did not hear her, but one of their daughters did. She says, "Imma returned from the cemetery along with the others, their eyes red and swollen from crying. Imma's eyes were red, too, but she tried to smile as usual. Then she went to one side of the large room, concealed herself behind the drapes that covered the window, and began to open her heart to Hashem.

R' Shlomo Zalman Auerbach

"I didn't hear it all, but I'll relate what I did hear," the daughter says. "'*Ribbono Shel Olam!*' my mother cried, in a voice that came from the very depths of her heart. 'If I were to sit *shivah* for my brother, Shlomo Zalman *ben* Tzivia, *chas v'shalom*, he would not benefit from it at all. But if my brother, such a *gaon* in Torah and *yirah*, were to sit *shivah* for *me*, *Ribbono Shel Olam*, *I will benefit from it.*' Between the curtain and the wall, she was proposing an exchange — her life for her brother's. She was doing it out of her appreciation for his Torah.

"A life, in exchange for a living Torah for all of *Klal Yisrael*.'

Years later, it was R' Shlomo Zalman who sat *shivah* for his younger sister. Rebbetzin Schwadron departed this world at the age of 63.

IT WAS R' CHAIM LEIB AUERBACH'S CUSTOM TO GO TO BED IN the early evening. Before midnight, he would rise with vigor, and

Hidden Practices learn until daybreak. Then, after reciting the *Shema*, he retired to his bed again until it was time to *daven Shacharis.*

Certain neighborhood residents adopted a critical attitude about R' Chaim Leib's penchant for rising "late" in the mornings, not knowing that he was poring over the Torah while they slept in the night. His son related the following incident: "I remember So-and-so knocking on the door of our house at 8 o'clock in the evening, looking for my father. We told him that he had already gone to bed. 'Come back tomorrow morning and you'll surely get to see him then.' He came knocking at the door again at 8 the next morning — only to be told, 'He's still sleeping.' The man was clearly astounded. 'He slept from 8 to 8?!'"

These were some of R' Chaim Leib's hidden ways.

Rebbetzin Schwadron, R' Chaim's Leib's daughter, told the following. "There were times when Abba returned home late because of his business on behalf of the holy yeshivah, Sha'ar HaShamayim. Every night when he walked in, even if it was very late, he sat opposite his wife and told her everything that had occurred to him that day. Everything! When she became hard of hearing, he spoke in a louder voice, right into her ear. And he continued to consult with her and seek her wisdom and intuition."

When snow fell in Jerusalem, it was R' Chaim Leib's practice, together with a small group of friends, all hidden *mekubalim*, to roll in the snow. And there were other secret practices. Rebbetzin Schwadron was reminded of the time her father lost consciousness. "There was a great uproar. They ran to fetch a doctor and everyone was *davening* in fear and trembling.

R' Chaim Leib Auerbach

My mother walked over to the *Aron Kodesh* that was in their house, and burst into tears. One member of the family managed to overhear a few words: '*Ribbono Shel Olam*, take me from the world before [my husband], because if, Heaven forbid, he leaves before me, I will have to tell stories in his praise and no one will believe what I have to tell about him.' She went on to heap praises on her husband. 'Who will believe that there were long periods when he wore a sack underneath his clothes, to mortify his flesh? Who will believe and know?'"

❦

R' Chaim Leib founded the Sha'ar HaShamayim Yeshivah at a young age. R' Sholom told the story of its founding, as he had heard it from Rebbetzin Tzivia, his mother-in-law and R' Chaim Leib's wife.

On the morning that the yeshivah was founded, R' Chaim Leib deviated from his usual morning practice of leaving through the front door to go to shul. Instead, he headed for the back door, which led to the street that ran past the back of his house.

"Chaim Leib, where are you going?" Rebbetzin Tzivia asked.

"I have to go," he said, and disappeared. Less than 10 minutes later, he had returned — together with R' Shimon Leider, *zt"l*. The two sat at the table.

"Tzivia, please bring us a '*l'chaim*'!" R' Chaim Leib requested.

She was a good wife who did what her husband wished, even

without understanding it. She went to the kitchen and returned with a bottle. The two men sipped their drinks to cries of "*L'chaim! L'chaim!*" Then they stood up, seized one another's hands, and began to dance around the wooden table. Afterwards, R' Chaim Leib accompanied his visitor outside, said his farewells, and returned to the house.

The Rebbetzin was stupefied. The instant she laid eyes on her husband she demanded to know what had just happened.

"While I was asleep," R' Chaim Leib answered, "I had a dream. I saw two men with radiant faces. One of them came close to me and spoke, while the other kept his distance, his face growing brighter and brighter. I greeted the first man and asked him his name. He gave it to me [R' Chaim Leib did not reveal the name he was told in the dream]. Then he told me, 'It says in the *Zohar* that when the study of Kabbalah becomes revealed, the Moshiach will come. The time is drawing near. We have come to you to let you know that you must open a yeshivah where Kabbalah will be studied.'

"When the man finished speaking, the two vanished. I woke up, wondering what to do. I decided to go see R' Shimon Leider, an expert in Kabbalah. I would tell him about my dream and have him interpret it for me.

"I left the house and began walking — when I suddenly saw R' Shimon coming toward me. 'I am on my way to see you!' R' Shimon told me.

"'And I am on my way to see *you!*' I said.

"In short, it turned out that he had had the same dream."

And that was how the yeshivah was founded.

DURING THE WEEK OF HIS *SHEVA BERACHOS*, R' SHLOMO Zalman Auerbach did not feel very well. Each evening, after the *seu-*

A Whole Egg? *dah*, he threw up everything he had eaten. When his wife expressed her surprise and concern, he explained simply, "Until I married, I never ate meat on a weekday. Only on Shabbos and Yom Tov was I ever served a piece of chicken. These days, they've been serving me portions of meat, day after day; it's no wonder that my stomach is unable to digest the food."

On another occasion, R' Shlomo Zalman remarked, "In my youth, I never felt full." He satisfied his soul with the holy Torah instead, and in this way managed to forget his physical hunger.

His brother, R' Avraham Dov, relates, "During my own week of *sheva berachos*, I was invited to breakfast at the home of my wife's relative. On the table were many kinds of cakes and pastries, cooked eggs, bread, cream, butter, jam, and more. I looked at the table and waited patiently. My host asked, 'Why don't you wash your hands to eat?' Innocently, I answered, 'The others have not yet arrived.' By the amount of food on that table, I was sure that they had prepared a *sheva berachos* breakfast for a *minyan* of people … In our home, I never once ate a whole egg. My mother, o"h, would scramble an egg with a bit of flour and divide it among three children. A whole egg? Who ever heard of such a thing?

"But the interesting thing is that our home was always filled with happiness. Even when there were no toys for the children or notebooks and pens for writing or other pastimes — even then, we lived satisfied and happy."

Rebbetzin Schwadron once recalled with emotion, "We received bread and milk from good Jews, and that's all we had at home. When my brother, R' Shlomo Zalman, grew up and went to yeshivah, our mother once hid a piece of halvah for him. 'When Shlomo Zalman comes home late at night, he'll have a little halvah and some cold water to refresh him,' Imma said.

"There was a time when the yeshivah's debts were very large. Merchants tricked my father, zt"l, causing heavy damage to the yeshivah's finances. Matters grew so bad that a small advertisement appeared in the newspaper inviting anyone who was interested to come buy used furniture in the Nachalas Tzadok section — in the Auerbach house. But even on that day, happiness did not leave our home. There was no panic; our daily life continued peacefully. Things were as cheerful as always. My parents' wisdom stood by them even in the most difficult situations.

"One *erev* Pesach, my father [R' Chaim Leib] returned home, saying, 'Ah, *baruch Hashem*, I managed to find money to support all the young men in Sha'ar HaShamayim. It wasn't easy!'

"My mother sat down and started crying. 'And what about your children?'

"My father grew excited. '*Oy! Oy!* I completely forgot!' And he immediately rushed out to obtain another loan before the time came to burn the *chametz*."

THE SPECIAL ATMOSPHERE OF *EREV* YOM KIPPUR IN R' CHAIM Leib Auerbach's home began at 3 in the morning, according to his

"May Your Desire Be ..." son, R' Avraham Dov:

"All of us children were awakened before dawn. We washed our hands and went out into the yard." There, he goes on to relate, they would find their father checking knives, with the *shochet*, R' Mendel Porush, *zt"l*, at his side.

R' Mendel would usually begin asking each child a short question about what he or she was learning. "I remember to this day one of the questions I was asked," says R' Avraham Dov. "It was the last year he *shechted* for us. This is what he asked: 'The Gemara tells us that if someone steals away another person's mitzvah of *kisui hadam* from a chicken, he is obligated to pay that man 10 gold pieces. What would the halachah be if he takes this mitzvah away from a Jew who is about to do it for the first time in his life — would he still owe 10 gold pieces? After all, on the first time we also recite the blessing of *Shehecheyanu!'*

"One of the children answered, 'Of course! The one who steals the mitzvah should pay double.'

"'Mistake! Mistake!' said R' Mendel the *shochet* warmly. His smile emerged to meet the rising wind of dawn. 'Losing the *kisui hadam* caused him a loss, while not being to recite the *Shehecheyanu* was no loss: He can say that *berachah* on another occasion when he does *kisui hadam.*'

The moving custom of *kapparos* touched every heart. You could have cut the tension with a knife as R' Chaim Leib twirled the chicken and said aloud, with great fear and awe, "This is my atonement, this is my substitute ..." When he was done, he put the chicken under the table and cried out in a trembling voice, "A life for a life!"

"There were tears of terror in our eyes when we heard those words! They shook up the quiet night. We stood ready to fulfill the *minhag* of *kapparos* 'in fear and trembling.'

"The chickens were slaughtered. During the course of the morning they were plucked, passed over a fire to remove insects, and then salted and cooked. By noon, all was ready. The girls of the family went about the mitzvos of the day that naturally brought about an unusual solemnity. By midday, we could see Abba sitting in his white clothes, his face filled with fear of Heaven. The house wore a special *kedushah*."

Then came the moment when the children went, one by one, to stand beneath their father's *tallis*. R' Chaim Leib stood and spread his hands over the child's head. Bursting into wracking sobs, he moved his hands over each small head. With tears pouring down on their heads, he said, "May Hashem make you like Ephraim and like Menashe." They could hear every word despite the tears. "May your desire be to Torah and mitzvos." His entire body shook with the force of his weeping and his hands grew heavy on their heads.

"I remember that Imma had bought me a new yarmulka in honor of Succos. I was granted her permission to wear it on Yom Kippur as well. Abba, *zt"l*, cried so hard over my head that the yarmulka grew creased and sodden with tears," R' Avraham Dov remembers emotionally. "In our home," he continues, "there was no concept of kisses. Only at the end of his Yom Kippur *berachah* would Abba put out his hand and say, '*Gib ah kush!*' (Give a kiss!) We kissed his hand, and then he immediately told us to go over to our mother and kiss her hand, too. We left the room and went over to

Imma, who was sitting near the door, crying profusely as she was saying *Tehillim*. She never did anything else during the *berachos*. We bent over her hand and planted kisses on it.

"On Yom Kippur night, Abba would give a *derashah* in shul. It was a stormy talk. He had a voice like a lion and would soon arouse the whole audience to *teshuvah*. It is a fact that, at the height of one fiery talk, a listener in the women's section fainted.

"With daybreak on Yom Kippur itself, the fear and tension began to subside. As children, we calmed down a little from the emotional state that had held us from the middle of *erev* Yom Kippur night, and that stayed with us all that day — and all the days of the year."

REBBETZIN TZIVIA, WIFE OF R' CHAIM LEIB, LIVED OUT HER entire life on a lofty plateau of piety, fear of Heaven, love for Torah,

Clothed in Glory

and an extraordinary trust in Hashem. She was also possessed of a remarkable wisdom — a wisdom of the mind and the heart.

"As a child, I thought that my mother had *ruach hakodesh*," one of her sons related long afterward. "We lived in the Nachalas Tzadok neighborhood, near Sha'arei Chesed, and we boys walked there regularly, every night, to learn in the Kehal Chassidim Shul in Sha'arei Chesed. When we returned from learning, there were times when Imma would tell me, 'Today you didn't learn so well. Other boys learned better than you.' On occasion, she would even tell me what I did in shul: 'Today you played a little with the big stove in the shul, throwing twigs of wood inside.' And sometimes there was a compliment: 'Today you learned with great intensity.'

"For years, I never knew the secret of her 'ruach hakodesh.'

"After a full day of difficult housework — washing clothes and ironing them [with a coal iron], preparing meals, scrubbing and cleaning ... and saying *Tehillim*, learning the *Kav HaYashar* and the *Menoras HaMaor* [which she knew by heart], she still found the energy to leave home after dark and walk over to the shul in which we were learning, to stand by the window and keep track of us.

She sewed shirts and pants for us with her own hands, because she had no money to buy any. Her hands were always full of work — and yet she found the strength for her children's *chinuch* with an extraordinary devotion," her son recalls.

Rebbetzin Auerbach had a special notebook, in which she wrote down the "miracles" that had occurred during her life — and particularly the ones attendant on her children's marriages. It was the day after one of her children became engaged that she sat down and filled an entire notebook. That notebook, alas, has vanished with time.

$$\approx \approx$$

A daughter, Rebbetzin Malkah Horowitz, *o"h*, once consented to relate an unusual example of her father's trust in Heaven:

When his daughter Malkah's *vort* was over, it became known that R' Chaim Leib had promised the *choson's* father a large dowry and support. Rebbetzin Tzivia asked him what he had depended on in making such a promise."

"We will depend on Hashem, as always," answered R' Chaim Leib.

Some days passed. The *tena'im* was fast approaching, but there was no money. What was to be? Confronted with this question, R' Chaim Leib was tranquil as ever.

Two days before the *tena'im*, there came a knock at the Auerbach's door. Standing in the doorway was a wealthy couple in need of marital counseling. The two had heard about R' Chaim Leib's wisdom and had come begging for his help. "We will pay whatever you want. Just save us!"

The three of them entered a room. Two hours later they emerged, the couple happy and uplifted. They took a large sum of money and placed it on the table, but R' Chaim Leib agreed to accept only the amount that he had promised his *mechutan*, plus an additional sum for a nice *tena'im*. That happy occasion took place with a lavishness that astounded all the family's friends. "Where did the money come from?"

On another occasion, R' Sholom, *zt"l*, said: "I was promised a dowry of 200 lira, in addition to three years of *kest* at my in-law's table. I received these with great devotion. R' Chaim Leib sold a piece of land he had and gave me the money with joy. When I married, the situation in the [Auerbach] home was very difficult. Simply put, there was *nothing*. Later, the situation improved slightly.

"My mother-in-law would remind me that before the wedding I told them, 'I am a Kohen; maybe blessings will come to your home through me.'"

Their constant and plentiful bread was their trust in the One above.

THERE WAS NO REFRIGERATOR IN THE HOUSE — AND NOT EVEN an icebox. The Shabbos food was kept in a box tied to a rope,

Chametz! which they would lower into the well in the yard. The water was cold and the well itself kept the temperature cool.

One Shabbos during the summer months, one of the Auerbach children was sent to the well to bring in the fish. He pulled at the rope tied to the box — and the rope broke! Turning pale, he ran indoors to tell the others what had happened. With one voice, everyone cried out in anguish, "There's nothing to eat! All the food fell into the well! *Oy!*"

Rebbetzin Tzivia also reacted with horror, but the words she cried were completely different from those of the rest of the family. She clasped her hands together, saying, "*Oy!* The well has become *chametz!* We'll have no water from it on Pesach!"

This incident took place at the height of summer. There were still long months to go before Pesach arrived. But this was the Rebbetzin's spontaneous reaction to the news. "*Chametz!*"

HER SON, R' AVAHAM DOV, DESCRIBED HIS MOTHER'S DEPARTURE from this world.

And She Will Laugh on the Last Day While still hale and healthy, she had once asked her son R' Eliezer to prepare a metal tablet and engrave the *seder haviduy* on it in his fine handwriting. "Engrave it in large letters for me, and also the *Shema Yisrael*," she said. "Sometimes, when a person is at the point of leaving this world, there is no one there to help him say the *viduy*, especially if death comes suddenly. Therefore, it's a good idea for me to have the text beside my bed," she said.

Her son shuddered at the whole idea, and tried to turn the talk to other matters. But Rebbetzin Tzivia was insistent. In the end, R' Eliezer engraved the text as she had requested, in clear, beautiful letters, and brought it to her. There was a large window in the Rebbetzin's room (as in all the old Jerusalem houses). On this, opposite her bed, she placed the tablet. It remained in place for the next 10 years, until her death.

Before she passed away, the Rebbetzin's memory grew dim and the tablet she had prepared was useless to her. But because she had worried about the day of her death for so long, Heaven helped her. About 2 hours before her passing, she suddenly opened her eyes, looked around, and called out emotionally, in the manner of a person who is seeing wondrous things, "*Heilige malachim!* [Holy angels!] *Heilige malachim!*" [It is brought down that righteous souls close to the dying person come to greet him near the hour of death.] Then she lifted her voice and cried out the *Shema* 10 times.

"*Kinderlach!*" she cried. "Children! There is nothing to worry about." And she pleaded for their forgiveness.

With the last of her strength, she recited *Ein Kei'lokeinu* and *Pitum HaKetores*. Then her energy failed her and her mind grew clouded again. Half an hour later, in the presence of many family members, Rebbetzin Tzivia Auerbach returned her soul to its Creator.

MANY TALES WERE TOLD ABOUT R' CHAIM LEIB AUERBACH'S wisdom and sagacity. R' Sholom himself would wax very enthusi-

R' Chaim Leib Tells a Story astic on the topic. One story he repeated often took place tens of years before. At that time, the Jewish Agency decided to put a halt to all appeals by *chareidi* Jews on behalf of their organizations. The heads of the Jewish Agency summoned *chareidi* leaders to an urgent meeting, at which they demanded an immediate cessation of fundraising efforts abroad. (Their goal was to have all funds funneled through a single source.) The Agency promised that the Torah institutions would no longer have any cause to appeal for outside funds: "*We* will attend to all your needs!"

The religious leaders were given a chance to speak at this meeting. Several leaders of the "Va'ad HeYeshivos" declared that they would agree to the Jewish Agency's demand only if they could be guaranteed the sum of a million lira per annum. "If we stop sending fundraisers to the Diaspora, this is the sum you'll have to give us," they said.

A secular Jew representing the Zionist leadership stood up in a fury. "You are not embarrassed to demand such a large amount? *Shnorrers!*" The man was derisive and contemptuous in the extreme.

The negotiations limped along with difficulty, each side struggling to attain the upper hand. R' Chaim Leib Auerbach, a participant, sat quietly and waited for his turn to speak. He decided to dispel the notion that the Jewish Agency could control these funds.

"I decided to pay that wicked, brazen man in his own coin," R' Chaim Leib told his son-in-law, R' Sholom, later. When his turn came to address the group, he stood up calmly and began, "Let me tell you a story." And he proceeded to offer a parable he had made up on the spot.

"There was a place called Alexot," R' Chaim Leib continued. "This was a large city that was divided in two — an upper section and a lower one. The distance between these two sections was great — so great that the upper section contained a large parking area where wagon drivers would gather before setting out several times a day to the lower city.

"In upper Alexot there lived a widow named Sarah. She had one daughter, Chana'le, who lived in the lower city. Chana'le was very poor. Her children wore ragged clothes and had no shoes for their feet, and Chana'le was reduced to supporting them by begging for alms. Sarah, her mother, would also collect pennies and send them to her daughter from time to time.

"One Yom Tov eve, Sarah went to the parking area and found Yankele, the wagon driver, waiting for his wagon to fill with passengers for the lower city.

"'Listen, Yankele,' she said in a pleading voice. 'Do me a favor. You are going down to the lower city in any case, and you know that I have a poor daughter there. I've baked a tray of fresh, round loaves of bread for her. Please, be a good Jew and bring it to her. It will hearten her for the holiday.'

"'All right, Sarah — for you!' Yankel answered. 'Give it to me.'

"'But Yankele,' Sarah went on, 'will you bring her dry bread? What kind of taste does dry bread have? I've prepared a jar of butter. If she can eat bread with butter, then she'll be contented.'

"'Sarah! I've hardly managed to find room for the bread. Where will I have space for a jar of butter?'

"'Yankele, don't be like that. Do a mitzvah, have pity on her — find the room.'

"Yankele cried, 'Enough! Put the butter here, beside the bread, and that's all!'

"Five minutes passed, and the wagon had its full complement of passengers. Yankele sat down, about to set out. Suddenly, Sarah called up to him again from the street below: 'Yankele, just a minute! What kind of taste does bread with just butter have? I've prepared some good, tasty cheese in honor of the holiday. My Chana'le will eat bread, butter, and cheese — *oy*, how that will revive her broken spirit. She'll have something for Yom Tov ...' And Sarah burst into emotional tears.

"'Sarah, you're driving me crazy! Take everything back and leave!'"

"'Yankele, don't be so hard-hearted! Have pity on us. You understand how important this is. Don't be wicked! Please.'

"'Oh, what do you want from me? Throw it in, and that's all!'

"'You shall be blessed — you'll be successful — may you and your family have everything good!' Sarah blessed him with all her heart.

"Just as the wagon wheels began to turn, Sarah came running back, shrieking, 'Yankele! Yankele! What good is bread to a poor woman who doesn't even have shoes for her children's feet? Please, take these three rubles and give them to her. May blessings be heaped on your head!'

"'All right,' Yankele agreed at once. For money, he had room. He put the coins in his pocket and started on his way.

"Days passed. A day, two, then three, with Yankele going back and forth dozens of times. Sarah was certain he had fulfilled her commission at the first opportunity. But one sunny day after the holiday, Sarah received a tear-stained letter from her daughter. 'Mother, what happened? Have you forgotten that you have a daughter living nearby? We have no clothes or shoes, we have nothing to eat, and you didn't send us anything.'

"Sarah's head swam and her vision grew dark. Something must have happened. She went out into the street to search for Yankele. She found him in his usual spot in the parking area.

"'Yankele! You wicked man, you thief, what have you done to me? You have killed me! What happened to the things I sent with you?'

"'What's all the shouting about?' Yankele asked calmly.

"Sarah sobbed, 'Where is the bread that I made, and the butter and cheese? And the three rubles — *where are they?*'

"'Why are you screaming like that?'

"'What do you mean, why am I screaming? Aren't you ashamed of yourself?'

"'Just a minute. Listen to me a minute, and I'll explain what happened,' Yankele said, his serenity growing more maddening by the minute.

"'What do you mean? Look at this letter? My heart is weeping blood! Are you not ashamed? Look how miserable she is in every word she writes!'

"'Sssh ... Listen, Sarah. That fresh bread you baked — what can I say? — you have golden hands!'

"'What are you babbling about? You're throwing salt on my wounds!'

"'And the butter ... Golden hands!'

"'*What?* You ate it? You wicked man!' the poor mother cried.

"'Just a minute. Wait patiently, and I'll tell you everything. You remember the day I went — of course you remember. It was an especially warm day. The sun beat down from above and the heat was unbearable. On the way to the lower city, I began to feel something damp near my feet.'

"'Stop telling me stories. I'm burning up, and you're telling me tales!'

"'Patience, and you will understand everything. I bent down to see what had happened, what was wet — and saw that the jar had cracked and the butter inside melted. It was dripping out — a real waste.'

"'I understand very well. Let's skip over the butter and all your stories. What about the bread I baked?'

"'Wait, and I'll tell you,' Yankele smiled. 'It would have been a pity to waste such good butter — really a pity, wouldn't it? So I took a small piece of bread, dipped it in the butter that was left in the jar, and put it in my mouth. But you were right — bread with butter is nothing without a little cheese. What can I tell you, Sarah? I suddenly had such an appetite — such golden hands — you make the most wonderful bread … I forgot myself entirely — such bread! — and ate piece after piece.'

"Sarah tore her hair out and screamed, '*Gevald!* All right, let's pass over the bread, the butter, and the cheese. But what about the money? I gave you three rubles. Where are they?'

"Yankele gave her a mocking look. 'And did you think that all this was worth no money? That I would transport it all for free?'"

R' Chaim Leib finished his story and sat down.

Everyone at the meeting who understood the meaning of this parable smiled. Some burst out laughing. The meeting broke up.

In this and countless other ways, R' Chaim Leib utilized his wisdom to strengthen Torah in every area within his reach. He also devoted himself to the support of young, spiritually aspiring men who would become the backbone of Torah institutions in Jerusalem. His life was one of suffering, but also one where love of Hashem and dedication to the Torah were never absent.

When his son-in-law, R' Simchah Bunim Leizerson, passed

away in front of his eyes at the age of just 29, R' Chaim Leib cried out in a fearsome voice, "I have lost the *Shas Bavli* and *Yerushalmi* in a single volume ... I have lost a holy *gaon!*" He went on to lament the enormity of the loss to himself, to his daughter, to the entire family and to *Klal Yisrael* as a whole, and everyone echoed him with a great weeping. From that moment, R' Chaim Leib's health deteriorated. Still, he did not cease his efforts on behalf of Torah or the raising of his beautiful family — sons and daughters and sons-in-law who were righteous and great of stature, and most of whom have not even been mentioned on these pages.

LET US CONCLUDE WITH A *"VORT"* THAT R' SHOLOM USED TO quote often, in his father-in-law's name:

The Essence of a Man "My father-in-law, *zt"l*, asked a question. On the face of things, it is a powerful question. On *erev* Yom Kippur, the most scrupulous people eat from the morning on; certainly, that is the mitzvah. It is the custom to pass out some cake in shul in the morning, etc. All day long, there is some sort of eating going on — and all the more so, of course, at the *seudah hamafsekes* (the meal before the fast).

"After this meal, we recite the *Bircas HaMazon* and prepare for shul. We put on a *tallis* and white clothes, like angels, and walk to shul.

"The *Shulchan Aruch* says that a wise man does not fill his belly except for practical purposes. At *Kol Nidrei*, our bodies are full of food, filled with the material, with *gashmius*. We continue in this way to *Ma'ariv* until *K'rias Shema*, where we say *Baruch Shem ...!* out loud, like angels. On and on — after *Ma'ariv* we say the *Shir HaYichud* and *Tehillim*, and there are those who remain to sleep in shul. And so on: *Shacharis, Mussaf, Minchah* ... Who spends any time speaking of trivial things? No one! If there is a short recess we go home to rest. In short, the entire day we are like holy angels. Until *Ma'ariv*.

"Before *Ma'ariv*, the shofar is blown — a great blast — "And He, the Merciful, will atone for sin." And we continue until *K'rias Shema*, where we recite *Baruch Shem ...* — **in a whisper!**

"There is something astonishing here. On *erev* Yom Kippur,

when we eat mighty portions of soup and forget the *Shulchan Aruch's* telling us not to fill our bellies — then we are considered like angels. But after a day packed with mitzvos and prayer, immediately with the first *Ma'ariv* we say *Baruch Shem* quietly. Why?

"My father-in-law had an answer. When we sit at the *seudah hamafsekes* and eat stuffed chicken, the food tastes very good. The mouth eats — but is the mouth the man? Are the hands, the feet, the mouth, the essence of a man? No and no! An animal also has hands and feet. What is the difference? What is a man?

"The Ba'al Shem Tov said, 'A man's thoughts are the man.' In that case, let us think. He is eating, true — but his thoughts are on Yom Kippur. 'Why am I eating now, why did I eat all day?' he thinks to himself. 'Because it is a mitzvah to eat on *erev* Yom Kippur in order to be able to fast on Yom Kippur.' And the Gemara states, 'He who eats on the ninth [of Tishrei] is as though he fasted on the ninth and the tenth.' In general, all our thoughts on *erev* Yom Kippur are devoted to the holy day before us.

"But when we hear the shofar on *motza'ei* Yom Kippur, what do we think? 'Ah, soon I'll be able to eat and drink.' The angel has departed, and the man has returned for coffee and cake.

"And so, he must once again say *Baruch Shem* in a whisper."

Chapter 3
At Home

THE MOONLESS NIGHT WAS VERY DARK OVER THE SHA'AREI Chesed neighborhood. Every house slept under the thickening cloud cover, and continued to sleep as **Night** a light drizzle began to fall. The streets **Watch** grew slick. Raindrops dripped slowly from the tree branches. All was quiet, save for the pitiful mewing of a cat seeking shelter in the gutters — and the creak of a gate as a lone figure passed through it and began to stroll peacefully up the street.

Before long, a second figure, wrapped in a heavy overcoat, followed up the same street. Soon the light of a street lamp illuminated yet a third, who stepped outside, hesitated as though becoming conscious of the inclement weather, and turned back. Within seconds, however, the figure reappeared wearing a raincoat.

And then came two more shadows in the night. The taller, taking

The entrance to the Sha'arei Chesed neighborhood

the silent street with a broad, vigorous stride, was father to the second, a young girl.

It was the same every night, rain or snow. The biting Jerusalem wind snapped at their faces as though trying to send them home, but they persisted. Who were these figures?

They were R' Sholom Schwadron and his four daughters.

Where were they going, and what was their secret?

~~

The modest Schwadron home, near the old entrance to Sha'arei Chesed, served as an emblem of grace and lovingkindness. The door swung open on its hinges from sunrise to sunset, and did not cease even when the stars were twinkling in the sky. And through that door, with clockwork regularity, four figures would exit … and sometimes five or six or seven: the Schwadron daughters.

Each daughter turned with willing steps toward a different house, to take advantage of the nighttime hours to perform acts of kindness. Each would spend the night under the roof of an unfortunate woman: Baila the widow, Reshka the lonely, poor Yenta, old Bilka, or Grishka the addled. If the girls were afraid to sleep there alone, they took a friend or a cousin along. R' Sholom's daughters, well-known rebbetzins today, are prepared to relate volumes about the education they received on those nights — an education in *chesed*.

Most of the women who needed help were righteous women, and their homes generally provided a pleasant atmosphere. Even when they did not, there was always much to be gained merely by spending time with these women, so wise in the ways of life. Occasionally, however, the girls ventured into homes where quarreling was rife and their nights were riddled with fear and distress.

"I'll never forget those nights," one of R' Sholom's daughters said, decades after that period in her life. "For months on end I slept at a certain woman's house, wrapped completely in a sheet, leaving only a small opening for air. Bedbugs were everywhere, but there was no way for me to give the house a thorough cleaning. That woman required very respectful treatment. I could never mention the lack of cleanliness, let alone the living creatures infesting her home. That's how I slept."

The figures left home quietly, without fanfare, night after night. One of the daughters had a long way to go — all the way from Sha'arei Chesed to the Machaneh Yehudah neighborhood. The route was dark and frightening, and it was imperative that someone accompany her. The girl's mother toiled from early morning and the father worked hard all day, yet they took turns marshaling their last strength for the walk, dodging raindrops and puddles and mud. Summer and winter, they trudged on undaunted — all for the sake of others.

"Why us?" The question, inevitably, popped into the minds of each of the girls from time to time. But the members of the Schwadron family knew that there were some questions you never asked aloud.

Said one of the daughters, "Our mother never neglected our upbringing for the sake of educating us in this mitzvah. She supervised everything we did, asking us who we were going to visit, when, and with which friend. The ends," she concludes, "were never allowed to justify the means."

A Special Kiss

FOR A LONG TIME, A CERTAIN WIDOW HAD INSISTED ON REmaining alone, refusing her neighbors' support. At last, growing afraid, she permitted one of the Schwadron girls and a friend to spend the night at her house.

The cold was piercing, accompanied by periodic heavy rains and thunderstorms. Inside, the house was warm. It didn't matter if a little rain seeped through the doorway or into the hall ... unless, like R' Sholom's daughter and her friend, you happened to be sleeping there.

As the night wore on, the hall grew progressively colder and damper. The girls' mattresses took up most of the width of the hall, making it impossible to keep from getting wet as rain dripped down from the ceiling. Icy and miserable, they cast longing glances at the room next door, where their hostess slept with a heater. That first night was a difficult one.

"I don't want to go there anymore," R' Sholom's daughter declared the next morning. "There's a limit to everything. To lie in the cold, with water trickling onto the edges of my mattress — I can't sleep that way!" In a forceful, pain-filled voice, she ended, "It's too much for me. I give up."

Rebbetzin Schwadron listened attentively to her daughter's complaint. A thoughtful silence descended. A little later, over breakfast, the mother's thoughts took verbal form.

"What do we do?" she asked her husband. "Leave the old woman alone? Our daughter is not required to suffer. True, we're not talking about something catastrophic. A little water on the bed isn't all that terrible — but she is suffering. Is that her obligation? And to what extent?"

R' Sholom and his wife considered the matter carefully. Finally, they came to their conclusions. It was clear they could not permit the respected widow to remain alone. As for their daughter, they would instigate a few changes in her sleeping arrangements. The mattress would be moved to make room for buckets to catch the dripping water. They would provide her with an extra blanket. The important thing was for the heart to keenly feel another's lack, and to beat with compassion for another's misfortune. It is not pleasant to sleep in a hall — but that, at times, is life. This whole world, after all, is like a hall.

Along with these arrangements, R' Sholom decided to pay his daughter a stipend for sleeping at the widow's house on a regular basis. "You'll get five *mil* [the coin used in that day] each night, or 25 *mil* per week," the Rebbetzin told her daughter. It took some coaxing, but the girl was persuaded at last to undertake the job for a trial period.

The money, of course, came out of R' Sholom's own pocket. At the end of each week, the girl received the stipend from her father. Gradually, she grew accustomed to sleeping in the hall. The money accumulated in her purse, and she began to daydream about the things she would buy one day. It was a sweet dream.

The dream lasted until 8 a.m. one Friday morning.

On her way to high school, the daughter stopped off at her house to pick up a sandwich for lunch. She overheard her mother, Rebbetzin Schwadron, speaking in the kitchen, her voice filled with anguish but trying not to inflict too much pain. "There's nothing — not a penny. I have nothing with which to buy food for Shabbos, not even a challah. Our money is gone, down to the last cent!"

"I have nothing, either," her husband said gravely. They were silent in this crisis. What to do?

Just outside the kitchen, quiet as a mouse, their daughter stood stock-still. She felt as though something were stuck in her throat; she felt perilously close to tears. Had her father and mother been paying her with coins of pain — with money they didn't have? Had they given her the bread they didn't have? Did they spend their last penny to provide the widow with a pleasant night's sleep?

In a few moments, she recovered. Going into her room, she returned with a small purse filled with pennies. Hesitantly she approached the kitchen. She stepped inside and in a voice choked with emotion, begged her mother, "Imma, please take this money you gave me ... so we'll have something to eat on Shabbos."

Astonished at this unexpected reprieve, the Rebbetzin stood up and bent over her daughter to plant a warm kiss on her cheek. It was a kiss of appreciation — and admiration. She remained still for a long moment, her arms around the girl, trying to conceal the tears of joy making their way down her face.

"But," the daughter says, "I saw those tears.

"And I will never forget that kiss."

Letting Go

THE SCHWADRONS HAD A CERTAIN NEIGHBOR WHO WAS downright wicked in her never-ending attempts to destroy Rebbetzin Schwadron's peace of mind and to generally poison the atmosphere.

One day, this woman became a widow. A week passed, then two, and it came to the Rebbetzin's attention that this widow was sleeping in an empty house at night, lonely and miserable. The

Rebbetzin empathized with the other woman's pain. She made up her mind that this woman had just spent her last night alone.

Two of the Schwadron daughters walked over to the woman's home and climbed the steps. Hesitantly they knocked on the door and offered their companionship for the night. From then on, the two girls slept at the widow's house, alleviating her loneliness.

"My parents were always talking about restraint and self-control," the daughter recalls, "and the prohibition against bearing grudges. You could say the slogan of our home was: 'Forget it, give it up, let it go.'"

JERUSALEM WAS IN THE GRIP OF A TERRIBLE EPIDEMIC. POLIO had claimed the lives of many. In a natural reaction, the city's res-

Epidemic idents kept their distance from anyone who had a sick person at home. The slightest rumor of possible contagion was enough to keep the neighbors at bay.

One Jerusalem woman tells of the time her brother fell sick with the dreaded disease. "When I approached the door of the grocery store, I was ordered not to come in. From inside the shop, the store-keeper would shout: 'Keep your distance! Stand away with your basket open, and I'll throw the bread into it.'

"I was completely ostracized. The fear was everywhere, and it was justified."

One of R' Sholom's friends relates that two of his children succumbed to polio. This upstanding *talmid chacham* was busy caring for his sick children on a round-the-clock basis. There were two other children at home. Who was to care for them?

The man said not a word to anyone, but his anguished eyes told their own story. He needed immediate and ongoing help in caring for his healthy children. Silently, he pleaded for someone to remove the children from his house and attend to them. It was a question of saving lives.

R' Sholom and his wife took the children in.

The Schwadron household consisted of 10 people at the time, living in two crowded rooms. Among them were young children. But R' Sholom did not hesitate in adding two more.

Apart from the physical inconvenience was the crushing worry: Was there a chance that these children were carrying the germs of the terrible sickness that was claiming so many lives? Would the Schwadron household become infected as well? The neighbors were shocked at the Schwadron's temerity in accepting the two children. Rebbetzin Schwadron herself worried silently. Each day brought its fresh burden of anxiety. Who knew what fate was in store for them?

"He who performs a mitzvah will not know anything bad," R' Sholom proclaimed. And, for an entire month, the Rebbetzin bathed, fed, and soothed the children of that *talmid chacham*. No sacrifice was too great for the sake of doing a *chesed*.

R' SHOLOM WAS ONE OF THE GENERATION'S FOREMOST LEADERS in the mitzvah of *hachnasas orchim* — welcoming guests into his

Open House

home. There was a period when he wished to devote a set portion of each of his talks specifically to this mitzvah. Though that plan never came to fruition, R' Sholom's personal example remained indelibly etched in the hearts of Jerusalem's residents.

The story is told of one oddly-behaved guest who suffered from a painful stomach disorder, real or imaginary, that required oil massages and frequent bandaging. He was also subject to strange and awful fears. At unexpected moments he would erupt in a shout: "*Gevald!* They want to kill me!" Normal people kept their distance. Even if the gates of compassion in their hearts were wide open to him, the doors of their homes were firmly shut.

Who would care for such an individual? Who would receive him into their home?

It was not long before he found the right address: 17 Sha'arei Chesed Street.

The Schwadrons cared for him devotedly. R' Sholom changed his bandages and the Rebbetzin washed them with her own hands. (She had no washing machine.) The Rebbetzin fed him and calmed his fears. His clothes reeked so unbearably that the family members were unable to be near him for more than a few minutes at a time. At night, all the Schwadron girls and their mother slept in one room, while R' Sholom slept in the other near their guest. According to a son-in-law, when this guest, or others like him — and there were many — came for a Shabbos meal, R' Sholom made sure to seat them at the head of the table, at his own right hand. He forbade his family to keep too far away (though he did allow them to maintain a certain distance at the table, in order to prevent them from succumbing to nausea during the meal). Quietly, but with unmistakable firmness, R' Sholom explained to his children how important it was not to embarrass their guests. In this house, his tone implied, we perform the mitzvah of *hachnasas orchim*. Anyone who finds that too difficult may eat at the neighbors.

R' Avraham Tovoleski, a relative of R' Sholom, relates:

"I once entered R' Sholom's house and found him, as usual, sitting and learning. Not far from his chair sat a simple Jew, reciting *Tehillim* in a loud, raucous voice. Later, the man told me that he distributed newspapers in the morning, which left him many free hours during the day. He would come to the Schwadron house, enjoy a meal, then sit reciting *Tehillim* — and R' Sholom would pay him for 'energizing' his morning.

"This routine lasted for many years ... with pay."

R' SHOLOM'S SON-IN-LAW RECALLS AN INCIDENT THAT OCcurred soon after he married into the Schwadron family:

One Seder Night It was the first night of Pesach, and after *Ma'ariv* in Sha'arei Chesed's "Chassidim" synagogue, R' Sholom noticed one man who had remained behind in shul. Though the fellow's appearance bespoke a man of sense, perhaps even a Torah scholar, both sight and smell of his soiled and threadbare clothing testified to the fact that their last cleaning was lost in the mists of time. In fact, on closer scrutiny, fleas were clearly visible on his suit. "Standing next to him," the son-in-law remembers, "was just horrible."

On the spot, R' Sholom decided to bring the man home for the Seder. To invite him to sleep over at their house was impossible, however, because of the fleas. This problem troubled R' Sholom to no end. Where would the man sleep that night? "We have to find him a place to sleep. The meal will be over late. Where will we send him after midnight?" he whispered anxiously to his son-in-law.

Back home, the family was impatiently awaiting R' Sholom's arrival before the little ones succumbed to sleep. But R' Sholom did not appear. As time passed, his wife and children told themselves, "Abba probably found some mitzvah to attend to. We'll wait."

Sure enough, R' Sholom was completely caught up in the momentum of the mitzvah at hand. Back at the shul, he thought for a few minutes, and came up with an idea. "Let's go," he told his son-in-law. "We'll track down the owner of the Yerushalayim Hotel." (The hotel was located a short distance from the Sha'arei Chesed neighborhood.)

Before he left, R' Sholom went over to the unfortunate Jew, shook his hand warmly, and said, "Good Yom Tov. You're invited to our house for the Seder! We'll be back in a little while and walk home together. Please wait for us."

The man mustered a grateful smile, then sat down at a table to wait, a *sefer* open in front of him. R' Sholom and his son-in-law left.

The streets were deserted. Everyone was already seated at their tables like kings, inaugurating the Seder by announcing *Kaddesh!* R' Sholom and his son-in-law hurried to the hotelier's home, where R' Sholom requested a single room for his guest. "We'll be responsible for any damage that may result," he promised. The man agreed; a key exchanged hands. The two returned to the shul and R' Sholom happily collected his guest.

Together, the three walked to the Schwadron home. As R' Sholom led his guest inside, the Rebbetzin and her daughters moved quickly away. The girls whispered among themselves in agitation.

"Who is he?"

"Where did Abba find him?"

"Look out, that chair is going to be full of fleas!"

"The smell is unbearable!"

The Rebbetzin stepped forward with a pleasant smile, offering

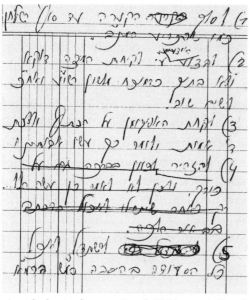

A notebook entry from erev Pesach, 1965 — reminders of halachos and minhagim

the man a seat. R' Sholom, as usual, seated the guest at the head of the table. The person at the man's other side surreptitiously moved his chair until a full meter separated the two. The stench was truly unbearable. Tiny creatures were already beginning to crawl around under the guest's chair.

Kaddesh. Ur'chatz. Karpas. Yachatz. Maggid. This was where R' Sholom ascertained that his guest's interior was indeed of far finer quality than his exterior: He was a learned man. Enthusiastically, R' Sholom engaged the man in a spirited dialogue on various aspects of the Haggadah and its commentary. The animated talk continued all through the Seder.

At midnight, R' Sholom and his son-in-law went out into the dark street to accompany the guest to his hotel, where they parted warmly.

After that night, the hotelier was forced to dispose of the mattress that the man had used, along with all the bedclothes. (At that time, there were few means of exterminating the bugs.) True to his word, R' Sholom paid for all the damages.

His son-in-law concludes: "If you want to know how far R' Sholom's aspirations in the area of *hachnasas orchim* went, I'll tell you what I heard from his own lips about that great mitzvah. More than once, R' Sholom told me: 'I envy a certain Jew from England, who welcomes so many guests into his home that he himself often has no bed for the night and has to sleep in his car. I truly envy him. If only I merited the same!'"

WHEN THE NEIGHBORHOOD CATS HAD FINISHED THEIR ROUNDS
of the garbage dumpsters, they made their way routinely to Dinah's

**Cats, Cats,
Everywhere**

house. She cared for them faithfully.

Who didn't know Dinah, an abandoned
and slightly addled old woman who hardly
ever went out into the street? Several times a day she stepped into
her front yard to feed the cats. The local children, as children will,
threw things at Dinah's cats. Her shouts and expostulations only
increased their antics. This situation went on for years.

To Dinah's good fortune, R' Sholom lived right across the street.
If anyone tried to chase away her cats, it was R' Sholom who was
summoned to help. He was also one of the few whom Dinah con-
descended to visit.

"R' Sholom!" she would call. "*Ich hub ah kashah!* (I have a question!) The Gemara says that visiting the sick removes a sixtieth of
his illness. Why not send 60 people to visit him, and he'll recover
completely! R' Sholom, what do you think of that idea?" An intelligent woman, if also a peculiar one.

One day, one of the cats followed her across the street. Suddenly,
it shot away from her, heading towards a Schwadron daughter.
Seeing the girl reacting, Dinah asked her angrily, "Hey, why are you
running away from the cat? He's not doing anything!" She then
turned, "R' Sholom, what's your opinion of Sha'arei Chesed today?"

R' Sholom and his Rebbetzin listened, smiling patiently.

R' Sholom's son-in-law tells of the time Dinah visited on the first
night of Pesach. Outside, the yard was dark, while inside, the
house was brightly illuminated. Haggadahs, wine, the Seder plate,
and the matzos were laid out royally and the family members were
seated around the festive table when, abruptly, Dinah appeared at
the door holding a glass. Behind her, as a matter of course, was a
cat, playfully chasing its tail.

"Rebbetzin!" Dinah called. "Please ask your husband if this
glass can be used for the four cups of wine. Ooh, what a pretty
tablecloth you bought." Then she thought of another question that
she posed to R' Sholom. "R' Sholom, this has been bothering me
for years. When we say *Ha lachma anya* ..." Another cat popped

into view and began weaving its way through the legs of a nearby chair. This odd mixture of questions and cats was liberally sprinkled with shouts from the grandchildren, who leaped out of their seats crying, "Help! I'm scared!"

R' Sholom and his wife acted with their customary patience. Quietly, they moved the matzos to a corner, lest one of the cats drop from its mouth bread crumbs which it had picked up from some dumpster. They answered all of the old woman's questions pleasantly. When she was satisfied, they escorted her, with warm smiles, to the door. Only then did they return to their recital of the Exodus from Egypt.

R' SHOLOM'S DAUGHTER STUDIED THE STRANGE LOOKING MAN standing in the doorway. "Apparently," she thought, "someone

A Different Kind of Guest

sent him here." Everyone knew that you could send anyone to the Schwadrons.

"It was Friday night," relates the daughter, "and the family was seated around the Shabbos table when the man appeared at the door. His demeanor was frightening: scowling face, red eyes, swollen cheeks, wild hair, gaping mouth. All were taken aback at this apparition, frozen in tension as Abba approached the stranger.

"'Good Shabbos,' he greeted the man.

"'I need to eat. I also have no place to sleep.' The man's voice was thick and pleading.

"'All right,' Abba replied apprehensively.

"This once, my father's joy at the mitzvah that had fallen to his lot was tinged by genuine fear and doubt. He did not seat the stranger with the others, leading him instead into the bedroom. There, at a small table, he served his guest a meal. The man's breathing sounded odd. Abba was conscious of a pang of anxiety.

"But — *hachnasas orchim!* That obligation superseded all else.

"The family completed its meal. Abba was scheduled to walk over to the Zichron Moshe Shul that night to deliver a lecture. Trembling, my mother said, 'No, you can't go and leave us alone.'"

R' Sholom was in a quandary. On the one hand, how could he chase a guest from his home — especially a guest who had expressed a need for a place to sleep? On the other hand, how could he cancel the talk for which people were already assembled and waiting? Both were impossible. Finally, he decided to enlist a relative to stay with the family and protect them from any harm until his return.

Before R' Sholom left the house, the family collected the knives, forks, and every other sharp implement they owned. These they hid in a concealed drawer. R' Sholom went into the bedroom, offered the man a bed, then left the house with his customary confidence. "The performer of a mitzvah will come to no harm!"

The house was quiet. The family waited patiently for R' Sholom's return. A light rain was falling and the streets were empty. When, at length, they heard his hearty "Good Shabbos!" everyone breathed a sigh of relief.

R' Sholom peeked into the bedroom and saw that the stranger was sound asleep. The room reeked of alcohol. The man was a drunkard.

Frequently, when this type of guest was in the house, R' Sholom would sleep in the same room as the guest while the remainder of the family crowded into the other bedroom. This time, however, he was leery of pursuing this practice. He joined the others in the second room.

R' Sholom's daughter continues: "Abba used to *daven* with the sunrise (*vasikin*) *minyan*. Very early the next morning, he prepared to leave for shul. Imma woke up and begged, 'It's dark outside, dark in the yard, maybe something will happen. Please … All night I heard rustlings. The man was wandering through the house. Sholom! Don't go out!'

"But Abba gathered his courage and left the room. On tiptoe he approached the guest's bedroom and peeked inside.

"'He's gone!' Abba announced. He hurried to the front door. 'He opened this door and left the house. Who knows what he might have taken with him.'

"In the darkness of early Shabbos morning, Imma walked around, checking to see if anything was missing. Suddenly, from the kitchen, she exclaimed, 'I told you I heard him walking around at night. It frightened me. Look, there's no food! All the fish is gone.' When we all rushed into the kitchen after Imma, we saw that the *cholent*, too, had been reduced by half. Our visitor had apparently taken a spoon to the pot as it stood on the *blech*, and had eaten his fill.

"That Shabbos, we all joined our uncle, Rav Shlomo Zalman Auerbach, for the lunchtime *seudah*!"

Switching Gears CHANAH WAS A VERY ADDLEBRAINED WOMAN. "WHEN THERE was no more room, she slept in our beds with us," R' Sholom's daughters recall. They treated her with respect, allowing her to ramble on for hour upon hour. She would remain with the family for days and nights, chattering, weaving stories, weeping, laughing, and shouting. She also ate a great deal. But R' Sholom would not hear of sending Chanah away.

However, in the course of her excessive talking, there reached a point when she would inevitably begin spewing coarse and vulgar language. This pierced R' Sholom's equanimity. "*Nivul peh* (coarse language)?" he roared. "Send her away at once!"

Chanah knew that there always came a point in time when she would have to leave. The Rebbetzin gently said, "Chanah, it's time to go home now. Come back tomorrow." Unoffended, the woman left, only to return several days later, as merry as ever.

Hachnasas orchim. The mitzvah derives not merely from kindness, but from an obligation imposed on us by the Torah. Yet when this ideal clashes with G-d's will, the goal is quick to change.

R' Sholom's sensibilities were very finely tuned.

Home Talk THE MAN WHO WAS THE EPITOME OF CONTENTMENT AND JOY — the man whom others loved to be near — the man who later became a *velt mensch* (a man of the world), was a modest Jew who tasted few of the pleasures this world has to offer. While many believe that this world is the fountainhead of happiness, R' Sholom knew otherwise. And this was the source of his contentment.

His kitchen was so small that it was exempt from the requirement to post a *mezuzah* on its door. It had, of course, only one sink. There were just two bedrooms for the entire family, and the bathroom was outside the apartment till the end of his days. Money was something you needed in order to live, but never something to be amassed.

Not everyone is capable of living as R' Sholom did.

WHEN WE CAME INTO THE HOUSE, A CERTAIN INDIVIDUAL RElated, the house was filled with serenity. The atmosphere was

Around the Table sheer delight, and you felt it the instant you set foot inside the door.

We stood in the doorway, a group of young *kollel* men, and looked around the giant room. From floor to ceiling, every wall was lined with *sefarim*, old and new. And in the midst of them all sat R' Sholom, radiating contentment.

It was *erev* Shabbos, and we had come to hear R' Sholom address us. Smiling through his beard, he looked at each of us as we came in and motioned for us to sit. We took our places around a large wooden table, on chairs that were strong, simple, and very old. The moment we sat down facing R' Sholom, we were overcome

R' Sholom in his book-lined study, addressing the members of Kollel Da'as Torah; to the left is the Rosh Kollel, R' Yitzchak Schwadron

with tranquility — a spiritual peace that filled the soul. On the table, opposite R' Sholom, was a piece of thick paper propped up at a slant. It read: *Shivisi Hashem l'negdi tamid.* (Hashem is before me always.)

The Rebbetzin remained modestly in the adjoining room, seated on a chair that squeaked, to hear her husband speak.

"You want encouragement?" R' Sholom began. "From me? Who am I? But I will pass on to you what I've heard from others, from my teachers and *rebbe'im*, from the great R' Leib Chasman. Thunder was created only to straighten out the crookedness in our hearts."

For a time, R' Sholom spoke of deep matters. Then, unexpectedly, he changed direction.

"People search for mitzvos outside, in the streets. They don't know that their own households contain everything there is. I will tell you a story.

"About 20 years ago, one of my small children fell ill. I did not want the other children to catch his illness, so I decided to send them to my mother's house for a day or two. I walked from Sha'arei Chesed toward the Beis Yisrael neighborhood, where my mother lived.

"On the way, I met R' Isaac Sher. 'Good morning, R' Sholom,' he greeted me. I returned the greeting.

"'Where are you going?' R' Isaac asked.

"I explained that my child was sick and that I was on my way to my mother's with the other children.

"There was a brief silence, and then R' Isaac asked simply, 'Well, what then?'

"I didn't understand what he meant. I had no idea what to answer.

"Apparently, R' Isaac wanted to ask what had driven me to this action. 'Why, and what for?' he asked again.

"Raising my voice slightly, I repeated my explanation. 'My child is sick so I'm taking the other children to my mother's house.'

"Narrowing his gaze, R' Isaac said, 'In other words, the big animal is leading the small animal.' (In the animal kingdom, parents also show concern for the well-being of their offspring.) He went on to explain, 'But what is the difference? *You* are on your way to do a *chesed* to a Jewish child, who also happens to be your own flesh and blood.'

"Do you understand?" R' Sholom asked the young men grouped around his table. "It's simple! You just do *chesed*."

"That same morning, on my return to Sha'arei Chesed, I saw my wife approaching with two buckets of water she had drawn from the well. I hurried toward her. Whispering, '*Hineni muchan u'mezuman la'asos chesed* ... I am ready and willing to perform a *chesed* for a Jewish woman, who happens to be my wife,' I took the buckets from her.

"Half a year later," R' Sholom continued, "I had taken R' Isaac's words to the point where I said, '*Hineni muchan u'mezuman la'asos chesed*' in my behavior toward my wife, my children, and in everything I did. All my actions have been tailored to this new attitude. A wise man can change dust to gold!"

R' Sholom raised his voice. "Everything that goes on at home can fall into this category! There are men and women who think they are doing nothing. They are 'only' raising their children. But every step in the home that is accompanied by a good intention is a gold mine. To raise children who are healthy and strong, to nurture them in Torah and fear of Heaven — this is *chesed. And* Torah.

"Let me tell you another story. This one involves R' Eliyahu Lopian. We were once walking in the street together when we saw a Jewish man repairing the street. R' Elyah turned to me and said, 'Look at that Jew who is so involved in doing mitzvos — specifically, the mitzvah of settling the Land of Israel. The only thing missing here is his *intent* to do a mitzvah! If our focus is only to earn a living, we lose the value of the mitzvah. It all depends on the intent.'

"Do you understand? There are mitzvos spread everywhere, and it takes only a drop of thought to have it all. The important thing to remember is: Don't run through the streets searching for mitzvos. You can *also* search in the streets, but not exclusively so.

"Here is the language of the *Ohr Yahel* in *Parashas Bamidbar*: A man who guards a city at night, shielding its citizens from all harm — imagine if he did this for the sake of the *chesed*. There would be nothing that could exceed it! To patrol the streets alone, night after night, through rain and sleet, never abandoning his job as protector. Sometimes we find a man who is a thief or a murderer or some other lowly form of humanity. Yet this man does his job well — he guards faithfully. However, even after years of faithful guarding, he remains his lowly self [and the kind deed he performed in protecting the people had no influence on him at all]! Why is that? It is because he did his job solely for the sake of the coin he was paid — and not in order to do good to others. What a tremendous loss! What has he sold for that trifling coin? Thousands upon thousands of exalted mitzvos — protecting men, women, and children, an entire city. Had he done this marvelous *chesed* for the sake of *chesed*, how rich he would be! Instead, for the sake of a coin, he has lost everything."

R' Sholom gazed around the table at the circle of intent faces. "I want to add another important detail about our day-to-day lives at home," he continued. "A man thinks that he is boss over his own home, over his wife, his children, and himself — and he forgets *HaKadosh Baruch Hu!*

"I will tell you a parable, based on a true story."

The *kollel* men stirred in their seats, their expressions filled with anticipation. R' Sholom began his story:

"For years, every day a certain man stood at the entrance to Jerusalem, holding an umbrella in the rain and wearing a cap to shield his head from the sun. Many people might recall him with a smile — a witless fellow who waved his arms to direct traffic, calling, 'Go! Go! Go!' He derived great satisfaction from the thought that all the cars were moving because of him. *He* was supervising them, and they were moving on his command. Wonderful!

"When the light turned red, the man would fall silent, waiting patiently. The instant the green light reappeared, he would begin waving his arms again, shouting, 'Go on! Drive!' He felt like a policeman, personally guiding the great flow of traffic into Jerusalem.

"A small deficiency in the brain, and you are convinced that all of Tel Aviv is following your lead into Jerusalem. Day after day, hour after hour, he stood there. Drivers liked to glance through their windows and smile at the unfortunate fellow at his post — a madman with a diploma in traffic patterns!

"This, my friends, is exactly how people appear. The normal man thinks: 'I am in control, I am the boss.' The children are sick and the father shouts: 'Go! Drive!' Pop some aspirin into the child's mouth and the fever leaves, and the father is convinced that he is the one who cured his child.

"In the course of a lifetime we convince ourselves that our private lives are steered by our own hands! *HaKadosh Baruch Hu*, Who leads the world all the time, gives the green light and lets the aspirin do its work. Health resumes, life goes on, a livelihood is obtained in wondrous ways, a thousand details sort themselves out in a personal pattern, and the man continues to stand there waving his hand: 'Go! Go! Go!' In his foolishness he smiles to himself, certain that it's all his doing."

Rav Sholom smiled sadly. "We, too, can provide a good laugh to the people driving into Jerusalem."

There was a silence as these poignant words sank into every consciousness. R' Sholom roused himself. "Let me say a few more words.

"The introduction to works of Kabbalah states that a person is first tested with the members of his own household. The head of a family is convinced that he is always right, that he must teach all the others and preach to them. It is all *I*. *I* will teach them, *I* will rebuke them ... *I*, *I*, *I*. But the Chazon Ish once told me: 'It is necessary to know *how* to teach.' Do you understand? You have to know *how* to teach!

"Whether you know how or you don't, the knowledge is readily available: There are two tractates in *Shas* that deal with *derech eretz*: one for the common man and the other specifically for *talmidei chachamim*." R' Sholom opened a volume to the latter tractate and began to chant, "How do *Chazal* begin this section? How does it open? With which behavior? *Yungeleit!*" He smote the table with his fist. "Listen to these simple words: 'The ways of Torah scholars are humble and industrious ... [they are] beloved of all men and ... subservient to the members of their households.'"

Here, once again, R' Sholom raised his voice. "Look further, and see what *Chazal* say in another place [*Maseches Kallah*, ch. 3]: 'A *talmid chacham* should be sweet to all people and not like a pot without salt.'" A smile overspread R' Sholom's face. "A pot without salt. Have you ever tasted soup without salt?

"When someone greets you with 'Good morning,' why do you answer with a scowling face?

"' He woke up on the wrong side of the bed,' they say about you.

"No, *rabbosai!*" He smacked the table again. "A *talmid chacham* must be sweet to everyone! And especially at home. At h-o-m-e. The walls of a person's home testify to his behavior. Be sweet and pleasant to everyone, your wife and your children. They are not your servants!" R' Sholom enjoyed a laugh along with his visitors.

Then he opened a volume entitled *Sha'arei Kedushah*, by R' Chaim Vital, and began reading aloud the following excerpt:

"Understand well that they are basic and essential [and therefore] were not included in the tally of the 613 mitzvos that are dependent on the intellect. It is even more necessary to be careful of bad character traits than to perform the positive and negative commandments, for the possessor of a good character will easily observe the mitzvos."

Seeing the tears in R' Sholom's eyes, one of those present was forcibly reminded of a talk that the *maggid* had given one Rosh Hashanah night. R' Sholom had entered the Kehal Chassidim Shul in Sha'arei Chesed, where the *gabbai* asked him to speak before the *Ma'ariv* service. R' Sholom walked over to the bookcase, removed a volume of R' Chaim Vital's *Sha'arei Kedushah*, and stepped up onto the dais. Opening the *sefer*, he then proceeded to read aloud the same excerpt about good character traits, enunciating each word slowly and clearly, and he began to cry. Upon concluding the excerpt, he went back and read it again, crying harder and harder. This was his entire talk. This is what he offered to rouse the congregants in preparation for the Day of Judgment.

The group of *kollel* men met at the Schwadron house again the following week. R' Sholom touched on matters relating to the time of the year — the month of Elul — with eyes closed and an emotionally charged voice. When at last he opened his eyes, the others saw that they were filled with tears. He looked directly at the young men and asked, "And you're *not* crying? You should cry over the fact that you're not crying!"

In his penetrating voice he continued to exhort the men, arousing their emotion. Just before concluding, he raised his voice and cried out tearfully, "*Rabbosai!* Let us repent! *My dear yungeleit*, let us ask all together — *hashiveinu* — bring us back!"

Together, in one voice, the entire group cried, "*Hashiveinu Hashem eilecha v'nashuvah, chadeish yameinu k'kedem!* Return us to You, O L–rd, and we shall return, renew our days as of old!"

"Good night," R' Sholom blessed them, "and a good week." They left respectfully.

R' AVRAHAM TOKER RELATED THE FOLLOWING INCIDENT TO R' Sholom Schwadron — a tale that gave R' Sholom a great deal of

Minute by Minute

pleasure. It stands as an interesting glimpse into the private lives of our great Torah personalities. Rabbi Toker relates:

I knocked on R' Yechezkel Abramsky's door. There was something I needed to discuss with him urgently. Rebbetzin Abramsky apologized: "The Rav is not at home. He should be back within a quarter of an hour's time. You can wait here in the house."

The minutes passed. Soon we saw the bright countenance of the *gaon*, author of the *Chazon Yechezkel*, in the doorway. I stood up and remained standing until R' Abramsky had sat down at the table.

The Rebbetzin came in with a glass of tea. She set the glass down in front of her husband and sat down at the table. I took my place there as well.

I listened as the great man began conversing with his wife. He began to tell her everything that had happened from the moment he had left the house, about 2 hours earlier.

"When I left home, I caught the number 21 bus," the *gaon* began. "I rode until Rechov HaNevi'im, where I got off, climbed the hill — *baruch Hashem*, it wasn't too difficult — and continued along Rechov Strauss in the direction of Meah Shearim until I reached R' Eliezer Yehudah Finkel's house." Rabbi Abramsky paused, took a breath, and continued. "I went over to sit near R' Leizer Yudel, and they happened to give me a low chair to sit on. After a few minutes another man came in. He explained that he was from South America, and he asked me my name. I told him it was Abramsky. He retorted: 'Your name is bigger than you look!' I answered, 'That's right, I know.'"

R' Yechezkel went on to describe his conversation with R' Eliezer Yehudah Finkel. "When I stood up to leave, R' Leizer Yudel told me, 'I'll walk you to the bus.' I told him, 'If you do, I won't come back here anymore.'

"'All right,' R' Eliezer Yehudah conceded. 'I'll just walk you out to the street.' I answered, 'If you walk me to the street I'll be distressed.' The Mirrer *Rosh Yeshivah* answered, 'I'll walk you to the door, and that's that!'"

Rabbi Abramsky went on to briefly discuss with his wife further details of his outing. When he was done, the Rebbetzin stood up and returned to the kitchen. Only then did I have my turn to speak with the Rav.

Rabbi Abramsky turned to me and said, "Avraham! I taught you an important lesson. When you return home, tell your wife everything that happened to you, to interest her, and to show that you want her to know about the things that occur in your life."

R' Sholom Schwadron, the man who so frequently spoke with such eloquence and passion about interpersonal relationships, was deeply moved by this story. "*Nu*, one thing is clear to see," he remarked. "The *Shechinah* certainly resides among them."

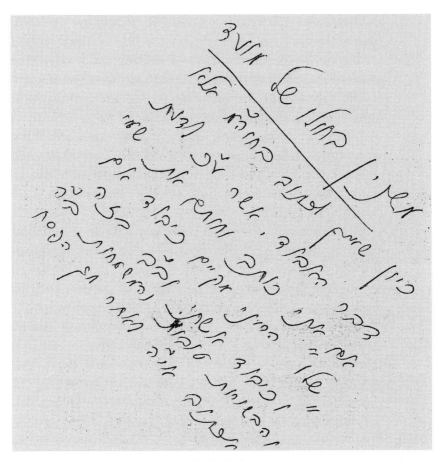

A letter to his family from overseas

R' SHOLOM'S DAUGHTER SPEAKS OF THE HOME SHE SHARED
with her parents and siblings:

Joy of Life The apartment consisted of a room and a half.
Abba's study — a room lined, floor to ceiling, with
thousands of *sefarim* — became a bedroom for all of us children at night. The beds were placed all around the table
where Abba learned. That's how we grew up.

Abba sat at that broad wooden table in the center of the
large room, learning at all hours of the day and night.
There were long stretches when he would sit there
wrapped in his *tefillin.* At night, when Abba realized that

the light was disturbing our sleep, he would get up, walk over to the doorway where the light switch was located, and switch off the ceiling light. Then he'd light the lamp that stood in the center of the table, beside the open volumes.

The light would illuminate his face, as the faint smell of kerosene from the lamp lulled us to sleep …

When did Abba sleep? That's a good question. There were times when he entered the room very tired and drained, sat down in his chair and dozed off for about an hour. When he awoke, he took a match, relit the lamp, and continued learning.

In the morning, he got up with the dawn. For many years he *davened* with the sunrise *minyan*. On his return home he had a routine of learning *Mishnayos* and then *mussar*. During the summers, when *Shacharis* ended early, we would wake to the pleasant sound of Abba's *Mishnayos*.

The sounds of Abba's early-morning *"mussar seder"* sweetened the atmosphere, while the tears that fell onto the table elevated our awakening. His voice was sweet and pleasant — the voice of *mussar* by a man of *mussar*. At times, his voice flowed; at others, it trembled and broke.

Afterwards, he was merry and happy all through the day. Whenever we entered the house we felt the joy of living emanating from him — a spiritual richness and happiness. He chanted each page of Gemara with a sweet joy, day and night.

He rejoiced in every new thing. Each fresh twist in his learning of Torah and *mussar* aroused tremendous enthusiasm. People used to call him a spiritual *"nosher"* because of his enormous hunger for each new crumb that would take him to new depths. It didn't matter if the crumb came from an old person or a young one. A fresh reading of *Rashi* or *Tosafos* would fill Abba with elation, and an apt saying by *Chazal* would intoxicate him. Hearing an additional inspirational nuance on any topic could reduce him to ecstatic tears.

What joy in living!

ONE OF R' SHOLOM'S DAUGHTERS, JUST 7 YEARS OLD, WAS BE-
having in a way that her father deemed inappropriate. One

Without Words

morning, on his return from the *vasikin minyan*, he took the little girl on his shoulder, carried her into the large, book-lined room, seated her opposite him at the table ... and burst into tears. After a few seconds, he began talking to himself through his tears.

"Why? Why has it come to this, that my daughter has sinned? What is my own crime and my own sin, to be punished this way? How have I failed, that my daughter should behave like this?"

With heartrending tears but not a single direct word to his daughter, R' Sholom drove home his message. From that day onward, the negative desire vanished in the girl. She was simply incapable of returning to her former behavior.

"THE WALLS OF HIS HOME TESTIFY ON HIS BEHALF," HIS DAUGH-
ter says. "At home, we saw his enormous efforts and his

A Personal Conversation

tremendous personal dedication. We often heard him scolding himself severely. It was fascinating to hear how he sought the central point in everything he did. For example, when we were seated at the Shabbos table and Abba said, '*lichvod Shabbos kodesh*' (in honor of the Sabbath) before eating, we could hear him whisper, immediately afterward: 'In honor of the Shabbos — or of my innards?' He scrutinized every step he took.

"Once, late at night, I saw my father go over to the refrigerator and take out something to eat. He stood beside the open refrigerator for a moment, then suddenly slammed the door shut as though in pain, saying out loud: 'Do not stray after your hearts and your eyes!' Who else would think that this applies to the refrigerator?!

"He never drank soda or any sweet drink, nor did he eat ice cream. 'Water from the tap is hard for me to drink — that's why I drink seltzer,' he would explain. Coffee, tea, or seltzer — that was the extent of his indulgence!"

R' Sholom was in the habit of talking to himself at home, words of introspection or self-rebuke. A yeshivah boy who once stayed at the Schwadron home was asleep in the room next to the study when he woke suddenly to the sound of R' Sholom pacing in the hallway outside his room, commenting aloud. Hesitantly, the boy opened his door and asked, "Did the Rav say something? Did he want something?"

R' Sholom smiled. "Have you ever seen a madman talking to himself?"

The boy beat a hasty retreat.

Another yeshivah student, paying close attention to R' Sholom's self-directed remarks, learned something of value. It was late one night when R' Sholom began to think aloud, in a *mussar*-like chant: "Ah, Sholom'ke, do you know that the world you're immersed in is only a corridor? No?" R' Sholom tapped on the table with a finger. "Not to know, but to *feel* that the world is only temporary!"

At that point R' Sholom noticed, out of the corner of an eye, that he had an audience. He smiled at the yeshivah boy and motioned for him to come closer. "Ah, you were listening? In that case, listen to something deep: A person can observe the Torah and mitzvos — for this world. He wants to be okay with *HaKadosh Baruch Hu*. His

In his succah

primary ambition is to get through life in peace. He believes implicitly that Hashem can ruin this so-pleasant world for him, and he is afraid.

"Good night to you," R' Sholom concluded, and returned to his thoughts.

The next evening, R' Sholom summoned the young man to his room to add another nugget. "I want to tell you a story.

"One of R' Aharon of Karlin's chassidim came to bask in his presence, and saw his Rebbe recite the blessing over fruit and then eat an apple. The thought flitted through his mind: 'I also eat apples and recite the blessing over them. What, then, is the difference between us?'

"R' Aharon sensed this thought, and turned to him immediately with a question. 'What really is the difference between us? Don't we both eat apples? The difference is small, but big.

"'I, moved by Hashem's marvelous creation, am ignited to the point where I yearn to bless Him and praise Him for creating trees, the earth, etc. That is why I take an apple and recite the blessing over it. You, on the other hand, desire to eat, and because it is forbidden to eat without a blessing, you recite one. We see that there are those who eat in order to say the blessing, and those who say a blessing in order to eat. We can categorize each individual according to his aspirations, ambitions, and desires.'

"Do you understand?" R' Sholom asked his guest. "Many people live for money or food, amassing money or eating in order to continue living — a cycle that runs into old age. Money for life and life for money, until life is gone along with the money. And then there are people ... Ah! They're the ones who have a part in this world *and* the next."

As the student waited, listening raptly, R' Sholom continued, "R' Shlomo of Zavil once said: 'Believe me, in my youth I used to put on my *tefillin* with such pleasure — like a man satisfying his greatest desire.' A person *can* reach this level." R' Sholom opened his heart to his young guest: "I am not a *tzaddik*, I am not holy, I am a person like all others — and yet, I can remember, as a young man at *Shacharis* on Shabbos morning, wrapping myself in my *tallis* and

Returning from Shacharis, accompanied by R' Kalman Krohn and Avraham Zelig Krohn

davening. And when I reached the words, *The soul of every living be-ing shall bless Your Name, Hashem our G-d; the spirit of all flesh shall always glorify and exalt Your remembrance, our King, from this world to the World to Come,* I would grow so emotional that my eyes began streaming tears of joy! My heart expanded in delight! What plea-sure!" Lifting his voice jubilantly, R' Sholom said, "I wouldn't sell those moments for any price!"

Smiling, he continued, "I'll explain something to you. An ac-quaintance once gave me a $5,000 check for *tzedakah.* At first, my happiness was great — $5,000! I had not held such a sum in a long time! After a few hours, however, I was used to the feeling. My happiness diminished. By the time a day or two had passed, I felt no special pleasure from the thousands of dollars in my wallet. Know this! A rich man who holds $50,000 in his hand and is ac-customed to it is about as happy as I was with my 5,000....

"How different is spiritual joy, joy in Torah, in love and awe of Hashem. ['I rejoice in Your Word as one who finds a great trea-sure.' One of our Torah giants explained these words: King David is saying that he always experiences a pleasure comparable to the moment of finding a great treasure. The pleasure does not diminish.]

"Yes! Yes!" R' Sholom ended. "When R' Aharon of Karlin and other Torah greats like him recite a blessing over a fruit, do they receive the *next* world? They receive *this* world!

"Good night, my dear boy."

And R' Sholom removed his glasses to read the small letters in the *Tosafos* he had been learning.

More Eloquent than Words

THE YESHIVAH WORLD ENJOYED HEARING R' SHOLOM'S SILENCES during his "speech fasts" (*ta'anis dibbur*). His silence, on these occasions, was more eloquent than the best talk he could deliver.

During these periods, R' Sholom would frequently express himself in writing. He kept an ample supply of paper and pens on hand for "talking" on paper. Often — especially on Shabbos and Yom Tov, when writing is prohibited — he would employ apt quotes from *Tanach*, *Shas*, or *Mishnayos*. He was generally careful, at such times, not to use these quotes in a way that

At a wedding, Elul 1989

"Speaking" — by writing — during Elul

would amuse those around him, but occasionally a situation would arise that spurred his sharp intelligence to quote a verse or saying of *Chazal* that brought a smile to his listeners' lips.

On one occasion, he let a woman know that she was not behaving appropriately with her child, quoting: "Merciful women cooked their children." And once, requiring his daughter's assistance, he phoned her, saying, "*Bo yavo b'rinah.*" (He will return in exultation.) Alarmed, she thought he might be feeling unwell.

"Abba, what happened?" she asked in agitation.

Raising his voice, he reiterated a reassuring, "*B'rinah!*"

There are thousands of incidents of this nature told about R' Sholom during his speech fasts.

His silences were not thunderous. It was pleasant being around R' Sholom during his *ta'anis dibbur*. For 60 years he refrained from speech twice a week — every Monday and Thursday! These fasts took place only during the daylight hours, never at night.

In others words, R' Sholom kept silent for at least 6,000 days over the course of his life: Mondays, Thursdays, and often also on Shabbos, along with the 40 consecutive days between *Rosh Chodesh* Elul and Yom Kippur. And this in a man who knew how to talk and loved to do so … the same R' Sholom who made a highly skilled craft of employing words to good effect — to draw his listeners closer to their Creator.

Even when knocking on doors abroad, collecting charity, R' Sholom did not break his silence. He would converse only on Torah matters, and write down the rest. If people gave a smaller donation because of it, he didn't care. The occasions when he did break his silence were ones where he might hurt a fellow human being's feelings, or in rejoicing with a groom, or in a case where his silence might wound a *talmid chacham's* honor.

On those days when he sealed his lips, his home was elevated in a special way. R' Sholom applied himself to his Torah study with extra diligence. He wrapped himself in Torah, submerged himself in halachah. Most of the time he was literally wrapped in his *tallis* and *tefillin,* his pen moving almost ceaselessly as he jotted down his thoughts on what he was learning. His *"mussar seder"* on those mornings was more penetrating than usual.

What he achieved by talking, he achieved sevenfold by remaining silent. And when he opened his mouth to resume speech, it was a more elevated, refined speech that emerged.

The Rebbetzin: Native Wisdom

ALL OF JERUSALEM SPOKE OF REBBETZIN LEAH SCHWADRON'S wisdom. It was a wisdom that came from the heart and it attained expression through the purity of her character.

Wisdom that is subjective loses its force. Rebbetzin Schwadron was a great woman, a woman who knew how to rise above jealousy, above the desire for honor. Her brother, R' Shlomo Zalman Auerbach, told her many secrets. Other great Torah personalities recognized her intelligence as well. "You have a smart mother-in-law," R' Yechezkel Levenstein told the Schwadrons' son-in-law, R' Moshe Ariel, after speaking briefly with her about an important matter. On another occasion, R' Sholom went to R' Meir Chodosh for advice. R' Meir listened to him, then responded with a smile, "You have wisdom at home. Why are you coming here to ask me?"

The Rebbetzin's home was a crossroads for numerous passersby. Many women came to pour out their hearts to her. There were those who came for advice and others who came only to find solace in her loving presence. She guarded the secrets of others assiduously, and the hinges of her door never stopped swinging open.

If we were to begin telling stories about the Rebbetzin's wonderful character, we would never end. Let us take just one illuminating example. The episode occurred near the end of her life.

Rebbetzin Schwadron was in bed during her final illness, wracked by suffering. Though she required a medical environment, R' Sholom did everything in his power to delay the moment she would have to leave the home she loved. Finally, however, her situation worsened to the point where she had to be transferred to the hospital. Her daughters and other relatives were there to help her, day and night.

At that same time, a relative of the Rebbetzin's — a *talmid chacham* of 80 years old — was also hospitalized. He was running a fever from some minor infection, nothing life-threatening or even very serious. Rebbetzin Schwadron was told that he was in the same hospital. Though he was elderly and she was only in her early 60's, the doctors were not holding out much hope for her recovery.

One day, the Rebbetzin noticed her old relative walking down the corridor, accompanied by his daughter. He was wearing a hat and his long, rabbinical coat. "It looks like he's going home," the Rebbetzin remarked to her daughter.

"Y-yes," the daughter stammered. "He — he was discharged today. His daughter told me that they're sending him h-home."

With great exertion, Leah Schwadron lifted herself in bed. "Please go after them, quickly. Ask them to wait a few minutes. I want to tell them something."

"Imma, you don't have the strength! Tell me — I'll pass the message on to them."

"No, no. Hurry and tell them to wait. I'll sit in the wheelchair and you can push me over to him. I want to talk to him. Please."

"Imma, this is not good for you."

But the Rebbetzin was adamant.

The daughter yielded. She hurried to the end of the corridor and stopped their relative before he left the building. The elderly *talmid chacham* sat on a chair to wait. "Who knows what Imma wants to say to him," the daughter wondered as she made her way back to her mother's room. No doubt she wished to solicit his blessing — to ask for the privilege of a long life, like his. She sighed. If only such a blessing would bear fruit!

It took a mighty effort to lift her mother out of bed and into the wheelchair. Droplets of blood dribbled from the Rebbetzin's mouth. Undaunted, she wiped her face and asked her daughter to wheel her into the corridor. She had something important to say to her relative.

Glimpsing the old man from afar, she grew very emotional. His pure and scholarly mien imbued him with a special charm. In her honor, he struggled to his feet. Then he approached the Rebbetzin with a pain-filled curiosity, to hear what the suffering Leah Schwadron had to say to him.

Her daughter waited, too. Soon, she hoped, he would bestow his blessing on her.

"I want to bless you with good health and a long life," the Rebbetzin said. "You should never have to enter this building again. You should enjoy much *nachas*, contentment, and blessings in a good old age."

She had said what she had come to say. Bowing her head as her strength waned, she added in a lower voice, "That's what I wanted to tell you."

Her desire had been to bless *him* with a long life!

At the Rebbetzin's funeral, that elderly *talmid chacham* cried without cease. He had seen her greatness with his own eyes.

The Rebbetzin found one of the hospital doctors unbearably arrogant. "My brother, R' Shlomo Zalman [Auerbach], is a *gaon* in Torah, yet he can bend his back to hear me. But this doctor, who knows how difficult it is for me to raise my voice, won't stoop to lower his head to minimize my suffering." In this small incident she saw the glaring contrast between the great men of Israel and those of other nations. Arrogance leads only to debasement.

Her body became covered with sores, spreading to include her tongue. Her suffering was terrible. That day, the doctor returned to her room, standing tall and proud as usual. "Mrs. Schwadron, please stick out your tongue!" he ordered.

"How," the Rebbetzin answered weakly, "can I stick out my tongue at such a respected doctor? Is it fitting for a simple woman like me to do such a thing right to your face?" She waited to see if the arrow had struck its mark — whether he had understood her allusion.

The doctor spun around and left the room, eyes downcast.

R' SHOLOM'S MOTHER WAS A GREAT PART OF THE INSPIRATION behind the atmosphere of his modest home.

His Mother The hall was packed to the rafters. Voices which until a moment before had been raised in hearty song were stilled, and the circles of dancers dispersed. The throng that had gathered to participate in the joyous occasion had prevailed upon R' Sholom to speak.

Rising, he began to address the crowd, which thirstily drank in his every word. Suddenly, he broke off. A door at the back of the room had opened. He left his place and ran to greet the newcomer. His mother had arrived!

With an almost holy awe, he approached his mother and bowed. Then he grasped both her hands and kissed them. The crowd looked on, incredibly moved. Though strangers were privileged to witness the scene primarily at public celebrations like this one, this was the way R' Sholom habitually greeted his mother: with submission, deep respect, and a kiss on both hands. In a letter he sent his mother from Belgium in the year 5716 (1956), he signed off, "From your son, Sholom Mordechai, who kisses your hands from afar."

He approached his mother and bowed

From where did this profound respect spring? What secret lay behind those reverential kisses?

She was a great woman. She was the daughter-in-law of the Maharsham. She was R' Yitzchak Schwadron's wife. She was R' Sholom's mother.

Many are the stories woven around this woman. Interesting new insights into Torah are brought in her name. Here is just one of them; the facts speak for themselves.

R' Yitzchak Schwadron (*Av*

Beis Din in Chatzmer and author of the *Ateres Yitzchak* on *Tosefta Zera'im, Mo'ed, Nashim, Nezikin,* and *Ein Haro'im*), became a widower with nine orphans to raise on his own. He left his rabbinical post in Chatzmer and returned home to his father, the leading halachic authority of his generation — the Maharsham of Berzan. In the year 5663 (1903) R' Yitzchak moved to *Eretz Yisrael* with four of his children, having left a few of the older ones with their grandmother in Galicia. The two eldest children, a boy and a girl, had remained behind on their own.

R' Yitzchak remarried. Rebbetzin Frayda, his new wife and later the mother of R' Sholom, undertook to raise the orphans as though they were her own children.

"I'm raising four children in any case," she told her husband. "Send for the other two; it won't be any extra work." Proud of her goodness, he allowed himself to be persuaded, and sent for his older son and daughter. The daughter, having just become engaged to be married, declined the invitation. The son traveled to *Eretz Yisrael* to join his father and stepmother.

These were the days just prior to World War One, when extreme poverty was the lot of Jerusalem's Jews. When R' Yitzchak's son, Gad, arrived at his father's home, he was accorded a joyous welcome. The Rebbetzin was in the kitchen, putting together a festive dinner in his honor. R' Gad overheard her murmuring to herself as she cooked: "Two beans for Yankele, two beans for Shmulke, half a carrot for … and another half for … Half a potato for everyone together."

R' Gad was appalled. He had heard of the poverty afflicting *Eretz Yisrael* at this time, but now he was witnessing it personally.

"Is it right for me to make my father and his wife's burden even heavier?" he thought. "Do I need this — to live in such poverty, and at the expense of others?" He made up his mind to return to Europe on the first boat. (He later perished in the Holocaust.)

"What can I do to repay you for all your kindness?" R' Yitzchak asked his wife.

The Rebbetzin had only one request. "Learn Gemara with me!"

"The Gemara forbids me to teach you Gemara," he answered. "But if you get such pleasure from Torah, I'll try from now on to learn out loud so that you can listen and enjoy."

She developed into a budding "*talmid chacham.*" Her grandsons attest to her comprehensive knowledge of the tractate *Beitzah*, for example, and describe a halachic debate with her *mechutan*, R' Auerbach — who ended the debate by conceding, "Rebbetzin Schwadron beat me."

The good years came to an end. R' Yitzchak passed away at the age of 63, leaving the Rebbetzin with six orphans — the six children she had borne in *Eretz Yisrael*. She was widowed at the age of 35 and was to remain a widow to the end of her days. Forty-two years of loneliness. Forty-two years of courage.

She had no money. If, before, there had been half a carrot for Sholom'ke, now there was none.

To earn her living, she sold bread, walking up and down stairs all day long with her loaves. Her great joy was seeing her sons involved in Torah learning.

"Once, when my mother was an older woman," R' Sholom recalls, "I found her crying. 'Imma, why are you crying?' I asked. And she answered, 'What will I bring with me to the Next World? Sholom'ke! What will I bring to the Next World?'

"I answered simply. 'Dear Imma! What did you work for all your life? Why did you labor so hard to sell bread? Why did you walk up and down hundreds of stairs on your swollen legs? Why did you knock on the neighborhood doors? You did it all so that you would have food to feed your sons so that they could learn Torah. If they take the weight of the bread and the number of stairs you climbed during those long years, there's no question that the scales will be tipped to your benefit in the World to Come!'

"A calmness descended upon her. My mother said, 'You have given me new life, my son! You have given me new life!'

When night fell, Rebbetzin Frayda became another person. Even without the presence of her husband, her home was filled with the sounds of Torah. The mother cast a last glance at her children tucked into their beds, stretched her aching legs, and then took her seat at the big, scrubbed table by the window. The room was dark except for the flickering light from a kerosene lamp before her. She opened a *sefer* and filled the room with the soft music of Torah. These were the moments that stayed with R' Sholom until his own final days.

Eulogizing his mother after her passing, R' Sholom said:

> I will write a few words about my honored, noble, and long-suffering mother, who raised orphans with love and good will, without screaming or hysteria, giving us a father's *mussar* along with a mother's Torah from her youth until her old age.
>
> Rashi, in his commentary on *Mishlei* (30:17), explains the words *"likhas em"* as referring to the lines and wrinkles that crease a mother's face. Let us look at the lines that have gathered on our honored mother's face over the 42 years of her widowhood — and tremble with awe and respect at the sight of such strength, such endurance, such a heroic spirit.
>
> She was like a foundering ship that has lost its captain and its sailors in one blow, and has no one to help her. Each day she had to struggle to provide for her family, to feed them, to dress them, to support and help them, and to educate them in Torah and fear of Heaven. But she did not stumble beneath this heavy load. Her feet did not falter, nor her hands weaken. She went her way with courage and strength, step after step, with faith in Hashem *Yisbarach* — Father of orphans and Judge of widows!
>
> On top of all this, a brother of hers — poor and sickly, suffering both physically and mentally — lived in her home. She tended to him and cared for his needs, faithfully and devotedly, as though he were one of her own children.

We saw the meaning of true *chesed*, of simplicity, of humility, of natural piety. She would reach out a hand to help the stumbler. Indeed, she behaved in this fashion in all that she did.

Above and beyond all this, we must stand in wonder at the level of her Torah knowledge, which was extraordinary for a woman even in the generations preceding hers. Hashem graced her with mighty talents, and she, with remarkable diligence, rose higher and higher. It seems incredible to relate that every day, after hours of hard work — physical work that entailed lifting and running about, climbing many flights of stairs in homes and courtyards selling bread, to earn a meager amount to support her own children, and thereafter performing the housework, the cooking, cleaning, feeding the children, and more — she would use the few moments that remained for herself to enter a new world: the world of learning, reading, studying, and reviewing. She found solace from all her troubles in the books that rested on her table. She drew from them profound comfort and encouragement for her spirit. In those volumes she found light to illuminate the darkness of her widow's life — because she was a great, wise, and educated woman!

It was wondrous, too, to watch her pour out her heart in prayer to Hashem morning and night, in a tone that pierced the heart and gave warning. When she pleaded with her Maker in the words of King David, the rhythm of every syllable punctuated by the tears that dripped onto the pages of her *Tehillim*, then we knew what it was her soul longed for … And it comes as no surprise, for she understood the significance of the words she murmured, and rose with them to heights of purity.

Believe this if you wish (and the stubborn may choose not to believe); it's all the same to us. But we know this, too: every week, she would learn the Torah portion with *Rashi's* commentary, and sometimes with other commentaries such as the *Ramban*, the *Ohr HaChaim*, and the *Kli Yakar*, and she grasped them and discussed their difficulties and resolutions like a rabbi. Similarly, she had a broad knowledge of *Tanach*, which she reviewed many times. She even dabbled in the Oral Torah.

Once, in a conversation, she mentioned several tractates that she had learned by herself (this was during my father's lifetime, when she was not as burdened). We would see her sitting at night with a copy of *Ein Yaakov* and other collections of *aggados Shas*; when she finished them she would return to the beginning and review them several times. In fact, it would be no exaggeration to say that in the area of *aggadah* she was more conversant than a number of men who call themselves Torah scholars!

Indeed, she deserves the descriptions we ascribed to her in our opening words: noble in her endurance, noble in Torah and mitzvos, and patient in her suffering. Praiseworthy is the people for whom this is so, praiseworthy is the people whose G-d is Hashem!

[The introduction to the *Da'as Torah Maharsham* sets down, in her name, riveting details about her husband and his father, the Maharsham. In the second section, R' Sholom quotes her original thoughts on the Talmudic *aggados*.]

Chapter 4

The Maggid's World

THE PARTING WAS TEARFUL AND EMOTIONAL. FOR A LONG
time, the woman and her children stood at the port in Haifa
Parting and gazed after the ship sailing off into the
distance. Beyond the stretch of blue
Mediterranean separating them, they could just discern R' Sholom
standing on deck, beard waving in the wind as he trembled with
weeping and prayer. His Rebbetzin succumbed to her own emotion, sobbing briefly into her hands.

It was winter's end in the year 5716 (1956) when R' Sholom
packed his bags and left Israel for the first time in his life. His destination: London. In all, he remained in Europe for eight
consecutive months. He returned to Jerusalem in Kislev, 5717
(1956), just in time to light the Chanukah candles in his own
home.

R' Sholom drew thousands of Jews to him in Europe, laboring in
community affairs day and night. But his longing for *Eretz Yisrael*
remained unabated:

"I never knew how hard it would be," he wrote in a postcard mailed from Manchester to Sha'arei Chesed. At times he was overcome with intense longing for the narrow streets of his native city, for his beloved family, and for his many students. He would take that powerful emotion and channel it into the talks he gave, transforming personal longing into passionate inspiration for the glory of Hashem.

Passport photo, 1956

Excerpts from R' Sholom's short letters from that period of his life have been preserved. They are filled with his impressions of a new world. In the Diaspora, he met zealous Jews living side by side with alienated ones. Chance encounters with individuals from the latter group left him in a welter of emotion, which erupted at times — usually during his prayers. "Blow a mighty shofar for our redemption!" These powerful feelings took root in his heart, where they flourished and sprouted fruit.

A Jew from Jerusalem, dressed in traditional Jerusalem garb, was no common sight in Europe. It is no wonder that when meeting R' Sholom, Jews who had strayed were drawn to him, as though mesmerized.

On his first night in France, he spent a long time *davening* the *Ma'ariv* prayer. As he completed the *Shemoneh Esrei*, R' Sholom noticed the *gabbai* waiting patiently for him to finish so that he could lock up the synagogue.

R' Sholom apologized — he had no idea that the shul was closing up for the night at such an early hour. Then he stepped out into the cold street, quietly murmuring *Mishnayos* that he knew by heart. Before long, a man appeared at his side, attracted by R' Sholom's face and his unusual appearance. The man noticed the way R' Sholom's lips were moving.

"Rabbi! What are you saying?" the man asked in German.

R' Sholom did not understand the language, but the obvious emotion in the man's manner spoke volumes. "I tried to answer him in Yiddish, which contains some German expressions, but we couldn't understand one another," R' Sholom remembered. "But I saw that he was very excited."

The man stayed close to R' Sholom, trying in every way he knew to formulate short sentences in Yiddish. At last, his efforts were rewarded: R' Sholom learned that the man was an assimilated Jew who served as a judge in civil court. "You know, Rabbi," the man said proudly, "I observe Pesach. On Pesach I eat only kosher cheese. I know a rabbi who is friendly with the priest, and even though my wife is a gentile, I keep a kosher Pesach."

It was clear to R' Sholom from the start that the man was interested in drawing closer to his Jewish roots. R' Sholom tried to explain that it was possible for the man's wife to convert to Judaism, but the man was frightened by the thought that she would have to immerse herself in a *mikveh* to do so. He responded to each of R' Sholom's suggestions with the same reluctance — yet did not leave R' Sholom's side during their entire long walk. Here was a Jew, R' Sholom concluded, who was living the life of a gentile — except when, from time to time, he was subject to a soul-shaking experience that urged him to return to the bosom of Judaism. Seeing a figure that symbolized that world to him, he had attached himself to R' Sholom like a moth fluttering around a light. But there was nothing R' Sholom could do to save him. The man decided, at length, to leave, and the two parted ways.

As he watched the other Jew turn his back and walk away, R' Sholom's eyes filled with tears. R' Sholom tried — in vain — to return to his *mishnayos*. His throat was choked.

This type of encounter made him feel the pain of the entire generation. He strove valiantly to help Europe's Jewry, infusing the fire of his rhetoric with his personal anguish.

An excerpt from another postcard that R' Sholom sent to his family in Jerusalem (Nissan, 5716 [1956]) reads:

Here in Sunderland, the *chazzan* and *shochet* have told me about a prosperous Jew who never comes to shul [his store is open on Shabbos] except on *erev* Pesach. He comes in a taxi and stays in shul until everyone else has gone. What's going on? Why? He's a *bechor* (firstborn son), and his memories of his father's home tell him that a *bechor* must eat in shul on *erev* Pesach.

With war threatening Israel, R' Sholom advanced his trip home by two weeks. His family celebrated, overjoyed to see him safe and well after an eight-month absence.

During the happy reunion, one of the Schwadron daughters noticed that her father was wearing the same torn sweater he had been wearing when he had left Jerusalem the winter before. She pointed this out to the family.

"Abba!" they cried in surprise. "You were abroad for months

Four of R' Sholom's sons-in-law — R' Tzvi Shenker, R' Moshe Ariel, R' Menachem Koenigsburg, and R' Nachum Sheinelson — greet him at the airport in 1975

and didn't buy yourself anything? Who goes traveling and doesn't buy himself what he needs?"

They surrounded him. "The same clothes — the same everything!"

R' Sholom apologized, but said nothing more.

A little time passed. Suddenly, R' Sholom called the family to gather round. He pulled a small tape recorder from his pocket — a rare object in those days.

He placed the tape recorder in the center of the table as the others stared in astonishment. When he pressed a button, voices sounded. It repeated the entire homecoming scene. R' Shalom had pressed the "Record" button as soon as he had walked into his house.

"Here you are!" he announced. "Here, my dear children. Until now, you've been used to large tape recorders with big batteries. Today you will see that it's possible to hear everything without anyone being the wiser. Here it is — 'An eye that sees and an ear that listens, and all your deeds recorded in a book.' Every time you speak, every time you get angry or tell a lie or say something coarse — permissible and forbidden conversations — it's all recorded."

With a triumphant smile, R' Sholom sat back. "That," he said, "is what I bought abroad!"

"I WAS A BOY OF NINE AT THE TIME," R' YECHEZKEL SCHLAFF RElates enthusiastically. "R' Sholom stayed at our home in London for

The Shtreimel a long time. I remember many interesting episodes from that period. I'll tell you one of them — the one that made the strongest impression of all on me:

"It was our custom during the summer to leave the city for a short holiday. R' Sholom agreed to join us. The place where we stayed was far from any Jewish community, and on Shabbos we were faced with a difficult problem: There was no *minyan* of Jews. We decided to walk to the nearest shul, a very long walk, indeed, to hear the Torah portion read and to *daven* with a *minyan*.

"As I stood by the door, I caught snatches of a conversation between R' Sholom and my father. My father was trying to persuade

R' Sholom not to wear his Yerushalmi *shtreimel* on his head: 'The English don't know what a *shtreimel* is, and they may feel agitated by the sight of a Jew wearing one,' my father explained. 'Even in our own neighborhood, we chassidim wear a hat or yarmulka on our head when we leave our homes, and not a *shtreimel*. Certainly it won't do to wear one here.'

"But R' Sholom refused to be persuaded. He was determined to dress just the way he had back home in Jerusalem. 'It doesn't matter, I'm not worried. I'll wear the *shtreimel* here, too.'

"We set out on our long walk.

"There was at that time a famous English actor who wore a trademark hat made of fur tails. The Jewish *shtreimel* was unknown to the general public. We had not gone far when the catcalls began to come from various windows. 'Hey! Hey!' Gentile youths gathered around us, calling out the actor's name, making scoffing comments and singing raucously. During all this, R' Sholom continued to walk peacefully along, discussing Torah and *mussar* topics as though nothing was happening. In the full majesty of his Jewish pride and distinctive Jewish garb he walked miles, both to and from shul — wrapped in the same serenity that had always accompanied him through the faraway streets of Jerusalem.

"That long walk with R' Sholom," says R' Yechezkel, "stays with me to this day. It showed my child's heart the nature of an inner Jewish pride that never falters. That walk was a signpost that points out the way for me even today — 40 years later."

≈

"Thirty years ago, R' Sholom was our guest in France," Rebbetzin Westheim relates. "At that time, we lived in an area where it was unheard of for a Jew to walk around on Shabbos wearing a *shtreimel*. There was a very real danger of being taunted, or worse. I tell you nothing new when I say that. On Shabbos, R' Sholom went out wearing his *shtreimel*. I'll never forget what happened on that *motza'ei* Shabbos.

"That night, R' Sholom had to visit a certain wealthy Jew's

Passport photo, 1961

home. As he stood in our doorway preparing to leave, he put on his *shtreimel*. We pleaded with him not to wear it: 'One is not required to wear a *shtreimel* on *motza'ei* Shabbos." But he was adamant. 'In Yerushalayim I also wear a *shtreimel* on *motza'ei* Shabbos!' With those words, he left the house.

"I accompanied him to show him the way. At first we walked on side streets. It wasn't until we reached a major thoroughfare that the trouble began. A husky gentile suddenly stood in front of R' Sholom, blocking his way.

"R' Sholom looked at him. Before he could say a word, the gentile struck him a ringing blow on the face. R' Sholom's head was flung back and his *shtreimel* fell to the ground. Laughing coarsely, the gentile moved on.

"R' Sholom bent down, picked up his *shtreimel*, and resumed his walk.

"And what do you think?" the woman asked emotionally. "Did he learn a lesson? On the way back, did he hide the *shtreimel* under his coat or at least hold it in his hand? Not at all!

"His meeting concluded, the Jerusalem *maggid* stepped out of the French Jew's house, put on his *shtreimel*, and started back the way he had come!

The following brief excerpt from a letter R' Sholom sent home from England contains another reference to the *shtreimel*:

If you'd like, I'll tell you a little about this past Shabbos — Shabbos *HaChodesh*.

I spoke in a shul that has a membership of 2,000, only 500 of whom actually come on Shabbos. They asked me to speak for only 20 minutes, and I managed to speak for just 18 — amazing! It's a very modern shul and most of its members are completely ignorant. I translated every word I said into Yiddish. Yet I hear that the *gabbai* quietly told my friend, R' Simchah, "Your rabbi, who spoke to us, is 100 percent the gentleman." This is the highest praise in England, especially for a man like me, wearing a *shtreimel*, etc. By the way, the *shammas* of the shul told me that in 20 years he had never seen a *shtreimel* with his own eyes.

In another letter, R' Sholom referred to his *shtreimel* in a different way:

Yesterday, I spoke at the Agudah shul on the topic of Pe'ilim. The shul is large, and so is the congregation … One of our friends wanted me to wear a stovepipe hat in order to be successful — but it turned out that my *shtreimel* and white *kaftan* made the most wonderful impression of all. There are plenty of stovepipes here … The main impact on the congregation was not me, but the "Berzaner *einekel*" (the Maharsham's grandson). Many of them are chassidim and there are those who knew my grandfather and my father.

At the end of my talk, I told them that [the Torah] states that one must be innocent in the eyes of both Hashem and Israel — so they must not suspect me of traveling abroad in order to tour … because that is forbidden by halachah.

R' SHOLOM ATTRACTED EUROPEAN JEWS OF EVERY STRIPE.

In Europe and America

"That year," R' Yom Tov Lipman Rakov relates, "R' Sholom spent the entire winter here in London. Each week, on Friday night, he spoke at the large shul in Graveline. I was young then, and I remember that the shul was packed to the rafters — both the men's and the women's sections."

Another Englishman speaks emotionally of that time. "It was 40 years ago. I couldn't believe my eyes! The shuls would fill up until there was no more room. Jews of every kind came to hear

Hashem's word. London's largest synagogue was crammed with Jews, many of whom had come for the first time in their lives to hear a *chareidi* rabbi speak … They all sat open-mouthed as R' Sholom's musical voice pierced their hearts."

He adds a vivid detail: "On R' Sholom's fourth or fifth visit to England, matters reached the point where, on one occasion, the police had to be called in to deal with the traffic jam that had sprung up in the street because of the crowds converging on the shul!"

American Jews saw R' Sholom as a providential messenger sent to burnish the image of yeshivah students, to prop up Jewish ideals, to decimate materialistic ambitions, and to sow fear of Heaven. "A stranger wouldn't understand," says R' Yitzchak Raskes of Baltimore, a faithful follower. "Torah students would stand crowded around him to absorb his every word. R' Sholom paid them back in kind, by going around from yeshivah to yeshivah, from *kollel* to *kollel*, and traveling long distances to every Jewish center. Thousands turned their thoughts to repentance in his wake."

In his talks, R' Sholom epitomized a style that might be referred to as "the left hand rejects while the right draws closer." On the one hand, he scolded and rebuked his listeners, while on the other hand he drew them near with overflowing love. The spectacle of hundreds and thousands coming knowingly to be rebuked was an extraordi-

R' Sholom — with R' Paysach Krohn — wearing his shtreimel on a Motza'ei Shabbos

nary one. R' Sholom's talks in the United States and Europe were a historical "first." Everyone came — proud men and ignorant men, side by side with learned scholars and upright householders.

R' Sholom himself was amazed at the incredible response he drew. His initial goal in traveling abroad was to garner funds for the struggle against secular attempts to undermine *Yiddishkeit* in Israel. The Pe'ilim organization was a linchpin in the war against assimilation, and R' Sholom was its shofar blast to alert and arouse. His voice would resound in shuls and study halls: "My teachers, my dear brothers! We learn in *Tanna D'vei Eliyahu* that in the future *HaKadosh Baruch Hu* will hold a Torah scroll and ask each and every Jew, 'What have you done so that Torah will not be forgotten in Israel?' My friends! The first thing a person must do is work on his inner self, so that Torah won't be forgotten in Israel — because he, too, is part of Israel."

R' Sholom would go on to exhort his listeners on the importance of establishing set times for learning Torah and performing mitzvos — only much later remembering that he must touch on the subject of rescuing Jewish youth in *Eretz Yisrael*. His rhetoric would soar emotionally: "*Oy! Oy!* And when *HaKadosh Baruch Hu* asks what we have done for the immigrants from Morocco, from Tunis, from Yemen, what will we answer? Who can say that he didn't know that thousands of Jewish children in the Holy Land are being turned away from their faith? The Gemara, in *Maseches Gittin*, says ..." Suddenly, the dam would burst and the tears begin to flow. While R' Sholom's tears were shed openly, many of his listeners bowed their heads to hide their own. These were tears that had lain in their hearts for years, never finding their way to the surface, not until R' Sholom reached the shores of America.

"To raise money, to sound an alarm about the awful situation — but to be careful not to speak ill of *Eretz Yisrael*," were the instructions he had received from the great man of his generation, the Brisker Rav (as quoted by his son). It was a formidable order — to shatter the barrel while preserving the wine. R' Sholom did his best to obey.

R' Sholom was unable to return to Israel until he had raised sufficient funds. As a novice in the field of fundraising, the task took many months.

In one of his first talks, he said, "*Rabbosai*, forgive me, I am not an English-speaker. I only speak Yiddish. But I do know one sentence in English: 'I am sorry, he is not at home.'

"Many people, seeing a Jew with a beard, realize at once that he is a fundraiser. The woman of the house steps out, or else she sends her maid, to say, 'He is not at home.'" (as excerpted from one of his letters sent from England to his family in Sha'arei Chesed, 5716 [1956])

But the arduous trip resulted in much good. It gave R' Sholom the opportunity to visit many different communities and to leave behind a legacy of love for Torah and fear of Heaven. As the Chofetz Chaim remarked: The shortage of funds in the yeshivah world, along with the *roshei yeshivah's* consequent wanderings through the world to fill that lack, brings great blessing, in that it leads to increased respect for Torah and its study in the wider world.

Surrounded by yeshivah students on a visit abroad

A Torah scholar in London tells the following story:

"In England at the time, hardly any families sent their sons to learn in yeshivah before they had completed their university or at least their secular high-school education. Some had their sons learn in *yeshivah ketanah* and then removed them so that they would start earning a living. The boy who sat in yeshivah from youth to maturity was rare indeed.

"R' Sholom undertook to change this situation, both in England and in America.

"One talk was particularly compelling. Comparing those who learn Torah to stones, as the Gemara does (*Ta'anis* 4), R' Sholom quoted a verse that speaks of holy stones rolling into the streets. 'When those who are engaged in learning Torah go out into the streets, when they leave the study hall to enter the marketplace, *oy, oy.*'"

Many years have passed since he heard R' Sholom speak, but one member of his American audience attests that he can still hear R' Sholom's plaintive, heartfelt voice to this day.

R' Sholom did not tailor his talks to the demands of the European or American communities that he visited. On the contrary! When he discerned a breach in the walls of Judaism or saw a clear field in which to strive for the sake of Torah, he promptly forgot his reason for being abroad and knocked on the doors of shuls and study halls, his voice penetrating in top form — all for the glory of the Torah!

"I was present at one of his talks, about 40 years ago," R' Chaim Schneider remembers. "R' Sholom was standing one Friday night on the steps of the central shul in Graveline. This time, uncharacteristically, he did not stop berating his listeners. What was their crime? An insult to the Torah! He rebuked London Jewry for flinging their sons into the alleys of the university. He spoke for a long time and was extremely articulate, as usual — only this time, more than ever, there was a distinct thread of anger running through his speech. He was crying out on behalf of the Torah."

With the conclusion of his lecture, R' Sholom allowed a conciliatory smile to play on his lips. "I have spoken the truth," he said.

It is all written in *Chazal*. But perhaps, in spite of this, I have of-fended someone. To placate you, I will tell you a nice story." The listeners relaxed as R' Sholom launched into a story that the Sha'agas Aryeh once related to his congregation in Metz:

Like many other Torah giants, the Sha'agas Aryeh under-took voluntary exile. He left the city of Minsk and wandered from place to place. At one point, he found him-self in the city of Hamburg for an extended period. One day, he confided to the city's rabbi that he hoped Hashem would rescue him from poverty.

"And why is that?" the rabbi asked.

"Because poverty and exile have caused me lost time from Torah study," the Sha'agas Aryeh replied. "The land-lady served me food, and because I was so immersed in my Talmud, I moved my hand and accidentally knocked the bowl off the table. The landlady cried out — and for that moment I neglected my learning. Therefore, in order to prevent future neglect, I am willing to accept the burden of the rabbinate."

The very next day, Heaven interceded. Messengers from Metz arrived with a rabbinical contract in hand.

Before undertaking the post, the Sha'agas Aryeh re-turned to Minsk to say goodbye to his congregants there. A righteous woman in that city, knowing of his great poverty, had personally baked and delivered two challahs to him every *erev* Shabbos. On his arrival in Minsk, he blessed the woman with wealth, and added that she would be privi-leged to build two shuls [corresponding to the two challahs she had baked for him every week], one in the Diaspora and the other in *Eretz Yisrael*.

In time, his blessing came true! That woman, Chanah, became very prosperous and built a shul in Minsk that was called by her name. At an advanced age, she traveled to *Eretz Yisrael* in order to fulfill the second part of the Sha'agas Aryeh's blessing. On her way she stopped in

Volozhin, where she went to see the great R' Chaim of Volozhin. Hearing her story, he asked, "What is your hurry?" There was no reason to rush. She was bound to merit long years of life, because life was assured her as long as the Sha'agas Aryeh's blessing had not yet come to fruition.

When in Minsk, the Sha'agas Aryeh also summoned his *shammas*, a simple and pious man who had served him long and faithfully. "With what would you have me bless you?" he asked. The *shammas* answered, "I own a cow which, until recently, supplied a good quantity of milk to earn me my livelihood. Now that she's grown old, there's less milk. I ask your blessing for the cow."

The Sha'agas Aryeh stood up and gave him the blessing he had requested — that the cow would live long and give more milk. Then he looked at his *shammas* and added, "And you, too, shall have a long life."

And, indeed, the townspeople spoke of a certain Jew who reached an incredible age — who was seen at the age of 102 walking down the street with a sack of flour on his shoulder. "There," the people would whisper to one another, "goes the Sha'agas Aryeh's 'cow.'"

R' Sholom on Sunday

HIS HANDS WAVED DRAMATICALLY AS HIS LIPS FRAMED QUOTES from every portion of the Talmud and *midrash*. His topic: Sunday — or, to use R' Sholom's own pained label, "the Diaspora's second Shabbos." American and European Jews who were present at one of his talks on this subject found his words unforgettable. Whatever else may have been lost in the recesses of their memory, "*Zuntig*" (Sunday) stands out in bold relief.

Shouting, laughing, or mocking as he saw fit, R' Sholom labored to instill in the minds of his thousands of listeners that Sunday was a wasted day. It was to his credit that many regular Sunday *shiurim* were established.

Another pressure-point was the Western idolizing of sports —

With R' Shimon Schwab at a convention of Agudath Israel of America

especially in the United States. Often, he would scathingly lump Sunday and sports together. The following is a portion of an outstanding talk in which R' Sholom decided to step beyond his usual limits and bring his audience to laughter. The talk took place in the 1970's in Boro Park, and concerns an incident that occurred the first time R' Sholom set foot in Belgium.

Unlike America, Antwerp custom left no time for a proper breakfast, and it was undignified to carry a sandwich in a brown bag. At lunchtime, therefore, R' Sholom went to a kosher restaurant.

"The first time I arrived in Belgium," he related, "I stayed in Antwerp and had to eat lunch in a private restaurant from time to time. One day, I entered as usual at 1 o'clock. The place was empty. Something unexpected must have occurred, I thought, as the restaurant was normally crowded at that hour. After about 10 minutes, one man walked in, then another, until slowly, some 10 men came in — all of them clearly in very low spirits. They exchanged no words and the atmosphere was gloomy.

"Living in Jerusalem, I was used to tragedies and catastrophes (which abounded during the first decade after the establishment of the State of Israel). My heart trembled. Who knew what had happened? Perhaps something had taken place in Jerusalem that I had not yet heard about ... I had no phone with which to call home ... I tried unsuccessfully to read their faces, then sat quietly, afraid.

"A few minutes later, another Jew walked in. He washed his hands and sat at the table. For the first time, one of the men there broke the silence.

"'Shimon,' he asked, 'how many people were at the funeral?'

"I understood that he was not referring to a funeral in *Eretz Yisrael* but rather in Belgium. Who had passed away, *Rachmanah litzlan*? I waited tensely.

"Shimon answered, 'By my estimate — about a million.'

"I concluded at once that they were not discussing a Jewish funeral. There were not even half a million Jews in Antwerp. I stood up, walked over to one of the Jews, and asked, 'What happened?'

"The man turned and said with a smile, 'R' Sholom, this is not for you.'

"I began to get angry. 'You've caused me to be so afraid that my heart almost stopped, and then you say it's not for me? *Tell me what happened!*'

"The man relented. The national passion of Belgium is bicycle racing, like football in America and horses in England. It seemed that a young Belgian had once biked several kilometers in the space of only 14½ minutes, to win a large cash prize. He was now a millionaire. He opened a bar, where thousands came to drink with the champion. Two years passed.

"'Yesterday,' my fellow diner informed me sadly, 'that same man tried his luck again, attempting to achieve a new record — to bicycle the same distance as before, but in a shorter time. On the way, he crashed into a wall, overturned, and was killed on the spot. Nearly a million people attended his funeral. We joined, too. The general atmosphere was one of mourning, and we got caught up in it.'

"Hearing this," R' Sholom continued, "a spirit of mockery

seized me. I told them, 'You wish to attend athletes' funerals? Please, come to Sha'arei Chesed. There's a cat there that climbs the tallest tree in the neighborhood in just half a second — from bottom to top, like lightning! Yesterday, the cat died. Go to its funeral.'

"I went on to explain, 'You are confusing skill with wisdom. A talent or skill is a natural thing that *HaKadosh Baruch Hu* grants a person, giving him the ability to jump or fly or run. It's not at all connected to the person's character, but simply to natural phenomena [and is an area in which the animal kingdom often outshines the human one]. What, then, is a person's task? To work on himself and with himself, to elevate himself and rise ever higher. That is human!'

"Come now! Form *that* kind of competition, and see who wins."

R' Sholom entered a local shul. There was something out of the ordinary: The shul was not filled to capacity. The shortage was easily explainable. It was summer, and many of the neighborhood families had traveled away for the summer.

R' Sholom climbed the steps before the ark and related a famous parable in the name of the Kelmer Maggid:

"I was strolling slowly through the city streets before sunset when, from one of the houses, I heard a quiet sobbing. Sharpening my ears, I tried to determine the source of the weeping. As I walked toward that house, the crying increased in volume. It was a sound filled with anguish and longing.

"I continued until I reached the doorway of the house. The cries had not ceased even for a moment. I knocked on the door, but there was no response. I rang the bell, but the door did not open. I tried my luck, twisting the doorknob with both hands — and it opened! The weeping grew louder.

"Who was crying here? What had happened? A child, a youth, or perhaps a lonely old person? What sort of weeping was this? I hesitated, unsure whether or not to go in. In the end, I gathered my courage and entered.

"I concluded at once that the crying was coming from inside a closet. Who was locked up there? Who could be sobbing inside? With tentative fingers I opened the latch — and, immediately, all became clear.

"There was a *tallis* in the closet and the *tallis* was crying!

"'What's wrong, *tallis*, to make you cry so long and so hard? What happened?' I asked.

"Sobbing even harder, the *tallis* said bitterly, 'My owner has gone off on vacation in the mountains. He packed up his belongings. He put his money in his wallet and the wallet in his pants pocket. He packed all his valuables in a suitcase and went on vacation. *I am the only thing he left behind!*'

"I was quiet for several moments, wishing to offer comfort but not knowing how. All at once, I grew bold. I bent down, came close to the *tallis*, and whispered, 'Don't cry, *tallis*. The day will come when your owner will leave everything here at home — the day when the man who owns this house will separate from everything he possesses. That will be a true separation. He will leave *everything* behind — except you. He will take you, his *tallis*, with him. Nothing else'"

In the audience, fingers dabbed at eyes damp with tears.

R' SHOLOM'S *YIRAS SHAMAYIM* — FEAR OF HEAVEN — WAS THE genuine article. His family, while not discussing the matter in de-

Always Scrupulous tail, will say this much: For R' Sholom, sin was a matter of *Gehinnom* opening beneath his feet. Even the slightest possibility of sin was, in his eyes, a tragedy.

His family and closest disciples had grown accustomed to his scrupulousness in halachah and the ever-present awareness of his accountability to his Creator. The tales they tell of R' Sholom are related with the simplicity of long familiarity. Those who knew or hosted him abroad, however, speak of those same traits with tremendous enthusiasm.

When it came to *kashrus,* R' Sholom did not yield an inch. Decades ago, when it was not easy to acquire food with the very high level of *kashrus* he demanded, he would insist on abstaining from certain products. Instead of seeking out ways to make the food permissible, he found dozens of fresh doubts. In light of this, his trips abroad, far from home, were not easy for him. As a long-time resident of Boro Park remembers, he would never ignore any possible problem in *kashrus.* Another recalls that R' Sholom never recited blessings over food without his hat on his head. Distance from home did not change his practices at all.

His greatest fear was wasting time that might be devoted to Torah. Reading a newspaper simply for the sake of reading, for example, was like burning up precious minutes. "Boxes of *sefarim* arrived some time before he actually set foot on foreign soil," one of his American hosts recalls. "They were volumes of halachic responsa and Talmudic commentary." These were the indispensable companions R' Sholom refused to do without.

R' Sholom's speech was always guarded and refined. Even when speaking to secular Jews, he never permitted himself the slightest laxity in his choice of words. The son of R' Moshe Soloveitchik tells of the first time R' Sholom was a guest in his home in Zurich. "I was just a small boy then. R' Sholom came over to me and asked, 'Where is the room without the *mezuzah?*' It's been decades, but the delicacy of his speech stays with me still."

R' Rephael Yitzchak Wasserman relates:

"I was with him in Switzerland on his first visit, in Elul 5716 (1956). R' Sholom stayed at the yeshivah in Lucerne and was given a bed in my room. What can I say? He sat from morning till night wrapped in his *tefillin,* learning Torah. It was the time of year — Elul — when R' Sholom had a practice of maintaining silence for 40 days. The sight of his face was very moving. He submerged himself in holy work without interruption … For the holiday of Succos, he was a guest in the home of R' Moshe Soloveitchik. Afterwards, I met him again in Belgium. There, too, his ways were wonderful to see — especially his diligence in Torah."

Emotionally, R' Wasserman continues: "Oh, how R' Sholom feared Heaven! Sharp and shrewd and experienced in the ways of man, no one could fool him in spiritual matters — and *he did not fool himself.* That was the way he operated everywhere he went in Europe — because the possessor of true *yiras Shamayim* will be listened to. It was so enjoyable to be near him, beloved Above and pleasant here below. He was always sanctifying the Name of Heaven. Thousands flocked to hear what he had to say in his wisdom and awe and love of Torah. Though there were many in Europe at that time who were already pious and G-d-fearing, many others, good people, needed the kind of spiritual cajoling they received from R' Sholom Schwadron."

R' SHOLOM SERVED AS A KIND OF LIGHTHOUSE WHEREVER HE went, spreading rays of illumination from on high.

A Lighthouse Late one Friday night, when R' Sholom was staying at the home of an American family, he walked into a room and noticed that the light was switched on. He was concerned that opening the door might have caused the light to turn on, making him the cause of electricity flowing on Shabbos (even if there was no halachic prohibition in this case). On Shabbos morning, in considerable distress, he approached his host to ask about the house's modern fittings. "Does opening the door cause the light to go on?"

Seeing R' Sholom's pale face and agitated manner, his host soothed him with a smile. "R' Sholom, there's nothing to worry about. Yankele, our little boy, accidentally turned on the light switch after Shabbos started. It wasn't you."

"A pity, a pity I didn't know," R' Sholom said with a sigh. "I was so upset that I didn't sleep all night. Had I known, I would have slept."

A lively dance during his first visit to the Telzer Yeshivah in Cleveland, Purim 1969

"THERE ARE ALREADY FIVE OR SIX RABBIS AND OTHERS WHO want me to stay with them for Pesach," R' Sholom wrote his wife

Lettuce and Water

from England. "But I haven't yet clarified where I'll be, *baruch Hashem*."

It was one of his first trips to England and the masses did not yet know how unique he really was — but they had heard of him. London's many willing hosts labored to find him a pleasant flat in a large apartment building, at his request, so that he could spend Pesach night there alone.

That was the start of a tale that ended in tears.

R' Sholom spent the week before Pesach learning Torah by day and immersed in community work (on behalf of Pe'ilim-Yad L'Achim) by night. On the morning of 13 Nissan, with Pesach practically on his doorstep, he collected cleaning materials and began a single-handed scouring campaign in honor of the approaching holiday. By the end of the day, his house was *chametz*-free. That night, he performed *bedikas chametz*, then went out to buy a large container to hold his drinking water for the entire festival, as had been his custom at home in Jerusalem. He found a large pail, carried it to his room, and filled it with water. On the morning of *erev* Pesach, after burning his *chametz*, he sat down to learn. He remained at that task until noon.

His hosts had arranged for all of R' Sholom's needs to be met. In these last hours before Pesach they went about their own preparations, confident that he was safe and sound in his apartment. In the early afternoon, a youth from the neighborhood came to visit him. In the course of their conversation, the boy discovered that R' Sholom was completely alone in the building. All the other Jewish tenants had left for Pesach. The only person left in the building was a gentile woman on the top floor. R' Sholom was living downstairs. There existed a possible problem of *yichud*. ("Not an actual prohibition," R' Sholom would relate later, "but a problem nevertheless.")

R' Sholom grabbed his matzos, wine, and the bucket of water. Because it was after noon, and thus past the time when one may have *chametz* on his premises, he was unable to pour out the water and fill the pail again later. Carrying the heavy pail, he went out into the street.

Where to?

He did not know his hosts' addresses or telephone numbers. They planned to come and meet him at the start of the festival, R' Sholom knew — but what now?

A friendly Jew passed by and greeted him with a smile. "R' Sholom! What's the matter?"

R' Sholom explained his predicament. The other man stepped back. "I'm sorry, it's impossible for me to host the Rav. Rav Schwadron is holding machine-made matzos, and at our house we consider that practically *chametz!* I'm sorry, really, and hope the Rav will judge me favorably. I just can't ..."

Alone and tired, R' Sholom walked down the street. He was far from his family, with no place to turn. In his hands he carried a large bucket filled to the brim with water, along with a bottle of wine and his Pesach matzos. He walked and walked, searching for someone who would agree to have him and his machine-made matzos.

In Jerusalem, he had a custom of visiting the *Kosel* on *erev* Pesach, to purify himself with tears as he recited the *Korban Pesach*. Now he was in the Diaspora, far from that holy spot, utterly alone, walking through the streets of London … to which destination? The possibility of returning to his apartment flitted across his mind, only to be firmly rejected. No, he would not go back! He would not involve himself with the possibility of a prohibition.

"Where should he go?" he wondered.

He already had a horseradish root, and he suddenly spotted a greengrocer selling lettuce for Pesach. Instantly forgetting his plight, he leaped into action, purchasing a large lettuce for the Seder (his custom was to eat the rib of the lettuce, not the bug-ridden leaves). He was smiling for the moment, but the smile soon gave way to his former nervous apprehension. The bucket of water was very heavy, and he was tired.

"That was the way I walked," he recalled. "I tried to flag down a taxi, but it wasn't easy. At last, I found one — and was treated to an earful from the cab driver about the pail of water I wanted to bring with me. Finally I located another taxi driver who agreed to take me and my water. *Baruch Hashem* that I found him — I didn't know my way around the streets in that section of town."

Somehow, R' Sholom managed to reach the house of a Jew he knew in the area. That man, although also refusing to host R' Sholom, found him another place to stay. A certain poor Jew granted permission for his guest to bring machine-made matzos into his home — on the strict condition that R' Sholom would not sit with him at the same Seder table.

Engrossed in Torah thoughts

With all due respect, the host arranged a separate table at one side of the room, presented R' Sholom with a rocking chair, and left him to conduct his solitary Seder.

"I said the Haggadah alone, and in the middle I cried," he remembered. His sleep that night was not a restful one.

After Pesach, R' Sholom described the whole episode in a letter he sent back home. His Rebbetzin wept when she read it, and all those who read the letter with her cried too. They assigned no blame to the good Jews of England, who had done their best to arrange things comfortably for him. It had all happened so unexpectedly, and in the last tense hours before Pesach.

R' Sholom did not permit the incident to bring him down. The great Yerushalmi continued on his travels, teaching, exhorting, strengthening European Jewry and spreading Torah wherever he went.

R' SHOLOM WAS EXTREMELY SCRUPULOUS ABOUT THE PROHIBI-
tion of *yichud*. Staying as a guest in strangers' homes made this

Yichud   strict observance uncomfortable at times, but he did not let this deter him. Says the London *dayan*, R' Aharon David Dunner, "R' Sholom told me that he had special permission from the Tchebiner Rav to follow Rashi's stricter ruling, which held that *yichud* is Rabbinically prohibited even if the woman's husband is in town.

"Even though it was not a very comfortable situation, he would check the door from time to time to make sure it was standing open. That was when we left home and he stayed behind to learn in our house." Rabbi Dunner adds, "Everywhere he went, we saw the image of a G-d-fearing man."

Another Torah scholar from England has his own story to relate on this topic. "When R' Sholom was our guest, I once met him coming down the stairs [from the upper floor of our house] at a dizzying speed. He was 70 years old at the time and wearing slippers, but he ran from the third floor to the first like a young boy. He was pale and clearly distressed. Seeing me, he stopped, breathing heavily.

"'What's the matter, R' Sholom?' I asked.

"'I thought there was no one home except for your daughter,' R' Sholom answered, so I was running to the front door. Ah, you're here — *baruch Hashem!*'"

R' Chaim Rosner adds: "I was an eyewitness. I saw R' Sholom refuse to return to the place where he was staying, remaining in shul all through an entire day, out of a remote possibility of *yichud*. It was the Vizhnitz shul in Stamford-Hill."

THERE WERE OCCASIONS WHEN R' SHOLOM FOUND HIMSELF abroad over Chanukah. His custom was to use a glass-enclosed

The "pushka" from Jerusalem menorah — a "pushka" — that stood outside the door. Knowing that many Diaspora Jews light their candles indoors and that there was a great risk of his not finding an enclosed menorah there, he decided to take his own along with him.

"Outside of *Eretz Yisrael*," R' Rephael Wolf says, "you don't find anyone lighting Chanukah candles outdoors, at the entrance to the house [as is the way according to the Rama]. But R' Sholom was of

R' Sholom in New York with his menorah "pushka"

the opinion that he must light his menorah outdoors, even in England. He bought a length of chain to secure the menorah against theft. He stood it on a chair by the front door, tied the chain, and lit the menorah.

"My father took me regularly to see those Chanukah candles, unique in all of London. He wanted me to see scrupulousness in halachah, up close."

R' Wolf adds, "We saw scrupulous attention to detail in halachah in every area. He was always thinking of halachic questions. Even the small children remember his care in matters of *kashrus* (such as eating a certain cooked dish at a *melaveh malkah*, and the like)."

R' SHOLOM WAS A GUEST AT A CERTAIN *TALMID CHACHAM'S* house in Belgium, where he requested a *melaveh malkah* meal on

Danger? I Won't Eat!

motza'ei Shabbos. The woman of the house sent one of her young sons to a store on a nearby street to fetch food for R' Sholom.

The meal was set on the table — and then R' Sholom learned that it had been a small child who had brought it. Gently, he pushed the plate away. Looking around to make sure the child was not present and would not be offended, he said, "I can't eat this."

Naturally, this occasioned surprise for the members of the household. R' Sholom explained. "In order to reach the next street, one must cross a large road. It seems to me that there is danger in that. Therefore, I cannot eat this food! I will not eat something that came to me through danger, as the Gemara says (*Bava Kamma* 61; King David refused to say a *devar Torah* in the name of someone who had brought it to him at personal risk. The same source also relates that King David refused to eat something that had come to him through something prohibited). It seems to me that there is an element of danger here. Perhaps you think differently; in that case, I apologize. But I cannot eat it."

His host, a local rabbi, went personally to purchase a fresh meal for him. Only then would R' Sholom consent to eat.

IN THE YEAR 5721 (1961), R' SCHWADRON'S VISIT TO ENGLAND coincided with the High Holy Days. Once again, he clung faith-

Sweet Symbols fully to every custom he had followed at home in Jerusalem. He asked his hosts to help him purchase — at any price — the symbolic foods eaten on Rosh Hashanah night. Most of these were unknown to the local populace.

R' Chaim Schneider speaks of his mother, who was devoted to R' Sholom. "She wanted to go to London's chief market to search for the things R' Sholom needed," he says, but was unsuccessful in deciphering the exact nature of some of those items. "For example, she didn't understand which vegetable was known in Yerushalayim as *silkah*, etc."

To compound his difficulties, R' Sholom traditionally maintained a strict silence during the month of Elul. His solution? He sat down with pencil and paper and spent many long minutes painstakingly drawing a picture of each vegetable. With these drawings in hand, R' Schneider concludes, his mother went to the market. She managed to find most of the symbolic foods.

R' Sholom was overjoyed at the goodness and piety of these Jews, who were willing to care so devotedly for his deepest needs.

THE RIMNITZER REBBE ONCE FELL DOWN THE STEPS IN HIS YARD. Afterwards, he sat down on one of the steps and did not move.

Fall — and Rise! Members of his household hurried to him, asking anxiously, "Does it hurt very badly?"

"No, no," the Rebbe answered.

Surprised, they asked, "In that case, why doesn't the Rebbe stand up?"

"I'm sitting down to figure out why I fell," the Rebbe explained.

R' Sholom enjoyed retelling this story. And when he himself fell on London's streets, he did not even remain in the city for Shabbos. He got up and left England. R' Yechezkel Schlaff of London tells the tale:

"R' Sholom's last trip to Europe was about 10 years ago. He was 75 years old then, elderly and weak. On Purim, as he walked through the streets, he tripped and fell. The next day, in his own room, the same thing happened again.

"'Why did I fall?'" R' Sholom asked himself over and over. '*Why?*'

"We explained to him that falling is common among older people. 'There's no need to worry that anything in particular is wrong with you,' we said. 'The facts are simple: Your blood pressure and sugar are not as they should be. There is no cause for special anxiety. You just got dizzy and fell.'

"As though he hadn't heard a word we said, R' Sholom repeated anxiously, 'Why did I fall?'

"Seeing that he was not absorbing what we were telling him, we decided to leave him to his own thoughts.

"Suddenly, he rose to his feet and said, 'I'm going to discuss this with the *Rosh Yeshivah*' — in other words, with the *gaon* of Manchester, R' Yehudah Segal (to whom R' Sholom was very attached).

"A short time later, R' Sholom announced with a festive air, 'We have decided together that my falling was caused by a lack of gratitude!' He went on to explain: 'An acquaintance of mine has just married off a son in the United States — a man who has been very

kind to me on many occasions. This man asked me repeatedly to join in his *simchah*, but my lack of strength prevented me from agreeing to make the trip ... But — gratitude! Gratitude! I should have gone!'

"The story was not yet over. R' Sholom informed us that he was going to fly to America at once, in time to be present at the last of the *sheva berachos*.

At the engagement of R' Paysach Krohn; to R' Sholom's right is the chasan's grandfather, R' Chanoch Henach Krohn

"R' Sholom asked us to phone his American friend to let him know of the plan, and to ask them to stretch the *sheva berachos* festivities until near sunset, at which time he calculated that he would be able to reach their home. 'Tell them to wait — I'm coming.'

"The elderly *gaon* packed a small suitcase and set out for America at once.

"They waited for him at the airport and drove him to the party. With Heaven's help, R' Sholom made it in the last moments. The great R' Sholom brought joy to the *chasan*, added joy to the *chasan's* father, and poured love of Torah and fear of Heaven onto the hundreds of people who had streamed to that *sheva berachos* to join with him.

"He returned to Europe the next day.

"On his return to London, he found it necessary to rest for several days. The back-to-back flights, old age, and ill health had weakened him. But his spirit was ebullient. He felt cleansed inwardly, he felt pure: 'I did what was required of me — wholeheartedly.'"

These are just a few of the tales, a sprinkling of golden nuggets told about the *middos*, the piety, and the love of Torah that his friends and admirers the world over, remember.

Giving a blessing to a child in the courtyard of the apartment in which he stayed in Kew Gardens, N.Y.

Right to Left: R' Chanoch Henach Krohn, R' Sholom, and R' Shmayah HaKohen Pekter, whom R' Sholom nicknamed "The Kohen Gadol"

In the Telzer Yeshivah Beis Midrash, Purim 1969, with R' Baruch Sorotzkin

Chapter Four: The Maggid's World / 125

Purim in the Telzer Yeshivah, 1969

Greeting R' Mordechai Gifter

With R' Chaim Stein

Purim in the Telzer Yeshivah, 1969

Chapter 5

The Voice of Torah

R' **Let's Dance!** SHOLOM HAD SEEN THE LIGHT. WITH HIS OWN eyes and the power of his mind he had just glimpsed the simple meaning of the *sugya* he was learning — and had realized that the great Maharsham's explanation constituted an awesome original thought.

Unable to contain himself, he went out into the dark night. His happiness lit the way to the home of his illustrious brother-in-law, R' Shlomo Zalman Auerbach. He stepped along merrily. "A fantastic *chiddush*!" he thought as he went. "Amazing!"

On this night, R' Sholom was simply incapable of remaining at home. He felt compelled to share his marvelous new insight with the "*shvugger*" (brother-in-law), as R' Shlomo Zalman was affectionately known in the family. He had to describe the difficulties he had encountered in learning the *sugya*, the different sides that had cried out for reconciliation, and the flash of lightning that had illuminated the whole matter for him — via his grandfather's wonderful remarks. (Some say that R' Sholom and R' Shlomo

Zalman had pondered this question a few hours earlier and had been unable, at that time, to plumb the depths of the Maharsham with real understanding.)

R' Sholom climbed the stairs leading to his brother-in-law's house — or rather, floated up. He knocked excitedly on the door without noticing that most of the apartment was already shrouded in darkness. He was not in a frame of mind to notice much of anything.

The door opened. R' Shlomo Zalman's son said softly, "You're looking for Abba. *Oy*, Abba just went into his room to lie down. He's not sleeping yet, but he's finished learning and he's gone to bed."

R' Sholom was adamant. "If your father is not yet asleep, allow me to make him happy. Let me go inside."

And in he went! As he approached the door of the bedroom, he called, "R' Shlomo! R' Shlomo! It's worth your while to get up!"

R' Shlomo Zalman got up and went to greet his brother-in-law.

Sparks seemed to fly around them as R' Sholom began discussing Torah. Triumphantly, he offered the Maharsham's explanation. R' Shlomo Zalman listened transfixed, his eyes glued joyously to R' Sholom's.

"*Nu*, that's some *chiddush*, isn't it!" R' Sholom said eagerly. "Isn't it *gevaldig*? It's incredible! Let's dance!"

R' Shlomo Zalman, no less caught up in wonder over the *chiddush*, never thought of refusing. Hand in hand, they circled the room in a joyous "*mitzvah tance*" — one, two, three, four times.

The scene epitomizes the secret of R' Sholom's existence: the fire of Torah and the love of Torah. All the

R' Sholom in a dance with R' Shlomo Zalman

ebullience that bubbled in his veins was given over to Torah. His very joy in living revolved around the moment of discovering a new *chiddush*.

An original thought in Torah would send him out of his senses. He could spring into a dance anytime and anywhere — at home, in the street, in the yeshivah and in the *kollel*. When he discovered a *chiddush*, floodgates would burst open, the air would roil like a volcano, and R' Sholom would rejoice like a young man at his wedding. He was tremendously moved by every twist in logic.

This, in a nutshell, was the secret of his famous *simchas hachaim*, joy of living.

R' DOV LANDAU TELLS THE FOLLOWING STORY.

Searching "A group of us from the Chevron Yeshivah were walking together when, across the street, we caught sight of R' Sholom. Seeing us, he immediately crossed over. As he approached, it became clear that he was very troubled. His face was serious and drawn with worry. His eyes never stopped darting to and fro. 'R' Sholom must be searching for something he's lost,' we thought.

"R' Sholom nodded in greeting, came nearer, and immediately revealed the reason for his worry.

"'Maybe you can help me. I've lost the Gra's *chiddush* on the redemption of *ma'aser sheni*. Maybe you know where it's located?' He waited expectantly.

"To this day, that scene is etched in my mind: the way R' Sholom looked as he walked through the city streets, troubled and anxious, searching ... We were young boys then, and that image made an enormous impression on us."

A CERTAIN YESHIVAH IN ENGLAND WAS HONORED WITH A VISIT by the *gaon* and *maggid*, R' Sholom. A few hours later, R' Sholom **Torn Shirts** returned to his lodging in London, caught in the grip of a powerful inner turmoil. He did not regain his composure until he had poured out his story. R' Chaim Schneider recalls R' Sholom's words.

"I entered the yeshivah hall. Near the door of the large room stood two young students debating the points of a *sugya* they were learning. The atmosphere was calm: a typical peaceful morning. The boys had their hands in their pockets as they discussed their topic. One boy said something, then the other took issue with him, until one of them emerged victorious. The one who had lost the debate looked at the other, thought a moment, then said, 'Why not? You're right.' With measured steps, the two returned to their places."

This was the essence of the episode. A quarter of an hour later, R' Sholom was standing up to address the yeshivah. He berated not only the two boys he had overheard, but the whole yeshivah!

"'*Toras chaim*' — the living Torah — what is that?" He described the scene he had just witnessed, then went on to cry, "Is this how we learn? Like *that?* Hands in pockets, a thought here and a thought there, and good day?!

"When we learned in yeshivah," R' Sholom continued, "and when R' Moshe Mordechai Epstein gave us a *shiur* — we tore our shirts! The very air was filled with thunder! A genuine Torah thought must be guarded like a treasure. A fundamental question is worth struggling with day and night. The Torah must be part of our identity, literally a part of our essence! To be involved in the study of Torah means to wake up with it, to go to sleep with it, to drink it, to walk with it — to lie with it even in our sickbed. It is a living Torah! *And we don't waste life with our hands in our pockets!*"

When R' Sholom returned to the Schneider household in London, R' Chaim Schneider recalls, he retold the story over and over. "Why not? Hands in their pockets! And their shirts," R' Shalom added, smiling sadly, "were crisp and pressed."

"R' Sholom's living pain," R' Chaim Schneider says, "is engraved in our memories to this day — 37 years later."

"I WAS A FEW YEARS YOUNGER THAN R' SHOLOM," R' MICHEL Yehudah Lefkowitz said, "and a piece of Torah that he told me as a young man still echoes in my ears.

A Burning Flame

"It was during the period between R' Sholom's engagement and his wedding. From time to time he

R' Sholom with R' Michel Yehudah Lefkowitz

would prepare a Torah thought to present to his future father-in-law, R' Chaim Leib Auerbach. When the thought was polished, R' Sholom would often tell it to one of his friends. "One of these stands out in my memory. It touched on the subject of a renegade Jew who slaughters meat. R' Sholom spoke with extraordinary passion — so much so, that I remember his words to this very day."

Diligence

WHEN HE SERVED AS *MASHGIACH* IN YESHIVAS TIFERES TZVI, R' Sholom made a habit of circulating among the study tables, an open volume in his hand and his eyes glued to the print. R' Moshe Kupshitz remembers, "I would see how he supervised the students in the afternoons, walking back and forth through the study hall learning pages of Gemara by heart. The sight influenced me greatly."

A certain Torah scholar reprimanded R' Sholom: "You have to watch [not learn]!"

R' Sholom got on the bus and traveled from Jerusalem to Tel Aviv and from there to Bnei Brak, to consult with the Chazon Ish. He described the rebuke he'd received at the hands of that other *talmid chacham*.

The Chazon Ish rendered his judgment: Personal example is the best kind of *hashgachah* there is.

I Learned It from You!

R' SHOLOM AND HIS FRIEND, R' LEIB FRIEDMAN (OR, AS R' Sholom called him, R' Leib Tzaddik), entered R' Yechezkel Abramsky's house to request his endorsement for a certain pious Jew in Jerusalem who was in need of financial aid.

The "Chazon Yechezkel" welcomed them affectionately, then turned to R' Sholom with a question. "Where have you been? I haven't seen you here in a long time."

R' Sholom thought a moment, then said, "I will answer the question, but first an introduction — a *midrash* from *Chazal:*

"The *Likkutei Shimoni* poses an interesting question. King David said the following words to *HaKadosh Baruch Hu: 'Achas sha'alti mei'eis Hashem, osah avakeish.'* (One thing I asked of Hashem, that shall I seek.) Hashem said to David, 'First you say *one thing,* and then you go on to ask *several* things, as it says, *"Shivti b'veis Hashem,* etc.'" Replied David: 'Master of the Universe, I learned it from You. At first, You said, "And now, Israel, what does the L-rd your G-d ask of you but to fear [Him]," then later you added many mitzvos, as it says, "To walk in all of His ways, etc." It is sufficient for a servant to be like his Master!'"

R' Sholom said, "From here, I chanced to hit upon a fundamental principle: 'I learned it from you.'" He turned to R' Yechezkel Abramsky. "*Rabbeinu* — I learned it from you! You sit and learn day and night and compose works. I learned from you! I also sit and learn and write books. I want to learn."

R' Sholom studying and teaching; to his right is his son R' Yitzchak

R' Abramsky derived great pleasure from this answer. He asked his visitor, *"Nu*, R' Sholom, what do you want me to do for you?"

When R' Sholom tendered his request, R' Abramsky wrote a special endorsement which achieved all that had been intended.

(As told by R' Avraham Toker)

What, indeed, is the simple meaning of this *midrash*? What is King David actually saying to Hashem? R' Sholom explained in one of his talks to the students of Chevron Yeshivah. "Hashem requests one thing of us: 'What does the L-rd your G-d ask of you but to fear [Him].' This carries in its wake all the other requests. It brings along with it all the other proper values. In the same vein, David HaMelech makes one request, which brings a whole train of other things in its wake. For when one sits in the house of Hashem, he attains everything else."

HERE IS AN EXCERPT FROM THE ENDORSEMENT (*HASKAMAH*) TO R' Sholom's first book:

A Breadth of Knowledge

This Rabbi and *gaon* is beloved to me, apart from his Heaven-blessed talents. Heaven has helped him because his piety precedes his wisdom. I have known him well since his youth, as he learned in our yeshivah and grew up there. While still young, a thirst for truth was already planted in his heart, along with a powerful desire to elevate himself in Torah and pure fear of Heaven. Indeed, he has risen from height to incredible height, for his soul is devoted to Torah and dedicated with genuine self-sacrifice to the quest for Divine awe. Afterwards, too, he has learned Torah with great intensity and diligence, day and night, and in that merit has attained greatness in both Torah and fear of Heaven and has brought merit to many others. Happy is he and happy is his lot. I discussed many portions of his book with him, and his words are filled with sweetness and delight.

My blessing is given to my dear and beloved one, that he may rise in Torah, and strengthen it, and spread its waters far afield.

His beloved friend and admirer,
Yechezkel Sarna
Adar 5706 (1946).

One winter's day, some 67 years ago, a group of yeshivah students entered the home of their *mashgiach*, R' Meir Chodosh. Among them was young Sholom Schwadron. The occasion: a meeting of their *va'ad*, or Torah "committee." R' Sholom enjoyed retelling the story of that meeting.

R' Meir asked each youth to figure out how long it took him to learn one page of Gemara. It might be one hour, or two, or perhaps even just half an hour. Each boy had to decide for himself, based on his own personality and learning style.

The boys fell silent, making their internal calculations.

After a suitable period of time had elapsed, R' Meir broke the silence. Quietly and with the simplicity of great wisdom, he said, "In the mornings we have a 4-hour learning *seder* (session), in which we learn a tractate in depth. Afterwards, there are still another 8 hours left in the day for learning Torah. Therefore, let us consider together: Whoever thinks he can cover a page of Gemara in half an hour can cover 16 times that in those 8 hours — or 16 pages. Simple arithmetic.

"By the same calculation, a person who learns a page in one hour can cover eight pages apart from the morning *seder*. And he who is slower than that — in other words, someone who can learn a page in 2 hours — can accrue four additional pages of Gemara each day.

"In light of these facts, the least amount of pages to be learned would be 28 pages a week — that is, of course, if he is really learning."

Then he went on to conduct *va'ad* business until its completion.

There were several youths at that meeting who took the *mashgiach's* words very much to heart. One of them was young Sholom

Schwadron, who much later related to his sons the changes that occurred in his spiritual world starting that day.

"Halfway through the month of Shevat, I began learning *Maseches Bava Basra* with my partner, R' Ezra Brizel. On *erev* Pesach, just a little while before candlelighting, we finished learning and reviewing the *masechta* for the fourth time! That was in the winter of 5691 (1931)."

The tractate *Bava Basra* comprises 176 pages. It is not clear whether R' Sholom and his learning partner began in the middle of Shevat or Teves. However, even if they began in Teves, in just three months the pair covered 704 pages of Gemara!

R' Sholom continued displaying amazing diligence in Torah, accruing the knowledge of hundreds of pages of Gemara — first learning, and then reviewing what he had learned. The result was the acquisition of a broad spectrum of Talmudic knowledge.

"When R' Sholom was young, a yeshivah student learning together with a group of other students, I urged them to undertake the study of *Shas* with *bekius*," says R' Yehudah Shenker. "They listened to me, and we guided their learning. With Heaven's help, within a short time they had grown and succeeded tremendously."

R' Sholom retained his notebooks from that time. He would cry out to his grandchildren, "Look into these notebooks and see how much we accomplished! How much we learned! How much it is possible to accomplish — to learn and to review your learning."

He covered tens of pages a week, hundreds of pages by the end of the *zeman* (semester).

The following figures are illustrative of the information found in those old notebooks:

"*Parashas Bo, Beshalach, Yisro, Mishpatim, Terumah*: 150 pages.

"*Vayakhel, Pekudei*: 50 pages.

"*Tazria*: 53 pages.

"The sum total of my learning this winter: 700 pages.

"Winter of 5693 (1932-1933): 450 pages, total.

"Summer of 5693 (1933): 575 pages, total.

"Winter of 5694 (1933-1934): 533 pages, total."

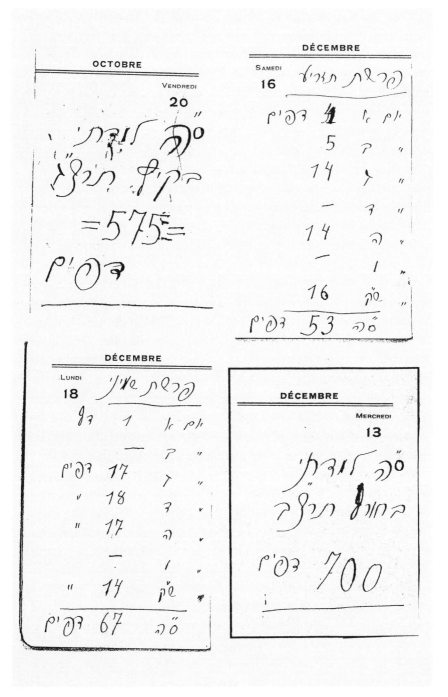

"We had a *va'ad* with R' Meir Chodosh," R' Sholom told a group of yeshivah students in a *mussar* talk. His voice rose in its customary chant. "R' Meir proved on paper that each one of us was capable of learning as much as 30 pages per week [or about four pages per day]. He said explicitly: I'm not talking about first *seder*. I am talking about the afternoons and nights. How is it possible not to manage 30 pages a week with full understanding — Gemara, *Rashi*, and *Tosafos?'*

"We were a group of youngsters. We began learning the way he had outlined for us, and saw that it was actually possible to learn 70 pages each week! That was the way we learned every week: 70 pages, with Heaven's help.

"Boys and young men learned and learned, but something troubled them. They were not satisfied. How was it possible to be satisfied, if over the course of five years they learned the beginnings of *masechtos* in the morning hours and several tens of pages in the afternoon? They'll learn the rest of *Shas* in the next *gilgul* (incarnation) ... They'll remain ignorant into old age. This is what troubled them.

"The soul is demanding, *'When will you learn?'* And that is why there is no feeling of satisfaction."

Acquiring a breadth of Torah knowledge — a crucial component for success in learning — was a burning issue for R' Sholom all his life. He exhorted on the topic constantly. Every grandson who visited him received his portion of *mussar* about it.

R' Rephael Wolf describes a short visit to R' Sholom's home in Sha'arei Chesed, approximately 25 years ago. R' Sholom greeted him warmly, then asked the question that every yeshivah *bachur* expects: "What did you learn in yeshivah this *zeman?"*

"I answered," R' Wolf says, "that we had learned 20 pages during the summer term. At once, R' Sholom became very serious. His eyes were angry. I was taken aback at his expression and tried to placate him by saying that on Simchas Torah I had undertaken to learn 700 pages of Gemara."

"'Ach, ach, 700 pages — what's that?' R' Sholom said. 'A boy who can learn more and more, who can accomplish and succeed —

and he decides to limit himself to 700 pages, no more? What's the matter with you?' he sighed.

"He didn't say a word about the 20 pages we had learned. It was the 700-page limit that pained him."

R' Sholom was, simply put, a *talmid chacham* who shared the aspirations of the previous generation.

"DURING A CERTAIN PERIOD IN YESHIVAH, SEVERAL GROUPS OF older students spent the mornings learning in Batei Horenstein," **Magen** R' Sholom related. "The Tepliker Rebbe learned **Avraham** there, too, along with another outstanding *talmid chacham*, I forget his name, who was conversant with *Shas*, both *Bavli* and *Yerushalmi*, and *davened* at extraordinary length. A full hour after we had come in to learn, he was still standing and *davening*.

"One morning, a man came in and said that he would like to put on *tefillin*. We had none with us, but found a pair inside one of the *shtenders*. We discussed the matter and decided that it was permissible to use someone's personal *tefillin* for this purpose. Then one of the *bachurim* raised another problem: Perhaps these were Rabbeinu Tam *tefillin*? We began debating this point to see what principle applied in this case.

"The Humler Rebbe (son-in-law of the author of the *Leshem* and father of R' Yosef Sholom Elyashiv) was sitting nearby. He raised his voice and called loudly, '*Magen Avraham! Magen Avraham!*'

"Noting our bewilderment, he explained, The *Magen Avraham* offers a sign: The *tefillin* hairs in a Rashi *tefillin* are located in the middle and in a Rabbeinu Tam *tefillin* are on the side. Don't you know anything?'"

R' Sholom finished his story and continued humbly, "The Humler Rebbe was astonished that grown yeshivah students, students of Yeshivas Chevron, didn't know. How could we know if we hadn't learned? We learned the *Shulchan Aruch* during mealtimes, but no more. It was a just grievance."

At the time of this talk, R' Sholom was already counted among the generation's Torah greats. His knowledge of halachah was outstanding. Yet he chose to mock himself in order to help others: "Teach your tongue to say I don't know."

One of his grandsons tells of an incident that demonstrates R' Sholom's incredible mastery of the *Magen Avraham*.

"In the wake of an illness, Saba (Grandfather) had begun to lose his powers of concentration. From time to time, he also forgot things. There were days when this wasn't the case, but then there were other days ...

"One Shabbos morning, Saba's body became bloated with six liters of water. He was taken to the hospital, where he remained in life-threatening danger. The doctors labored to save his life, and Heaven had mercy: His lungs were drained, the great danger passed, and he was transferred to a ward.

"One of his students came to visit him just as he had turned his face to the wall in order to sleep. Seeing him turned away, the student stood at his bedside reciting *Tehillim*. When he was done, I went over to him and remarked, '*Nu,* because you're *davening* by a sick person's bedside, you can pray for him without mentioning his name [*Berachos* 34].' We had begun to discuss the point from a halachic standpoint, when Saba's voice suddenly cut in, '*Magen Avraham!*'

"We didn't understand what he meant by this. I assumed that he wasn't sure whether or not he had *davened* that morning and, in his weakness, had decided to *daven* again in bed. I went to him, bent over, and said, '*Saba,* you already *davened Shacharis.* There's no need to *daven* again.'

"'*Magen Avraham!*' came his voice again. I explained quietly to the visitor that R' Sholom was apparently repeating *Shemoneh Esrei.* Perhaps his illness had overcome him to the extent that he had forgotten that he had already *davened.* But Saba insisted, '*Magen Avraham!* That's the *Magen Avraham!*'

"At last, I understood — the halachah that we had been discussing is mentioned in the *Magen Avraham!*

"'Where in the *Magen Avraham?*' I asked. And Saba answered, 'What's the difference where? It's the *Magen Avraham!*'"

The Torah was a part of his identity. Just as we don't "forget" our own foot, so we do not forget the *Magen Avraham*.

(The *Magen Avraham, Siman* 119, says that one who prays on behalf of a friend need not mention his name if he prays in front of him, but if he is praying elsewhere, he must mention the sick person's name.)

R' SHOLOM'S SWEEPING TORAH KNOWLEDGE DID NOT CONFINE itself to halachah; he was also particularly conversant in *aggadah*

Your Mother's Teaching

and in *midrash*. "In my young days," R' Sholom told a learning partner, "I reviewed the *Ein Yaakov* very well." When did he find the time? "Each night, before I went to sleep, I would read the *Ein Yaakov* in bed. I managed to study every page of that slim work well." In addition, R' Sholom was also remarkably well-versed in latter-day works of *mussar*, such as the *Reishis Chochmah*, the *Tomer Devorah*, the *Sha'arei Kedushah*, and more.

R' Sholom, as we know, grew up without a father's guidance or personal example. His father, the famous *gaon*, R' Yitzchak Schwadron, passed away in Jerusalem in the year 5680 (1920), when R' Sholom was only seven. R' Sholom's righteous mother would study the *Ein Yaakov* assiduously, and she was unusually knowledgeable in all the Talmudic *aggados*. As a child, he would fall asleep to the sight of his mother poring over the *Ein Yaakov* and the *midrash* by candlelight. This image helped rouse his own fear of Heaven and love of Torah, and created a strong, unconscious bond to the *Ein Yaakov*. Thanks to his mother's early example, R' Sholom became, almost incidentally, one of the generation's leading lights in *midrash* and *aggadah* as well.

R' SHOLOM STUDIED THE *MISHNAH* EXTENSIVELY — 18 CHAPTERS a day. He established certain regular patterns of learning for him-

Mishnayos and R' Elyah Lopian

self: five pages of Gemara, 18 chapters of *Mishnayos*, and *Tanna D'vei Eliyahu*. He also took care not to partake of food until he had completed his morning learning session. During the rest of the day he pursued his other, in-depth, studies.

Of particular interest are the cassette tapes he prepared, in which he recorded himself learning 18 sequential chapters of *Mishnayos* in his inimitable chant, followed by 10 minutes of *mussar* and then another 18 chapters of *Mishnayos*. These tapes covered all the tractates of *Zera'im* and *Mo'ed*. R' Sholom listened to these tapes on his travels. Whenever learning out loud was impossible or impractical, he would place the recorder in his pocket, conceal the earphones behind his long beard, and learn.

One of his grandsons relates an interesting episode. "One Friday afternoon, when Saba visited our house, I saw him seated beside the bare table. Being just a child, I went up to him and asked if he wanted a *sefer*. Saba smiled, motioned for me to come closer, and pulled the earphone wires from under his beard. He was listening to his *Mishnayos*."

Among R' Sholom's belongings was a notebook in which he recorded a resolution to undertake a certain learning agenda over a specific period of time. Included among the topics he planned to study were some of those found on his tapes. Here it is, in his own words:

> Until I go to sleep at night, learn five pages of the *Rosh* or one page of the *Rif*, except for *erev* Shabbos and *erev* Yom Tov, Shabbos and Yom Tov. Also 18 *perakim* of *Mishnayos*.

And 12 on *erev* Shabbos, with eight from *Maseches Shabbos*. And on Shabbos *kodesh*, the remaining 12. Either by heart or in writing, either spoken or in thought — but if I listen to the tape I have to make sure to speak the words … Also, learn one new *mishnah* by heart … from *Maseches Terumos*, and specifically on the *seder*; and three times a day, morning, noon, and evening: once before eating, once in the middle [of the day], and once afterwards.

Why did R' Sholom combine *Mishnayos* and *mussar* in this particular way? He learned continuously from morning to evening, but it was only at night or in the early hours of the morning that he engaged in the study of *mussar*. Why?

The answer is simple: Rabbi Eliyahu Lopian used to do it that way! The following incident occurred decades ago (as told by R' Tzvi Frankreich):

Over a certain period of time, R' Elyah Lopian would

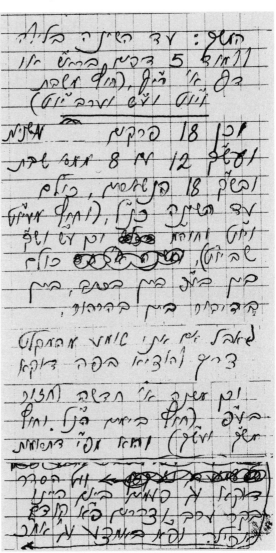

give *mussar* talks at the Lomzhe Yeshivah in Petach Tikvah. Though he lived in Kfar Chassidim, far to the north, he agreed to travel to the yeshivah on a regular basis for this purpose.

"I went with him several times," R' Frankreich recalls. "The trip down from the north to Petach Tikvah began with a bus from the Kfar to Haifa, where we took a public taxi [*"sherut"*] to Tel Aviv. For an extra sum, the cab driver agreed to stop in Petach Tikvah.

"On one occasion, we took the taxi in Haifa as usual. *Rabbeinu HaMashgiach* R' Elyah sat in the front passenger seat while the rest of us sat in the rows behind. It was a 2-hour trip. An unusual silence filled the car, as though the other passengers recognized that they were in the presence of a great person. There was no conversation on the road, only a respectful silence.

"And R' Elyah? His lips were whispering *Mishnayos* by heart the entire time. And that's when I noticed something interesting: Every

15 to 20 minutes, R' Elyah took the *sefer Sha'arei Teshuvah* from his pocket and learned from it for several minutes. When he was done, he would return the book to his pocket and resume reciting *Mishnayos* from memory!"

Here is behavior reminiscent of R' Sholom, his student.

"It's worthwhile going on to describe R' Elyah's visit to the Lomzhe Yeshivah in detail," R' Frankreich continues, "and to see how R' Sholom acted similarly.

Studying Mishnayos

"We arrived in Petach Tikvah. R' Elyah said a gentle good-bye to his fellow passengers and left the taxi. The others looked after him with awed respect, then continued on their journey to Tel Aviv.

"In Petach Tikvah, he stayed at the home of the famous Zaks family. (Many Torah leaders were guests in that home; R' Elyah was related to the family.) R' Elyah gave a lecture at the yeshivah and stayed in Petach Tikvah overnight. R' Sholom, hearing that his Rebbe had come down from Kfar Chassidim, traveled up from Jerusalem at once, and was seated opposite R' Elyah at the breakfast table by 8:30 a.m., absorbing his every word.

"He asked R' Elyah all sorts of questions. I remember that he asked about a certain oral tradition that had been transmitted, one man to another, from someone in Kelm. Rebbe and student sat by that breakfast table for an hour, two, three ... until 2:10. They could have sat longer, but the time had come for R' Elyah to give his lecture at the *kollel*.

"The elderly R' Elyah left the house and R' Sholom and I accompanied him to the yeshivah. On the way, we passed the home of Rebbetzin Jacobsky, wife of R' Berel Yanover. R' Elyah stopped and suggested that we go in and see how the widow was faring since we still had a few minutes to spare. When we came back downstairs after our visit, R' Elyah noticed that it was late and began walking as quickly as a young boy, with us following, until we reached the *kollel*.

"I will take this opportunity to point out that one of the fascinating things about R' Elyah was the way he could walk quickly when the need arose. He once hurried up the steps of the Chevron Yeshivah in Jerusalem to *daven Shacharis*. R' Yechezkel Sarna tried to follow at the same pace but couldn't catch up with him. Astonished, he said, 'That old man! That old man! Look at the way he runs ... And us ...?'"

R' Sholom used to tell a similar tale about his mentor. "People say a lot of things about R' Elyah's characteristic of *zerizus* (quickness, zeal), but I saw an example of it with my own eyes during the funeral of the Chazon Ish, in the year 5714 (1954). There was a tremendous crush; some 50,000 people had gathered together.

Along with R' Elyah (who was 78 years old at the time), we followed the bier. Suddenly, R' Elyah began walking ahead with amazing energy. We tried to keep up, but we couldn't! I remember that we discussed it afterwards, and were embarrassed that we, the younger men, lacked his zeal."

Labor of a Lifetime

HARD WORK WAS R' SHOLOM'S ESSENCE FROM HIS YOUTH ON-ward. "I toiled tremendously over the course of several years, wiping the sleep from my eyes." (From the introduction to R' Sholom's first book, 5706 [1946].)

R' Sholom used every opportunity to drive home the need for hard work on behalf of Torah. As one example, he described the way the Chazon Ish, a man who, in his weakness, could scarcely move his arms and legs, and sometimes lacked the strength to recite *Bircas HaMazon*, nevertheless managed to stand up from his bed and learn a different *mishnah* each day for two consecutive weeks. The Chazon Ish told those close to him that he had studied a certain tractate 14 times, though he was unable to lift his arms or legs afterwards! "Once," R' Sholom recalled, "I saw him lying on the floor of the balcony in his home, utterly spent. Then he decided that he was obligated to rise — and he got up like a hero! I was astonished. How did he manage to do all this? 'Because the thing is very close to you …' When? 'When your mouth and heart are engaged in doing it.'"

R' Sholom continued on the topic. "Go over to a person whose feelings are only for his business, and tell him, 'Sit and learn.' For him, that would be like splitting the Red Sea. Yesterday, a man told me, 'I don't see any other way of life except to sit and learn (Torah) — but I'm just not cut out for it.' What does that mean, 'not cut out for it'? For that man, the Torah is across the sea, it's in the sky, it's far away. It must be on your lips and in your heart. It's not enough to simply say that you see no other way than to learn. You have to understand it and feel it. It must be very close to you."

R' Sholom advocated caution in working beyond one's physical capabilities. "The Chazon Ish taught me that one must sleep 7 hours in the course of every 24, plus an extra hour's rest — there's no need to sleep then, it's enough to lie down and rest. There were others whom the Chazon Ish told to sleep only 6 hours in 24, but he recognized that I need 7. I didn't heed his instructions very well. I didn't sleep enough, and in the last decade of my younger years, I sensed a disturbance that had arisen as a consequence: I began to need an afternoon nap. R' Elyah also used to say that if one does not sleep well during the good years, he gains nothing: Revenge is taken later!" (As related by R' David Mor)

R' Sholom added, "I spoke with R' Elyah about reducing one's appetite. One of the things he said was, 'A person requires food, that's simple. One of my children decided to subsist on bread and water. He did this for a certain period of time, and ended up falling ill.'"

ONE NIGHT, IN HIS LATER YEARS, R' SHOLOM REQUIRED EMERgency care. The need was so pressing that he struggled out of his

Bitul Torah chair and walked heavily to the adjoining room to wake the grandson who was staying in the apartment with him.

Opening the door to the room, he found his grandson sitting at a table, learning. R' Sholom was silent.

"Saba, what is it?" his grandson asked. "What do you want?"

"Nothing, nothing! I don't need anything."

The younger man urged him to answer, but R' Sholom persisted in his refusal. In a weak but determined voice, he said, "*Bitul Torah!* In that case, I don't need a thing from you."

And he maintained this stance despite all his grandson's coaxing.

Torah Tales — as Told by R' Sholom

IT WAS *ROSH CHODESH* TAMMUZ, 5714 (1954). MANY PEOPLE were gathering in Jerusalem for a wedding in the Bnos

"I Want to Serve" Yerushalayim hall, as it was then known, near the Jordanian border. Among the guests were R' Aharon Kotler — who was to be the *mesader kiddushin* for his student — and R' Yechezkel Levenstein.

R' Aharon dancing with a talmid at the young man's wedding

R' Sholom was present as well, and was therefore able to relate, emotionally, what occurred at that wedding.

Suddenly, a great noise sounded. Artillery boomed from the direction of the Old City. The Jordanians were shaking up the entire area. All the guests fell flat on the floor, and the lights were doused. From the streets, strangers poured into the building. Tables were overturned, food and drink fell and spilled. There was noise and terror, both inside and out.

"We could hear the explosions clearly," R' Sholom related. "Everybody was lying on the ground. The man next to me asked fearfully, 'What do we do now?'

"'We say *viduy*,' I answered."

Those were very difficult moments. One man scanned the crowd with his eyes, trying to locate his father; another shouted that he had lost his wife. The element of surprise had caused a terrible panic. There were no Jewish soldiers patrolling that area. Every new sound aroused further fear.

"R' Aharon Kotler was also lying on the ground," R' Sholom said. "And what did R' Aharon Kotler say? What was the leader of the generation thinking about during the pandemonium and the terror?

"Ah, R' Aharon, R' Aharon!" R' Sholom banged on the table. "R'

Aharon was pleading with *HaKadosh Baruch Hu* to spare his life: '*Ribbono Shel Olam*, I want to learn your holy Torah!'"

One of his students was beside him on the floor; in fact, he was the one to lift R' Aharon up later. R' Sholom and others went to this student's house to ask what he had heard during those moments of prayer.

"After a long lull in the shooting, I bent down to the *Rosh Yeshivah*, R' Aharon, to help him to his feet. I heard him say, '*Tatteh*, I want to serve You and work for You.' Then I heard a few more snatches, in which he seemed to be talking to *HaKadosh Baruch Hu* and saying that there was still work for him to do in this world."

About an hour after the shooting had commenced, the all-clear sounded. The crowd breathed a collective sigh of relief. Then R' Sholom stepped into the picture. In his deep voice, he recited, "*Lamenatze'ach mizmor l'David ya'ancha Hashem b'yom tzarah ...*." The others echoed him, word for word — and their prayers flew straight up to Heaven.

On another occasion, R' Sholom commented on the above incident.

"*Rabbosai!* The Tchebiner Rav once *davened* to Hashem in this same fashion. 'I want to learn the holy Torah.' I plead for life in order to learn Your holy Torah. That's what they wanted!" R' Sholom raised his voice as he told the story:

"R' Chaim Shmulevitz and another Torah scholar once visited the Tchebiner Rav to invite him to join a conference of *Moetzes Gedolei HaTorah*. This happened about two years before the Tchebiner Rav departed this world. The Rav declined the invitation, but did not reveal his reasons. After much pleading on R' Chaim's part, the Rav finally opened his heart.

"'Thirteen years ago, I fell ill with a life-threatening illness. I did [what King Chizkiyahu did in his time]: I turned my face to the wall and asked for another 15 years of life — in order to learn Torah. "*Ribbono Shel Olam*, I want to live and to learn Your holy Torah," I pleaded. And *HaKadosh Baruch Hu* answered me. 'Therefore,' the Tchebiner Rav concluded, 'I am not free to busy myself with anything other than Torah study!'

"That," R' Sholom finished, "was two years before the Rav's passing. Thirteen years, plus another two."

"Let me tell you another amazing story," R' Sholom said in the same speech. "An awesome and moving story: Together with my son-in-law, R' Eliyahu David Reichman, I went to the ask the Brisker Rav a question on the *Rambam* concerning the laws of *korban Pesach*. It was a difficult question. The Rav listened attentively, then turned to his son, the *gaon* R' Yosha Ber, seated beside him and said, 'Tell them the answer — and the circumstances under which we found it.'

"The Brisker Rav's son told the following story:

"'During World War Two, when we were running for our lives toward Vilna, enemy aircraft were bombing the area ceaselessly. Though our fear was overwhelming, we had no choice but to keep going. Together with thousands of other refugees, we continued along the main road to Vilna.

"'We were still on the road when the enemy pilots noticed large numbers of people walking. Without much hesitation, they began to bomb the road itself — literally right over our heads.

"'In the grip of a deathly terror, we tried desperately to turn our wagon off the road to find shelter from the enemy. We searched for concealment beneath the trees. At the very moment that we drove beneath the thick foliage and stopped, my father announced, "I understand the *Rambam's* meaning!"

"'That was the very *Rambam* you asked about just now.'

"R' Yosha Ber," continued R' Sholom, "explained the *Rambam* to us. Then we got up and left."

He ended the story without further elaboration or commentary — except for the two tears of emotion trickling slowly down his face.

They Learned Torah!

"THE *GEDOLIM* LEARNED TORAH ... *THEY — LEARNED — TORAH!*" R' Sholom was at his most emphatic. "I recall a wonderful fact. At one of the most difficult moments in my father-in-law's life, R' Chaim Leib Auerbach continued to come up with profound Torah insights."

During World War One, the small Jewish community in *Eretz Yisrael* was struggling with a grave situation. The *yishuv* was ruled by the Turks, who were at war with the English. Jews were drafted into the Turkish army, never to return. Their wives remained *agunos* for the rest of their lives.

R' Chaim Leib Auerbach, *Rosh Yeshivah* of Yeshivas Sha'ar HaShamayim, began devising ways to save Jews from the cruel draft. Studying Turkish law, he found that the Turks did not draft foreign subjects. He decided, therefore, to befriend an employee of the Persian Consulate.

R' Auerbach worked assiduously to forge a personal bond with this man, "buying" his friendship with gifts and bribes. (Indeed, the employee once remarked, "Well, you probably want something from me.") When he felt that the time was right, he asked his new friend to arrange a meeting with the Persian Consul. The "friend" set up several long meetings between the two. In the course of these meetings R' Chaim Leib found favor in the Consul's eyes and was raised to the status of friend, to the extent that the consul appointed R' Chaim Leib his assistant.

R' Auerbach utilized his new position well, distributing Persian passports to some 70 Jews, and saving them from certain death.

An announcement was made by the government at that time, warning that the punishment for draft evaders and for those who aided them in their evasion was death. Fear was widespread. There were those who made their fortunes by offering the government information on draft offenders — including, among others, R' Chaim Leib Auerbach. (The identity of his informer is known.) Upon hearing that R' Auerbach was distributing Persian passports to Jews, the Turkish government sent a contingent of soldiers to his home to arrest him. The house had a back door. With Heaven's help, R' Chaim Leib managed to slip away at the last minute.

He ran toward the Batei Hungarin, where a friend lived. There, behind a broad closet located in a room inside a room, R' Chaim Leib hid.

"I stayed there for several days," R' Chaim Leib later related to his son-in-law, R' Sholom Schwadron. "Hunger and thirst beset me — and fear, of course. There were moments when I felt as though my soul was about to explode." Opening his heart still further to his son-in-law, R' Chaim Leib added, "R' Sholom! The Shach said that when running from the Cossacks, he came up with a certain insight into the Torah. I, too," he said, pointing at a sheaf of pages filled with his writing, "wrote down my *chiddushim* that came to me while hiding from the Turks in that closet."

When the tongue sticks to the palate from thirst, when hunger is overwhelming — the brain explores the byways of Torah!

"Let's continue the story," R' Sholom said.

After several days in hiding, R' Chaim Leib was informed that the Turks had threatened to execute his family in his place if he did not give himself up. R' Chaim Leib immediately left his hiding place and was arrested.

It was decided to put him on trial along with R' Leib Dayan, whose signature appeared alongside R' Auerbach's on the passports. Fear gripped the Jewish *yishuv* in Jerusalem as the trial date approached. Public prayer meetings were held. The students of Yeshivas Sha'ar HaShamayim gathered a huge crowd for a tearful *Tehillim* rally. Words of prayer resounded in every corner of the Old City. The Jews were well acquainted with the Turks' cruelty, and the fate that was met by those who crossed them.

At the appointed hour, R' Chaim Leib and R' Leib Dayan entered the courthouse. A map was spread out on a table, with a long-barreled gun resting on it. Behind the table sat two officers. One of them was Gamal Pasha, the governor.

At once, R' Leib Dayan fainted from fear. He was dragged from the court. The trial rested squarely on R' Auerbach's shoulders.

One of the judges read the indictment aloud for a crime punishable by death. "What do you have to say about your guilt?" the judge demanded of R' Chaim Leib. ("You can just imagine how my heart was pounding!" R' Chaim Leib said later.)

To the judge, he answered, "Those men are *really* Persian citizens!"

Gamal Pasha leaped up in a rage. "Liar!" he bellowed. "How

can you say that they're Persians? They are all white-skinned, while Persians are dark!"

R' Chaim Leib, quaking with terror, nearly fainted as well. But all the *tefillos* and *Tehillim* had incurred Heaven's compassion. Mastering his fear, he managed to meet the question with a smile. After a moment, calmer now, he began speaking in fluent Arabic, weighing his speech heavily with terms of respect and making frequent use of the governor's title.

"I will explain to you, Your most exalted Honor. You know that the Russian pigs (the Russians were then fighting on the enemy's side, hence R' Chaim's Leib abusive reference) have been causing great problems for many of the Jews. Many Jews, therefore, wish to escape from Russia but are unable to do so. What do they do? When the time approaches for a Jewish woman to give birth, she travels to Persia, which is close to the Russian border, and has the baby there. Therefore, the baby is a Persian citizen! But his skin is still white."

Gamal Pasha listened to the explanation, then turned to R' Chaim Leib and said, "Listen! I know that you are a liar, but a mind as sharp as yours should not be buried underground. Get out of here."

There is no describing the joy that flooded the Yeshivah Sha'ar HaShamayim and the entire Old City when R' Chaim Leib left the courthouse a free man.

THE RIDBAZ, ONE OF THE TORAH GREATS OF THE MAHARSHAM'S time, expressed his opinion of the Maharsham's unique abilities: "We

Around the Maharsham's Table: R' Sholom on His Grandfather also know [how to learn] … but the ability to find the precise halachic source to apply to a new situation — in this the Maharsham is unique."

One example among the thousands will illustrate this quality.

A certain gentile squire wished to borrow a large sum of money from a Jew who, knowing how much trouble compliance might cause him, asked another Jew to lend the required sum to the squire. Naturally, the second Jew had the same reservations as the first: When the time came to ask the powerful gentile to repay the money, the squire was liable to do him harm. Then the first Jew took it upon himself to guarantee the loan. Hearing this, the second Jew agreed to lend the squire the money.

When the loan came due, the second Jew came to the first and asked for his money. The first Jew said, "I did not agree to be responsible for the loan. I am simply a guarantor. Go to the squire and ask for your money; if he refuses to pay, then come to me."

The second Jew screamed, "I didn't understand it that way! My whole point was to avoid having to deal with the squire. When you agreed to guarantee the loan, I understood that to mean that *you* would deal with the squire, and that if I want to, I can come to you for the money." Unable to resolve their differences, they brought the case before the Maharsham.

On the surface, the halachah seemed to fall clearly on the side of the guarantor, for even the lender admitted that the other had said only that he would guarantee the loan. But the Maharsham replied that there was room for placing the law on the lender's side. (I don't know if he ruled thus, but the parallel that he cited was marvelous.) He cited the Maharsha's commentary on the *aggadah* in *Maseches Pesachim* 118b. The Gemara there relates a conversation between *HaKadosh Baruch Hu* and the ministering angel of the sea.

Hashem ordered the angel to spit the Egyptians' drowned bodies out of the Yam Suf, onto dry land, so that the Children of Israel could see that they were truly dead. The angel protested, "Is there a servant whose master gives him a gift and then takes it back?" Hashem promised to return one and a half times as many bodies at a later date.

"But can a servant demand payment from his master?" the angel asked.

Hashem said, "The Kishon River will be my guarantor." The angel immediately caused the sea to hurl the bodies ashore.

The question that springs to mind parallels the case of the two Jewish

The Maharsham

moneylenders and the squire. How could Hashem promise that the Kishon River would be the guarantor for the "loan" of the bodies, when that would mean that the lender would still have to apply to the borrower first for repayment — and the servant did not wish to apply to his master? But the Maharsha dealt with this question: "Although one applies first to the borrower in the case of a simple guarantor, in the case where a servant cannot apply to his master, the guarantor becomes responsible for the loan."

In the case we have just examined, the lender's primary fear was in demanding payment from the squire — turning the simple guarantor into the responsible party.

In his book, R' Sholom presented another brilliant story:
A certain prosperous Jew hired laborers to work in his fields.

One morning, the landowner went out into his field and saw his workers brushing their teeth with brushes and toothpaste. It was their habit to perform this rite every morning, though at the time it was more commonly reserved for the rich and pampered.

Seeing them engaged thus, the landowner shouted, "These are not farm laborers, they are university graduates!" Such pampered individuals, he believed, would not do a good job in his fields. He fired them.

The workers did not go quietly. "Tell us," they demanded, "where we have not performed the work as well as any villager — and *then* fire us!" But the landowner refused to have anything more to do with them.

The workers brought the Jewish landowner to court, and the *din Torah* was interesting in the extreme. Eventually, the case was brought before a large gathering of prominent rabbis, headed by the Maharsham.

One day, as the discussion on the legal ramifications of the case continued, the Maharsham stated, "There is an answer to [the workers'] claims. Indeed, these pampered ones do not work the earth as required — and it says so clearly in the Gemara!"

The other rabbis were taken aback. Where could such an explicit Gemara be found without their knowledge? One of their number, who knew much of *Shas* by heart, began to go through the tractates: *Berachos, Shabbos, Eruvin,* etc. He concluded, "With all due respect to the Berzaner Rav, we have not found such an explicit Gemara."

The Maharsham was not fazed. "Seeing as the respected rabbis are working hard to contradict me," he said calmly, "I'll give you a hint. The Gemara [to which I refer] is found in *Maseches Shabbos!*"

Other rabbis joined the one who knew *Shas* by heart. They went through the entire *Maseches Shabbos* without finding the reference to which the Maharsham had alluded. The Maharsham said tranquilly, "In that case, I will mention the precise *perek* where the Gemara is located. It is the *perek* that begins, *Bemah beheimah!*"

A great commotion ensued. The *perek* he had cited comprised no more than five and a half pages. They went through the entire *perek* before announcing unanimously that the reference to which the Berzaner Rav kept alluding was simply not there.

Smiling, the Maharsham said, "In that case, here is the language of the Gemara itself, in that *perek*, on *daf* 54." And he went on to discuss the Gemara's definition of the term *eretz kabul*. "Rav Huna says that [the land] had people who were *mechubalin* (covered) with silver and gold. Rabbah asked, 'Why does it say that these individuals did not find favor in Hashem's eyes?' And R' Huna replied that because they were pampered and spoiled, they did not work properly!"

Hearing these words fall from the Maharsham's lips, the other rabbis raised a great cry, tugging at their beards and *peyos* and asking, "Where are our heads?"

[R' Sholom wrote down this story as told to him by R' Herzog, who heard it from R' Meir Shapiro, who was present when the episode occurred.]

R' Sholom added:

"Despite the fact that the Maharsham possessed a phenomenal memory, he constantly reviewed the halachos in which he was well versed — even to the point of counting their letters. My honored mother, Rebbetzin Frayda Leah, told me that she heard from my father that the Maharsham used to study, from memory, the laws pertaining to the washing of hands before he ate; during his meal he would review the laws of *Bircas HaMotzi*, etc.; and before reciting *Bircas HaMazon* he would review its laws. On Shabbos he would review the tractates of *Shabbos* and *Eruvin* and the laws pertaining to Shabbos, and on *motza'ei* Shabbos, during the *melaveh malkah* meal, he would finish *Maseches Eruvin*.

"In his booklet, *Oholei Shem*," R' Sholom continued, "my brother writes that he heard from the Maharsham himself that after his marriage he did not wish to become either a rabbi or a teacher, and instead opened a wine shop. During the two years in which he managed this shop (it subsequently burned down and he was forced to accept a rabbinical post), he sat and reviewed all four parts of the *Shulchan Aruch 400 times!*"

R' Sholom went on to relate an episode that he had heard from one of the great men of his generation, who remarked on the Maharsham's uncanny grasp of all of Torah. He illustrated his point with a story he had heard from R' Meir Shapiro, who lived in the Maharsham's home for a period of several months. (The Maharsham's second wife was R' Meir Shapiro's grandmother.)

It happened once that the Maharsham fell ill and took to his bed. Several Torah scholars gathered in the adjoining room, where they began an animated discussion of a certain halachah in the *Even HaEzer*. The discussion became heated and voices were raised to the point that they reached the Maharsham's ears. He asked R' Meir Shapiro what the others were arguing about. R' Meir told him.

"Why do they have any questions on that?" he wondered. "The law is explicit in the *Darkei Moshe* on the *Tur* on *Yoreh De'ah, hilchos mezuzah, siman* so-and-so." He commanded R' Meir to bring him the *Tur* so that he could show him the law. R' Meir was very excited by the Maharsham's ability to pinpoint the precise halachah in the *Tur* — whereupon the Maharsham flipped to the back of the *Tur* and showed him where he had written: "With Hashem's help, I have completed the *Tur* 101 times." And he added, "In that case, what is there to get excited about? If one learns the *Tur* 101 times, one can remember the *Darkei Moshe*."

Indeed, it is no wonder that he merited all the honor he received and that his edicts were accepted as halachah throughout the world!

In referring to King David, R' Sholom expounded, the Gemara says that "Hashem was with him" — in other words, that his was the final word on halachah everywhere [see *Sanhedrin* 93b]. Why was this? Because "David was small." Our Sages, in *Megillah* 11, add that he was small from beginning to end: He made himself small in comparison to those who were greater than he was in Torah, and in his kingship he made himself small with reference to those who were greater than he was in wisdom. Similarly, *Eruvin* 13 cites Beis Hillel's lowliness as the reason they merited to have the halachah decided according to their way.

"My grandfather, the Maharsham," R' Sholom says, "is another example." As one of his generation's Torah giants expressed it: "He was a genuine chassid who submitted himself with all his heart and soul to his teachers, and stood before them like a servant before a master. He humbled himself before the *gaon* of Ziditchov and Sar Sholom of Belz, even when he himself was already renowned the world over. In his old age, he would humble himself before the *gaon* of Chortkov.

Most people, R' Sholom says, do not humble themselves even to those who are greater than they in Torah! The fact that King David did so was considered a remarkable and praiseworthy trait, for most people bloat their own importance until they consider themselves kings! They find it extremely distasteful to subjugate their own "kingship" to someone greater.

King David was willing to see himself as a small man in comparison with one who knew more than he in Torah, and almost as a commoner in contrast to one who was wiser than he. That is why it says, "David was small." And that is why "Hashem was with him" — and the halachah was decided according to his opinion everywhere!

Torah Tales

THE FOLLOWING WAS RELATED BY R' DAVID KLEIN, A BOYHOOD friend of R' Sholom from their years in the Chevron Yeshivah:

Three Tractates

R' Moshe Mordechai Epstein, the *Rosh Yeshivah* of Chevron Yeshivah, met with Rav Kook on many occasions.

In those days, *Eretz Yisrael* did not boast health spas or vacation resorts, as such. One of the few such spots that served the public was the *Mizrachi*, perched on the crest of the Carmel. One summer's day, three great men were staying there at the same time: R' Moshe Mordechai, R' Isser Zalman Meltzer, and Rav Kook.

The three sat in the courtyard breathing the clear mountain air. To avoid tiring their minds with a deep discussion, one of them suggested that they each recite one tractate of the Talmud — from memory.

The other two turned to R' Moshe Mordechai first. The *Rosh Yeshivah* of Chevron recited the entire tractate of *Bava Basra* by heart. Then came R' Isser Zalman Meltzer, with *Maseches Yevamos*, followed by Rav Kook with *Maseches Shabbos*, from beginning to end.

A true story ... and a glimpse into the glory and the mastery possessed by the previous generation's Torah greats.

R' SHOLOM TOLD A STORY THAT HE HAD HEARD FROM R' YEHUDAH Kravitz, whose father, as a young man, had learned in yeshivah to-

He Didn't Feel a Thing

gether with R' Yechezkel Levenstein.

The yeshivah's dining room was a long walk from the *beis midrash*. After *Minchah* services, the boys would walk over to the dining room for lunch, and then they would return to the study hall.

In general, R' Yechezkel (or, as he was known in the yeshivah, "Yechezkel Warshaver") was ahead of all the others. Before the boys had even completed the walk to the dining room, R' Yechezkel had already finished his meal and was on his way back to the *beis midrash*.

One day, the boys arrived for lunch to find the cook dis-

traught. "I have no food for you today." In distress, she explained, "I poured salt into the pot of food, and then my assistant made a mistake and poured more salt in, so that the food is extremely salty. Take some bread and something to drink," she advised sadly.

Immediately, she asked, "But where is the boy who was already here and ate?"

R' Yechezkel Levenstein in his later years

The boys thought this a fine tale. Look at Yechezkel Levenstein — he practices abstinence by eating salty food and saying not a word! Upon completing their own meager meal, they returned to the *beis midrash* and approached R' Yechezkel.

"How was lunch today?" asked one fellow student.

"Good," Yechezkel answered. "Very good."

"You didn't notice anything wrong?"

"No, nothing."

The other boys were amazed. He didn't do it to deprive himself of pleasure. He simply did not notice.

A FINAL TALE FROM R' SHOLOM'S COLLECTION:

Saying Good-bye

In his youth, the Beis HaLevi went into voluntary "exile." Lacking the necessary funds for transportation, he hired himself out to wagon drivers to whip the horses in return for passage.

On one occasion, the Beis HaLevi arrived in the city of Brod, where he met with R' Shlomo Kluger. The two met daily at R' Shlomo Kluger's home, where they took on the following custom: One day, the Beis HaLevi would ask a question (*"ah kasha"*) on the Talmud and R' Shlomo Kluger would search for the answer; the next day R' Shlomo Kluger would pose a question and his guest would answer. This practice continued for two weeks.

On the last day, R' Shlomo Kluger said, "This time I will ask a *kasha* that you won't have an answer for: *Kasheh alai preidaschem* (literally: Your parting is difficult for me). Do you have an answer?"

Some add [though the authenticity of this portion is unclear] that the Beis HaLevi responded, "It's true that I have no answer for that one — but I already asked it before you did."

Chapter 6

Of Good Character

THE TORAH WORLD OF PETACH TIKVAH WAS DRESSED
for festivity. R' Dov Zokovsky

To the Last Ounce
of Strength

("R' Berel Yanover") was
marrying off a daughter.
Many residents of the city, and many from outside it, came to
celebrate with the *tzaddik* from Yeshivas Knesses Yisrael-Chevron.
R' Sholom Schwadron, a former student of the yeshivah, traveled
from Jerusalem for the event.

The mitzvah of rejoicing with a groom was one for which R'
Sholom was famous. His extended arms upraised, he lifted his legs
in his trademark dance. It was a dance filled with devotion. The
joy of the mitzvah was stamped on his shining face as he smiled
and bowed and kicked and waved.

At that particular wedding, R' Sholom would not stop dancing
for the groom. As happiness flowed through him, he felt a special
desire to dance … dance … dance! Perspiration bathed his face and
his heart pounded powerfully. Filled with his mitzvah, he exerted

himself still further. His arms and legs moved until they could move no more.

After an hour, he moved aside at last. Weakness engulfed him, making him fling himself into a chair at one end of the large hall. R' Sholom was near collapse. R' Ze'ev Eidelman went over to see if he could help.

Interviewed about this incident, R' "Velvel" Eidelman sighed. "Ah! If you want to hear about R' Sholom's greatness, no matter how much we talk we'll never finish. R' Sholom was great in every area but especially in Torah. He demonstrated mastery over every topic about which he was asked. R' Sholom was a *gaon* in Torah."

R' Velvel went on, at the interviewer's request, to speak of the Petach Tikvah wedding. "As you know, R' Sholom was especially enthusiastic about observing the mitzvah of rejoicing with the bride and groom. That night, he danced for a full hour, until he lost his strength." He paused. "I know a little about medicine. I saw that R' Sholom's condition was not good. I took him into a side room, stretched him out on a bed and made sure he rested. R' Sholom lay in terrible weakness — in genuine danger. Afterwards, I took him home with me and he slept there till morning.

R' Sholom dances with R' Ze'ev Eidelman

"As soon as he awoke, I saw that he was truly an ill person. I gave him a small amount to eat and drink before *tefillah*, until, little by little, his strength was restored. He could not be allowed to travel back to Jerusalem, he needed rest. We sent a telegram to his family to let them know about his condition, and R' Sholom remained in my home for about two weeks. A two-week stint of rejoicing with the groom!"

R' Velvel's warm friendship with R' Sholom dates from that episode. During their two weeks together, the pair engaged in long, profound Torah discussions. They talked about man's obligation in this world. In these serious conversations were sown the seeds of a bond that would survive for decades.

With a tranquility that spoke of a peaceful heart and mind, R' Sholom said to R' Velvel, "I'll tell you a story from the Vilna Gaon's life — a story that will help you to understand the significance of the mitzvah of rejoicing with a *chasan*."

This is the story he told:

> During a certain period in his life, the Gaon went into voluntary exile, traveling from city to city. One day, he arrived in a small town in Russia to find a wedding taking place. All the townspeople emerged from their homes to celebrate and rejoice with the groom. The Vilna Gaon attended with them. He stepped off the road and entered the wedding hall, sitting in the area reserved for the local paupers.
>
> During the wedding feast, a valuable object disappeared from one of the tables. Suspicion at once fell upon the Gaon, a stranger who had appeared out of nowhere and was sitting on the sidelines saying nothing. Nobody in the town recognized him. He must be the thief!
>
> One Jew who fancied himself clever took it upon himself to go over to the stranger. "Return what you have taken!" he demanded.
>
> The Gaon was silent.
>
> Raising his voice, the man repeated, "Return what you have taken!" Still the Vilna Gaon said nothing.

R' Sholom dancing at a wedding as R' Reuven Gershonowitz looks on

Another of the merrymakers assured his host that *he* would make the stranger speak. He reached out a hand, seized the Gaon by the arm, and lifted him from his seat. Then he pulled him over to sit by the *chasan* at the eastern table, in full view of all present. Angrily, he said, "Return what was stolen!"

The Vilna Gaon remained stubbornly silent. Tension gripped the hall and its occupants.

One guest, a man devoid of wisdom or piety, was unable to contain his rage. Flinging open the door, he booted the Gaon out, to the tune of general laughter.

Turning, the Gaon saw that the groom, too, was laughing. He reflected, and later related to others, "It was worth it all for the sake of making the *chasan* happy."

"We see from this story," R' Velvel continued, "how great is the mitzvah of making the groom rejoice."

(Incidentally, the Gaon later explained why he refused to answer his accusers. "Had I answered them, I would have been reincarnated as a dog." The Gaon believed that any words he might say in his own defense could fall into the category of speaking *lashon hara* against the actual thief — and that the punishment for those who speak *lashon hara* is to come back to this world as a dog.)

166 / VOICE OF TRUTH

"I WAS WILD," R' SHOLOM OFTEN SAID WHEN SPEAKING OF HIS childhood. "My rebbe, R' Leib Chasman, removed half of my wildness."

Forgive Me!

And the other half? R' Sholom just smiled.

What lay beneath this early wildness? What was the nature of R' Sholom's personality during that period? We can learn some of the answers from a story his friends have preserved from their days in the Talmud Torah of Meah Shearim.

R' Sholom himself authenticated this tale and repeated it to one of his beloved grandsons.

"The *gabbai* of the *chevrah kaddisha*," he recalled, "was a very tall man. He also had an unusual walk, which, together with his height, gave him an extraordinary appearance."

The boys were playing in the Talmud Torah schoolyard when the *gabbai* climbed the stairs of the nearby Ohel Sarah Synagogue. Seeing him, the young Sholom started imitating the *gabbai's* movements. His appreciative classmates doubled over with laughter at his antics.

At first, the *gabbai* swallowed the insult in silence. As the laughter grew louder, however, he spun around and asked angrily, "Who is making fun of me?"

R' Sholom was rendered mute, but his friends exploded in frightened cries. The man descended the stairs, walked toward them at a rapid pace, and entered the Talmud Torah yard. At once, all the boys fled into the building.

"I was scared," R' Sholom said. "I still remember how I felt that day. He was a giant of a man, chasing me in fury … To my friends' credit, they did not tell on me. The *gabbai* searched the Talmud Torah for a while, then left, frustrated.

"I could have let myself forget the incident, but the man's humiliation bothered me deeply. Regret gnawed at me all that day and night. A Jew had been hurt because of my wildness … The next morning, I made a daring decision. I would find the *gabbai* and ask his forgiveness. The problem was, I didn't know where he lived."

The young Sholom searched for the *gabbai* across the length and breadth of Meah Shearim. Finally, while searching near a shul, he stepped inside it and glimpsed the man he sought, standing at his full height in the center of the room.

Sholom fled in a panic.

In both age and stature, Sholom was small. And the *gabbai* was a giant of a man. Sholom was afraid of his own idea, of what he was planning to do. He was terrified at the notion of entering that shul again. What if the *gabbai* decided to "repay" him as he deserved? The boy's heart pounded and his breath became short. More than anything, he longed to return to *cheder*. He wished with all his heart to vanish from the spot and run back to school. But the regret that had filled Sholom's heart all the preceding day held him firmly in place.

"I gathered my courage, stepped back into the shul doorway, and stood looking inside. I lifted my head, cupped my hands around my mouth, and cried [in Yiddish], 'I am the boy who laughed at you yesterday. Forgive me!' With that, I turned tail and began to make my escape.

"The giant man came after me. He took giant steps. Before I could get far, he had caught me in his two hands."

Young Sholom trembled with fear. He tried to struggle, but the man's grip was too strong for him. The *gabbai*, a good and honest man, patted him vigorously. Then he lifted the boy almost to the ceiling, brought him close, and kissed young Sholom on the forehead. To the other congregants in the shul he said in a ringing voice, "Look! Have you ever seen a boy ask for forgiveness?" He set Sholom down on the floor.

Worn out from the mental and physical struggles he had just experienced, Sholom left the shul, chastened, but far lighter in spirit than when he had arrived.

EACH SHABBOS, JUST BEFORE *MINCHAH* SERVICES, R' SHOLOM conducted a *shiur* in *Mishnayos* in Sha'arei Chesed's Gra Shul. After

"I'm Sorry" *seudah shelishis*, the third Shabbos meal, he would return to the shul to lecture the congregation until *Ma'ariv*.

One Shabbos, before the *shiur* was over, a man came into the shul and pounded on one of the tables as a signal to R' Sholom that it was time to finish. "It's time for *Minchah!*" the man announced.

At first, R' Sholom paid no attention to the interruption. When the disturbance grew louder, however, he decided to react. Turning on the newcomer, he rebuked him sharply for his insolence. Insulted, the man desisted, and the *shiur* wound to a close.

An hour later, the lecture between *seudah shelishis* and *Ma'ariv* services began. As usual, only a small number of people were present at

R' Sholom speaking, as his brother-in-law, R' Shlomo Zalman Auerbach, listens

the start, with more people coming in from the neighborhood as time passed. The shul was soon filled to capacity. A regular attendee was R' Sholom's brother-in-law, R' Shlomo Zalman Auerbach.

Suddenly, in the midst of his talk, R' Sholom fell silent. His eyes swept the roomful of filled seats. "*Rabbosai!*" he exclaimed. "At the end of the *shiur* before *Minchah*, I did not behave properly. I insulted a certain man (R' Sholom named him). I'm afraid that I transgressed and shamed my fellow man in public. Therefore, I would like to beg his forgiveness here, in public. If possible, I would ask him to forgive me verbally. I am sorry!"

The members of the audience exchanged incredulous glances. "I remember," one eyewitness recalls, "that R' Shlomo Zalman Auerbach, who was among those in the shul, was visibly moved by R' Sholom's words. As soon as R' Sholom finished apologizing, R' Shlomo Zalman displayed signs of tremendous admiration and emotion."

This story is not unique in its kind. It happened again and again — at home, with his wider audience, and among his students and acquaintances. R' Sholom never hesitated to apologize or to plead for forgiveness.

Who Was Right?

HIS REGULAR GEMARA *SHIUR* — SPANNING DECADES IN Sha'arei Chesed — was another place where one could savor R' Sholom's sparkling purity and wonderful character. One incident involved R' Chaim Yosef Kreuzer.

During one *shiur*, R' Chaim Yosef corrected R' Sholom, informing him that the words he had just quoted were found on a different page than the one R' Sholom had cited. R' Sholom listened courteously, then replied, "It seems to me that I was not mistaken, and that I cited the correct page. However, bring the Gemara and let's look inside."

Rabbi Kreuser rose with alacrity and fetched a Gemara. He spread it open on a table, searched for the quote, then cried, "My teacher, R' Sholom! You were right!"

R' Sholom then whispered to a man seated beside him, "I know R' Kreuser. Even if *he* is right, he'd say that I was in order not to embarrass me." Aloud, he said, "Please bring the Gemara here. I want to see for myself."

R' Sholom had not erred in his assessment. R' Yosef Chaim's original claim had been correct: The words quoted were indeed found on another page. We know this with certainty, for R' Sholom announced it for all to hear. "*Rabbosai!* He was right. I was wrong!"

That was R' Sholom in a nutshell: a firm commitment to the truth.

The Mission

R' GEDALIA SHENIN RELATES:

During the repetition of the *Mussaf Shemoneh Esrei* one Rosh Hashanah, a boy was wandering near the Holy Ark in the Chevron Yeshivah. He repeatedly climbed and descended the steps in front of the Ark, until R' Sholom gestured for him to leave the area. The sensitive child was wounded.

"R' Sholom," R' Gedalia told him quietly after the services were over, "the boy who was jumping around and creating a disturbance is an orphan."

"*Oy, oy,* what have I done?" R' Sholom exclaimed. "I caused pain to an orphan!" His face creased with anguish as he went on to explain a further source of distress: To ask a young child for forgiveness posed a halachic problem. What to do?

"I sent him off to the side because I was afraid he might not be clean, in which case I would be prohibited from *davening* near him. But I ended by causing him pain. *Oy v'avoy!*"

For some 20 minutes, R' Sholom pondered deeply. Then his face cleared. Turning with a smile, he said, "Gedalia! I hereby appoint you my messenger to ask for forgiveness. No, not now … At his bar mitzvah!"

He shared his reasoning: "You, R' Gedalia, know this boy and often help him. You will certainly be invited to his bar mitzvah celebration [while I do not know if I'll be in this world by then]. In that case, you have been given a mission — to beg his pardon for me!"

The following year, during the *piyutim* of *Mussaf* on Rosh Hashanah, R' Sholom caught sight of the same boy. He immediately motioned, with obvious affection, for the boy to come closer. When he came, R' Sholom patted him warmly and seated the boy beside him for a long time.

The years passed, and the boy's bar mitzvah was upon them. R' Sholom was still numbered among the living, and he remembered the incident. R' Gedalia went to his house to tell him that he, too, remembered his mission: to ask the boy for forgiveness in R' Sholom's name. R' Sholom took a *sefer* out of his closet as a gift for the bar mitzvah boy, and inscribed it. *Sefer* in hand, R' Gedalia went to the bar mitzvah celebration directly from R' Sholom's house, to rejoice with the boy and his family — and to beg his pardon.

"R' Sholom had been concerned about cleanliness," R' Gedalia thought. "Look at the cleanliness of R' Sholom's soul!"

"I WAS A MISCHIEVOUS LITTLE BOY," A CERTAIN MAN RELATES.
"At 6 years of age, I filled my pockets with sunflower seeds and

A Pocketful of Seeds walked to the Zichron Moshe Shul hand-in-hand with my grandfather, to hear one of R' Sholom's famous sermons. I actually sat myself down right on the *bimah*, no less!

"During the talk, I suddenly remembered the treasure in my pocket ... and began cracking the seeds energetically right in front of R' Sholom.

"About 20 minutes passed before I heard a great voice cry out, 'You came here to crack sunflower seeds?' Every eye was directed at me, a small boy. I was embarrassed down to my fingertips. Naturally, I stopped eating the seeds and sat dreaming until the talk was over.

"R' Sholom decided that it was incumbent upon him to placate me. Immediately after his talk was completed, he brought me

near him and patted and stroked me. As usual at the end of a talk, people came over to speak to him, and he listened to them while patting and caressing me the entire time — perhaps 20 minutes in all! — until I had had my fill, and was comforted.

"Twenty-three years have passed since then, and those caresses have accompanied me to this day."

R' Sholom at the upsherin of his great-grandchild, Shimon Katzenelenbogen

WE WOULD LIKE TO TAKE THIS OPPORTUNITY TO QUOTE FROM a certain marvelous letter sent by R' Yaakov Yisrael Kanievsky, the

The Steipler Steipler, to R' Sholom Schwadron. It is an electrifying letter, as is the story that goes along with it.

A great *hesped* was held for R' Avraham Yoffen, son-in-law of the Alter of Novardok. The *hesped* took place in the Tel

Aviv yeshivah. Though he was hard of hearing, the Steipler Rav made the effort to come and participate. He did not come to hear, but rather to honor the passing of the man being mourned.

The eulogy lasted long, and the hour was growing late. When one of the eulogizers finished speaking, the Steipler rose to leave. At that moment, it was R' Sholom's turn to speak. He rose to the dais just as R' Yaakov Yisrael Kanievsky left the hall — and several dozen others after him.

Two days passed. The Steipler, in his greatness, wrote the following letter asking R' Sholom's forgiveness:

"To my friend, the famous Rav *HaGaon*, whose mouth spews pearls ... R' Sholom Schwadron, *shlita*, grandson of the minister of Torah, the Maharsham.

"I beg forgiveness from your Torah Honor. I am distressed because one night, when attending the *hesped* of *Moreinu Harav* Yoffen, I did not come to listen because I could not hear a single word; as everyone knows, I only came to show respect for the *niftar*, as I had learned in his yeshivah for several years, and also to comfort his son, in fulfillment of the mitzvah to comfort a mourner. I was not feeling well, and I sat there for perhaps an hour and a half, and it was difficult for me. When your turn came to speak, I thought that you, being a celebrated speaker, might continue for another hour, and that would have been very difficult for me. Therefore, thinking to myself that I had already fulfilled my obligation, I wished to go home. I did not think that this would be construed as an insult to you, as everyone knows that I cannot hear and that I had only came in order to show respect to the *niftar*.

"But when I began to leave, another *minyan* of men, perhaps more, were drawn to follow, and I imagine that most of them did not return to the *beis midrash* but returned home instead; so it came about that through my actions your honor was wounded. Had I known that my departure would draw others to do the same, I certainly would not have left.

"I request strongly from Your Honor that you tell me you forgive me, because an insult to a great man in Torah is very, very serious.

R' Sholom at the hesped for R' Eliyahu Weiner

"My warmest regards to Your Honor, and my heartfelt blessing that you achieve great success on behalf of good, and multiply your activities for the sake of Torah through increased wisdom and much *nachas*, and the blessing of the Almighty's peace.

"Awaiting Heaven's mercy and the full redemption ...

"Yaakov Yisrael Kanievsky."

The end of the story came about 10 years later.

In the Lederman Shul in Bnei Brak, a *hesped* was being given for R' Eliyahu Weiner. The Steipler arrived to join those present. At this late stage in the Steipler's life, this was a rare public appearance. R' Sholom, the last of the speakers, stood up and began making his way toward the Holy Ark to deliver his eulogy. He noticed that the Steipler had remained seated. He could not hear a thing, yet he remained out of respect for R' Sholom.

R' Sholom did not step onto the *bimah*. Instead, he walked over to the eastern wall, where the Steipler was sitting. The audience held its breath, waiting in astonishment to hear what R' Sholom would say.

Removing a piece of paper and a pen from his pocket, R' Sholom wrote a brief note, saying that he begged the Steipler not to trouble himself to wait for R' Sholom to speak. R' Sholom assured him that he would not judge such a thing severely — on the contrary.

The Steipler indicated his deep satisfaction with R' Sholom's pure heart, then rose and went home.

THE SWEETNESS AND THE HUMILITY OF R' SHOLOM'S CHARAC-
ter requires a chapter in itself.

Humility   After a sermon that had inflamed and inspired thousands, he could never understand what the audience wanted from him. "Why?" he would ask, red-faced. "Why are they following me?" He was simply incapable of understanding the urge that impelled them to dog his footsteps.

R' Sholom knew that the Jewish world eagerly awaited his inspiring words, and how, at every gathering, the people anticipated the Torah insights that emerged from his lips. He witnessed the way his talks brought so many to tears, to dramatic change, and clearer thinking. Yet, despite all this, he was never haughty. He knew that he was a faithful transmitter of the previous generation's teachings, yet he was never arrogant. In the posters advertising his weekly Friday night talks in the Zichron Moshe Shul during the winter months, he insisted that he be listed only as "rabbi," with no additional titular flourishes. And the poster itself was small.

In the year 5724 (1964), the *chareidi* newspaper, *Hakol* ["The Voice"] announced that R' Sholom would be speaking at a certain place. The announcement referred to him in the most glowing of terms: "The rabbi, *gaon* and *tzaddik*, whose mouth spews pearls and who speaks with Heavenly grace and brings merit unto the many." The newspaper reached R' Sholom's hand. When the time came for the advertised talk, he opened with a scathing mockery of these ornate terms of respect, ending with, "How do they write such things about me? What chutzpah!"

Always, as he lectured, the humility would radiate from his countenance, reflecting that which resided within. It was this that made others love to hear him. When raising his voice to rebuke, he always added emotionally, "Who am I to stand before you like this? I am not telling you, I am scolding myself, too."

Incidentally, he was able to let pass the title "*gaon*" if absolutely necessary — but the title "*tzaddik*" was one he categorically refused to accept.

R' Sholom and R' Yehudah Zev Segel (right) visting R' Moshe Feinstein (left)

When the Steipler would see R' Sholom's figure in his doorway, he would gather his strength to stand in greeting — while R' Sholom grew pale as a sheet. When great Torah personalities rejoiced to see him, he was unable to utter a word. He simply did not believe the evidence of his own eyes. When R' Yehudah Zev Segal spoke of him with admiration to his face, R' Sholom's reaction was, "*Nu*, he knows how to encourage people."

The Steipler once remarked to R' Sholom's son-in-law, R' Moshe Ariel, "Your father-in-law brings merit upon a great many people in our generation by inspiring within them *yiras Shamayim*." R' Moshe passed this compliment on to his father-in-law. As the years passed, R' Sholom conveniently "forgot" it. Whenever it was mentioned, he would say, "Really, did he say that?" R' Sholom remembered everything except remarks such as these.

The Chazon Ish once asked R' Sholom to act as *Rosh Yeshivah* of a certain famous yeshivah. On a different occasion, he suggested a position as spiritual administrator in another large yeshivah. R' Sholom declined both positions: He had no wish to adorn himself with this kind of honor.

Upon his return from the *Knessiah Gedolah* of Agudath Israel, R' Sholom related emotionally, "I entered the convention hall. R' Benzion Abba Shaul was sitting there, and as I came in he gave me his place. It seems to me that his humility goes beyond the natural. Here he is, a world-class *gaon*, outstanding in his diligence and filled with the talents of the previous generation — and he gives *me* his place! A humility that goes beyond nature!"

As R' Tzvi Tauber attests, whenever the name of R' Abba Shaul was mentioned at R' Sholom's table, he would exclaim with feeling, "Did you know? The *gaon* R' Benzion is an *anav* (a humble man) beyond the bounds of nature."

⌒⌒

Pride and arrogance could not touch him — and one of his sons-in-law explains why.

R' Sholom was always prosecuting himself, even while accumulating a wealth of Torah and *yirah*, even when influencing the masses. He lived his life wondering what his obligation was and which path he was being led to follow. At the end of his life, as he stood on the brink of leaving this world, he was constantly afraid of what the next world held for him. A doctor who was treating him once entered his room and asked, "What is troubling the Rav?" R' Sholom was not prepared to answer, but the doctor pressed him until R' Sholom lifted his eyes.

"Troubling me! I *am* troubled: *What will be in the next world?*"

The doctor, in confusion, stammered something. R' Sholom looked at him and repeated, "What will be? What will be?" And his tears soaked the pillow.

R' Sholom would often explain the difference between learning *mussar* out of sadness and learning it with a broken heart. Sadness, he said, was like a great darkness. How does one tell the difference between the two?

"If after learning *mussar* you *daven* and learn better — that's a sign that you're on the right path. But if, immediately after you finish learning *mussar*, you light up a cigarette and feel bored, that's a clear sign that sadness has wormed its way in."

Together, his giant heart and tremendous mind forged the state that he termed a "broken heart." He demanded of himself incessantly, never allowing himself to rest on his laurels or to feel complete — though he did take genuine joy in the things he accomplished. To a discerning mind, the two do not contradict one another.

R' Sholom once said, "R' Eliyahu Lopian told me several times, in the name of R' Simchah Zissel, the Alter of Kelm, that there is a kind of person who really should be thrown out the window to shatter to bits. But if he has a broken heart, it says, 'Do not scorn a broken heart.'"

AN INCIDENT OCCURRED THAT FILLED RAV SHACH WITH WONder at R' Sholom's humility.

Mixed Messages   Rav Shach had been asked to serve as *sandak* at the *bris* of R' Sholom's grandson. During the meal, the two engaged in a prolonged Torah discussion,

R' Shach (right) speaking with R' Shlomo Zalman Auerbach at the wedding of R' Sholom's daughter to R' Nachum Sheinelson. R' Moshe Deutsch is at left.

in the course of which R' Sholom ventured his opinion on a certain *Rambam* on the laws of *bris milah*. Rav Shach was jubilant. *"Baruch shekivanti!* I think the same way!"

Baruch shekivanti? R' Sholom was surprised. " Is the Rav making fun of me?"

Appalled, Rav Shach replied, "Heaven forbid! Am I the kind of person who would make fun?" Then he added, "Let me tell you a story about R' Akiva Eiger."

"R' Akiva Eiger and his son arrived at the home of a man whose daughter had been suggested as a match for the son. The girl's father spoke with the young man in order to get a sense of who he was. When the conversation was over, R' Akiva Eiger asked the girl's father, 'Well, what do you say about my son?'

"Smiling with satisfaction, the father said, 'If only the groom's father pleased me as much as the groom does.'

"'And why don't I please you?' asked R' Akiva Eiger.

"The father was quick to acquit himself. 'No, no — I was joking! Just kidding around. I truly respect you with all my heart.'

"'*Leitzanus* (levity)?' R' Akiva Eiger was shaken. 'I don't want to make a *shidduch* with jokers!' Immediately, he got up and left the house. The match was off."

Rav Shach went on to relate an incident from the life of the Sha'agas Aryeh. Two young men came to him to receive ordination at his hands. The Sha'agas Aryeh tested them and was satisfied with the results. The young men's joy was great, as was the Sha'agas Aryeh's satisfaction. He offered to toast the occasion with a *"l'chaim!"*

Searching the cupboards of his home, the Sha'agas Aryeh found only a small amount of liquor and some cooked eggs. There were no baked goods in the house. He placed the drink and the eggs on the table, then asked, "What shall we make the blessing over?"

Laughing, one of the young men answered, "On the egg, of course! It says so clearly in *Parashas Lech Lecha*: *v'ha'ai* (in Yiddish, an *'ai'* is an egg) *mikedem* (first)!"

The Sha'agas Aryeh was taken aback. *"Leitzanus?!"* He refused to ordain them, and they left in humiliation.

Rav Shach finished the story and fell silent. R' Sholom realized that the other man's words had truly emerged from the depths of his heart. *Baruch shekivanti!*

～～

It is well known that R' Sholom was R' Leib Chasman's devoted student. "I never missed one of R' Leib's talks or learning groups," R' Sholom attested. Then he added, "Even on the day my very good friend, R' Avraham Roth, got married, I went to the *chuppah* in the Old City and then returned to the yeshivah in Geulah to hear the *mashgiach* deliver a Friday night talk. After *Ma'ariv*, I returned to the Old City to rejoice [with the *chasan*]."

R' Sholom began writing down R' Leib's talks during the latter's lifetime. He showed his teacher what he was doing. "After R' Leib read through the pages, he told me, 'This is not exactly what I meant.' I got upset and asked him if I should erase it. 'Erase it? No, no! Leave it the way it is!'"

It is interesting to note that R' Sholom received the *mashgiach's* tacit endorsement for the work, despite the fact that R' Leib did not think R' Sholom had properly understood everything he had said. In his introduction to the three-volume *Ohr Yahel,* R' Sholom writes, "I knew clearly that [R' Leib] liked my transcription of his talks in my own style, because I showed him one of the transcripts and he said that I had not understood … And yet, when I wanted to hand the work over to someone wiser, he ordered me not to change it, adding other remarks that made me sure that this was his wish."

WHENEVER R' SHOLOM DISCOVERED THAT HE HAD BEEN MIS-taken, he revealed a greatness of spirit in admitting his mistake

I Was Mistaken with no sense of loss of self-respect. One example can be found in the margins of the Maharsham's responsa (Section 8, *siman* 222) concerning the laws of *pidyon haben* at night. His celebrated grandson wrote: "In *Da'as Torah, siman* 568, I wrote about this law … and in truth, I was completely in error, and where I had intended to rectify, it is clear that

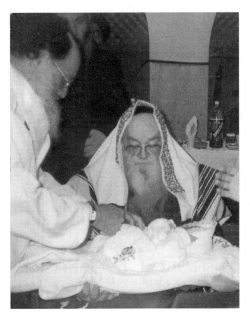

I did damage ... Similarly, in another place I wrote about this law of *pidyon haben* at night, and I answered the question erroneously, and have already been informed of my mistake ... I admit it again here. May Hashem understand and forgive me."

⌒⌒

R' Sholom used to travel regularly to Kfar Chassidim to spend time with R' Eliyahu Lopian. Many of these trips were made in the company of his friends, R' Hirsch Palei and R' Leib Friedman. R' Lopian would ask R' Sholom to deliver a *mussar* talk in the yeshivah.

One evening, R' Sholom was giving such a talk and the students, as usual, were absorbing his every word. The topic was Korach. When he was finished speaking, one boy came over with a question on what he had said. R' Sholom reflected a moment, then said — apparently as a delaying measure — "It's already time for *Ma'ariv*. I'll answer your question afterwards."

When the *Ma'ariv* service was over, the boy returned to R' Sholom and waited for him to speak. R' Sholom acted as if he did not see the boy. Instead, he went over to R' Lopian and asked for permission to address the student body once again. R' Lopian agreed.

R' Sholom faced his audience and said, "Before *davening*, a boy came over to me and asked a powerful question. The boy's point was correct! What I had said was not valid! I thought about what might have led me to make a mistake ... and immediately understood the reason.

"Everything I said in my earlier *mussar* talk was based on things that my rebbe, R' Leib Chasman, had said. I wanted to put a 'sugar coating' on my teacher's words. I tried to pretty up his wonderful thoughts — and in this, I stumbled and erred.

"I will now briefly clarify only what my teacher actually said. The rest was a mistake."

A true story.

NEIGHBORHOOD RESIDENTS FLED, FRIGHTENED, AS THE FIRE trucks roared through their streets, sirens screaming. A house had

Ahavas Yisrael burst into flames. It was only with difficulty that the firefighters managed to salvage a small number of the unfortunate homeowner's belongings.

That particular man was an individual who had caused the Schwadron family untold aggravation. His wife, too, had the habit of walking all the way to the Schwadron house to hurl insults and complaints, and even to dirty their clean laundry. There was no question that this couple was a thorn in R' Sholom's side.

And yet, when neighborhood groups met to discuss ways of helping the distressed family, none other than R' Sholom himself stood at the forefront of every effort!

"You had to see him in action," his son-in-law says of R' Sholom. "You had to see the energy and enthusiasm with which he tackled the problem. He behaved as though the man was a relative or family member. But that man did not know that the person thinking about him for long hours through the day and night was R' Sholom. And even if they had told him, he would never have believed it."

In that same period, a eulogy for a Torah leader took place in the Chazon Ish *kollel*. The great hall was packed to capacity as R' Sholom rose to speak. However moving were R' Sholom's regular talks, they did not hold a candle to one of his eulogies. At such times he was reverently referred to as "the great *maspid* (eulogizer)."

In the middle of that *hesped*, as the audience was held fast in the grip of profound emotion, R' Sholom suddenly switched to the topic uppermost in his mind. Raising his voice, he cried, "*Rabbosai!* Something has happened in Jerusalem. A fire has destroyed a *frum* person's home … Charity! Support for the unfortunate! This is a positive commandment in the Torah!" Then he did something he rarely did. He said, "I am going to circulate among you. Everyone give what you can."

Removing his hat from his head, R' Sholom turned it upside-down and began moving through the crowd. The people contributed generously. R' Sholom was astounded at the amount of money he was able to collect in that session. Thousands … for his "friend."

The money made its way to its recipient in stages. R' Sholom bought the man a new stove and other appliances, and sent over a great deal of cash … all in secret.

IT WAS *EREV* ROSH HASHANAH. IN THIS PRE-DAWN HOUR, THE streets of Sha'arei Chesed were utterly still. Suddenly, the quiet

Love of Chesed

was shattered by a group of secular Israeli youths who had come to see the spectacle of Jews getting up early for *Selichos*. There was some time to go before their desire would be granted. It was still so early that the streets were devoid of movement.

Then a single figure appeared. He was an elderly Jew, white-bearded, walking briskly along with a hammer in his hand.

The youths and their group leader stared at him in astonishment, then exchanged curious glances. What was the old man up to?

R' Sholom continued on his way to shul. All at once, without warning, he stopped, stooped to the ground, and hit the asphalt with his hammer. The boys' amazement grew sevenfold.

"Maybe this is some kind of ritual connected to *Selichos*," the group leader suggested to his bewildered charges. The boys scrambled to pull their cameras out of their backpacks.

The mystery was solved by a student from Yeshivas Ma'alos HaTorah, who happened to emerge from the study hall at that moment after learning there all night (*"mishmar"*). He, too, was taken aback by the sight of R' Sholom — red-faced with exertion — beating the ground with his hammer. He took a few steps closer, the better to see — and then he understood.

Turning to the group of secular boys, he explained, "This street was recently paved with fresh asphalt, and a piece of wood accidentally became attached to the ground at this spot. It sticks out above sidewalk level and obstructs people as they walk by. The man you see here decided to take upon himself the responsibility for removing this obstacle from the public domain. That's why he's hammering like that."

R' Sholom had been confident that he would meet nobody at such an early hour. In the end, however, not only did the students of the yeshivah see him, but also the group of nonreligious boys — who received a powerful message about the meaning of true *chesed*.

R' DOV SCHIFF, ONE OF THE SCHWADRONS' NEIGHBORS IN Sha'arei Chesed, relates the following in his own words.

The Midnight Feast

"On the night before *erev* Shavuos, I finished learning in shul after midnight. An old Jew, dressed in rags, approached me. 'Reb Yid,' he said, 'can you arrange a place for me to sleep tonight?'

"It was very late. I could not bring him home without waking the whole family. Distressed, I looked around the dark neighborhood, searching for one house that was still lit. To my joy, I saw a light in R' Sholom's window. He was sitting and learning.

"'Try knocking at that door,' I suggested to the unfortunate stranger. 'If he can put you up for the night, fine. If not, I'll be waiting for you here and will try to find another place.'

"The man made his way to the Schwadron home. My curiosity grew stronger as some time had passed and he had not returned. I walked up to R' Sholom's window and peeked inside.

"Disbelieving, I rubbed my eyes. R' Sholom was carrying cakes and sweets from the kitchen, along with fish and salads — setting out a full meal for this stranger at midnight. These, apparently, were some of the Yom Tov foods his family had prepared.

"The next day, at *Shacharis*, the same ragged man came over to me and asked, 'Tell me, who is that *tzaddik*? I knocked on his door, and he took me in and immediately set out a whole feast for me. Every time I tried to apologize for bothering him, he said in his sweet voice, "*Chazal* say: More than the householder does for the poor man, the poor man does for the householder." Afterwards he prepared a bed for me to sleep in, left me a cup and towel for *netilas yadayim*, and did not leave my side this morning until he had given me a sum of money to go on with. His mind was eased only when he saw me put the money into my pack — provisions for the road.'"

R' SHOLOM WAS INVITED TO A *CHANUKAS HABAYIS* CELEBRA-tion at one of the Bnei Brak yeshivos, and was asked to speak

First and Last

there. Spellbound, the audience drank in a riveting lecture surrounding the words of the psalm, "*Mizmor shir chanukas habayis.*"

When he had finished speaking, a prominent Bnei Brak rabbi walked up to the dais and apologized, "R' Sholom has already spoken on the topic I was going to touch upon. I will therefore be brief in my good wishes on this memorable occasion."

R' Sholom's son-in-law recounts that at that moment, R' Sholom came to a decision. "From now on," he said, "I'm the last speaker. I am not going to steal someone else's speech, *chas v'shalom!*"

"WE HAVE A TEACHING," BEGAN R' SHOLOM, PASSED DOWN from one man to another: If we are confronted with the biggest

To Build the Beis HaMikdash

mitzvah, such as building the *Beis HaMikdash*, but doing it would cause strife or a weakening of the faith — then

R' Yechezkel Levenstein (right) and R' Eliyahu Lopian (left)
at the PonoviezherYeshivah in Bnei Brak

R' Yechezkel Levenstein (left) and R' Elazer Menachem Shach (third from right) at a wedding
of a talmid

we do not perform the mitzvah. It is better to leave it for another time. This is what I heard from the *mashgiach*, R' Yechezkel Levenstein."

R' Sholom added, "It was a time when I worked at one of the yeshivos. The yeshivah's *mashgiach* was abroad, fundraising for the yeshivah, and the students asked me to give them *mussar* talks. The question that came to my mind was whether to be more concerned with the fact that the boys would lose spiritually by not hearing *mussar*, or to worry whether I would be very successful and the students would say afterwards, 'We want to hear R' Sholom,' causing the *mashgiach* pain.

"I went to see R' Yechezkel Levenstein — and the above was the answer he gave me!"

The answer served as a beacon for R' Sholom in everything he did.

Pollution

AN UPSTANDING NEW YORK JEW BECAME EMBROILED IN AN INternal struggle within a certain institution which he, personally, had established. He stood at a crossroads, uncertain how to behave in this impasse. Hearing that R' Sholom Schwadron was residing as a guest in R' Paysach Krohn's home, he jumped immediately into his car to seek his advice.

R' Sholom listened to the details of the story, then said, "Many years ago, I was also a member of a certain Torah institution, when dissension arose. From that day to this, I carry in my wallet a souvenir of that time. I would like to show it to you."

R' Sholom (right) on his first visit to New York,
with R' Yisrael Grossman (center) and
R' Avraham Zelig Krohn (left)

Pulling his wallet from his pocket, R' Sholom drew out a small slip of paper on which he had written a brief excerpt from the Rambam's letter to his son. Without any further explanation, he handed his visitor the paper. The man read the following lines:

"Do not pollute your souls with strife, which consumes body, soul, and money, and what is left then? ... I have seen white turn to black, families destroyed and officers removed from power and great cities made desolate, groups separated and chassidim laid to waste and men of faith lost, respected individuals scorned — all because of dissension. Prophets have foretold and wise men have counseled and philosophers have sought endlessly to tell of the evils of strife, without reaching its end. Therefore, detest it and run from it and stay far from all those who love it and are its friends."

Without further elaboration, R' Sholom returned the slip of paper to his wallet and parted warmly from his visitor.

(as told by R' Paysach Krohn)

Fifty Pairs of Slippers

ONE DAY, R' SHOLOM SLIPPED ON THE TILES IN THE SHA'AREI Chesed *mikveh*. He fell flat on the floor, but sustained no serious injury. It is the habit of most people in his position to blame the whole world for the fact that they slipped and fell. R' Sholom was different.

Upon his return home, he told his daughter, "I have undertaken to buy 50 pairs of slippers — half for the *mikveh* here in Sha'arei Chesed and the other half for the *mikveh* in the next neighborhood." He asked her to find a store prepared to sell 50 pairs of slippers at one time.

With the help of her son, R' Sholom's daughter managed to locate such a shop at some distance, and brought back a sackful of slippers to her father's house. That very day, they were delivered to their destinations.

R' Sholom had reasoned in simple, logical fashion: "I am the one who personally experienced the dangers of slipping. Therefore, it is up to me to take care that others don't fall. I have already fallen. At least others can be spared."

The simplicity of greatness.

One day, R' Sholom pressed a sum of money into his son-in-law's hand and said, "Please, go buy 30 pairs of slippers for the *mikveh* in Zichron Meir (in central Bnei Brak)." Without a question, the young man went to carry out his father-in-law's bidding.

After R' Sholom passed away, an interesting notation was found in his wallet — a note that shed light on those slippers:

"This lira and a half does not belong to me, and I must do some mitzvah with it to benefit the public — buy slippers for the *mikveh*." (To this sum, he added more money of his own for the purchase of the slippers.)

Incidentally, the Sha'arei Chesed *mikveh* acquired fame through R' Sholom's talks, in which he related an incident that occurred there more than a half-century ago. In R' Sholom's own words (as transcribed from a recording of a eulogy):

> There was a Jew in Sha'arei Chesed, a *gevaldiger* great man by the name of R' Yosef Shimsholovitz. He was one of the first young men to join the famous *kollel* of R' Yitzchak Elchonon of Kovno. His nickname was "R' Yosef Shas'l" because he knew all of *Shas* by heart, and they told me that he also knew the *Rambam* and all four parts of the *Tur* by heart. I did not know him personally, as he passed on before I arrived in Sha'arei Chesed, but many stories were told of his greatness.
>
> Near the end of his life, afraid that he would soon depart this world, he asked for young boys to come and test him. He would recite the *Shulchan Aruch* for them, the *Shach* and the *Taz* in their proper order, from memory ... to test himself and see whether he remembered! He once revealed to someone that on his walk to yeshivah each day, from Sha'arei Chesed to the Old City, he would review all of *Maseches Kesubos* by heart. That was the man — R' Yosef.
>
> My brother-in-law, R' Shlomo Zalman Auerbach, related

to me that he once went to the *mikveh* on *erev* Shabbos and saw R' Yosef Shimsholovitz standing there, teeth chattering. R' Yosef was an old man by then, and R' Shlomo Zalman was afraid that he wasn't feeling well. Going over to him, R' Sholom Zalman said, "I see that you're cold. I'll help you out." R' Yosef answered, "It's nothing, it's nothing."

A few minutes passed, and then R' Shlomo Zalman again noticed R' Yosef trembling — trembling! He went over and, without a word, took his arm and helped him to get dressed.

R' Yosef said, "It's nothing, it's nothing ... It's just that someone before me stuck his foot into the water and said, '*Oy*, it's burning like *Gehinnom!*'" His voice shook. "*And then I remembered Gehinnom.*"

These are great men, these are *tzaddikim*, these are *talmidei chachamim!* R' Sholom concluded. Today, it's not fashionable to remember *Gehinnom*. It's not nice, not suitable. *Oy*, the modern *Gehinnom*!

A Friendly Face

Like Old Friends

THOUSANDS OF PEOPLE MET WITH HIM; TENS OF THOUSANDS in Israel and the Diaspora shook his hand over the decades, asking eagerly, "R' Sholom, do you remember me?" The question was one that arose at least once a day. "R' Sholom, we traveled to Flatbush together last year! Remember?"

And R' Sholom would smile. "Really? How are you? How do you feel? How's the family? Do you live in the same place as you did then?" R' Sholom would focus all his attention on the other person, as though they were dear old friends.

R' Sholom with R' Pesach Ackerman, who made the new collar on the coat R' Sholom is wearing

Not infrequently, when the brief encounter was over, R' Sholom would ask whomever he was with, "Do you know who that man was?"

Once, his family members asked him about this behavior. "I learned it from my teacher, R' Yitzchak Meir Petziner (Ben Menachem), son-in-law of R' Isser Zalman Meltzer. And *he* learned it from his father-in-law! Here is what happened:

"I was once walking with him on a city street. On our way, we met the widow of a well-known *talmid chacham*, walking with a young relative. R' Yitzchak Meir inquired after her welfare and that of each of her children, then went on to ask the young man who was with her detailed questions about himself and his family.

"After we had parted from them, R' Yitzchak Meir asked me, 'Who was that young man?' I was astounded at his ability to converse in a way that made the other feel he knew him. I remarked, 'This is something I need to learn — how you carry on a conversation with a young man whom you had never seen before, leaving him with the good feeling that you've known him a long time. Usually, when one meets two people who are walking together, and only knows one of them, one tends to talk freely and gladly with the one he knows, while saying only a polite "Hello" to the one he doesn't know.'

"'This,' R' Yitzchak Meir said, 'is something that I learned from my great father-in-law, author of the *Even HaEzel*: *V'hevei mekabel es kol ha'adam b'seiver panim yafos.* [And you shall greet every person with a pleasant countenance.]'"

R' YITZCHAK RASKES, OF BALTIMORE, TELLS THE FOLLOWING

The Broken Bottle

story.

"During one of my visits to *Eretz Yisrael*, on Purim, I sent my young daughter to R' Sholom's house with a loaded tray of *mishloach manos*.

"As she entered the house, her hands slipped and the

R' Sholom with talmidim of Telzer Yeshivah in Cleveland on Purim

tray clattered to the floor, spilling all its contents. The bottle of wine shattered to bits and the rest was scattered far and wide. Misery and shame flared up in the girl's cheeks.

"R' Sholom, who was in an inner room, realized what had happened. Immediately, he ran to the door, calling jubilantly, 'Wonderful! *Gavaldig!* How good that the wine bottle broke! The Gemara [in *Eruvin* 65] says, "Any house where wine is not poured like water is missing a symbol of *berachah.*" *Baruch Hashem!* Wine has been spilled in my house — and on Purim! A *siman berachah!* We haven't had such a Purim in ages!'

"His enthusiasm infected the others, and the Purim joy grew without bounds as the entire household rejoiced over the shards of that wine bottle and its attendant mess. Anyone happening to walk into the Schwadron house at that moment with *mishloach manos* would have broken his bottle, too, just to please R' Sholom!"

R' Raskes went on to add, "The good *middos*, the *menschlechkeit*, the thank-you for everything that was done for him, the pleasantness that everyone felt around him — ah! Ah!" And his voice becomes choked with tears of longing as he recalls the special times he shared with that great man.

AT THE COMPLETION OF THE EULOGIES FOR THE STEIPLER RAV in Bnei Brak, the organizers found someone who volunteered to

Never Enough! drive R' Sholom — then an elderly man — back to Jerusalem. R' Sholom got into the car, and the trip began in silence. Suddenly, he turned to the driver and said, "Whenever someone agrees to drive me back to my home in Sha'arei Chesed, I'm always afraid of stealing, because sometimes that willingness comes from the desire to hear some sort of '*vort*' or story from me during the trip."

The driver reacted enthusiastically. "Yes, yes, that's right. Of course, I'd love to hear something."

Exhausted from the eulogy he had just delivered, R' Sholom gathered his strength and said a nice *vort*.

"Enough?" he asked tiredly.

"No, no. How I enjoy hearing the Rav speak!" R' Sholom's eyes were closing, but he roused himself once more to tell a good story.

"Okay, is that enough? Did you enjoy it?" he asked warmly.

"No, no — more, more! I will never have my fill of R' Sholom's stories!"

In short, R' Sholom was forced to keep talking all the way to Jerusalem — words of *mussar* and inspiration to dispel any suspicion of stealing as he made his way home.

THEY ALL FILED OUTSIDE, GATHERING ONE BY ONE NEAR THE main entrance. Only there did they burst into heartbreaking wails.

Kosher Tears An hour earlier, the entire family had gathered by the bedside of Rebbetzin Schwadron. "Any time now," the doctor had told them. Her great brother, R' Shlomo Zalman Auerbach, had come to part from his older sister, as did all the Schwadron children. There were about 25 people present.

R' Sholom and his son, R' Yitzchak, remained outside the hospital, as entry was forbidden for Kohanim. R' Sholom summoned his daughters for a last request before their mother died. "What could Abba want at a time like this?" they wondered weakly.

He did not leave them to wonder for long. Time was short.

"My precious children! Imma is about to leave us. The pain is deep, the anguish is very heavy — yet know this! None of the sick people near her have to suffer for our sakes. Be careful not to break out in loud tears. The patients in the ward do not have to sense her death." Thus spoke their father, and the Rebbetzin's husband.

The Rebbetzin murmured the *viduy*, her frail hand pounding lightly against her heart. Then her hands fell and special verses were recited with great fervor. The family, led by R' Shlomo Zalman, parted from the righteous Rebbetzin with the *Shema Yisrael*.

Silence fell — the silence of death. The daughters walked out of the hospital — and only then permitted their suppressed tears to fall. R' Sholom wept along with them.

Kosher tears ... for a kosher human being.

When it came time for R' Sholom to depart this world, the group gathered near his bed read with fervor the verses declaring Hashem's Oneness ... and then remembered the great man's instructions: "Do not disturb others!" They glanced around and into the adjoining rooms, to make sure they were not creating a disturbance — just as the *tzaddik* would have wished.

A Widow's Heart

"I FOLLOWED HIM, AND HE NEVER STOPPED MURMURING HAPpily, 'And I shall gladden the widow's heart,'" R' Sholom's

Up the Hill   son-in-law relates.

It was Shabbos, and a new son-in-law was about to be called up to the Torah. R' Sholom arrived in Bnei Brak, where he *davened* with the *vasikin minyan*, as was his custom. Afterward, he walked over to the shul where the celebration was being held. The service lasted a long time — until nearly noon. R' Sholom left with all the other guests, stepping into the heat of the Bnei Brak day. Tired and weak, he walked slowly.

Suddenly, he remembered: "Oy, we're walking near the hill where the Ponoviezher Yeshivah is located." Turning to his wife, he said, "You're acquainted with the Rebbetzin, the Ponoviezher Rav's wife. Come, let's climb the hill and enter her house to make her happy."

The Rebbetzin agreed at once. Exhaustion fled, and happiness took its place. R' Sholom began climbing the hill with a radiant face, his mouth never stopping its joyful murmur: "And I shall gladden the widow's heart! And I shall gladden the widow's heart!"

R' Sholom and his wife were perspiring profusely. The Rebbetzin was wearing a Jerusalem head covering. She had never encountered the Bnei Brak humidity. The walk was difficult, but they took no notice. They were completely wrapped up in the happy prospect of gladdening the widow's heart!

~~

R' Sholom was extremely careful to maintain purity in thought and word. If a woman called on the phone, he made sure to speak briefly, and occasionally scolded members of his household for not exerting the same kind of care.

But when a widow was on the phone, she found she could speak to R' Sholom for any length she wished. A learning partner of his was once surprised to overhear a long phone conversation between R' Sholom and a woman. Noting his astonishment, R' Sholom explained. "What don't you understand? She's a widow!"

WIDOWHOOD WAS AN ESPECIALLY IMPORTANT ISSUE FOR R' Sholom. He was always apprehensive lest he cause a widow even

A Night Among Nights

the smallest distress, and rejoiced unabashedly over the chance to make one happy.

R' Paysach Krohn talks about one Pesach night when R' Sholom was a guest in his home. That year, the Seder night fell on a

Motza'ei Shabbos. The Seder was delayed because the preparations could begin only after Shabbos had ended. R' Sholom returned from shul and waited with affable patience, as was his habit, until the elder widowed Mrs. Krohn finished her preparations. When everything was ready, R' Sholom sat down to conduct the Seder, with the entire family — brothers, sisters, and grandchildren — sitting around the table.

"Knowing that R' Sholom was very scrupulous about eating the *afikoman* before midnight," R' Krohn says, "I urged the younger ones to cut down on their *'vorts'* on the Haggadah so that we could serve the meal and finish it before midnight. I also urged my mother to hurry. R' Sholom, noticing my efforts, gave me a severe look. 'Don't rush them,' he ordered. This happened several times. I would take pity on R' Sholom and try to hint to the others to speed things up, but he would always stop me."

It was very late by the time the family ate the *afikoman* — well after midnight. R' Krohn was positive that R' Sholom would be very upset, but there was nothing to be seen on his face except for holiday joy and the exalted mood brought on by the Seder.

When the Seder was over, R' Krohn went over to R' Sholom and said hesitantly, "R' Sholom, forgive us for causing you to eat the *afikoman* after midnight for the first time in your life."

With a serious face, R' Sholom replied, "To eat the *afikoman* before midnight is a Rabbinical law — but causing distress to a widow is prohibited in the Torah itself. Let me explain: I was extremely anxious not to cause your mother, the widow, any pain. This night, the Seder night, is the one special time of the year when she derives *nachas*. She waits all year long for the Seder night, when her children and grandchildren will sit around her table engaging in Torah matters, which gives her joy. Was I permitted to take all that away from her? I was afraid of transgressing a prohibition stated clearly in the Torah!"

"When he said those words," recalls R' Krohn, "I could see the fear in his face, and bowed to his greatness. I understood that not everyone is capable of behaving this way, nor is everyone supposed to behave this way. But R' Sholom, who possessed the

qualities of character that allowed him to measure the Torah's re-
quirements in the light of his personal circumstance, was able to
do it."

On other occasions, R' Sholom would relate the following: "I
heard from R' Eliyahu Lopian that he once heard R' Naftali
Amsterdam say that he had noticed R' Yisrael Salanter breaking
from his usual schedule. When R' Naftali asked him to explain, R'
Yisrael replied that his wife had brought into their home a maid
who was a widow. If he rose early in the morning to leave the
house, as was his custom, he would wake the widow as he closed
the door, and he was afraid that this would fall into the category of
distressing a widow or orphan [prohibited by the Torah]. R' Yisrael
then went on to describe other things he refrained from doing for
the same reason.

"R' Yisrael concluded, 'And if you suggest, R' Naftali, that I fire
her and ask her to leave my home, in that case, we will find that it
is forbidden to hire a widow or orphan to work in a Jewish home,
for fear of causing them distress. How can we say that?'"

R' SHOLOM TOLD A WONDERFUL BUT LITTLE-KNOWN STORY
about the Alter of Slobodka's incredible *middos*.

Magnificent Middos — Neither In nor Out

R' Moshe Schneider, a student
of the Alter of Slobodka, heard
that the Alter was staying at a
German spa to improve his health. He traveled there immediately,
taking along his young son, R' Gedalia. R' Moshe rented a room
for three days in the same hotel where the Alter was staying, and
went down from time to time to bask in his presence.

"On the third afternoon," R' Gedalia later related, "I saw the Alter
go up to my father's room. He knocked on the door, opened it, and
put one foot inside. He saw at once that my father was asleep."

The Alter of Slobodka stood frozen in place, neither going in nor
leaving, afraid that closing the (squeaking) door might wake his
student. He stood there for a long time, unmoving, until R' Moshe
awoke.

R' Sholom was awestruck at this eyewitness account of such a refinement in *middos*, such greatness as the Alter of Slobodka possessed. He heard the story when he was staying in England. Upon his return to Jerusalem, he met with R' Meir Chodosh and told him enthusiastically, "You were the Alter's student. You have something to say about the way he lived, about every step he took — but I have something to say, too! I heard a story about the Alter that you've never heard."

On the same subject, R' Sholom would add the following story, which he heard from R' Reuven Miltizki, who, as a youth, traveled extensively to visit the great Torah personalities of his time.

One day, R' Reuven arrived at the home of the *tzaddik*, R' Leib Chassid. He knocked lightly on the door and waited respectfully.

"Who's there?" the youth heard from inside. Almost immediately, there came the sound of running footsteps. Then the door was opened by R' Leib himself. "Yes, yes, please — *Sholom aleichem!* How do you feel? Perhaps you would like a hot drink?" R' Leib grasped his visitor by the shoulder and escorted him joyfully into the house, talking about how wonderful it was to have him there.

The welcome extended to a full 10 minutes. Only afterwards did R' Leib turn to his guest and ask, "And what is your name? Where are you from?"

"The first thing is to greet every person pleasantly," R' Sholom would conclude. "Afterwards you can find out who he is!"

THE ALTER OF SLOBODKA WAS ONCE SEEN PRAYING NEAR THE home of one of his students. When asked for the reason, he ex-

Carrying the Burden plained, "We know that this student is experiencing trouble at home. We see him in yeshivah day after day, and it is difficult to ascertain the true extent of his pain. That's why I came here, to his house, where the feeling is deeper. One who 'carries a burden together with his friend' gets a more accurate sense of things, and can therefore pray with much greater depth."

(As told by R' Sholom)

TWO CHEVRON YESHIVAH STUDENTS WERE CELEBRATING THEIR weddings on the same night. The study hall was empty as all the youths went off to join in the happy events.

Your Brother   One student decided to remain behind. "How can we leave the *beis midrash* without Torah?" he thought, and sat down to learn.

Some time later, R' Leib Chasman entered the study hall. Walking over to the lone student, he said one word. "*Chasunah?* (Wedding?)"

"There was no one left in the yeshivah, so I decided that I, at least, would be the one to stay and learn Torah," the youth answered.

"Don't be a fool," R' Leib retorted. [In other words, don't pat yourself on the back and think that there aren't other considerations involved here.] "If it were your brother getting married tonight, would you think the same way?"

Chapter 7

Refined Silver

THERE WERE TWO WATER CARRIERS IN A CERTAIN
small town. Yankel hauled water from a well in the south-
All for ern part of town, Alter from a well to
the Public the east. Yankel the water carrier was a
valued member of the neighborhood.
His long black beard gave him a respectable air, and the children
enjoyed following him around town. He wore tall boots, and a
stout rope tied the hem of his long coat securely about his hips.
Tugging at this rope, the children would call, "Reb Yankel, a *berachah*! Reb Yankel, give me a *berachah*!"

With a good-humored smile, Reb Yankel would place his hands
on the children's heads and humbly bless them. On festival eves,
as well as on Rosh Hashanah and Yom Kippur eve, the town's
grownups would wait for Yankel's "Good Yom Tov" or "*Kesivah
v'chasimah tovah!*" as he handed them their pails of water.

In stark contrast to Yankel was Alter, the other water carrier. He
was a dusty figure who dragged his water buckets around town
from morning to night. Apart from a rapidly muttered "Thank you

very much," the townspeople did not exchange a single word with Alter. The children took pleasure in teasing him, and he would respond by flying into a rage and sometimes chasing them.

What was the difference between these two men? If we point to the lowly nature of the work they did, then what accounts for the respect that Yankel the water carrier garnered?

Children are always looking for someone to tease. The water carrier was the first person they encountered on the street. This was why Alter was privileged to be on the receiving end of their taunts and jokes.

And Reb Yankel?

By profession, Reb Yankel was not actually a water carrier. He had another source of livelihood. But for some reason, he had made up his mind that there is no greater *chesed* than providing pure water for other Jews. And so, one day, he began trudging from house to house, two pails dangling from a yoke slung across his shoulders. At each doorway he would humbly call out, "Water? Is anyone interested in a pail of water?" If the answer came back positive, he would deposit the bucket and leave.

"Money! Money, Reb Yankel!" the townspeople would call after him.

"No, no. Pay me another time," he would answer as he hurried away.

There were those who ran after him and slipped money into his pocket, while others grew accustomed to receiving water from such a seemingly gullible individual who was not concerned with payment. But both groups accorded him respect. "Reb Yankel, a *berachah!*"

Is it forbidden to request payment for drawing water? The answer, of course, is that it is not forbidden at all. It is not only permissible to ask for money, it is the correct thing to do. But Reb Yankel was not a water carrier. He was a *ba'al chesed.*

The "international *Maggid,*" R' Sholom, was not a "*maggid.*" He was not a lecturer. He was, in his essence, a man who cared about bringing merit to the public.

"If I have been privileged to serve others, my soul is at peace; and if Hashem has given me a tongue for teaching, how can I not transmit what I have learned?" (From the introduction to his *sefer*, *Da'as Torah*)

His sermons did not belong to him; they belonged to others. They were the property of all of *Klal Yisrael*. "I? Who am I?" he would repeatedly ask. He spent full days walking — traversing *Eretz Yisrael* from top to bottom and side to side — and many months crossing the sea to visit Jewish communities in the Diaspora. For many years, he distilled all his strength and all his talent in the service of the public. And all without payment. The sermons did not belong to him.

R' Yehudah Landy says, "I heard R' Sholom speak in Flatbush. When he was finished and the audience was starting to disperse, R' Sholom returned to the podium, asked the people to remain, and requested their permission to speak. He had decided to say a few words on the subject of charity, which had, after all, been his purpose in traveling to America on behalf of Chinuch Atzma'i. The audience settled down and waited to hear what he had to say.

"I will tell you a story," he began. "A man went into a bank with his small son, and the two waited in line for their turn. Suddenly, the boy cried, 'Father, look how rich that clerk is over there! Look at that great big stack of money he's holding. How rich he must be!'

"'Silly boy,' the father thought. 'That money does not belong to him. True, he's holding a great deal of money in his hand — but it is other people's money. If he were to take even a cent of it for himself, he would immediately be thrown into jail.'"

R' Sholom stopped speaking and said no more. The audience understood.

What R' Sholom demanded from others, he demanded also from himself: "If I were to take even a 'cent' of my talks for myself, I will have betrayed my purpose."

R' Sholom — a berachah!

THE SCHWADRON HOUSEHOLD DID NOT KNOW WHAT EASE and plenty were. Their home was constantly beset with difficul-

Payment ties, the prime one being a lack of money. There were times when the Rebbetzin could not find money even to buy a loaf of bread.

One night, R' Sholom returned home from a lecture he had given and went to the closet to hang up his coat. As he put his hand in his pocket to draw out the small *Mishnayos* he always kept there, his fingers touched upon a slip of paper.

What was this? He reached inside again, and pulled out — a check for 1,500 lira (a very large sum in those days). Putting on his glasses to read the name on the check, he understood what it was and where it had come from. It was his payment for the lecture he had just delivered.

R' Sholom was aghast. His hands trembled as he lifted the check, held it tightly in both hands — and ripped it into pieces. Then he strode over to a corner of the room and deposited the shreds in the wastepaper basket.

R' Simchah Nosson Segal, his son-in-law, witnessed the entire episode. He was shaken to his depths. "Who knows better than I what straits they are in financially," he thought. When R' Sholom left the room, the young man went to the wastepaper basket, retrieved the pieces of the torn check, and put them into his wallet — where they remain to this day. Decades have passed since then, but those pieces of paper stand as testimony to the kind of greatness we rarely have the privilege of seeing today.

The torn check

THE STATE OF ISRAEL WAS GEARING UP FOR ITS SECOND ELEC-
tion campaign, and Sha'arei Chesed was one of the centers of activ-

**I Never
Asked**
ity for Agudas Yisrael's campaign efforts. One evening,
with the elections not far off, a large, impressive gathering was held in the plaza near the Gra Shul in that
neighborhood.

R' Sholom's house, adjoining the plaza, became the focus of the
rally. The Schwadrons had donated their home to the election effort. Loudspeakers were affixed to the windowsills, and the
campaign workers stood inside to address the crowd.

The speakers — with R' Sholom himself at their head — were
eloquent in their appeals to the gathered throng to back the party
to their utmost. When the rally was over, the crowd dispersed with
renewed enthusiasm to fight for the cause in which they so wholeheartedly believed.

The rally was held on a Tuesday night. On Thursday, as she did
every week, Rebbetzin Schwadron went to the Machaneh Yehudah
shuk, an open-air market, to purchase what she needed for Shabbos.
On her way, she met the wife of one of the rally's speakers.

Smiling, the woman called, "Rebbetzin Schwadron! I'm sure
you were paid more than I was. After all, the whole rally was
based in your house, and for that alone you should get a nice payment. What have you bought yourself this week?"

The Rebbetzin looked at her with a smile, and returned the
question, "And what did you buy?"

"I've always wanted to exchange my old Primus stove for a new
gas range. Cooking with gas is more efficient, and certainly a lot easier. Till now, I've never been able to afford such an expensive
appliance — so I was very happy to see the nice amount my husband
received! Immediately after the rally I went out and bought myself a
gas range." The woman rubbed her hands with patent satisfaction.

Rebbetzin Schwadron, lost in thought, forgot that she was standing in the middle of a busy street. "Gas?" she mused. "As long as
our old Primus works, and as long as we can buy kerosene in the
market, my husband would never agree to such luxury. We don't
even have a refrigerator, and now we're talking about gas ranges?"

R' Sholom addresses a pre-election rally

She was pleased with herself for being content with her lot ... until a sudden thought struck her. "Why hasn't my husband told me that Agudas Yisrael paid him for speaking at the rally? Who's talking about a refrigerator or gas range — we hardly have enough money to buy chicken and fish for Shabbos! Why didn't he tell me about this stroke of good fortune?"

Her friend, seeing the distress on the Rebbetzin's face, murmured a few hasty words of apology for keeping her so long, and went on her way.

"My dear husband!" the Rebbetzin said to R' Sholom upon her return home. "I have a question. After the big rally this week, did you get paid or not?"

R' Sholom lifted his eyes from the page he was writing, set aside his pen, and said with a smile, "I didn't ask, so I didn't get. I did not get so much as a *grush*, because I didn't ask for it." He lowered his head and resumed his work.

The Rebbetzin left the room with mixed feelings. "I know he doesn't ask for payment for his talks," she thought. "But isn't it acceptable to receive payment for an election speech? Should the money go to others who work only half or a third as hard as my husband does on behalf of the party?"

It was true that R' Sholom had not received payment because he had not demanded it. But his wife knew all too well that, had payment been offered, he would have refused to accept it. "I never asked for money, so don't give me any." She could hear the words as if he had spoken them aloud in her presence.

⌒⌒

With the passage of time, R' Sholom's reputation grew. Invitations to speak increased daily, giving him no rest. One day he would speak in Tel Aviv, the next day in Tiberias, and then in the heart of Jerusalem. One lecture would follow hard on the heels of another, with eulogies for illustrious Torah personalities interspersed in between.

One family member thought of a way to make life easier for R' Sholom. "Charge money for each talk. That way, you'll get fewer invitations to speak."

R' Sholom's reply was unequivocal: "No. Under no circumstances."

After a moment, he added, "But I will ask this much: that someone drive me to and from the lecture in his car. Until now, I've been spending a lot of time riding buses and walking all over Yerushalayim. I'm not convinced that this request will bring in fewer invitations to speak, but I do think it's permissible for me to ask this much."

From that day forward, whenever anyone came to his house to ask him to speak or to eulogize, he would agree as graciously as ever, then add his small request: "I don't have the strength to walk. Please send someone with a car."

The invitations continued to pour in.

The public was unaware of his policy about accepting payment. Once, R' Sholom said with a smile, "They say I own acres of land between Bnei Brak and Yerushalayim!" He was not far off. Had he agreed to accept even one dollar from every person who came to hear him speak, he could have been the owner of numerous properties.

The Rebbetzin once confided to R' Sholom's learning partner, R'

Tzvi Tauber, with quiet pride, "I don't know what it is — my husband has absolutely no desire for money. When he travels abroad, they offer him $500 for each talk, but he refuses to accept even one dollar. He just doesn't take money. He could be living like a king ..." Her admiration was apparent.

A grandson relates that he once saw a man plead with R' Sholom to accept payment for a lecture. When R' Sholom refused, the man tried to shove a few bills into his pocket and make his escape.

R' Sholom's face, his grandson says, changed instantly from its usual smile to an expression of tremendous anger and pain. Shocked, the man quickly took his money back and, inclining his head with respect tinged with awe, walked away.

Not even when he was hard-pressed for money with which to feed his family did R' Sholom find it within himself to request a small salary for his regular appearances in the Zichron Moshe Shul, or to take even a dollar for all his public appearances in Europe and the United States.

ON THE OCCASION OF A FAMILY SIMCHAH, R' SHOLOM ONCE spent a Shabbos in Kiryat Gat. Over the course of that Shabbos, he

A Potent Parable
spoke a total of seven times. One of the local people whispered into his son-in-law's ear, "How much are they paying him?"

"Paying him?" the son-in-law repeated incredulously.

The other man was equally disbelieving. "I don't believe it! Seven speeches in one day, for a man who's no longer young ... Surely they must be paying him."

Somehow, this exchange reached R' Sholom's ears. He said nothing, though his eyes spoke volumes.

The next morning, he noticed that the *Daf Yomi shiur* given following the *Shacharis* service in Kiryat Gat was much better attended than usual. Men who generally did not attend were hunched over their Gemaras.

"What's so special about today?" R' Sholom asked one of those present.

The man smiled as he answered, "After hearing you speak yesterday, how could I not take it upon myself to establish regular times for learning Torah?"

R' Sholom looked around for his son-in-law and cried out in an emotional voice, "Here! Here it is! *This is my payment!*"

It is worthwhile to pause here to share a golden nugget from one of the speeches R' Sholom delivered in Kiryat Gat — the lecture that inspired among its listeners such an outpouring of renewed dedication to learning. After lecturing on the importance of establishing regular times for learning, R' Sholom ended with the Chofetz Chaim's parable. This parable was something he had undertaken to present in his first lecture in any new place.

The story tells of a downtrodden and poverty-stricken Jew by the name of R' Zalman. Early one morning, R' Zalman ran into an old friend of his, R' Baruch, one of the city's most prosperous citizens. As his name implied, R' Baruch seemed indeed to be blessed. He was blessed with talent, with intelligence, with wealth, and with Torah knowledge.

"Good morning to you, R' Baruch," R' Zalman greeted him.

"Good morning," the rich man responded courteously.

R' Zalman launched into an emotional speech. "*Oy*, you've doubtless heard of my unfortunate situation. How hard is my lot! I have no bread, I hardly have any water. I need an urgent loan for a business that may help me out of my difficulties. You have no idea what a salvation it will be if you help me, R' Baruch!"

The rich man thought for a moment, then said, "My old friend, I can't pass up an opportunity to help. I have no ready cash on me at the moment, but I'll get it for you by 10 this morning. Don't be ashamed — what Hashem has given me is not for me alone, and if I can help another Jew, I'll do it gladly! Come to me at 10 a.m. and you will get what you need."

With heartfelt thanks and blessings, R' Zalman parted from his friend and went on his way.

At the appointed hour, R' Baruch stopped conducting his business and made sure that no one would be present when R' Zalman arrived, so that the man would not feel embarrassed. He waited impatiently for his chance to do the big mitzvah. But 10 minutes passed, then a quarter of an hour, and then half an hour, with no sign of R' Zalman.

"The poor man," R' Baruch sighed. "Something unforeseen has probably come up to prevent him from coming." He went back to his own business.

The next day, at 7 in the morning, R' Baruch's phone rang.

"Good morning, R' Baruch! How are you today? How are the wife and kids?" It was R' Zalman.

R' Baruch returned his greeting, then listened as the poor man explained, "This isn't pleasant for me, but I have to marry off my daughter and things are very difficult for me. I need an urgent loan. It will be the saving of me!"

"Ah! Certainly, R' Zalman. I waited for you yesterday, but please come by today. I'll see you at 10, with the sum you need. Don't worry, Hashem will help you find a way out of all your difficulties. Come at 10!"

R' Zalman blessed him emotionally, "You're saving my life! May Hashem bless you with everything good!" After adding other blessings, he hung up.

At 10 o'clock, R' Baruch was waiting. But R' Zalman did not turn up by 10:15, or by 10:30. "Maybe someone in his household is ill," R' Baruch thought in distress, "or something else has kept him from coming here or sending word. He'll probably show up tomorrow."

The next day, at 7:30 in the morning, the phone rang again. "Good morning, R' Baruch! How are you? And the family?" Then, beginning to cry, R' Zalman said, "My friend, my situation is desperate. If you help me, there will be no end to your reward!"

"But I've waited for you for two days now," exclaimed a bewildered R' Baruch. "All right, come here at 10 this morning — that's two and half hours from now. I'll be waiting!"

But once again, 10 o'clock passed, and 10:15, and then 10:30, but R' Zalman did not come.

At 7 the next morning, R' Zalman was on the phone again. "Good morning, R' Baruch! How's everything? How are you feeling — and the wife and kids? Listen, I'm in a very pressing situation ..."

R' Baruch interrupted forcefully, "Fool! Leave me alone!"

"The man," R' Baruch thought as he slammed down the receiver, "is crazy!"

Here, R' Sholom's voice would take on its magical, chanting quality. "This is the way it goes in shul each morning. This, the Chofetz Chaim tells us, is the way we appear every day!

"Every morning, we recite the *berachos* of *Shema* — 'Love us with a great love' — a love that is great and eternal — 'grant us great mercy!' We begin to arouse Heaven's compassion. The angels themselves are moved to hear us plead each day: 'Merciful father, Who has pity' — please, have pity on this Jew who needs so much mercy! 'Merciful One, have pity on us! Bestow in our hearts ...' We rattle off a list of eight requests: 'to understand, to grasp, to listen, to learn, to teach, to safeguard, to perform, and to keep ... *all* of Your Torah with love'! Every morning, Reb Yid pours out his heart for success in Torah. Even more, he adds: 'And illuminate our eyes with Your Torah, and let our hearts cleave to Your commandments, and unite our hearts to love and fear Your Name ... so that we may never be humiliated or destroyed.'

"We ask for everything, for this is life itself — and where life is concerned, there are no partial requests.

"The angels, who are not able to discern a man's thoughts, hear such a prayer and immediately beseech Hashem to grant them permission to fulfill it. They fill barrels with wisdom and understanding, then stand in long rows — waiting. As soon as that Jew completes his *davening,* it will pour down onto him. After all, see how earnestly he pleaded. He deserves it! In just another minute, he will receive the "big loan" he requested.

"Well, he reaches *Ashrei* and *U'va L'Tziyon,* and the man is already thinking about which exit to take from the shul. Soon he is kissing his *tefillin.* The kisses echo in the emptiness, and the snapping of the *tefillin* boxes reverberates through the shul. He respectfully winds up the straps. By the time they reach *Aleinu* he is outside — until late at night.

"And above, the angels wait ... and wait.

"So they judge him favorably. No doubt the man had some urgent reason to run off to work today. Perhaps tomorrow he'll open a *sefer*. He was rushed today, but tomorrow he will surely sit with his Gemara. Don't the Sages say that even if a person is a *tzaddik*, if he does not busy himself with Torah he has nothing? (*Midrash Tanchuma*)

"And so, at the same time the next morning, the prayers are soaring up to the Heavens once again. 'Have mercy! Please, have mercy on us! Bestow Your wisdom on our hearts!'

"'*Nu?*' the angels say. 'Open your Gemara already! We stand ready to pour down a sea of Heavenly assistance.' But the man is already on his way — to the business!

"*Oy, oy, oy,*" R' Sholom would chant. "*Oy,* the business ... He stands ready to have mercy on us and to give us what we ask — and we run off to our businesses ... just like the fool who called R' Baruch every morning. *Oy.* The business ..."

In a ringing voice, he concluded, "May we never be humiliated or destroyed!"

TO PROVIDE FOR HIS FAMILY, R' SHOLOM SERVED AS *MASHGIACH* in a yeshivah. "*HaKadosh Baruch Hu* can bless me with money

Making an Effort at Making a Living through my sole salary as *mashgiach,*" he once declared to his daughter. "It's enough."

On the topic of earning a living, he once told a relative, "One of the people who comes regularly to hear me speak at the Zichron Moshe Shul is an older man who decided to consult with me about various questions that came up in his life. He had become a 'chassid' of mine, he told me with a smile. By profession, he was a tailor."

One day, the man came to R' Sholom for advice. "I have a shop, and a certain individual has come along suggesting that I take him in as a partner. What do you think — should I join forces with him?"

"Do you have enough to live on without him?" R' Sholom asked.

"Yes," the tailor responded. "I earn about 300 lira per month" (a very nice living in those days).

"In that case," R' Sholom inquired, "why do you need a partner?"

"He is prepared to invest a certain sum. According to my calculations, I could then make something like 600 lira per month."

Characteristically, R' Sholom answered indirectly, with a story.

"A Jew came to the Chofetz Chaim and told him that he had a shop on a certain street and was thinking about opening a second shop on another, more distant street, in order to make twice the profits. The Chofetz Chaim told him, 'This is like a man who has a barrel of wine with a spigot from which to pour out the wine. The man thinks: I need twice as much wine to live on. I'll insert a second spigot in the barrel so that twice as much wine will come out.

"'*Another spigot will not bring more wine.* A person's livelihood is decreed for him. If he has a shop, he has a spigot from which to earn his living. Another spigot will only make the decreed amount come in faster, but it won't increase it.'"

The Jew listened to R' Sholom's advice and refrained from taking in a partner. Heaven smiled on his business. Later, it came to light that the man who had offered himself as a partner was a thief.

Still on the topic of wealth and livelihood, R' Sholom said simply, "There is no rich man who does not see Hashem's Hand in his livelihood, none who will claim that his own hand accrued lira after lira, dollar after dollar, until he was rich. Wealth always comes about through business successes over which no man has full control. Our Sages speak of three types of people who are loathed by Hashem, and one of them is the rich man who denies his faith in Hashem. He is the one who, with his own eyes, has had an opportunity to witness Hashem's Hand in his affairs. Who is he to deny it?"

It's Not Mine

"DOES CHINUCH ATZMA'I BELONG TO ME MORE THAN TO ANYone else?" R' Sholom would ask. "I won't ask them to give you a job." This was his answer to relatives who wanted him to pull strings for them. "It's true, I raised money for them, but ..."

This brings to mind a story told about the Ponoviezher Rav — one which R' Sholom enjoyed relating.

The Ponoviezher Rav was staying in a central Chicago neighborhood while he attempted to raise funds for his yeshivah. His routine was to deliver a Gemara *shiur* to a group of householders, only afterwards asking for their contributions in the support of Torah.

During that same period of time, a fundraiser for the Novardok Yeshivah in Bnei Brak came to Chicago, and happened upon the shul where the Ponoviezher Rav was delivering his *shiur.* Understanding the scenario, the fundraiser realized he had nothing to seek in this place. If the Ponoviezher Rav was already here, he was wasting his time.

"But as long as I'm here," he thought, "it would be a pity to miss out on a *shiur* by the *gaon* of Ponoviezh." He pulled up a chair and listened.

When the *shiur* was over, the Ponoviezher Rav raised his voice and said, "Here in the shul with us is a respected Jew, a *talmid chacham* from Bnei Brak. He came in quietly and is sitting on the side. You should know that this man has come all this way in order to help support Torah, as a representative of the Novardok Yeshivah in Bnei Brak." The Rav went on to praise that yeshivah and exhort the group as to their obligation to help support it. By the time he was done, he had moved his audience to give generously to the man sitting on the side. The Novardok Yeshivah benefited handsomely that day.

As they were leaving the shul, the fundraiser ran over to the Ponoviezher Rav and burst out emotionally, "You worked so hard, devoting your precious time — many, many hours — on behalf of your own yeshivah, Yeshivas Ponoviezh. You traveled all this way … and in the end, with the money practically in your purse, you directed it all to the Novardok Yeshivah. To my yeshivah, not yours! What have you done? And why did you do it?"

The Rav gazed at him through eyes that were filled with love and caring for all Jews, and answered, "My dear man, is there a 'yours' or a 'mine' when it comes to Hashem's Torah? In supporting the

Torah, is there 'yours' or 'mine'? Our goal is to increase Torah among our people. Let the students increase at every location and in every corner."

R' Sholom embraced the same approach. He toiled endlessly on behalf of holy Jewish institutions, but he never turned it into a personal crusade. Were his speeches "his"? Was Chinuch Atzma'i "his"?

"I don't belong, personally, to any institution that I work for. Let those in charge of the institutions decide what to do with the money I collect and make up their minds about whom to hire or not to hire. Who am I?

"I have given my efforts for *Klal Yisrael* — in this specific instance, in the form of Chinuch Atzma'i. But I will not toil for them on behalf of my children and grandchildren. Never."

"IT'S PURIM ALL YEAR." THAT WAS THE WAY R' SHOLOM'S daughter described her father's approach to giving *tzedakah*.

Charity Whoever held out a hand for charity was granted it. When he would walk in the street and he would be asked for *tzedakah*, R' Sholom would begin at once to search through his pockets. And when his pockets were empty — a frequent occurrence — he would ask his companion to do him a favor and lend him a few pennies.

"My father gave, and gave ..."

"My father gave, and gave, and gave to others," his daughter recalls. "Once, when there was no money in the house to buy clothing for Yom Tov, my mother smiled and told my father, 'I also fall into the category of a poor person. I'm sure you will try to find a few pennies for me.'"

One of the character traits R' Sholom particularly abhorred was stinginess. He would deride this trait with all his might. When he spied signs of it in any family member, he would immediately work up a storm over it, doing everything within his power to make this bad *middah* as hateful to the other as it was to himself. He would tell (in the name of R' Eliyahu Lopian) of a man who groped under his father's *tallis* after the father's death, groping and searching, until he found what he was looking for. "A button fell off my shirt," he explained, holding it up. A button — worth less than a penny.

To be stingy was bad enough — but to be stingy when it came to giving charity was a thing utterly loathsome to R' Sholom.

R' SHOLOM LOVED THE MITZVAH OF GIVING *TZEDAKAH* WITH all his heart. "To give to others gave him a special joy," his son-in-

One Holiday Eve law relates. And he told of an interesting incident:

One *erev* Yom Tov, the son-in-law arrived at R' Sholom's house to spend the holiday with him. Just after he had entered, he heard a knock on the door. A poor man stood in the entrance.

The son-in-law had continued on into the house to deposit his belongings, when he suddenly heard a soft cry emerge from the room, and saw one of R' Sholom's daughters wringing her hands. "*Oy!* Look what Abba's doing! Why is he doing that? Oh, come see what Abba's doing!"

In some confusion, the son-in-law went to the front door, where he saw R' Sholom unfolding a brand-new shirt before the poor man's happy eyes. It was a shirt he had purchased in England, and which had sat unused in the closet for four months, waiting to be opened in honor of Yom Tov!

After he had shown the poor man how beautiful the shirt was, R' Sholom refolded it and returned it to its wrapping. "Take it! Take it! You should have a new shirt. Good Yom Tov!"

The poor man accepted the shirt and left. Turning back inside, R' Sholom met his daughters' reproachful eyes. "Abba! If you had no money and had to give a shirt, *why* give him the beautiful shirt from England? Why?"

R' Sholom saw their pain, and was silent. A moment later, he summoned the son-in-law over to the bookcase, where he removed a *Rambam* and opened it to the laws of prohibited sacrifices. Bringing the volume close to his eyes, he began to read. Silence fell over the household as they listened.

"Listen to the *Rambam's* language. 'One who wishes to [offer a sacrifice in his own merit] should … bring of the best quality there is of the type he is offering. It says in the Torah that Hevel brought the best of his flock and of the fat, and Hashem preserved Hevel and his offering. This is the law with everything … If one builds a house of prayer, it should be more beautiful than his dwelling place. When feeding the hungry, he should give of the best and sweetest food on his table. When dressing the naked, he should offer his nicest clothing.'"

R' Sholom finished reading in his mellifluous voice, leaving his son-in-law with a profound impression that has accompanied him to this day, decades later.

The Many Faces of Tzedakah

R' SHOLOM'S LOVE OF CHARITY ALSO EXPRESSED ITSELF IN ways other than the actual giving of money. Money is the physical expression of charity, but there is also the great gift of an encouraging smile, a listening ear. The mitzvah of *tzedakah* belongs not only to the hand, but specifically to the heart — as well as the mouth and the rest of one's limbs and faculties. In this form of charity, R' Sholom was unique.

When there was money in his purse, he gave it generously. But when his physical resources ran out, he would bestow his entire spirit and soul on the needy: his sweetness, his expressive face, his smile, the eyes that brimmed with good-heartedness. Anyone who drew close to him felt the outpouring of friendship and love that was his way of "giving" — all the time. Just being in R' Sholom's presence filled one with good-will and peace of mind.

All his actions were sweet as honey. When he rejoiced with a groom, he danced with all his might. When he sat down to comfort the bereaved, he would cry with them and share in their pain. His weeping would lead the mourners to renew their own bitter tears — but when the tears stopped, they felt a lightening of their grief and a measure of comfort.

"When there was money in his purse, he gave it generously." To R' Sholom's left is R' Ze'ev Eidelman.

This is the way R' Sholom gave *tzedakah:* All his money, all his possessions, all his heart, and all his emotions went to others who needed them.

He would expound wryly on the way the man in the street "carried his friend's burden with him." The scene: the Machaneh Yehudah open-air market, crowded with humanity. One Jew meets his neighbor at a vegetable stall.

"How are you?" he asks.

"Thanks, thanks, *baruch Hashem!*"

And then the two of them continue the solemn business of selecting cucumbers.

Does he really want to know how his neighbor is faring? Is he interested in finding out whether there is anything troubling him? When he asks "How are you?" — does he really care at all?

"No!" R' Sholom flung out his arms in an attitude of denial. "He doesn't really care. He is merely being polite — a superficial behavior."

But our Sages, he is quick to remind us, have taught us otherwise. They told us to carry our friend's burden together with him. They want us to think about our neigh-

R' Sholom shows interest in the needs of a young boy

bor ... to *really* think about him!

R' SHOLOM'S SCRUPULOUSNESS IN MONEY MATTERS WAS LEGendary. It was with genuine fear that he avoided even the shadow

Kosher Money of a suspicion of anything that might smack of theft. Any money that fell into his hands was as good as stamped, "kosher Money."

R' Sholom liked to tell about the time that the Chofetz Chaim, on one of his trips to serve the public, was presented with a silver tray. Someone close to him noticed that the Chofetz Chaim was murmuring something with great emotion. Listening attentively, the man heard the Chofetz Chaim repeat joyously, "Ah! Ah! Kosher money!"

"Yaakov *Avinu* returned [over the river] to retrieve some small containers that he had forgotten there. From this we learn that a *tzaddik's* money is more precious to him than his own body. And why? Because they do not touch stolen money" (*Chullin* 91). R' Sholom would chant happily: "Here is the Chofetz Chaim, who distanced himself from 70 permissible gates in order to avoid entering one small prohibited one." The Chofetz Chaim's hands would shake when he held money whose owner was unknown. He felt as though hot coals had scorched his hands when they came close to touching "unkosher" money. And he would beam with pleasure when his hands held kosher money. A *tzaddik's* joy.

EVEN IN HIS YOUTH IT WAS POSSIBLE TO DISCERN THE SIGNS OF R' Sholom's meticulous care in money matters. A classmate

I.O.U. once loaned him half a shilling. R' Sholom scrupulously noted the loan in his personal memo book: "I owe half a shilling to ... who lives in America." That note remained in his notebook for the next 15 years. By this time, both the American boy and R' Sholom had married and had children. One Purim night, they met by chance in the Chevron Yeshivah.

"I owe you half a shilling!" R' Sholom cried out at once.

"My dear R' Sholom, I pardon the loan. All is forgiven," the other man said with a smile.

R' Sholom went home, took the notebook out of his closet, searched for that single line written so long ago, and erased it.

ON ONE OF HIS TRIPS TO LONDON, R' SHOLOM VISITED R' Rephael Mayerson and presented him with a new volume of the

He Couldn't Sleep Maharsham's work — the fruit of R' Sholom's labor. When R' Mayerson asked the price of the *sefer*, R' Sholom quoted a figure that seemed unusually steep. The Londoner decided to pay it; if R' Sholom said so, there was no reason to argue ... and the money was doubtless going to a worthwhile cause.

R' Mayerson still has an interesting letter, sent to him several days later together with a "refund." He has kept that letter for 35 years as a precious memento. (Our thanks to R' Benzion Benedict for passing it on to us.)

"I was greatly distressed tonight, and I can't go to sleep until I have said my piece. And this is it: Because I am used to the currency of *Eretz Yisrael*, it simply did not occur to me that I am charging a great deal for the books that you bought from me ... And therefore, I am hereby fulfilling *'al tashkein b'ohalecha avlah* — do not keep an illicit thing in your abode and enclosing 10 liras in return."

R' Sholom goes on to explain the nature of his error, and concludes, "And afterwards I thought that it is really terrible to charge a person such an amount. I beg your forgiveness and hope that you will understand and forgive and pardon me."

The letter was signed, "With thanks and blessings ... Your friend, Sholom Schwadron."

⌒⌒

Any money that bore the suspicion of interest was immediately removed from his wallet. When a bank clerk tried to credit his account with interest, R' Sholom wrote a polite letter to the bank management, asking them to refrain from doing so. "I stand on my legitimate right not to accept the money," he explained. At a later date, he began to harbor suspicion that one of the bank clerks was taking for himself the interest due to R' Sholom's account. He withdrew all the money at once, and closed the account.

WHEN R' SHOLOM HAD COMPLETED THE NINTH VOLUME OF HIS *Da'as Torah Maharsham*, he asked the head of a well-known printing

Dollars and Sense house to evaluate the work and give him an estimate of the costs involved in publishing it.

The printer studied the work, then told R' Sholom with a satisfied smile, "The way I see it, the new book will comprise such-and-such number of pages. There will have to be plates made up, and we will do the printing and binding. The work will take several months; I estimate that the book will be ready by the end of the winter.

"As to the price, Rav Schwadron, it is $12,000. I will receive the money in installments: $2,000 after the plates are made, a further sum at a later point in the process, and the rest when the job is finished. Should you wish to pay the full amount in advance, I will reduce the price to $10,000."

The printer concluded his speech and waited for R' Sholom's answer.

R' Sholom summoned his grandson for a consultation. They were discussing the printer's proposal from every angle, when R' Sholom suddenly jumped out of his chair as though bitten by a snake.

"Interest! *Oy*, we are close to the sin of taking interest!"

"What do you mean?" his startled grandson asked.

R' Sholom's face was pale as he resumed his seat and explained, "I have the full amount that's being charged for the work, and it is my inclination to give it all to the printer now. It is advantageous for us to do so as this way we are not afraid of losing the money and are also able to pay less. But there is a suspicion of interest here. We must not sit talking even one minute longer." R' Sholom raised his voice. "Quick! Run to R' Shlomo Zalman and ask him to tell us the halachah in this case. Hurry, my son! When you come back we can continue to discuss the other details."

The grandson, after a quick review of some of the laws of interest, went to R' Shlomo Zalman Auerbach and poured out the whole story. The *gaon* answered, "There is a way to get around the problem of interest, but it's not so simple."

The young man returned to find his grandfather tense and impatient. "Nu, nu, what did the *'feter'* say?" (*"Feter"* — uncle — was the affectionate term by which R' Shlomo Zalman was known in the family.)

"He said it's possible, but it's not simple," the grandson replied.

R' Sholom was soon sitting opposite the printer once again. "This is what we have decided," he said. "We will conclude the matter according to your suggestion: printing, binding, transportation, and distribution. You will receive $12,000 cash. We will pay a certain sum in advance and add the rest with the completion of each stage of the work. *Baruch Hashem*, we have the full amount in hand and can pay you in stages until the job is done. Under no circumstances, however, can I pay you a discounted price of $10,000 up front."

The printer rose to leave but R' Sholom was struck by a new thought: It was certainly permissible to pay the printer the *full amount* in advance! R' Sholom had originally intended to pay for the work up front, then had realized that he could not pay the discounted price of $10,000 because of the possible problem of interest. Since he could not pay the lesser amount in any case, why not give the printer the $12,000 right away? R' Sholom would not lose by it. Let the printer enjoy the money!

R' Sholom called the printer back. A few minutes later, the printer left again, this time holding the full $12,000 in his hand. As he left the house, he thrust the money into his pocket, thinking with wonder, "What kind of people are they — they have absolutely no idea about money! I'll never understand the minds of these rabbis. They live in another world."

A world of halachah and truth.

"I REMEMBER ONE TIME WHEN I HAD A STANDOFF WITH R' Sholom," R' Yehudah Ilan relates. "It was after a lecture he gave in the Chazon Ish *kollel* on *Chol HaMo'ed* Succos. I wanted to call a taxi to take him back to Yerushalayim. But R' Sholom was adamantly against this: 'Public funds! You are responsible for public funds that people donated to an important cause — to promote Torah *shiurim* during *Chol HaMo'ed*. I won't take a cent, not even for transportation!'

Standoff

"R' Sholom walked slowly to the public taxi stand, took his own money from his pocket, and sat down with the other passengers. We managed to sneak a sum of money to one of the other people, asking him to order a taxi for R' Sholom to take him from Geulah, where the taxi would let him off, to his home in Sha'arei Chesed."

For many years, R' Sholom suffered from elevated blood sugar. R' Sholom explained to his grandson the way this condition had developed.

"When laboring to publish the work of my teacher, R' Leib Chasman, I exerted tremendous physical effort. There were many nights when I hardly slept at all, and even when I collapsed from exhaustion it was only for a short time. When I finally completed the work, I was sick in bed for half a year (having apparently suffered a mild stroke).

"After my recovery from that episode, a painful thing happened to me in Antwerp:

"A young man came to the house where I was staying and asked for a place to sleep. 'It is Shabbos today, and I have no place to go.' A man standing near me whispered in my ear, 'He looks like a suspicious character; better not let him in.' But because I was not sure that there was really anything to be suspicious about, and because it is a mitzvah to welcome guests, I welcomed him inside happily, while adjusting my attitude to one of 'Honor him and suspect him.'

"I watched his movements carefully, and noted that he had a special bag which he carried around on Shabbos. When he fell asleep, I peeked into the bag and saw *tefillin* — and a knife. The sight caused me no little amount of distress. On Shabbos morning, when I stood ready to leave for shul, he declined to get up, saying he was tired. But I stood over him and gave him no rest until he got up and left the house with me.

"As the time for the third meal approached, I became suspicious that he might try to use the time when we were all in shul enjoying our meal, so I decided to stay and eat the meal at home. As it grew dark, he came in and lay down on his bed. The room was dark, and I followed him inside. Suddenly, he got up quickly and went carefully to the door. Then he stepped back inside as though he had forgotten something. He opened the closet, reached into my [weekday] coat pocket, and left the room. By the time I was on my feet he was running at top speed toward the street — along with all the money I had collected for Chinuch Atzma'i!

"The trembling and distress that I experienced then raised my blood sugar to tremendous heights. I wandered around the house in great anguish, until I remembered something I had once heard from a man at the port of Haifa, just before I set sail for Europe. Before that trip, I waited at the port together with my family, who had come to see me off. Suddenly, a man came over and asked if he could tell me a wonderful *vort*. With Heaven's help, I remembered that *vort* in my hour of anguish and pain in Antwerp, and was immediately comforted. [Unfortunately, although that *vort* was recorded by R' Sholom, the tape has been lost with the passage of time.]

"I do not regret the kindness I showed to that young man," R' Sholom asserted. "I worked many hard years in order to refund that lost money to Chinuch Atzma'i. I committed no actual transgression, because I did watch over the money and followed the man's movements. I thought, logically, that my presence would deter him from taking the money. Still, because the matter came about through me, I obligated myself to pay it all back."

R' Sholom's son, R' Yitzchak Schwadron, tells of another theft, this one taking place in Sha'arei Chesed. "At that time, they also stole a sum of money from my father. I went over to his house the next morning to commiserate with him, but he seemed unperturbed. I asked, 'That other time, in Europe, you were broken. And today?'

"He retorted, 'This time, there are no *public funds* involved.'"

On the other occasion, it had been public money that was stolen from him. This time, it was his own money, and, therefore, it did not unduly disturb him. "Hashem gives and Hashem takes away — blessed be the Name of Hashem!"

CHAPTER 8

Small Stories About a Great Man

THE WORLD OF *MUSSAR* WAS CONSIDERABLY ENRICHED by the publication of *Ohr Yahel,* a compilation of R' Leib **In a Dream** Chasman's *mussar* sermons. It was his student, R' Sholom Schwadron, who labored long and hard to bring this hidden treasure to the light of day.

R' Sholom began writing down these sermons during R' Leib Chasman's lifetime and continued working on them after his rebbe had passed from this world.

The Alter of Slobodka had called R' Leib an *ilui* (genius) of *mussar,* so it is not surprising that R' Sholom found the task of putting his words into writing a monumental one. It took a certain genius of his own to grasp the essence of what his teacher was saying, and to present the ideas in the precise fashion that would offer R' Leib's insights with all their original intent. To this end, he exerted enormous effort: "Know and believe that it has been nearly seven months since I turned my attention away from my other concerns and I have sat day and night to prepare and present [this work] with great and mighty effort." These were R' Sholom's own words in his introduction to the work. Members of his household are quick to add that R' Sholom collapsed at the end of his labor on the *Ohr Yahel*, and required extensive rehabilitation.

Thousands of copies of the books were published. They constitute a rich jewel in the treasure house of *mussar*.

R' Leib Chasman never got a chance to thank his student during his lifetime; the three-volume work was published only after his death. But there were those who were certain that R' Leib had come in a dream to thank R' Sholom.

During a meeting with R' Sholom, R' Eliyahu Lopian remarked, "R' Leib, your rebbe probably came to you in a dream to thank you for publishing the *Ohr Yahel*."

He did not notice the shudder of emotion that swept through R' Sholom at these words. To R' Eliyahu, it was a simple matter for R' Leib Chasman to come in a dream to thank R' Sholom — such a simple matter that he related an interesting story on the spot.

"R' Eliyahu Dessler regularly observed the *yahrtzeit* of his father-in-law, R' Nochum Ze'ev [Velvel] of Kelm. On that day, he would lead the service in the Kelm shul, and learn *Mishnayos* for the elevation of the departed soul.

"Once," R' Lopian continued, "R' Dessler was required to leave town urgently for the sake of a mitzvah, and he asked me to observe his father-in-law's *yahrtzeit* in his place. I agreed to do as he asked.

"On the night of the *yahrtzeit*, R' Nochum Velvel came to me in a dream. I understood that he wished to thank me for *davening* and saying *Kaddish* for him." His story concluded, R' Lopian turned to R' Sholom with interest. "Probably R' Leib Chasman came to you, too."

R' Sholom related this incident to his family and friends, but declined to reveal how he had answered R' Lopian.

It was a question that occurred to several bright minds. "You've also published the works of R' Eliyahu Lopian, in the famous *Lev Eliyahu*," one of them later remarked. "Did *he* come to thank you in a dream?"

R' Sholom replied with a slight smile — and silence. Humbly, he said only, "One must be worthy," and would add no more.

⌒⌒

About another dream, however, R' Sholom did not choose silence. He opened his heart, saying, "I saw my rebbe, R' Leib Chasman, in a dream. I dreamed that I was going up to *duchan*, to say the *Bircas Kohanim* (the priestly blessing), and the Rebbe was standing and leading the *davening*. When I finished the *duchan*, the Rebbe turned to me and said, "Say *Kaddish*."

"At the time, I didn't know how much importance to attach to this dream. Then, in the morning, I received the bad news: R' Leib Chasman's son had died. It was his only son, and this son had left no son to say *Kaddish* for him.

"All the rest of that year," R' Sholom finished, "I said *Kaddish* for R' Leib's son every single day."

(Incidentally, R' Sholom also had the custom of standing up in front of the shul each year and saying *Kaddish* on R' Leib Chasman's *yahrtzeit*.]

⌒⌒

Right to left: R' Nissim Karelitz, R' Sholom, R' Shmuel Auerbach, R' Peretz Ariel

Chapter Eight: Small Stories About a Great Man / 227

R' Peretz Ariel, *Av Beis Din* of Gadiel and Hod HaSharon, once saw the Chofetz Chaim in a dream. This was after a mass gathering during which he had signed on hundreds to strengthen their observance of *shemiras halashon*.

When R' Sholom heard this story from his grandson, he smiled and said, "I had the privilege of seeing the Chazon Ish in a dream, and he was delivering a *derashah* (sermon) on *shemiras Shabbos*. Heaven smiled upon me: When I awoke I remembered every word, and have passed them on to the public. "[It is clear that this material did, indeed, come from a dream, as the Chazon Ish did not as a rule make speeches or deliver sermons.]

R' ELIYAHU LOPIAN, R' SHOLOM'S TEACHER AND MENTOR, once told him that he had something special that he wished to trans-

I Am Ready mit to him orally, from the last of the Kabbalists, the "Leshem." R' Lopian instructed R' Sholom to make certain preparations and to come to his room at a specific time.

R' Sholom was flustered. "It seems to me that I am not worthy of this. I'm not yet at that level."

R' Eliyahu Lopian, apparently, did not agree. He was silent.

R' Sholom went on his way. Despite a powerful desire to receive this "transmission" from his rebbe, after further reflection he decided, in his humility, that he was not yet worthy.

Nine years passed before R' Sholom decided that the time had finally arrived. He was now worthy of being on the receiving end of such material. He went to his great teacher and said, "I am ready." In distress, R' Lopian said, "The hour has been lost. Time has passed and I am already old. Now I will not pass on what I have received."

(as told by R' Avraham Erlanger)

Anguished, R' Sholom told his grandson later, "I may have been in error when I declined R' Eliyahu Lopian's request that other time. I lost out."

The young man, not knowing the full story, was at a loss to understand his grandfather's reference until R' Sholom's passing, when the story came to light. Only then did he comprehend his grandfather's pain.

DIAGNOSTIC IMAGING OF R' SHOLOM'S 70-YEAR-OLD NECK showed four clogged arteries. The two remaining arteries were not in **The Scent of** satisfactory condition, either. A short time later, **Spirituality** dangerous signs were found on his legs, indicative of further distress in his blood system — signs that might, Heaven forbid, result in the need to amputate a foot. A highly qualified, internationally known doctor was brought in to care for R' Sholom in order to prevent the condition from progressing.

R' Sholom, who knew how to honor every person with a pleasant demeanor, was respectful to every doctor who walked into his room, whether religious or not. Always. This time, however, his attitude was different. He did not receive this doctor with his usual affable manner. He answered the physician's questions with cool indifference. After he had gone, R' Sholom commanded, "Don't bring him to me anymore. I don't want him. I don't like him."

"R' Sholom, he's an expert!" his family protested. After a great deal of pleading and persuading, R' Sholom finally consented to let the doctor return to his home to treat him. But he sighed, "What can I do? There is something that repels me about him. I feel repugnance toward him."

Investigating further, the family learned that the doctor was indeed a morally degraded individual.

A month later, they told R' Sholom what they had found out. He responded with pain: "I felt a repugnance toward him, but I didn't know why."

(as told by his son)

A 70th birthday comes along once in a lifetime, if one has the merit to live that long. R' Sholom had that merit. How did he celebrate his birthday?

There are differences of opinion among our Torah luminaries as to the correct way to celebrate a birthday. The Chasam Sofer believed that it was not necessary to mark the day with a festive meal. He cites Avraham *Avinu,* who made a feast each year to commemorate the anniversary of his son Yitzchak's *milah,* but not his birthday, as was Pharaoh's custom. But there were some Torah leaders who did celebrate their birthdays.

A 70th birthday, however, is a special day by anyone's standards. In his *Chavos Ya'ir (siman* 70), even the Chasam Sofer refers to the celebration of that day.

R' Sholom was not a man accustomed to repressing his joy. On his 70th birthday, he shared his feelings with several friends. His first call was to a good friend who was also among the day's great men of *mussar,* R' Hirsch Palei.

"R' Hirsch!" he exclaimed "Today I had the privilege of turning 70! My dear R' Hirsch, I have such a special feeling. Today a mitzvah is leaving me, and the Gemara tells us that Palti ben Layish cried when a mitzvah left him."

Who was Palti ben Layish? And what was the departing mitzvah to which R' Sholom referred?

The Gemara, in *Sanhedrin* 19, presents an argument between King Saul and King David on the subject of Michal, Saul's daughter, who was married to David. King Saul objected to the *kiddushin* by which David had married his daughter, while David felt that it had been a legitimate *kiddushin.* In accordance with his own opinion that David and Michal were not truly married, Saul gave Michal as a wife to Palti ben Layish.

Because of the doubts attending this controversial halachic ruling, Palti ben Layish decided to refrain from living with Michal as husband and wife. He adhered to his resolution with rigid discipline, until David became king and sent a messenger to bring Michal back. When that hour came and the test was taken away from him, Palti ben Layish wept as he accompanied Michal out of his home. "What," the Gemara asks, "was the reason for those tears?" And the Gemara explains the answer: "He was crying over a mitzvah that was leaving him." Palti wept because a personal challenge had now departed from his life. He shed copious tears over the loss of merit that came from withstanding that challenge. The Gemara showers him with high praise for this attitude.

"In my own case," R' Sholom told his friend, "we're talking about a completely different mitzvah. But we see from the Gemara that one can cry over the loss of a mitzvah. The *Yoreh De'ah* (*siman* 244) says that two Torah scholars or two elderly people have no obligation to stand up for one another, though they may choose to do so as a sign of respect. Now that I am seventy," R' Sholom lamented, "I am not obligated in the mitzvah of standing up for an elderly person!" His voice held genuine pain at the thought.

There were other telephone conversations after that first one. In each of them, R' Sholom shared his pain over the loss of a mitzvah. This was how R' Sholom marked his 70th birthday. These personal talks were not publicized for the world to hear; they belonged to R' Sholom's private and modest world. It was only by chance that his grandson happened to overhear them.

His family heard other things from him on that day. R' Sholom smiled joyously as he called, "*Rabbosai!* Things that my rebbe said casually have come true! R' Leib Chasman told me once, 'When you reach the age of 70, you will understand that one additional minute in yeshivah will make you a happy man.' He said that I would reach the age of 70 — and I have!"

With his incomparable smile, he added, "My rebbe told me another thing about turning 80, but I'm not telling anyone what he said."

THE ATMOSPHERE WAS CHARGED. STUDENTS WERE BESIDE themselves with excitement as the great R' Eliyahu Lopian entered

Honoring the Torah   the hall of Yeshivah Tiferes Tzvi, where R' Sholom had served as *mashgiach* for many years. Their eyes were lifted with reverence, their ears alert to catch every word.

R' Eliyahu spoke to his young audience, showering them with words of *mussar* and piety. After the *Ma'ariv* services, he prepared to leave the great hall, accompanied by the respectful students. Suddenly, something strange happened — something that would never be forgotten by anyone who was present.

Without warning, R' Sholom stretched himself out on the floor. The students exchanged bewildered glances. What was this odd behavior all about? But before they had time to speculate, the *mashgiach* rose to his feet and continued accompanying R' Eliyahu to the exit.

When they had parted from R' Eliyahu Lopian, R' Sholom saw the question marks on his students' faces. He knew he owed them an explanation.

"I wanted to fulfill the simple meaning of *Chazal's* words: 'And you shall lie in the dust of the Torah scholars' feet.'"

One of the students who was present on that occasion could not erase that extraordinary image from his mind, even decades later. Who had ever seen such exemplary *chinuch*? R' Sholom took the most direct means to show his students, by personal example, how seriously they should take the teachings of our Sages. With the hammer of his own personality, he pounded into those impressionable young hearts a powerful reverence for Torah scholars. And the unforgettable impression, as he had hoped, stayed with them for many years afterwards.

(as told by R' Menachem Tzvi Berlin)

R' SHOLOM'S PERSONAL EXAMPLE OF REVERING TORAH LEADers blazed the trail others would follow. This approach influenced

Reverence his every interaction with the individuals of whom he stood in such awe.

On one occasion, while waiting with a group of people for a *bris milah* ceremony to begin, he was chatting with his friends, R' Ze'ev Eidelman and R' Ezra Brizel, when a family member came to the door to announce: "The *sandak,* the *gaon* R' Eliezer Shach, will be here in a moment."

Visibly excited, R' Sholom placed a hand on each of his companions' shoulders as though to include them in a tremendous privilege, and said, "Let's sit down on this bench. If we're seated, we will be able to honor Rav Shach by standing up when he comes in."

The three men sat. And when Rav Shach walked in, they all

R' Sholom shows deference to R' Moshe Pardo

stood up at once in honor of the Torah.

CONTROVERSY BROKE OUT IN A CERTAIN TORAH INSTITUTION, and along with several other prominent Torah personalities, R'

"I'm Getting Out!" Sholom — much against his will — was forced to become involved.

"One day, during the month of Elul," an acquaintance recalls, "I drove R' Sholom back home from that institution. R' Sholom was sitting silently beside me. I decided to seize the moment to denounce a certain *talmid chacham* who was part of the controversy. My diatribe began gently enough, but soon turned harsh. R' Sholom signaled sharply for me to stop speaking in this vein about a Torah leader, but I persisted in explaining my position [as he did not disagree with my point, only with the style in which I was presenting it].

"As a rule, R' Sholom Schwadron was soft as butter. This time, he hardened like a rock. With a motion of his hand that could not be misunderstood, he let me know that he wanted me to stop the car. 'I'm getting out,' he stated. I stopped.

"R' Sholom lifted himself up with some difficulty, stepped out of the car, and began to walk. I drove after him, trying to coax him back into the car. It was clear that walking was not easy for him. Pity overwhelmed me and I regretted ever having brought up the subject — but it was no use. R' Sholom walked all the way home."

R' SHOLOM DID NOT TAKE A SINGLE STEP IN HIS LIFE WITHOUT consulting the great men of Torah who were his teachers. In mat-

Emunas Chachamim ters of halachah he turned to the Tchebiner Rav and to R' Shlomo Zalman Auerbach, his brother-in-law. To help him carve his ethical and moral path, he looked to R' Leib Chasman, R' Eliyahu Lopian, the Chazon Ish, the Brisker Rav, the Tchebiner Rav, the Steipler *gaon*, R' Yehudah Segal of Manchester, and others. Even as an elderly man near the end of his days, he came to R' Chaim Kanievsky for advice. The following incident took place on one of his visits to R' Chaim's home:

> The line of waiting people snaked from the room where R' Chaim sat, all the way to the front door. R' Sholom stepped inside the house and asked, "Who's last?"
>
> "The honored R' Schwadron can go in immediately," the others responded with one voice.
>
> As if he had not heard, R' Sholom asked again, "Who is last in line?"
>
> "I'm last," someone answered finally.
>
> R' Sholom sat down on a chair to one side of the room.
>
> One of those ahead in line, when his turn came to meet with R' Chaim Kanievsky, told him, "R' Sholom Schwadron is waiting outside." R' Chaim rose at once and went out into the waiting

With the Steipler

With R' Chaim Kanievsky

area to see what R' Sholom had come to see him about. R' Sholom stood up to greet him, raised both hands, and said, "No! No! I'm waiting my turn. A line is a line! I will go in when my turn comes."

But his protests were to no avail. R' Chaim led him into his office. Outside, in the waiting area, awed onlookers repeated details of the incident, until it eventually became widely known.

~~

In the area of *emunas chachamim*, faith in our Torah leaders, R' Sholom displayed extraordinary greatness. In talks too numerous to count, he transmitted facts about these spiritual giants to audiences everywhere.

His son describes a boat ride with his father on the Yarkon River.

"As a young boy, I was dangerously ill with a protracted cough which the doctors were unable to cure. My father went to see the Chazon Ish, to ask for his advice and his blessing.

"'Go to the Yarkon,' the Chazon Ish told him. 'There, near the water and the eucalyptus trees, the special air will help him breathe easier.'

"So my father and I went out in a rowboat. Neither of us knew much about boating. As my father made his way with difficulty into the boat, he kept murmuring, 'To listen to the words of the wise.' We sat in that boat on the Yarkon for half an hour, and all that time his sweet voice kept repeating, 'To listen to the words of the wise.'

"When the half hour was over, we asked a passerby to help us climb out onto the bank. We passed through tall reeds as we left the area. Amazingly, within the next half hour my coughing was reduced to short bursts — and an hour later, the cough was gone!

"'Tatty,' I said, with all the feeling a 4-year-old can muster, 'Tatty, now there is a cure for coughing! Everyone can come here to be cured.'

"My father gazed at me with piercing eyes. 'No, my dear son. No, no. It's not the Yarkon that cured you, but *HaKadosh Baruch Hu*, listening to the Chazon Ish's prayers. What quality does the Yarkon possess, apart from the blessing of the Chazon Ish?'

"His voice, as he spoke, was rich with his profound *emunas chachamim*."

R' YECHEZKEL LEVENSTEIN, THE *MASHGIACH* OF PONOVIEZH, was invited to serve as *sandak* at the *bris* of R' Sholom's grandson.

Changed Plans Noting the grandfather's absence, R' Yechezkel inquired after R' Sholom and was told that he had been unable to attend because of severe pains in his legs.

Some two weeks later, R' Sholom went to take his leave of R' Yechezkel before embarking on a trip abroad.

R' Yechezkel looked at him and said, "I heard that you had pains in your legs — and now you're traveling?!"

R' Sholom wasted no more words. Humbly, he left the room and hurried home. His wife was packing one final suitcase, while several others already stood locked and ready.

"I'm not going!" R' Sholom declared suddenly.

His wife looked up, startled. "What? Why not?"

"The *mashgiach* said…" And he went on to tell her the story.

"But your legs don't hurt you anymore!" she exclaimed in astonishment.

"I'm not going."

"But why not?" The question seemed to reverberate through the house.

R' Sholom answered with simple decisiveness, "R' Yechezkel is well aware of the fact that two weeks have elapsed since the *bris*, and that it's quite possible that my pains have passed. If he still found it necessary to make that remark — I'm not going anywhere!" Then he added, "Besides, I can't leave without a parting blessing from him, which I always get before traveling abroad."

The suitcases were emptied, the ticket was canceled — at the price of a hefty penalty — and the plans were put into storage along with the luggage.

Later, it was discovered that canceling the trip actually constituted a stroke of great good fortune for R' Sholom.

A similar episode took place in the Steipler's study. R' Sholom would not go abroad without a parting blessing from the Steipler, as from a rebbe to his student. Before one of his trips, R' Sholom entered the Steipler's room in Bnei Brak, but the Steipler did not bless him. "What do you want from me?" he asked again and again. R' Sholom decided to postpone the trip for a later date.

The following day, R' Sholom phoned his son-in-law, R' Moshe Ariel, and said with excitement, "Listen! I wanted to sail to America for the express purpose of meeting with a certain wealthy Jew who I hoped would cover the expenses for publication of my sefer, *Da'as Torah Maharsham*." Joyfully, he continued, "Today, on my way to a *pidyon haben,* who should I meet but that very same philanthropist! He told me, 'R' Sholom, there in America you would never have managed to meet with me. Here, take the entire sum and use it to benefit the public.'"

On the topic of self-abnegation and of placing one's complete trust in one's spiritual leader, R' Sholom liked to repeat something that the Chazon Ish once told him. "The chassidim," he said, "are happy. They listen and accept advice about every matter, without doubt or argument."

THE FOLLOWING IS FROM ONE OF R' SHOLOM'S FIERY SERMONS on the topic of *emunas chachamim*.

A Widow's Pleas *And one woman from among the prophets' wives screamed at Elisha, saying, "Your servant, my husband, has died!"* The *Radak* brings down a *Tosefta* that discusses this episode at length. He starts out by saying that this woman, the wife of Ovadiah, screamed 265 times — the numerical equivalent of the word *tza'akah* ("she screamed").

The prophet Ovadiah passed away, leaving unpaid debts behind. During his lifetime, he would borrow money, with interest, from King Achav's son, for the purpose of supporting the 100 prophets he had concealed in a cave. On his passing, the lender came to take away Ovadiah's sons as slaves, in payment of his debt. It was at this juncture that Ovadiah's widow screamed in anguish to Elisha, pleading 265 times for his help.

"Why?" R' Sholom asked. "If Elisha did not respond to her pleas, did she continue shouting?"

The answer, he said, was that the widow knew that this man, this *navi* of Hashem, was her sole recourse. That was why she pleaded so desperately and so persistently — once, twice, 10 times, 20 times, 50, 100, 200, 265 times!

All this was by way of introduction, leading into the following story, which R' Sholom had heard from the learning partner of the man involved. This man was a resident of Kfar Saba, and was close to the Chazon Ish. He came to see the Chazon Ish one Friday afternoon. He found a woman there who had come before him, standing beside her baby son asleep in his carriage. The boy, it seemed, was ill, and she was begging the Chazon Ish to bless him with good health.

The Chazon Ish sat silently, listening to her pleas without answering. She persisted, crying and pleading repeatedly. This went on for a quarter of an hour. At last, the man went over to her and said, "Please, don't you see that the Rav isn't answering you? Why are you continuing like this? Go on home."

Abruptly, the Chazon Ish roused himself from his silence. Turning sternly to the man, he scolded, "Who did she come to see, you or me?" Then he turned back to the woman and gave her his blessing.

The young man returned home to have what he referred to afterwards as a "Black Shabbos." "I was very distressed at having caused the Chazon Ish any pain." Immediately after Shabbos, he returned to Bnei Brak to see the Chazon Ish again.

The Chazon Ish received him warmly, his eyes laughing. The man began to apologize profusely for his behavior the day before. After hearing him out, the Chazon Ish said, "A woman is standing completely immersed in *emunas chachamim*. Why stop her?"

"This," said R' Sholom, "is the explanation for the 265 cries the widow cried. They were 265 shouts of belief in her spiritual leader — 265 screams of *emunas chachamim*.

"And so," he concluded, "our Sages have said that were it not for the merits of Ovadiah's widow, all of Israel might have been lost, Heaven forbid, in that hour. The power of *emunas chachamim!*"

IN THOSE DAYS, THE *MOSHAV* MOVEMENT IN ISRAEL CONtrolled the financial resources for new immigrants. The decision

Two Dances makers divided the available land among these immigrants, settling new arrivals from Yemen and North Africa in organized settlements, or *moshavim*. Every family head was entitled to a portion of land for his family's use. Those with little knowledge of farming were offered guidance by those experienced in farming.

The State attended as well to the educational needs of these immigrant families. The *moshav* children were provided with spacious, modern classrooms in state schools, where they were given every opportunity to become — to quote the Israeli national anthem — "a free people in our land" (instead of, as R' Sholom once pointed out, a holy people).

Chareidi Jewry was anxious to offer these immigrants a different kind of education. Pe'ilim representatives visited the various settlements to inform religious families that there were other educational options — religious ones — and that it was within their rights to demand them. From a legal standpoint, they explained, there was nothing to stop them from making these demands. The immigrants became fired up and prepared to do battle.

The matter reached the ears of the left-wing government, which immediately launched its counterattack. Government representatives went from house to house, explaining to the new settlers that persistence in their obstinate demands for religious education would leave them in danger of losing their rights to housing and settlement. They would have to live in huts, they would be denied seeds for sowing, and they would starve. There were some pious Jews whose stubbornness on this point brought them to the point of actual starvation. As R' Menachem Cohen described those difficult days, strong persuasive powers were needed to help the new immigrants stand firm in demanding their right to religious education.

Pressure both in Israel and abroad led to an interesting, historic

An evening class run by Pe'ilim voluteers in Jerusalem

meeting between Moshe Nissim — son-in-law of Koren, chairman of the *moshav* movement — and the original Pe'ilim. Nissim related to them some things he had heard from his father-in-law:

"It doesn't matter to us, personally, if your children learn Torah. The problem is that we need votes. The moment you take your youth and establish independent institutions, the votes shift over to you, and your parents and youth will bring the religious parties into power. This is why we are fighting. Your public struggle has caused us irreversible damage.

"Therefore, this is our proposal. We will erect separate institutions for religious youth. Your children will learn in these institutions. They will learn Torah, in any manner you wish and according to your own curricula. In this way, we can cut our political losses. You will vote for those who are doing things on your behalf — in other words, for us. You will agree to add your vote to the party that built you religious schools.

"Let us make peace between us, and peace in Israel — and all of us will profit by it."

The meeting was historic from every aspect. It set the stage for a *chareidi* triumph such as had never been seen before. The "enemy" had laid all its cards on the table ... and was willing to infuse unlimited funds into the establishment of Torah institutions. The left was beginning to yield. The price: a vote for the left, but without any curtailment of religious freedom. On the contrary, the religious right would benefit tremendously.

Anyone familiar with that particular epoch in Israeli history will understand the significance of this victory. Pe'ilim had started with nothing. A battle entered into by a few staunch individuals had forced the hard-headed left to show its first sign of fear. It was a bright ray of light in the shadows that shrouded that period.

The Pe'ilim board met in a stormy session to debate the proposal. At the height of the debate, R' Sholom's voice suddenly rang out. "Are we looking for votes? No, no! We have a single ambition: to learn Torah. And now we have that absolutely, with no one to object!" He stood up, raised his stick, and broke into a small dance of joy.

Still, whatever happiness might reign in the Pe'ilim boardroom

A study group taught by religous immigrants in a refugee camp

was not the determining factor; the leaders of the Torah world must be consulted. "Let's ask the Brisker Rav," they decided unanimously.

Smiling, R' Sholom offered to bring the entire story to the Rav. "I will present it from every angle, past and future," he said. "Let us go to his house and ask him."

R' Menachem Cohen was with R' Sholom when he visited the Brisker Rav. The Rav listened attentively to the story, then offered his answer in the form of a parable:

"A man took his young son into the forest. Suddenly, the father became aware that his son had disappeared. He glanced from side to side, searching — but the boy was gone! 'Yankele! Yankele!' he shouted. In the distance, he heard his son's voice: 'Father, here I am … but I can't return right now. I have caught a Cossak, and I'm holding him tight. I mustn't leave.'

"'Yankele, leave the Cossak!' the father shouted in a panic. 'Let him go, and come back to me! Otherwise, you'll lose your way and become completely lost.'

"A minute passed. Then the boy's voice came through the forest:

'Father, Father, I can't. He's grabbed me! The Cossak is holding me. I thought that I had caught *him*, but ...'"

The Brisker Rav concluded his incisive parable. There was no need to add anything further. The meaning was clear. However, he did wind up his thoughts with one final sentence: "*Yiddishkeit* is not bought with money. *Yiddishkeit* is bought with *mesiras nefesh* (sacrifice)."

"We had just left the house," R' Menachem Cohen relates, "when R' Sholom broke into an irrepressible dance of tremendous happiness. *Baruch Hashem* for these great men of Torah who watch over us! *Ashreinu, ma tov chelkeinu* (How happy we are, how good is our portion)."

This was the same R' Sholom who had earlier danced with joy over the opposite point of view. Without blinking an eye, his attitude underwent a complete reversal — a total, sweet surrender to the Torah leaders of his generation. He was able to negate his own self entirely, with joy.

His was a dance of *emunas chachamim*.

❦

R' Sholom's enormous respect for Torah scholars led him to decline acceptance of their services in any way. This held true for

A stormy session in Pe'ilim's offices. At right is R' Shlomo Noach Kroll, third from right is R' Yehoshua Sklar.

young scholars as well, and even for those who were members of his own family. R' Sholom refused to allow his sons-in-law to serve him. "You serve me? Heaven forbid! You are a *talmid chacham!*"

The same rule applied to his learning partner of many years. "I was never able to serve him," the *chavrusa* remembers. "I once chanced to pour him a cup of tea, and he refused to drink it."

One of the young men who stayed in R' Sholom's house after the Rebbetzin passed away tells of the many complex strategies he was forced to employ in order to serve his host. R' Sholom was adamantly against the notion of being served by any guest of his: "*Hachnasas orchim!*" he would state with resolution. "You will eat my bread and drink my water, but only as my guest. That is the condition under which you may enter my home."

And that was the way it was. At the Shabbos meals, for example, R' Sholom (then in his 70's) was the one who served the meal, cleared away the used plates, and brought each new course to the table. "R' Sholom would learn the weekly Torah portion at the table during the *seudah*," one such "guest" recalls. "Sometimes, he became completely absorbed in his learning, and I would have a chance to bring something to the table. I would then be reprimanded for doing this, and would wait a week or two before seizing the next opportunity to do it again, when R' Sholom was again immersed in his learning."

AS ON EVERY FRIDAY NIGHT, R' SHOLOM STOOD BESIDE THE HOLY Ark in the Zichron Moshe Shul, delivering his lecture. This time, the

Words of Wisdom topic was: "Bringing merit to the many: How does one accomplish this?" The following is a true story: A young man walked Jerusalem's narrow streets with drawn face and hunched shoulders, his attitude consonant with the time of the year: the period just preceding the days of judgment. He was lost in introspective thought.

"Time is short," he reflected. "How can I best use it to acquire additional merit?" Suddenly, an idea sprang into his mind. "Bringing merit to the many! That's a way to add a great deal of merit all at one time."

It was a Shabbos day, the last one of the year. The young man continued his walk, sunk in his thoughts. He had to find a way to tilt the scales of justice. Entering a local shul, he found the service near the end. Some of the worshipers were already folding up their prayer shawls and placing them in their *tallis* bags. A number of them were heedless of the halachic ruling that expressly forbids folding the *tallis* on Shabbos on the exact fold lines. The young man formed a resolution.

He waited for the *davening* to finish. The worshipers, busy wishing one another a "good Shabbos," were startled to hear a pounding from the front of the shul. Silence descended.

"My dear Jews," the young man began, "it is just a few days until Rosh Hashanah, and it is worthwhile to refresh our memories about a certain explicit halachah in the laws of Shabbos. On Shabbos, it is forbidden to fold one's *tallis* precisely — that is, on the fold lines. Good Shabbos."

Most of the congregants, simple people, gazed at each other in astonishment. "We never knew such a halachah existed. Have we been performing a forbidden act every Shabbos for all these years? May Hashem have mercy!" One pious man, who had also been unaware of this law, brought forward a suggestion on the spot. "Every Shabbos, right after *davening*, let's have a short *shiur* on the laws of Shabbos!" The others agreed at once. The *shiur* was launched on the Shabbos during the Ten Days of Repentance. The weekly lesson lasted only 10 minutes, but it became a firmly established ritual.

Congregants of a nearby shul heard about the *shiur* and thought, "There, in the shul where the 'simple' folk *daven*, they have a *shiur* — and we don't?" An immediate resolution was adopted: a weekly *shiur* on the laws of Shabbos.

Soon after, a third shul followed in the footsteps of the first two.

When R' Sholom related this story in the Zichron Moshe Shul on Friday night, he added in his melodious chant, "That young man got up and left. He probably had no idea of the many merits swelling his account. After hearing about these *shiurim,* I, too, thought about learning the *Chayei Adam* — *Hilchos Shabbos* (every Shabbos before delivering my lecture).

"Bringing merit to the many is an awesome thing, and it all began with a single pounding of the fist and a few good words," R' Sholom concluded. "The power of a few words before Rosh Hashanah."

Who was the young man whose identity R' Sholom was so careful to conceal — the young man who was so eager to bring merit to his fellow men, but whose name was never mentioned in the story?

He was none other than R' Sholom Mordechai HaKohen Schwadron.

(as told by R' Eliyahu Katzenelenbogen)

R' SHOLOM ONCE TOLD AN INTERESTING TIDBIT ABOUT R' Yisrael Salanter. On a certain occasion, R' Yisrael remarked that he thanked Hashem for not having made him a rich man.

Don't Make Me Rich!

"Wealth is a heavy burden," R' Yisrael said. "I have a neighbor who lives in abject poverty. During the winter he trembles with cold, day and night. His children walk around in torn shoes. His wife, after childbirth, requires several glasses of milk a day, but there is nothing. If they ask me in the Heavenly Court why I did not help this family enough, I will have a partial excuse: *I, too, do not have a penny.*

"No, it is not a full excuse. But it *is* a partial one, and even half an excuse is better than none. If I were rich, however, I'd undoubtedly get a sharp rebuke: 'Your neighbor is drowning in anguish, and you're hiding your gold under the floorboards?' How would I answer such a simple accusation?"

As he finished his story, R' Sholom grew emotional. He went on to describe, vividly and at length, the great responsibility that the rich bear. Suddenly, he raised his voice. "Ah, ah, R' Yisrael Salanter was right!" He waxed eloquent on the truth of R' Yisrael's words, and then lifted his eyes Heavenward and cried out, "*Ribbono Shel Olam* — don't make me rich!"

One of his students, a man of property, could not hold back. "R' Sholom, I don't believe you really mean that."

R' Sholom was silent for a moment. Then he smiled and said, "You're a smart one. If I were to ask you, right here and now, to say what I just said, out loud — to ask *HaKadosh Baruch Hu* in front of this group not to make you rich — you would refuse to do it. And why? Because you'd be afraid that Hashem might actually grant your request. But I — I am not afraid." He raised his voice once again and called, "*Ribbono Shel Olam, don't make me rich!*"

R' AVRAHAM TOKER TELLS THE FOLLOWING STORY. "A NEW fashion style (found in inexpensive clothing) appeared on the **"Not a** streets of modern Jerusalem, eventually penetrating **Chance!"** the edges of the *chareidi* sphere as well. I was sitting in *kollel* one day when three well-known *talmidei chachamim* [R' Moshe Kupshitz, R' Simchah Bunim Waldberg, and R' Aviezer Piltz] came over to me.

"Urgently, they said, 'R' Avraham, you know R' Yechezkel Abramsky. Come with us and ask him to deliver a *mussar* sermon to warn against the new style of dress. We will gather the Bais Yaakov students together so that the Rav can speak to them.'

"Nothing I could say deterred them from their determination to have me come along. I went with them, and we entered the Rav's house.

"R' Yechezkel raised his eyes and looked at us in surprise. There were four of us — a real mission! 'What happened? What do you want?' he asked.

"I gave him the details of the matter. 'This is the situation. We would like to hear the Rav's thoughts.'

"The *gaon* thought for a moment, then said decisively, 'You want

R' Yechezkel Abramsky; to his right is the Lutzker
Rav, R' Zalman Sorotzkin

me to speak in front of women? No! I don't speak to women!'

"We knew there was no point in arguing. There was no use in our pointing out, for instance, that the Chofetz Chaim had delivered talks to women, as had other Torah leaders. He knew all of this without our help; if he had made his decision, that was that.

"As we moved from topic to topic, R' Yechezkel raised a question about one of the verses of *Shir HaMa'alos* in *Tehillim*. He offered an explanation, then went on to explain another verse, '*Harchev picha va'amalehu* — Open your mouth wide and I will fill it.'

"'It is possible to ask for anything,' R' Yechezkel exclaimed. 'Anything! Open your mouth! We have only to *daven*, and *HaKadosh Baruch Hu* fulfills our requests. *HaKadosh Baruch Hu* gives and gives. Open your mouth in prayer — and I will fill it! We must only ask in earnest.'

"Seizing the moment, I asked hesitantly, '*HaKaodosh Baruch Hu* gives what we ask — but a human being? (In other words, we have asked for what *we* want.)'

"R' Yechezkel was quiet for a moment, and then referred apologetically to his refusal to speak in front of women. 'I am a man of full years,' he whispered, 'and the *yetzer hara* has a special interest in people at this time in their lives.' He paused, then added, 'I have known great men who reached this age, and the *yetzer hara* grabbed them. I won't give it a chance to make me stumble. I will not speak in front of women!' And he concluded sharply, 'I use the strengths that Hashem has given me only for Torah.'

"We were taken aback, both by his obvious fear and by the words that he spoke. We discussed other options, such as recording a speech to be heard by many. When we were finished threshing out the details, we left the *gaon's* home in a state of respect that bordered on awe.

"Days passed," R' Avraham Toker continues. "I knocked on R' Sholom's door in Sha'arei Chesed, and told him the whole story. R' Sholom derived great pleasure from it.

"'Such a story — what a story! And you haven't told it to me until now?' he complained energetically.

"'No, no,' I protested. 'It happened just this week.'

"R' Sholom thanked me warmly for telling him, and we parted."

The next day, on his way to yeshivah, R' Avraham saw R' Sholom standing, apparently idle, at a large crossroads. He was astonished at the sight.

"It's you I'm waiting for," he explained the moment his friend was close enough to hear. "R' Avraham! I told the story to my brother-in-law, R' Shlomo Zalman Auerbach, and he was greatly moved. He and I would like to hear again, in exact detail, the whole sequence of events: why you came to R' Yechezkel's house, what he objected to, and the precise language that was spoken: 'I won't give the *yetzer hara* even a chance.'"

R' Avraham Toker reviewed the whole episode with him until he left, satisfied. R' Sholom had waited in the street only for this.

Some two months passed. In the Sha'arei Zion hall, on Yaffo Street in Jerusalem, a large assembly took place for the purpose of welcoming newly arrived immigrants from Russia — a very unusual event in those days. R' Sholom was asked to speak at 9 p.m.

At 9:30, R' Avraham Toker saw him standing outside, near the steps.

"What's the matter?" he asked. "Why are you standing here?"

"There's some mixed seating," he answered.

R' Avraham reminded him, "These are *tinokos shenishbu* (Jews who don't know much about *Yiddishkeit*). It's very important to speak to them, especially since they're waiting for you in there."

Immediately, R' Sholom smiled, a smile filled with fear of Heaven. "Have you forgotten? *Not a chance!* What did you tell me, in the name of the *gaon*, Rav Yechezkel Abramsky? 'I won't give the *yetzer hara* a chance.'"

R' MOSHE ILIVITZKY, A MAN CLOSE TO THE CHAZON ISH, HAD A stringent custom of never eating anything that was cooked outside

Halachah and "Frumkeit"
the walls of his own home. He was careful to be discreet about this in front of outsiders, but the members of his own household were naturally aware of his personal stringency. He was a great and modest individual.

For 50 consecutive years, R' Moshe managed to observe this, without anyone being the wiser.

One time his son visited R' Sholom and related the following:

> I was once amazed to see my father pick up a fork and, without blinking an eye, begin eating in someone else's home! It was at a party to celebrate his son's engagement to the daughter of a certain well-known Torah scholar.
>
> Dumbfounded, the son asked, "Abba? In someone else's house? Have you changed your custom?" The sounds of merrymaking and celebration formed a background for his astonishment. "Abba, tell me, what happened? Fifty years … and now … What's going on? Why have you departed from your habit?"
>
> R' Moshe smiled. Leaning toward his son, he whispered in his ear, "My dear son, your new father-in-law — my *mechutan* — is the Rav of this neighborhood. This celebration is taking place in his home, with dozens of householders from the neighborhood in attendance. If they notice that the *mechutan* isn't eating the host's food, that would be a direct insult to the Rav!
>
> "The *chumrah* (stringency) that I've exerted myself to observe these past 50 years — so much so, that it has become part of my identity — is an admirable thing, but it does not

even carry the weight of a Rabbinical injunction. On the other hand, insulting a Rav and Torah scholar is forbidden in the Torah itself. That is why I am eating."

R' Sholom's eyes lit up. "*Gevaldig!* Wonderful! This is what is hinted at in the verse in *Tehillim*, 'Not in the strength of the horse does He desire, and not in the legs of man does He favor. Hashem favors those who fear Him, those who hope for His kindness.' What, one might ask, does the first thing have to do with the second? Aren't a horse's strength and fear of Heaven opposites?

"The story you've just told me about your father sheds light on the meaning of this verse. David HaMelech was not talking about horsepower and men's leg muscles. The verse is referring to serving Hashem foolishly, with a horse's strength — that is, *frumkeit* without fear of Heaven. If a *chumrah* is not rooted in genuine fear of Heaven, then a person runs here and there until he ends up running into a wall. He ends up being stringent even when such stringency is forbidden. These are not the ones that Hashem wants; He wants, rather, those who fear Him."

"EXCUSE ME, SIR," A WOMAN WHO WAS NOT YET OBSERVANT OF the mitzvos asked Rav Sholom. "The Rav has agreed to give

Those Who Fear Him me a blessing, and I know that the one who blesses places a hand on the head of the one being blessed. Why hasn't the *tzaddik* placed his hand on my head?"

R' Sholom smiled, and answered at once, "Have you ever made the blessing on the Shabbos candles?"

"Yes — on Yom Kippur eve I lit candles and said the blessing," the woman said.

"When you said the blessing, did you lay your hands on the fire?"

This answer appears to be the spontaneous fruit of a lightning-quick brain, but it has an added depth that is worthy of being addressed. Something that is forbidden is likened to fire. One does not rest his hand on fire! The reply was not merely the fruit of R' Sholom's mind, but also of his heart — the heart that burned with piety and fear of Heaven. The moment he was asked why he would not place his hand on her head, he saw a consuming fire rise up before his eyes.

(as recounted by his grandson)

THE MERE BREATH OF SIN WAS ENOUGH TO OPEN THE YAWNING chasm of *Gehinnom* beneath R' Sholom's feet. Doubts as to the

Scrupulous in Every Detail *kashrus* of certain foods deeply disturbed his equanimity. R' Yehudah Landy relates a story in which he was personally involved:

> About 20 years ago, I spent a Shabbos with R' Sholom in Netanyah. He was staying in a temporary rental apartment together with a group of *talmidei chachamim,* and during the course of Shabbos he spoke at several shuls throughout the city.
>
> During the Friday night meal, R' Sholom summoned me to his room and said. "My friend, the landlord [who provided the food], promised me in advance that all the food served here would carry the *hechsher* (*kashrus* certification) of the *Badatz*. But it seems to me that the challah I just ate came from a different bakery. Please, do me a favor and check it out for me." His face was the picture of distress and fear.
>
> As I left his room, I was afraid, too — afraid that I would find out the challahs were, indeed, not under the *Badatz* supervision and that I would be forced to tell R' Sholom the bad news. I couldn't bear to see his pain. I was ashamed to return to his room. In the end, R' Sholom himself went in search of the landlord, to clarify the situation.
>
> About two hours later, R' Sholom tracked me down. As soon as he saw me, his face was wreathed in smiles that presaged the good news he brought. "Don't worry, my friend — I checked it out, and *baruch Hashem* everything's

all right. The challos do carry the *Badatz hechsher.* We can relax."

⁐⁐

During the summer of 5718 (1958), it was R' Sholom's habit to travel to Tel Aviv every Wednesday. He would reach the city at an early hour in the morning, making sure to visit the head Pe'ilim offices on Rechov Allenby in the afternoon.

"During those hot summer days," R' Menachem Cohen relates, "R' Sholom refused all offers of food or drink that did not pass the *kashrus* criteria he had set for himself. He would refrain from eating or drinking all through the day, from early morning until his return home late at night. All he would consent to drink was water from the tap."

⁐⁐

From the year 5737 (1977), when the halachic questions were raised regarding the injections given to chickens, R' Sholom tried to avoid eating chicken until the end of his life. It is interesting — and edifying — to note the perfection of his *middos* in light of this resolution.

When his wife, the Rebbetzin, passed away, R' Sholom agreed to have a young Torah scholar live with him in his home on a regular basis. On the first *erev* Shabbos, this young man informed R' Sholom that, because of *kashrus* considerations, he refrained from eating cow's meat. "I eat only chicken," he said.

R' Sholom displayed no sign of distress at this news. Calmly, he informed his guest that he, on the contrary, refrained from eating chicken.

"So what do we do?" he asked aloud. He paused for reflection, then said genially, "In the soup and the cholent, we will put my meat and your chicken in separate bags. That way, they will both get cooked. And even though the meat will absorb the flavor of the chicken and flavor is halachically like the food itself, in the case of my *chumrah*, I will rely on Rashi and the Rambam, who rule that this halachah is Rabbinically mandated [in other words, not prohibited by the Torah itself]."

"He didn't owe me a thing," the young man marveled later. "He could have sent me away together with my *chumrahs*. Instead ..." The guest was visibly moved.

That same young *talmid chacham* continues his story. "During the period I lived with him, R' Sholom did not have the custom of being stringent with uncovered milk and water. He would cover some things and keep others uncovered. I was young then, and had the effrontery to tell him, 'The electric water kettle is always open. The water gives off steam when it boils, and the place where the steam is released is always open, even if the main portion of the vessel is covered. It is my custom to be careful about water being covered.'

"R' Sholom did not get angry with me. He went over to the cabinet, took out some aluminum foil, rolled a piece into a ball, and

R' Sholom with R' Yaakov Galinsky

used it to seal the mouth of the electric kettle. Moreover, he told his daughters when they came to help him in the house that from then on, they were not to leave the kettle open under any circumstances. 'There is a boy here who is stringent on this point,' he said firmly."

Incidentally, because R' Sholom was careful about covering water during that period, he continued this practice to the end of his life, long years after that particular young man had left his house. (He was careful from that point on to always keep his basin of morning *netilas yadayim* water covered overnight, basing this practice on the *Sha'arei Teshuvah, siman* 4; see also the *Shemiras HaGuf V'HaNefesh, siman* 44, *se'if* 6, with an explanation by Rav Kanievsky.)

⁓⁓

One Yom Kippur night, decades ago, the lights suddenly went out in the Chevron Yeshivah *beis midrash*. It was a complete electrical blackout. Within a few minutes, the problem was fixed by the electric company, and the lights went on again. But R' Sholom closed his eyes and continued his prayers by heart, in order not to benefit from the desecration of the Shabbos. When the service was over, the congregation was amazed to see R' Sholom walking toward the exit, his eyes still closed. That night, an unusually heavy rain was falling. The crowd waited inside the building's entrance for the downpour to ease up. R' Sholom waited along with the others — but with his eyes closed.

"I watched him for a quarter of an hour, and he didn't open his eyes even for a minute," recalls the teller of the tale. "Only when the rain stopped and he left the building did he open them."

Other Shabbos tidbits about R' Sholom:

R' Sholom was careful always to drink wine at the third Shabbos meal, in accordance with the Rambam's view. He also made *Kiddush* at every *seudah*, and at the third meal left the cup for *Havdalah*. He cut two challahs at every Shabbos meal, according to the custom of the Gra.

⁓⁓

R' David Mor relates: "I once borrowed R' Sholom's *tefillin*. After I had put them on, R' Sholom noticed that I was inspecting the *batim* from all sides. He smiled and said, 'I, too, once delved deeply into the matter of *tefillin*.' And I understood from this that he was referring to the stringency he had taken upon himself, pertaining to the type of parchment used in his *tefillin*."

An especially famous innovation of R' Sholom's with regard to *tefillin* was his suggestion for a method of forming the *"shin"* on the *bayis* in a manner calculated to remove certain potential problems. His suggestion quickly spread among the ranks of Jerusalem's *tefillin*-makers, and was implemented for many years (until recently, when a more modern method was instituted in its place).

∾∾

R' David Mor further relates: "R' Sholom took particular care in the area of *mezuzahs*. On his frequent travels, those close to him knew that his entry into a new house always necessitated a quick look at the placement of the *mezuzahs* and the manner in which they were put up.

"I once accompanied him to a place in Telz-Stone where we would be staying over Shabbos. Immediately upon reaching the doorstep, R' Sholom noticed a small problem. He raised his eyes to the *mezuzah* and, lifting his stick in its direction, brought to our attention the fact that the *mezuzah* had not been properly placed according to all opinions."

R' Yisrael Katzenelenbogen related the following story, which he heard from his grandfather, R' Sholom. R' Sholom spoke of the *mezuzahs* in his own home. "When I learned the laws of *tefillin* and the way the letters must be written, as described by my grandfather, the Maharsham, I decided to check my *mezuzahs*. I sat down and inspected the letters — and discovered that they were not perfect, especially the letter *yud*. According to the Maharsham and other halachic authorities, there was a small suspicion that the *mezuzahs* were *pasul* (disqualified for use).

"What was I to do about this halachic suspicion?

"Financially, we were in very difficult circumstances. We had no money even for meat or chicken. I thought about this as I walked down the street. Not a penny in my pocket, but … the *mezuzahs*! I took a few more steps, then entered Rechov Betzalel, near Sha'arei Chesed. It was at this point that I decided, 'Throw your burden onto Hashem.' For the purposes of a mitzvah it is permissible to borrow money, even when one is in the kind of dire financial straits that I found myself in at that time. I went to see a pious *sofer* (scribe) who was good at writing new *mezuzahs* according to specific instructions. I ordered the *mezuzahs*.

"I left the *sofer's* house and walked back toward my own home. When I reached my doorway, a man was waiting there for me.

"I greeted him, and asked what he wanted.

"He was interested in my book, *Da'as Torah Maharsham*. We went inside. The man was English; he bought my books and paid me 42 pounds sterling.

"That was the exact price — no more, no less — of the five *mezuzahs* I had ordered! I went back to the *sofer* that very night and paid for them."

❧

R' Sholom related an enlightening episode regarding a *mezuzah* and R' Leib Chasman, his rebbe.

> We were to accompany our elderly rebbe, R' Yehudah Leib Chasman, *mashgiach* of Chevron Yeshivah. We left the yeshivah building on Rechov Chaggai, and walked behind him in respectful silence. We had traversed about 100 meters when, suddenly, the *mashgiach* stopped, turned around, and began retracing his steps — all the way back to the yeshivah.
>
> When he reached the doorstep, he lifted his hand, brought his fingers close to the *mezuzah*, and let them rest

on it for a moment. Then he did another about-face and re-turned the way he had come.

The reason for his behavior was simple: The *mashgiach* had forgotten to rest his hand on the *mezuzah* when we'd left, and had returned for that purpose. (His custom was not to kiss the *mezuzah*, but only to rest his hand on it, in ac-cordance with the language of the *Shulchan Aruch*.)

⁓⁓

On one of his tapes, R' Sholom tells another interesting episode about *mezuzahs*:

My friend, R' Yitzchak Greenberg, once approached me in the Chevron Yeshivah *beis midrash* and said, "R' Sholom, do you want to see something nice? Come, and I'll show you."

From his bag, he removed a *mezuzah* and showed me the letter *beis* that appears in the word *levanecha*. The letter had a tiny hole, rendering the *mezuzah* unfit for use.

"What is the meaning of this *mezuzah*?" I asked. "What's the story behind it?"

"We have a neighbor in Petach Tikvah," R' Yitzchak said, "a secular Jew who does not observe the Shabbos. His wife had suffered repeated miscarriages, and he was broken-hearted.

"I suggested," R' Yitzchak continued, "that he go see the Chazon Ish. The man had heard of him, and decided to ac-cept my suggestion. He would travel to Bnei Brak to see the Chazon Ish.

"I went on ahead of him," R' Yitzchak said. "I went to the Chazon Ish and told him that a certain man was planning to come to see him, a man who desecrated the Shabbos. Here was an opportunity to help him mend his ways.

"A number of days passed, and the man duly went to see the Chazon Ish to pour out his story. The Chazon Ish lis-tened intently. When the man had finished, the Chazon Ish told him, 'Ask your neighbor, R' Yitzchak Greenberg, to check your *mezuzahs*. If he finds one that is unfit for use, he is to replace it with another.'

"My neighbor came to me," R' Yitzchak went on, "to ask me to do what the Chazon Ish had suggested. I asked him whether the Chazon Ish had discussed any other subjects with him, and he replied in the negative. 'The Chazon Ish just suggested that I ask you to check my *mezuzahs*, nothing more,' he said.

"I went into his apartment and began to inspect the *mezuzahs*. On one of them — the one I showed you just now, R' Sholom — I found a hole in the word *levanecha* — 'your sons.'

"I traveled back to the Chazon Ish," R' Yitzchak said, and asked him, 'But you had a chance to turn him into a *ba'al teshuvah!*'

"The Chazon Ish responded with a few brief words: 'We are not merchants.' (In other words, when a man comes to ask a specific question, we may answer that question without receiving anything in return — even spiritually.) 'Hashem made us straight and that is the way we must always deal with people — straight!'"

R' Sholom concludes, "I told this story to R' Dov Yaffe, who said that he, too, had had a similar experience. He had sent a secular neighbor to the Chazon Ish for the same problem, and the Chazon Ish had told him to be careful not to throw his fingernails onto the ground (as this is said to lead to miscarriages). From that time, the miscarriages stopped.

"I, too, pointed out to the Chazon Ish that he had had the chance to make a *ba'al teshuvah* out of the fellow. To which the Chazon Ish replied, 'We are not merchants.'"

R' SHOLOM'S NATURAL *YIRAS SHAMAYIM* RAISED A GREAT many halachic questions in a wide variety of different areas of the
Questions Torah. In these matters, it was his practice to consult with his brother-in-law, R' Shlomo Zalman

R' Sholom discussing halachah with his brother-in-law, R' Shlomo Zalman Auerbach

Auerbach. There were periods when he established regular telephone appointments with his brother-in-law every day after *Shacharis* to discuss these questions. R' Shlomo Zalman was his rabbi and halachic authority (after the Tchebiner Rav had departed this world).

A grandson, R' Meir Stern, relates that R' Sholom once told him that R' Shlomo Zalman had the habit of saying to those close to him: "If one knows the halachah with clarity, many doubts fall away. Many questions that arise for young people learning Torah derive from the fact that they do not know the ins and outs of the *sugya,* in all its detail."

"But those who are great in Torah also find halachic questions sprouting up all the time," R' Sholom added on another occasion. He told of R' David Baharan, who once said, "I don't know how people can walk down the street peacefully, without doubts about the very practical halachos that are around us all the time — the halachos of the blessings said over fruit. For me," R' David said, "not a day goes by without a new question on the laws of *berachos.*"

We will take this opportunity to draw a thumbnail sketch of R' David Baharan, in R' Sholom's own words:

> R' David Bahran was born to R' Nachum of Shadik and, like his father, was a pure and holy man. He knew *Shas* by heart and was known as the "expert in halachah." In eulogizing him after his death, the words of *Chazal* were applied to him: "Everyone who saw David remembered the halachah." When people looked at R' David, they saw

halachah. When he walked, when he sat down, when he ate, and when he recited a blessing, you saw halachah. "The expert in halachah! A walking *Shulchan Aruch!*"

It was well known that R' David had the custom of separating *terumos* and *ma'asros* (tithes) from fruits and vegetables on behalf of all of *Eretz Yisrael*. In this regard, he came up with many wonderful and original twists of halachah. "He showed me," said R' Sholom, "where he had written in his *siddur*, just before *U'va L'Tziyon*: 'Remember to separate *ma'aser* for everyone.'"

It was R' David Baharan who supervised the *mikveh* in Sha'arei Chesed. It was he who stepped inside the *mikveh* before it was filled, to check the walls and floors. He personally filled the *mikveh* with the proper amounts of water of the appropriate types. He took full responsibility.

"One *erev* Shabbos," R' Sholom related, "I had just returned from the *mikveh* when my wife said, 'R' Sholom, I see from the window that R' David Baharan has been following you all the way to our house.' I ran out to meet him, to see what he wanted. Though I begged him not to bother himself to come inside, he walked to the doorway with me. Near the door, he took off the slippers he was wearing and left them beside the door, explaining, 'Friday is when the floors get washed.' (R' Chaim Todros Hirschler would do the same when entering his home.) We sat down.

"'R' Sholom, I want to ask you a question,' R' David said. 'How much do you pay to enter the *mikveh* on Fridays?'

"Astonished at the question, I nevertheless answered immediately, 'Half a shilling.'

"'*Oy vey!*' he lamented. 'You pay half a shilling, and apparently everyone pays the same thing — but they charge me just two *agurot!* The reason, no doubt, is because I concern myself with supervising the *mikveh*. In that case, I have to worry about the Gemara that says that if a person receives compensation for rendering judgment, his judgment is nullified; if for acting as a witness, his testimony is void... I am afraid.'

"I saw the pain on his face and tried to ease his mind by saying confidently, 'No, no, it's possible that other people also pay the small fee of two *agurot*. The fact that I pay what I pay is no proof of anything. You may be calm!' But I had not only *not* reassured him — I actually added to his pain.

"R' David left my house and walked the long distance to the neighborhood where his son lived, in order to ask him the same question: 'How much do you pay?'

"His son's answer: 'Half a shilling.'"

It was R' David Baharan's custom to go to shul at midnight, in accordance with the teachings of *Chazal* that says, "I have never spent a midnight in sleep."

"At different times in my younger days," related R' Sholom, "I would follow him to shul at this hour. Once, when R' David encountered me at night, he turned to me and said, 'I've been wondering if I should stop *davening* in shul. Maybe I should *daven* at home instead. Why? I am already old, and there is a mitzvah in the Torah to rise for the elderly. When I walk into shul, there are some who do not rise. In other words, I am causing them to stumble. Why do I need to make others fall into error because of me? I've been thinking and thinking about whether or not I should stop coming to shul.'

"On another occasion, too, I met R' David at midnight and was again privileged to speak with him. He told me that, on that particular night, he had been in shul all night (as opposed to his usual habit of coming at midnight and remaining until dawn). What had occurred on this night to change his pattern? There was a simple answer. Ever since his wife had passed away, R' David had made his home with his daughter-in-law. On that night, there was a possibility of *yichud*, and he refused to remain in the house for a minute — making his way, instead, to shul."

R' Sholom concluded his remarks with another story.

"When I was a young boy, I happened by chance to enter the shul where R' David Baharan sat. It was on a weekday, between *Minchah* and *Ma'ariv*. While the congregation prepared for *Ma'ariv*, I sat and learned. Then I stood up, washed my hands, and returned to my seat. Glancing over at R' David, I noticed that he was preparing for *Ma'ariv* but had not washed his hands for *davening*. The *Shulchan Aruch* cites this as obligatory. I was amazed.

"A moment later, I found the *tzaddik* himself beside me.

"'Young man,' he said pleasantly, 'I washed my hands before *Minchah* with the intention of including *Ma'ariv*. That's why I did not wash my hands just now.'

"It was as though he had read my mind.

"That was R' David Baharan."

R' SHOLOM'S SON, R' YITZCHAK SCHWADRON, TOLD THE FOLlowing story.

What to Do? Just Stop! R' Sholom was in a taxi on his way to the airport to begin one of his trips abroad. After traveling some distance, R' Sholom suddenly remembered that he had left his cigarettes at home.

He couldn't go back. R' Sholom was very careful about R' Yehudah HaChassid's injunction never to return home after setting out on a journey.

He couldn't buy cigarettes on the plane. It was a *shemittah* year, and R' Sholom smoked only those cigarettes that he had ascertained were free of any suspicion of halachic impropriety. What, then, was he to do?

The answer was clear. "I'll stop smoking!"

His son adds: "The next time he traveled abroad (this time, via the port at Haifa), he had already left Sha'arei Chesed when he remembered that he had neglected to see a certain person whom it would be a mitzvah to visit and encourage.

"We're going back to Sha'arei Chesed," he informed the driver. "You'll receive your full payment. I just forgot something."

R' Sholom stepped into the room of the man he had forgotten to visit, his face glowing. He said not a word about the taxi waiting outside to carry him off to Haifa.

"R' Sholom, you came at just the right moment!" the man said. "I am feeling so depressed. You're bringing me back to life! No one else has come to visit, and the loneliness is very hard for me. You have earned a very great *mitzvah*."

R' Sholom sat down and began conversing tranquilly with the man. After all, was it possible to leave after such a welcome? Was it possible to get up and go, when his abrupt departure was liable to cast the man back into depression again?

He drew out his visit as long as he could. Eventually, there was a knock at the door, and the impatient driver announced tensely, "Honored rabbi, the boat is about to set sail. You'll be late."

Even then, R' Sholom lingered another few moments. He reached the port half an hour late — only to learn that an unexpected delay had prevented the boat from sailing on time.

THERE IS A STORY RECOUNTED BY R' SHOLOM'S DAUGHTER that offers an appropriate capstone to our discussion of R' **The Sure** Sholom's fealty to Halachah. It speaks for itself as **Route** testimony to how his every action was guided by the Shulchan Aruch:

> Before a Yom Tov, there was a simple way to ask Abba for money without making him upset. For example, I had one Shabbos dress, and there was no money to buy another one. What did I do? I waited patiently for *erev* Yom Tov, then went over to my father and said, "It's forbidden to wash laundry on *Chol HaMo'ed*, but I have to wash. I have only one dress!"
>
> The halachic problem instantly galvanized Abba — and I got my new dress. That was the way to approach my father. *Halachah!*
>
> Incidentally, during the rest of the year, Abba did not let us play instruments (as explained in the *Shulchan Aruch*). But when the holidays came, he was always careful to give us money to rent an accordion for *Chol HaMo'ed*. Our family celebrated with great joy during all the days of the *chag*.
>
> Our personal happiness came to us by way of the *Shulchan Aruch!*

IN THE TWILIGHT OF R' SHOLOM'S LIFE, AFTER SUFFERING FROM a second severe illness, it was decided that the most sensible course of action was to move him into the home of one of his daughters. He left the hospital, climbed into a taxi, and traveled to his daughter in Bnei Brak. Weak, exhausted, and ill, he arrived at her house, *davened Ma'ariv*, and immediately afterwards fell into a deep sleep. The coils of sleep held him fast until morning.

Strong as a Lion

His grandson described that morning to us:

"The time had come for saying *K'rias Shema*, and I went over to wake Saba. But Saba was sleeping so soundly that nothing I did woke him. I pounded on the blankets, I blew in his ear, I pleaded with him to awaken — all to no avail.

"I summoned another family member and he tried, too. At one point, Saba finally opened his eyes, but quickly fell asleep again.

"'His daughter entered the room and said, 'Come, I'll show you how to wake my father.' She walked over to the bed and called loudly, 'Abba! It's time to say *K'rias Shema*! In a few minutes, the *zeman* will be over!'

"At once — and this is no exaggeration — R' Sholom fully opened his eyes, lifted his hands, and used them to push back the thick blanket that covered him. Drowsy and weak as he was, he nevertheless eased both legs off the bed at once, set them on the floor, and sat up.

"'*Oy! Oy!* Why didn't anyone tell me? In just a few minutes the *zeman* will be over.' He peered at his watch in anguish.

"The others soothed him, telling him that there was still enough time to *daven*, and that even if he was late, he would certainly be in time for the second *zeman*, according to the Gra. R' Sholom's calm was restored. With his ever-present smile, he beamed, 'Thank you! Thank you all!' and shakily stood up."

That was the Jerusalem *Maggid*'s first morning in Bnei Brak. From then on, he made every effort to rise regularly for the *vasikin minyan*, the way he had for scores of years back home. It was an awesome sight: Each morning, in the darkness before dawn, someone would tiptoe over to his bed and whisper in his ear, "Saba, we're going to *vasikin*." And he would stir, then sit up quickly, strong as a lion to conquer his own weakness, and rise to meet the day. And that was the way it continued for him, until the day when half his body became paralyzed and he was unable to function in the same way.

⌒⌒

One Shabbos, also in his latter days, after a meal shared with his daughter, R' Sholom grew tired and lay down to sleep. Suddenly, he sprang up in bed, climbed out, and went to sit at the table. Here, too, he nodded off, but roused himself and made a powerful effort not to sleep.

His grandson, who was staying with R' Sholom, asked him to explain his actions.

"You, my dear grandson, are off to the yeshivah to learn. Your mother has left the house, and will return only a few hours from now. I don't remember whether or not I asked her to wake me for *Minchah*. I'm afraid that I won't wake up in time."

The daughter returned some 3 hours later and went directly to her room for a Shabbos nap. It was not until she was sound asleep that R' Sholom realized she was home. He refused to wake her in order to ask whether she had promised to wake him for *Minchah*. Instead, for 5 hours on a long summer Shabbos afternoon, R' Sholom struggled against his own exhaustion, determined to stay awake.

When his daughter woke from her nap, R' Sholom told her, "I couldn't rest, because I didn't remember whether I had asked you to wake me for *Minchah*. Please wake me in half an hour." Only then, half an hour before *Minchah*, did he lie down, completely spent.

Thirty minutes later he rose like a lion to go to shul.

NEAR THE END OF HIS DAYS, R' SHOLOM BECAME TOO WEAK TO walk. He was taken to shul each day in a wheelchair. When the time **To Stand and** came to recite the *Bircas Kohanim* (the priestly **to Serve** blessing, recited daily in *Eretz Yisrael*), someone would bring him water to wash his hands, after which he would stand up on trembling legs to say the blessing in his place. Battling his own monumental weakness, he tried with all his might to stand whenever standing was required during the service.

R' Yeshaya Bronfeld describes *davening* beside R' Sholom during that period of his life:

R' Sholom on his last visit to the Kosel HaMa'aravi. To his right is R' Yisrael Chinkis.

I was standing beside him. At the beginning of *Pesukei D'Zimrah* I saw him try to stand up, and fail. He tried again — and this time, succeeded in getting to his feet. Moving closer, I heard him say *Mizmor L'sodah*. The next day, at the same place in *davening*, R' Sholom took hold of his *shtender* and tried to rise, his face turning red until he managed to get his footing. It's true that the *Shulchan Aruch* says to stand at *Mizmor L'sodah*, but I couldn't believe my eyes when I saw that the *gaon hatzaddik* R' Sholom had not attempted to find a loophole for age and illness that would permit him to sit.

During that period of his life, R' Sholom's physical condition deteriorated still further. He tried mightily to stand during *Kiddush Levanah* but, with the entire left side of his body paralyzed, he was unable to rise. Despite his almost nonexistent energy, R' Sholom began to call out, "Stand me up! Stand me up!" None of those present was able to refuse. Two of them supported him from either side. R'

Sholom murmured a few words from a standing position — all he was capable of doing. But even those few words spread a blanket of tranquility over his suffering features.

IN THE FINAL YEAR OF HIS LIFE, WITH HALF HIS BODY PARAlyzed and the other half in frail condition, his head bowed with **The** age, R' Sholom regularly participated in every **Last Year** Shabbos *seudah,* together with his family (in his daughter's home in Bnei Brak). Once, just months before he left this world, he raised his voice suddenly and shouted: *"Borer! Borer!"* He was staring across the table at one person's plate, where he had observed a transgression of the Shabbos prohibition of *borer* (separating the bad from the good).

And again, just a week before his passing, in the hospital's intensive care unit, he opened his eyes and cast his still penetrating gaze at his grandson, a signal to indicate that he had noticed an alteration in some halachic point. The grandson grew very excited. It was hard to believe that his grandfather, lost in a fog of illness, was not lost at all when it came to the *Shulchan Aruch.*

To the very end, where halachah was concerned, R' Sholom's vision remained clear and true.

Chapter 9

A Penetrating Voice

STRONG WIND BLEW INTO R' SHOLOM'S FACE, AND flakes of snow danced around him in the frigid air. The streets were silent. The *Maggid* walked slowly, taking care not to slip. Suddenly, he stopped short, struck by a thought. Suppose he would turn around and go back into his warm house? The walk was long and difficult — and who, after all, would be coming out to hear him speak in such weather?

Hesitantly, he resumed his walk. "Who knows? Maybe a few people will show up. I have to be concerned with whoever wants to listen. It's worthwhile making the effort even for one individual!" He continued slowly, step by step, his breath escaping in small puffs into the freezing air.

Wrapped in dripping overcoats and walking briskly in the cold, Jerusalem's Jews came to the Zichron Moshe Shul. One by one they entered, deposited their *shtreimels* in their accustomed places, and took their usual seats. There was one pressing question on everyone's mind: Would R' Sholom put in an appearance tonight? He was no longer a young man. Would his strength permit him to walk such a long way in such stormy weather? From time to time, expectant glances were directed to the door. Each new person entering represented a fresh burden of disappointment. No, it was not R' Sholom. He had not yet arrived.

By the time R' Sholom himself stepped through the door, the shul was filled to capacity. Men stood in the aisles and sat on the steamy windowsills. The weather had not deterred this crowd. To put it quite

simply — they loved him. They loved his sweet words, and his fiery love for Torah, which no Jerusalem snowstorm could ever dampen.

R' Sholom walked up to the Holy Ark. From his place in front of the Ark, his voice sliced through the air, slowly at first, as was his custom. Soon, he was drawing a portrait of a mythical man named "Yankel." Reb Yankel learned in a *kollel* in the mornings and studied further on his own in shul in the afternoons. His livelihood was not thriving, however, so he made a decision. He would take up accounting at night.

"That Shabbos, between the reading of the Torah and the Mussaf service," R' Sholom related, "R' Baruch, seated next to him, clapped him on the shoulder in a friendly fashion. 'So what are doing with yourself these days, Reb Yankel?'

"Reb Yankel hesitated, reflected, blushed, and finally stammered, 'I'm in accounting.'"

R' Sholom's voice rose. "He is ashamed to say that he wastes his time! It's not easy for him to look his friend in the face and announce, 'I'm a yeshivah man!'" The *Maggid* fell into a melodious chant. "What is he ashamed of? What is he avoiding? Why is he walking around depressed? He's learning Torah, and that should be the pinnacle of pride! Why is he setting his sights lower? Instead of rejoicing and standing tall because he is performing Hashem's will — he is depressed. Amazing!

"Reb Yankel himself senses no problem with his reaction. Instead of pride, he feels embarrassment. Instead of understanding that the world exists in his merit, he casts his eyes down. The walls of the *beis midrash* do not appear worthy in those eyes. All day long, he carries the world upon his shoulders — yet he draws pride from his secular work. 'I'm in accounting.'"

The atmosphere in the Zichron Moshe Shul was rife with hidden pain. Beneath the *Maggid's* keen eye and incisive words, men stirred uneasily in their seats. Then, suddenly, a broad smile flashed onto R' Sholom's glowing face — a smile that caused the tension to dissipate all at once. "I just remembered a fantastic story!" The crowd breathed deeply, relieved at the introduction to this other side of R' Sholom. He was a man of many aspects, a man who, by turns, could rebuke and caress, criticize and soothe, pierce the heart and then make it rejoice.

In Eretz Yisrael 60 or 70 years ago, the concept of a *kollel* was almost unknown. The old *yishuv* was poverty stricken and apathetic. Today, *baruch Hashem*, the story is far different. "Yes, I'm an accountant — but I learn in the evenings. I'm a yeshivah man!"

R' Sholom was instrumental in bringing about this revolution. He traveled great distances in order to spread his love for Torah. His message began in Sha'arei Chesed and spread throughout the world. Zichron Moshe, Bucharim, Tel Aviv, Boro Park, London, and Antwerp were some of the places where R' Sholom raised his flag for the Torah revolution. He laid down roads and paved highways leading directly to Torah and piety. "A yeshivah man" was the dominant image in the talks he gave. R' Sholom poured the foundation that would allow these men to stand with pride. "A yeshivah man!"

The words are carved in the memories of all who heard them. They flew from the *Maggid's* heart to penetrate the hearts of his listeners. Many began to view their own lives and the source of their contentment in a new and different light.

"A yeshivah man!"

REB SHOLOM WAS NOT CONTENT WITH SIMPLY SPEAKING TO those who came to hear him. Often, he went to them to insure that

Into the Lions' Den the Torah's message was heard. And often his influence was profound and long lasting.

"A long striped coat, an old *shtreimel*, and a long beard. These were my impressions as I gazed up at the figure standing before the crowd in the great Yeshurun Synagogue. He was crying aloud from his heart."

That scene remains clearly etched in the memory of the *talmid chacham* who shared this story with us. He was 10 years old at the

time and was at the Yeshurun Synagogue one Shabbos when, at the end of *davening*, a strange sight met his young eyes.

"Shabbos, Shabbos!" resounded suddenly through the great hall. The worshipers exchanged startled glances. What was going on?

R' Sholom — though at the time the lad did not know who he was — had entered the shul. He stepped briskly up to the *Aron Kodesh*, then turned to face the audience.

"Shabbos!" he cried. "There are people who drive here on Shabbos. They are sitting among you and *davening*. After *davening* is over, they get into their cars, *Rachmanah litzlan*. Shabbos! Shabbos!" His strong voice echoed through the room.

Many of the shul's most prominent and distinguished members were among those present. They, along with others, were outraged. A total stranger had dared address them without bothering to request permission, and was standing there berating and attacking them! He was criticizing them for desecrating the Shabbos. What chutzpah! The congregation stirred uneasily in their seats.

All at once, a commotion broke out. Worshipers began shouting out their opinions — some in support of the stranger's words and others just as vehemently opposed. A few men decided to take action. They approached R' Sholom with the intention of removing him by force.

R' Sholom remained calmly in place.

"I stood among the others and listened as the decision was made to remove the speaker by force," relates the teller of the tale. "But Mordechai Frieman of *Kol Yisrael* stopped them. He calmed the crowd and asked them to let R' Sholom finish what he had to say."

R' Sholom concluded his remarks. Then he stepped away from the podium and left the shul.

"The incident aroused many emotions within me," the man recalls.

"Here was a man who had delivered a spontaneous rebuke, with no ulterior motive and at great personal risk. No one had asked him to worry about the whole world. He could have gone home to enjoy his Shabbos meal together with his family instead of volunteering to endanger himself in such a fashion.

"R' Sholom did not need any witness to his heroism. It was Heaven's honor that burned in him — and that brought him right into the lions' den. And that lesson has stayed with me since then."

AT THE HEIGHT OF HIS ORATORY, R' SHOLOM FELL ABRUPTLY silent. He had been talking about R' Eliyahu Lopian. The silence

Explosion stretched.

Even when he was not speaking, his audience

found him interesting to watch. They saw him push his glasses up, then lift a finger to the corner of one eye to wipe away a tear. Perhaps the tear came from the words of *mussar* he had just been quoting — or was it a tear of longing for the days he had spent with R' Eliyahu Lopian?

The audience was still wondering, when R' Sholom blurted out, "Ah, R' Elenkeh, R' Elenkeh (his respectfully affectionate nickname for R' Lopian) — how smart he was! How he knew how to plumb the depths of the human heart." He straightened his back, stroked his beard, and began speaking fluently once more.

"A Jew places his Chanukah lights higher than 20 *amah*. He takes the trouble to climb up and place his light just there. Why? What happened? The Gemara tells us that a candle like this is *pasul* (disqualified). Let us open the Gemara and read inside." As a rule, R' Sholom did not read aloud from the Gemara during his sermons, preferring to quote passages from memory. This time, however, he removed his glasses, brought the volume close to his eyes, and read:

"Rav Kahana said in the name of R' Tanchum that a Chanukah candle that is placed higher than 20 amah is disqualified. And R' Kahana said in the name of R' Tanchum: Why does it say, 'And the pit was empty, it contained no water'? If it says that the pit was empty, don't I know that it contained no water? Rather, it is coming to teach that it contained no water, but it did contain snakes and scorpions."

"What," asked R' Sholom, "is the connection between these two statements? Everyone asks that question — an intriguing one. *Talmidei chachamim* have already offered their explanations, but I want to ask again: Why would a Jew decide to place his candle higher than 20 *amah*?

"He is embarrassed. Ah, ah, he is embarrassed. He doesn't want the people in the street to see. Now we come to the continuation of R' Tanchum's words: 'And the pit was empty, it contained no water.'" A hand came down forcefully on the *shtender*, the blow resounding in the quiet shul. R' Sholom roared, "The pit was empty, it had no water. It had no Torah! Not only is it empty, it is a void, an abomination! It contains snakes and scorpions! What is that man afraid of? Why is he ashamed?"

R' Sholom's smile was tinged with visible anger. "To eat a pita in the middle of the street doesn't embarrass him. To sit on a chair in the middle of Rechov Yaffo and lick an ice cream in the faces of the passersby is not embarrassing. But lighting a Chanukah candle is something to be ashamed of. Who are you trying to hide from, you fool?" He might almost have been speaking to a particular person in the room.

In a lowered voice, he continued sadly, "I was walking down the street near a certain school and I glanced into the schoolyard. What did I see? Two groups of unfortunate children, *tinokos shenishbu*, who have not yet sinned. A teacher stood in a clearing between the two groups. I stopped to watch what they were doing. Suddenly, two boys — one from each group — ran into the clearing. Before I could blink my eyes, they began to fight with all their might. Their fists rained blows on one another, and their feet kicked each other with youthful energy. On both sides, the other boys were shouting, 'Give it to him in the teeth! Give it to him in the teeth!'

"This is Culture?" R' Sholom exclaimed. "Is it for *this* that you are embarrassed?"

With a sigh, he finished, "'And the pit was empty, it contained no water.' As our Sages have explained, there is no water but Torah."

The "street" was a powerful phenomenon in R' Sholom's day, attracting young people like a magnet. R' Sholom did his best to try and break the spell. To young Jews, he said, "Let's take the 'street' that so intimidates you — the policies, the political parties, the desires, the fantasies, and drag them all into the *beis knesses!*" He showed young people exactly what the "street" was, then exploded the illusion right before their eyes. The whole shallow edifice shattered into a million tiny pieces at one blow. That was R' Sholom's unique power.

His method of mocking secularism gave strength to many, and blazed the way for others to follow in their own sermons. R' Sholom was the supporting wall on which numerous families leaned, and the foundation upon which countless homes were built. He spread his word not only in *Eretz Yisrael*, but abroad as well. One native Israeli chanced to be in London years ago, and went into a shul on a Shabbos afternoon.

"The shul was packed from end to end, so that I could hardly walk in. R' Sholom stood on the steps leading to the *Aron Kodesh*, relating to everyone exactly what it was that filled the streets of London. He made fun of the race after money, the empty wealth ... This is one of the gifts that R' Sholom has given our generation."

"I'll never forget," another man says, "the time R' Sholom read aloud to us from the *Mesillas Yesharim*."

"'Because man was not created except to take pleasure in Hashem,'" R' Sholom read. "*Rabbosai!* A person was created for pleasure, for enjoyment — that is his purpose. It is Hashem's will that we enjoy. That we take pleasure!" He paused. "To take pleasure in what? In a cup of ice cream? In a cigarette? In sleeping 18 hours at a stretch? In what, exactly, shall we take pleasure? In foolishness? In emptiness?

"No, no, *rabbosai* — 'in Hashem!' To take pleasure in Hashem and bask in His *Shechinah*, which is true pleasure and the greatest delight of all. And the true location of that delight is the World to Come."

R' Sholom had a special power to help others view their own pathetic desires and fantasies in their true light. He took lofty concepts and carried them down to where the simplest person could grasp them. He gilded the depths of *mussar* with a golden patina that made them accessible to all.

A well-known Torah scholar relates, "I knew an unfortunate individual who struggled with all kinds of difficulties, and who rose and fell spiritually, over and over again. He wandered abroad, passing through different phases in his mitzvah observance.

"This man told me that whenever he would find himself in a particularly difficult situation and wished to rise above it, he would seize a few moments of quiet, close his eyes, and imagine one of R' Sholom's sermons: the pleasing voice, the melodious chant, the emotion. The vision carried him back to earlier good times in the Zichron Moshe Shul with R' Sholom. In this way, the man felt strengthened and was able to stabilize his life."

Wherever he may be, across the length and breadth of America, a forlorn man can close his eyes, concentrate on a particular talk delivered once, long ago, and far away, by R' Sholom, and emerge strengthened.

And this is only one such story among thousands.

One Newspaper Reporter

ONE SUMMER'S DAY IN THE YEAR 5718 (1958), A SECULAR NEWS-paper reporter entered R' Sholom's house and asked him the secret of his successful sermons.

R' Sholom smiled at the question. "I don't know if I'm successful or not. Let's try an experiment. I will deliver a talk to you, and when I've finished, you will decide for yourself what the secret of success is."

The sermon was delivered in his house in Sha'arei Chesed, in the tranquil atmosphere engendered by the thousands of volumes of *sifrei kodesh* lining the walls. The table, too, was covered with holy books. As the reporter sat opposite R' Sholom on one of the ancient wooden chairs, his host, radiating love of Torah and deeply felt piety, spoke at length.

When the sermon was over, the reporter's eyes filled with tears — Jewish tears. He went home and composed a long article for *Ha'aretz* newspaper. The article quoted a sermon which, he said, R' Sholom had delivered in the Zichron Moshe Shul, but which he had actually heard all by himself, an audience of one, in R' Sholom's own home.

Here is the article:

Preaching Without Reward

As is well known, people are not eager to hear a sermon, not from those close to them and certainly not from a stranger. But great crowds stream to hear the sermons of R' Sholom Schwadron, the famous Jerusalem "*Maggid*," especially when a Jewish holiday is approaching in the capital city.

המטיף שלא על מנת לקבל פרס

מאת שלמה גרבר

בידוע שאין בני-אדם להוטים לש־
מוע. הטפת מוסר, לא מקרוביהם ו־
על אחת כמה וכמה לא מזרים. אולם
את דרשות המוסר והסטורי של ה־
רב שלום שבדרון, "המגיד" הירושלמי
הידוע, נוהרים לשמוע המונים רבים,
בעיקר מקרב החוגים הדתיים בעירה.
בכל ליל שבת, לאחר הסעודה,
מגיעים לבית הכנסת הגדול בשכונת
זכרון-משה, שם נושא הרב שבדרון
את דרשותיו, מאות רבות של זקנים
וצעירים, נשים וטף מכל חלקי העיר,
יושבים ועומדים דחוקים וצפופים ב־
משך שעות, ומאזינים בפה פעור מ־
מש לדברי חוצב להבות ואמרי הנו־
עם של הרב שבדרון. תורת הנאום נ־
היתה לו. "הוא נואם בחסד עליון",
אומרים עליו הבקי-ז־ת. יודע הוא מתי
להרים קולו ומתי להנמיכו, מתי לס־
פוח בחזקה על השולחן שלפניו, מתי
לנופף בידיו, מתי להשמיע דבריו בנ־
גון חסידי, ומתי לנענע את גומו לק־
צב דבריו — ולכבוש את קהל מאזיניו
ולהחדיר ללבם את דברי המוסר הח־
ריפים, המתובלים בדברי חז"ל, ב־
פסוקים, בסיפורי חסידים ומתנגדים,
וכדומה.
ניכר בו ברב שבדרון, הן בדרשו־
תיו הן באורח חייו, כי כואב הוא את
כאבם של אלה הראאים, ועיניהם לוט,
את חוסר האמונה והכפירה בבורא־

בקופסת גפרורים? ואילו העולם הפלאי
והנורא — זה נברא מעצמו? אין
חושבים ואין יודעים הדבר הברור, ש־
כל איש העומד על דעתו יודע זאת, ש־
הכרת הוא שיש בורא עולם!" מטיח
הוא כלפי הכופרים האלמונים.
"הייתי ילד כבן שבע" — מעלה
המגיד זכרונות מימי ילדותו, כשעיניו
יורקות אש — "זכורני שישבתי על
מדרגות ביתי, בלילה, כשלוש שעות.

הרב שלום שבדרון

יצרו. בהתבוננות׳ במסירות ובכנות,
כמובן לא ברגע אחד, יכול הוא לשנות
את טבעו על ידי התרגלות במעשה —
כמו שאמרו חכמים, הרגל נעשה טבע
שני. כל המידות הטובות, אם אינן מו־
שרשות באמונת בורא-עולם סתורות
ונסתרות במעשי האדם, שעל פי הרוב
הוא גולד גם עם מידות מגונות".
לדעת הרב שבדרון אין עצה אחרת
אלא "לא להתברייש, להשפיל את הגא־
וה ולהתתודות: זנחנו את דעת אבו־
תינו. חשבנו כי חכמים אנחנו מהם, כי
הם הטועים ואנו המבינים. עתה אנו
רואים עד כמה צדקו, רצונם היה חזק
להחיות אותנו, לרומם אותנו, לעשות
אותנו ל... איך אומרים גליקליך? לע־
אשרים, בעולם הזה ובעולם הבא. טי־
עינו בטי"ת ותעינו בתי"ו. היתענו ב־
טי"ת והיתענו בתי"ו. אפילו התודעה
היהודית, ששר-החינוך מנסה להכניס
לבתי הסתר, אין הוא יכול להמליץ
עליה בפני תלמידים מוכשרים, כיון
שהם עשויים לשאול אותו: האם גם
אתה נוהג לפי מה שהינותך? רק אם
מנהיגי העם יראו את ההכרח הגדול,
שישרבו הם לפתוח ליסודות האמונה
בבורא עולם, שידעו, בלבם פנימה,
שברצונם לקיים כל התורה — רק אז
יוכלו לחנך אחרים בדרך הנכונה".

נאה דורש ונאה מקיים
זוהי דוגמה אחת של דרישה אחת

The article

Every Sabbath eve, after the meal, they come to the big
neighborhood shul of Zichron Moshe, where R' Schwadron
preaches his sermons. There are hundreds of them: the elderly and the young, men, women and children from every
part of the city, sitting and standing in crowded conditions
for hours, listening open-mouthed to R' Schwadron's
words, at the same time both fiery and sweet.

He is fluent in the art of oratory. "He speaks by the grace
of Heaven," say those in the know. He knows when to raise
his voice and when to lower it, when to pound powerfully
on the table before him, when to wave his hands, when to
express himself in a chassidic chant and when to sway to the
rhythm of his own words — to hold his audience captive
and drill into their hearts his message of pungent *mussar*, liberally sprinkled with quotes by our Sages, with verses, with
stories of chassidim and *misnagdim*, and the like.

It is clear to see that R' Schwadron, both in his sermons and in the course of his own life, shares the pain of those who witness people lacking in faith — denying the existence of the Creator — and especially when this is seen among the youth. He follows every new development in the State and weaves it into the words he preaches against the "heretics." But let us allow R' Schwadron to speak for himself:

"The first question" — this is the way he opened his remarks — "is how a person can wander the face of the earth for the 70 years of his life, without ever asking himself even once — and this, to our sorrow, is the bitter reality — 'Who am I, what am I, how was I created, and where am I going?' In the past, there were heretics and philosophers with twisted minds, but for all that, most of them were important people. But today?" Here R' Schwadron raises his voice and spreads his hands — "Today, nobody wants to think. They live their lives like animals. They eat, drink, sleep, and make money ... The adults grasp at whatever comes to hand, and are smitten with [spiritual] 'illnesses,' just like children. And all this because they don't want to think, because if they think, they will be forced to deny themselves some things that they have grown accustomed to." Rav Schwadron sighs.

Youth and Values

As he continues his speech, he presents several real examples, the most actual of them being, of course, the mixed swimming pool — standard fare for the public. Then he moves on to a different topic — that of our youth. "Today, young people are not searching for the good, but rather for the sweet and pleasurable. Like I said — they're licking ice-pops." As R' Schwadron grows more excited, his voice becomes excited, too. "And for this reason I began to understand what had surprised me at first: How people with a head on their shoulders, living in such a large world, claim that the sky and the earth, the stars and the moon, the plants and every living thing — were all created by themselves, Heaven forbid. A box of matches cannot create itself. If you suggested otherwise, people would laugh at you. And what, after all, is the big deal about a box of matches? But our wondrous and awesome world — that was created by itself?

"They do not think, and so they do not acknowledge the clear fact that anyone who uses his mind knows: It is necessary for there to have been a Creator!" He preaches at the anonymous heretics.

"I was a boy of 7" — the *Maggid* recalls the days of his childhood, his eyes igniting — "and I remember sitting on the steps of my house, at night, for about 3 hours, thinking and thinking about matters of faith. I thought until my head ached. But today? Boys of 16 and 17 don't even think about the creation of the world — 'What, who, how.' Previous generations had their share of apostates, but they were few in number. Today, for our sins, they have become many — from a few who denied our faith, to many who believe in denial of faith. They wish to deny the faith that has been transmitted from generation to generation. And it is a confused apostasy, which cannot under any circumstances claim that there is no G-d, an apostasy without substance. This — how do you say it? absurdity? — is what they believe in. Yes, the great absurdity! This is intoxicating our youth today. The youth seeks out all sorts of desires to fill his soul, in order to forget that his soul is crying out, against his will: '*A'yekah*!'"

Cruelty — Apostasy's Outcome

Rav Schwadron has no lack of examples to illustrate the results of clinging to apostasy. "We have never before heard of Jews behaving cruelly, the way we have heard it in our time, here in *Eretz Yisrael*. I am not talking about gentiles. Without Torah — that's the way it is. But the story about the young people who caught a boy from another political party trying to enter their meeting, and cut out his heart in cold blood — have we ever heard such a thing in Israel? Is it possible that, for a trash can on *erev* Yom Kippur, after midnight, a man will kill his neighbor? Is it possible that because of a dog's barking a man will murder his friend? Has it ever been heard that young people break into their schools at night and steal money, until the schools are forced to surround themselves with iron bars, like a prison?

"As for the good children ..." Here, R' Schwadron pauses a moment. After a brief halt for reflection, he continues, "Today, hundreds of children are being educated to steal. Robbery, murder, and the destruction of *middos* — all these things come from the theaters and the cinemas. Fathers without sense and mothers without wisdom stuff their children with all sorts of desires. And from this, our children begin to sink into the depths. The youth slides into the chasm in order to forget the cry of his own soul."

And again, R' Schwadron lifts his voice and shouts: "All the efforts of educators and police who know this hopeless situation and want to repair it, all their efforts are to no avail. Why? Because a person's inclination is evil from his youth. It is only when a person fears the punishment he can expect from the Creator of the world that he succeeds in mastering his inclination. With reflection, with dedication and with awareness, and naturally not in one minute, he can change his nature by habitual action; as our Sages have said, habit becomes second nature. All the good character traits, if they are not rooted in faith in a Creator, contradict and are contradicted by man's actions, because the majority of men are born with lowly traits as well."

In R' Schwadron's opinion, there is no other course but "not to be embarrassed, to cast down pride and admit: We have abandoned our father's faith. We thought that we are smarter than they, that they were the mistaken ones and we are the ones who understand. Now, we see how right they were. They had a strong desire to give us life, to elevate us, to make us — how do you say? — *gliklach*, to make us happy in this world and in the next. We were mistaken. Even Jewish consciousness, which the Minister of Education is attempting to introduce into the schools, is not something he can recommend to intelligent students, who are liable to ask him: 'Do you live according to what you are recommending?' Only if the leaders of our nation see the great need, if they return at least to the fundamentals of faith in a Creator, if they recognize, in their innermost hearts, that their desire is to observe all of the Torah — only then will we be able to educate our youth in the proper manner."

Practicing What He Preaches

This is just an example of one sermon among the many that R' Schwadron has been preaching in various shuls throughout the Sha'arei Chesed neighborhood for the past 20 years, and for the last four years in the large Zichron Moshe Shul. He does not repeat himself, and this is his strength. Every sermon arouses its listeners' interest. From time to time he is invited to speak in shuls in different cities, and to different sectors. He speaks in a juicy Yiddish and also in fluent Hebrew. And he is outstanding in another quality: in his observance of the saying, "Practice what you preach." He is scrupulous in his observance of all the mitzvos, large and small. Though his means (he is the father of seven daughters and a son) are strained, he lectures without payment, gives a tithe of his earnings to the poor, performs acts of lovingkindness, and extends a helping hand to anyone who asks. Money is not a consideration to him; the important thing is learning Torah for its own sake. During the month of Elul, he has decreed silence upon himself, except for Torah study, and will not exchange a word even with his family members, answering them in writing instead.

Born in Meah Shearim

Rav Schwadron is 46 years old. He was born in the Meah Shearim neighborhood of Jerusalem, to Rabbi Yitzchak Schwadron, son of the *gaon* of Berzon, R' Sholom Mordechai HaKohen Schwadron, author of halachic works that have earned widespread fame throughout the Diaspora and *Eretz Yisrael*, and by whose name he is known. He lost his father as a child, was educated in a Talmud Torah in Meah Shearim and afterwards in a yeshivah in Petach Tikvah. From there, he moved on to Chevron Yeshivah, where he was a student of R' Chasman who guided and taught him after he stood already revealed as outstandingly zealous in Torah. The time he has remaining after learning Torah and serving as *Rosh Yeshivah* of a Sephardic *beis midrash gavohah* in Mekor Chaim, is dedicated to publishing his grandfather, the *gaon's*, manuscripts and to composing his own halachic works, three of which have appeared in print thus far. He is now working on another book.

On Friday nights, after the meal, he hurries off to the shul in all kinds of weather, to preach his sermon to the hundreds who have come to hear him, and who listen thirstily to what he has to say. He is prepared to appear and to preach and to deliver talks anywhere he is invited to do so, as well as to write for newspapers, even the *Al HaMishmar*, though under a pseudonym. Those close to him relate that he is afraid of writing under his own name since the time he was dismissed after an appearance — a thickly bearded man with *peyos*, wearing a long coat and preaching about faith and religion — with the words, "Ah, *Neturei Karta*." They emphasize that he is *not* a member of the Neturei Karta sect, despite the fact that he is zealous and extreme in his faith, and does not belong to any other religious political party, though his views tend to Agudas Yisrael.

These were the impressions of a completely secular newspaper reporter, representing the best efforts of a non-observant man to acquire a grasp of who R' Sholom Schwadron was. R' Sholom's true essence was something that a reporter could certainly never touch. But his article is testimony to the powerful spirit behind R' Sholom's sermons, and to the changes that they were capable of bringing about even in those outside the religious camp.

THE TRUE SECRET BEHIND R' SHOLOM'S SUCCESS AS A SPEAKER and a mover came from the fact that he had erected an internal
Heart to Heart value system in his own heart, and from that vantage point was able to sway the hearts of others. He was also granted *siyata d'shemaya* — a helping hand from Heaven.

In a letter (to R' Shlomo Stentzal), R' Sholom expounded at length on matters connected to the preparation of a site from which to speak in Tel Aviv. He ended with a single, short, but illuminating sentence:

"May Hashem grant that we succeed in arousing ourselves to return in full repentance before Him, so that our intentions will be for the sake of Heaven; then we are guaranteed that what emerges from our heart will enter the hearts [of others]."

And in a different style, in another letter he wrote: "May Hashem grant that we are able to return to Him wholly and truly ourselves, and afterwards bring others' hearts back into His service."

In other words, R' Sholom demanded from himself and spoke to his own heart first. Only afterwards did he speak to others. *That* was the reason he was so successful. Even during the talk itself, he would be arousing R' Sholom Schwadron along with the rest of the crowd. In this, he was a giant of a man.

R' Sholom once spoke to an audience and felt afterwards that he had succeeded in rousing them more than he had roused himself. Immediately, he began seeking new ways to internalize his sermon to rouse his own self.

Left to right: R' Shneur Kotler, R' Sholom, R' Yisrael Grossman

The week of mourning for R' Shneur Kotler was at an end, and a *hesped* (eulogy) service was being held in Lakewood. R' Sholom Schwadron, staying in America at the time, was one of the eulogizers. His words rose up in tongues of flame, a powerful and bitterly mournful speech, accompanied by a storm of tears.

At the conclusion of the *hesped*, R' Sholom got into the car that would take him back to where he was staying. They were halfway there when R' Sholom turned suddenly to the driver, an acquaintance of his, and asked if he had a tape recorder in the car. Receiving an affirmative reply, he took a cassette from his pocket and asked the driver to play it. "They taped my *hesped* and gave me a copy of it. I want to listen to it," he said.

R' Sholom sat quietly, listening to his own words. All at once, he began to cry. The weeping grew stronger, the tears falling copiously.

The driver, in an impudent mood, said jocularly, "R' Sholom, you are already in the car. You don't have to cry anymore."

The tears dried up. R' Sholom turned and said, "Let me explain. When a person speaks in front of an audience, it's hard for him to hear himself. He invests a lot of energy in being heard and in arousing his listeners, but he doesn't manage to internalize the talk for himself. But I, too, want to hear a powerful *hesped* for R' Shneur Kotler."

He turned on the tape recorder again. As the car wound its way home, it was filled once more with a storm of emotion as R' Sholom listened to the eulogy.

(as told by R' Chaim David Ackerman)

≈≈

The people of Jerusalem loved R' Sholom, and they came by the hundreds to bask in his presence. Torah scholars sat side by side with the unlearned, the elderly alongside the children. All came on Friday night to the Zichron Moshe Shul to hear R' Sholom speak.

Many young people came with their pockets filled with sunflower seeds, prepared to have a good time. There were those who came with their eyes half-closed, having fought back the exhaustion that threatened to overtake them at the Shabbos table. After the meal, they struggled against their fatigue, donned their *shtreimels*, tied their belts, and set out for Zichron Moshe. Once inside, they often as not dozed off again ... until a blow to the *shtender* from the *Maggid's* hand startled them into wakefulness, and they started listening again.

In his tasteful, sweet manner, R' Sholom told them about the vital ingredients of a Jew's life. He knew how to touch the place inside where a person feels most deeply. Sometimes he dug deeper than people felt comfortable doing themselves, exerting pressure on each individual according to that person's unique personality and particular inner strengths. From that deep place, he would rouse his audience to reflection, introspection, and self-motivation. Even those who lived wild lives, lives without emphasis on good character or fear of Heaven, enjoyed refreshing their wandering souls with a good Friday night sermon in Zichron Moshe.

Every person left with a wonderful sensation in the depths of his innermost being. *Talmidei chachamim* and simple folk alike would emerge with strong new resolutions to carry them through the coming week. R' Sholom's sermon nourished them for the next seven days. In his presence, they tasted the *Olam HaZeh* (this world) that is in *Olam HaBa* (the World to Come).

R' SHOLOM OFTEN EXPRESSED GREAT ANGUISH IN HIS *SHIURIM* concerning the desecration of the Shabbos and the apostasy that he saw around him. From time to time, householders would try to comfort him. "It's not so bad. Hashem will help."

"My Meyer'ke"

One day, before the *shiur* began, R' Sholom's ears picked up some angry whisperings.

"What is it?" he inquired. He soon had his answer: "Ah! They're charging a tax for everything. Every loaf of bread comes with a state tax. What's going to become of our country?"

Smiling, R' Sholom spoke to them in their own language. "Don't worry, it's not so bad. Hashem will help."

He faced the assembled group. "I want to tell you," he said, "about something that happened to me a number of years ago. Two children from the neighborhood were playing 'horse and buggy.' One boy was the horse, and his friend pulled him with a rope as they ran around. The two of them galloped near my front yard and as they did, the boy in front tripped on a step, fell to the ground, and cut open his forehead.

"My wife ran into the house, calling out, 'Meyer'ke fell on the stones outside and is bleeding profusely! Let's take him to the doctor!' She took a towel, soaked it in water, and we went outside. I held the boy in my arms while my wife pressed the hole in his forehead with the towel. In this way, we began walking quickly toward the home of a doctor at the edge of Sha'arei Chesed.

"In the distance, we saw the boy's grandmother, a respected woman well beloved in Sha'arei Chesed. We said nothing to her. Seeing us from afar, she grasped the situation at once: R' Sholom and his wife were rushing to bring a hurt child to the doctor. She called out encouragingly, 'Hashem will help. It's nothing, it will pass.'

"Still we were quiet. Soon we were closer to the grandmother, and she saw that the blood-covered child looked familiar to her. Again she said, this time hesitantly, 'It's nothing terrible, Hashem will help.'

"Then we were right beside her, and she saw that the child was her own grandson. Immediately, she forgot all the comforting things she had said to us, and broke into piercing screams: 'Meyer'ke! Meyer'ke! *Gevald!*'

"What happened next?" R' Sholom asked. He continued, "All the neighborhood women ran out in a panic to see what the screaming was about. They took one look, then said, 'Don't worry, it's nothing, Hashem will help, it will pass.'

"I learned a valuable lesson from this episode. If it is not my Meyer'ke, it's nothing terrible.

"When a man does not feel that *chilul* Shabbos is his Meyer'ke, he takes comfort: Hashem will help. But when his taxes are 'my Meyer'ke,' he kicks and shouts.

"It is the same in every area of life. 'My Meyer'ke.'

"A valuable lesson."

≈≈

"I just remembered a story."

Everyone smiled to hear that expression. It was R' Sholom's habit to switch instantly into storytelling mode the moment he thought of one, even if it had no direct bearing on the topic at hand. When he was done, he would return smoothly to the original subject of his talk. He was acting on instructions from his teacher, R' Eliyahu Lopian, a man who, like R' Sholom himself, lived his life in the service of his community.

"If a thought enters your mind while you are speaking — even if it is a side point — say it aloud," the older man had advised. His reasoning was simple: It is the watchful Eye of Heaven, *hashgachah*, that directs all our steps and places a certain idea or story into our heads. Perhaps the listeners need to hear it — or perhaps only *one* listener does. It is Hashem's will that the speaker mention that particular story at this particular moment. R' Sholom adhered to this custom for scores of years.

Many, many individuals found the right moment in which to approach R' Sholom and tell him, "R' Sholom, what you said yesterday was exactly what I needed to hear. You have no idea why you happened to remember that particular *vort* in the middle of your talk." This was their reaction to hearing something that the *Maggid* had mentioned spontaneously, almost incidentally. *Hashgachah.*

A Jerusalem resident related to us a fascinating tale, one that R' Sholom had remembered "especially" for him.

The man owned a printing press. Every morning, after *davening Shacharis* with a *vasikin minyan* and learning the *daf yomi*, he went to his shop to earn a livelihood for his family. After his workday he would return to the *beis midrash* for a few more hours of learning and prayer.

Once a year, this man was called upon for reserve military duty in the Israeli Defense Forces. He never tried to avoid his service when called upon. His army job was that of watchman, which allowed him to spend many hours in learning.

Then came the day when he found a notice in his mailbox: reserve duty for three weeks. The service would fall out in the month of Nissan. Making a rapid calculation, the man realized that he would be gone from home on the night of the Pesach Seder, as well as all the remaining days of the holiday. At the prospect, a shadow fell across his face.

The notice arrived on a Friday. "I haven't had such a Friday in a long time," he thought. His spirits plummeted sharply.

That night, he ate his Shabbos meal, sunk in gloomy thought. He pictured his family's Seder table, minus his presence. Who would be there to answer his sons' *Mah Nishtanah?* And what would he himself eat during all the days of Pesach?

Friday evenings usually found the printer in the Zichron Moshe Shul, listening to R' Sholom speak. On this gray night, however, he decided to diverge from his custom and take a walk instead. After

בית־הכנסת הגדול „אהלי־יעקב" זכרון־משה
ירושלים ת״ו

מודעה

מודיעים בזה לקהל הרחב, כי בליל ש״ק פ׳ ראה
בשעה 9

·דרוש

הרב שלום שוואדרון שליט״א

בבית־הכנסת הגדול, בזכרון־משה.

הגבאים

דפוס קלישר — ירושלים

a long stroll in the company of his melancholy thoughts, he found his legs carrying him, as though by habit, to the shul. He hesitated at the door, then went in.

Zichron Moshe has a book-lined foyer at the entrance, from which one enters the main sanctuary of the shul. The printer stood in this foyer, listening to R' Sholom's clear voice roll out to reach his ears:

"I just remembered a story," R' Sholom was saying, "and when that happens, you already know what we must do. The story has nothing to do with our topic, but ..." R' Sholom embarked on his tale:

When yeshivah students would visit the Chofetz Chaim to discuss the problem of the Polish military draft, he would return a variety of answers. There is a wealth of stories concerning these amazing responses, and the *ruach hakodesh* that often prompted them. If the Chofetz Chaim placed a copy of the book *Machaneh Yisrael* in the student's hand, then he knew nothing would avail him; he would be drafted. But if the Chofetz Chaim's response was

290 / VOICE OF TRUTH

to say, "Whoever accepts the burden of Torah is released from the burden of the government and *derech eretz*," then the young man knew he must not spare any exertion in Torah — and his freedom from the draft would be assured.

"Whoever accepts the burden of Torah!" R' Sholom's voice rang out. "Whoever accepts that burden — whatever happens!" He continued to relate two examples of men who undertook the burden of Torah and were spared the draft. When he was finished, he asked where they had been up to before he began his story, and resumed the thread of his original topic.

"My heart was pounding very hard," the printer told us much later. "My whole body was covered with a cold sweat. I had never before felt such a personal *hashgachah pratis*. R' Sholom remembered the story at the very instant that my feet crossed the shul's threshold, and everything he said was directed at my own difficult situation. As he returned to the original subject of his talk, I saw that it really had no bearing at all on 'whoever takes upon himself the burden of Torah.' In other words, the thing had not come about through natural means, one topic leading naturally into the next.

"But apart from any considerations of *hashgachah pratis*, I was greatly encouraged by what R' Sholom had said. I decided at once to add an hour of learning to my regular schedule — one extra hour every day. I didn't wait for Sunday, or even for Shabbos morning. Immediately after the lecture ended, I went into the *beis midrash* and learned for an hour. I believed with a powerful faith in the words of *Chazal*, 'Whoever takes upon himself the burden of Torah ...' All my worry fell away.

"On Sunday, I told my partner at the printing press that I had some news for him, and a request. The news was that I had received a draft notice for the month of Nissan. And the request was that we close up shop an hour early each day, so that I would be able to use it for the study of Torah."

A week passed, then two. One morning, the man's partner walked in with his own startling announcement. "R' Yaakov, I've also received a notice for reserve duty in the month of Nissan!"

The army rule is that two business partners do not have to serve

R' Sholom addressing a Chol Hamoed gathering

at the same time. In such a case, one of them is released from duty. "The two of us took all our papers and went down to the army office," the printer relates. "A few days later, the letter came: I was released! I would be home for Pesach with my family. Unfortunately, to my distress, my partner was still required to serve his time.

"I was grateful to Hashem for helping me, in a natural way, to be free of my army duty. But it soon became clear that we had not yet come to the end of the marvelous *hashgachah* in this episode. My letter of release was only the first stage in the story.

"On the day my partner left for his reserve duty, I parted painfully from him. None knew better than I what he must be feeling at such a time."

The next morning, the printer walked to his printing shop as usual, and placed his key in the lock. To his surprise, the door wasn't locked! Slowly he twisted the knob and opened the door, then stepped instead, hesitant and afraid. A few steps into the room, he saw something amazing. There was his partner, working busily away!

"*Shalom aleichem!* Good morning!" the man greeted his partner, in open astonishment.

Front row, left to right: R' Yosef Shalom Elyashiv (seated), R' Shlomo Zalman Auerbach, R' Sholom, R' Avraham Shapiro

"What happened? Have you gone AWOL?" the printer asked

The partner smiled. "I arrived at the base yesterday," he said, "and an hour later, they sent me right back home! The supervisor came over and told me, 'There's been a mistake — some sort of misunderstanding. Your draft notice was for two months from now, and was sent to your address by accident.' I was dumbfounded. Such a thing had never happened to me before. But the supervisor apologized and sent me respectfully home, saying, 'Sorry about this mistake. You are released!'"

When he had finished telling his story, the partner stood up and cried out emotionally, "We have just seen, with our own eyes, the amazing results of following the words of *Chazal*, 'Whoever takes upon himself the burden of Torah is exempt from the burden of *derech eretz*.' In order for you to be released from your duty, I received a draft notice by mistake."

The printer himself adds a final note to this story. "When we took financial inventory several months later, it turned out that, from the time we began closing up shop an hour early each day, our income had increased greatly." Raising his voice with great feeling, he concludes, "Whoever takes upon himself the burden of Torah ...!"

THE SWEETEST MOMENTS R' SHOLOM SHARED WITH HIS LISteners were those in which he traveled back in time with them,
The Fire to an earlier world, a previous generation. At such times, he wove silken cords around his audience, enchanting them with visions of a glorious past. They would sit spellbound, rising at least 10 feet off the ground, together with the *Maggid...*

The flame surrounding R' Nachum'ke of Horodna was virtually visible to their naked eyes. The circle that the Chofetz Chaim made in the forest became the circling of R' Sholom's finger in the stillness of the Zichron Moshe Shul. In these magical moments, tears of longing filled the listeners' eyes — a longing to be better, to be higher.

Under the influence of R' Sholom's feeling voice, the city of Chevron spread out before his audience, and they were standing together with the "Sdei Chemed" as he stood up to his challenge and merited a great light. And then, once again, the transported listeners were filled with a deep desire to understand more, to learn more, to observe more. The melody that the *Maggid* chanted ignited a flame in the holy soul residing inside each and every individual in the shul ... until the last word was spoken into the hush, and the sermon was over.

Chapter 10

Chevron Yeshivah

R'Sholom Schwadron was a "Chevroner." It was in Chevron Yeshivah that he took his first real steps on the road to Torah and his own personal service of Hashem. It was here that he became an ardent student of R' Leib Chasman; it was here that he achieved the stature of a man. The Chevron *bachur* was Chevron, to the depths of his heart.

The yeshivah was comprised of an impressive mix of students from Europe — chiefly Poland and Lithuania — learning side by side with Jerusalemites. In time, they achieved a harmonious blend of outstanding Torah scholarship, a keen fear of Heaven, and towering character. It was Rabbi Yosef Chaim Sonnenfeld who consecrated the ground upon which R' Sholom Schwadron and many others like him were able to learn and grow.

Jerusalem at that time was busy erecting protective walls in the face of the secular influences that threatened traditional Judaism. The influx of students from the Slobodka Yeshivah to *Eretz Yisrael* frightened the old community, which trembled at any change in its age-old atmosphere. Suddenly, in the very heart of Jerusalem, a strange sight could be seen: clean-shaven yeshivah boys, dressed in short, European garb, and wearing gray hats with broad brims. Jerusalem's pious turned in anger to these young men, plastering posters on the streets that bore blistering denunciations of yeshivah boys who dressed like Germans.

Fortunately, Israel's teacher and leader did not share this point of view. R' Yosef Chaim Sonnenfeld, the man who stood on the front lines in the battle against dangerous change, recognized that these young men posed no threat. On the contrary, he was loath to insult individuals who had left their families abroad and had come to dwell and to learn Torah in Jerusalem at great personal cost. R' Yosef Chaim protected not only the Chevron Yeshivah, but also, in essence, all of Jerusalem. By embracing, instead of rejecting, the boys from Slobodka, he helped significantly to raise the level of Torah in that venerable city.

R' Yosef Chaim took a Chevron boy, R' Hirsch Kupshitz, as a husband for his granddaughter — the daughter of R' Shmuel Hillel Shenker. [In his eulogy for R' Kupshitz, R' Sholom said that he had earned the title of "*tzaddik*" by men who were themselves of the highest stature. A *tzaddik* has been lost!] R' Yosef Chaim's

R' Yosef Chaim's great-grandson, R' Moshe Kupshitz, giving a chaburah in the Chevron Yeshivah

grandsons also learned in the yeshivah when it was still located in Chevron.

Toward the end of his life, R' Yosef Chaim embarked on a personal and historic visit to the yeshivah. Those in the know point out that the visit took place after R' Yosef Chaim Sonnenfeld learned of the greatness of R' Nosson Tzvi Finkel, the "Alter" of Slobodka. Hearing about the Alter's purity and piety, both on the personal and on the communal level, R' Yosef Chaim gathered his failing strength and traveled to Chevron. In the yeshivah, he met first with the Alter of Slobodka in a private session, and then spoke to the yeshivah boys in learning. His appearance aroused tremendous excitement among the students, as well as a deep appreciation and admiration for their special visitor.

One day R' Yosef Chaim was sitting in his room surrounded by a group of Jerusalem's elite, when several Chevron Yeshivah students unexpectedly dropped in. Finding themselves in the presence of these honored men, the *bachurim* wished to leave at once. But R' Yosef Chaim invited them in, sat them down beside him, and engaged them in a profound halachic discussion of the laws pertaining to *Eretz Yisrael*. When the young men were ready to leave, he walked them to the door, remarking, "I know a Jew who dresses in the 'German' style, to whom Eliyahu revealed himself several times." (He was referring to R' Asher Bachrach.)

The hint was taken. R' Yosef Chaim's personal support for the Slobodka contingent became well-known, and denunciations of the newcomers ceased from that date. There was also no doubt in anyone's mind about R' Yosef Chaim's attitude toward the yeshivah as a whole. Any incipient rejection of Chevron Yeshivah dried up in the face of that venerable leader's wholehearted acceptance of it. An atmosphere was engendered, and a giant slice of Jerusalem's population became caught up in it. Many joined the ranks of Chevron Yeshivah boys, including R' Sholom Schwadron and numerous others like him. They joined at just the time when the yeshivah relocated from Chevron to Jerusalem.

R' Yosef Chaim's son-in-law, who had previously been on friendly terms with the Alter of Slobodka, came to see him as well.

An interesting episode is told about one of these visits to the city of Chevron:

> After traveling from Jerusalem to Chevron, R' Shmuel Hillel Shenker entered the Alter's room together with one of his young children. The boy, who had made the trip just for the privilege of being near the Alter of Slobodka, emotionally stepped up to where R' Nosson Tzvi sat, bent and kissed his hand. He did this naturally, having seen other great men of Torah treated in this manner in the home of his grandfather, R' Yosef Chaim. The Alter, however, was not prepared to accept such a token of respect. He took the boy lovingly by the hand, brought the hand up to his lips, and kissed it. By this simple method, he managed to remove the significance of the boy's kiss without evincing the least rejection of the boy's gesture.

From the year 5690 (1930) onward, when the yeshivah moved to Jerusalem, the bond between R' Yosef Chaim and the students of the Chevron Yeshivah deepened. When thousands from Jerusalem's old *yishuv* thronged to R' Yosef Chaim's succah each year, the Chevron boys did not hesitate to join them. Together, they danced and sang for hours before the rabbi of Jerusalem.

R' Mendel Sheinen, a Chevron student, remembers: "We, too, made sure to join the great celebration. This was during R' Yosef Chaim Sonnenfeld's last years. Among the thousands that passed before him, R' Yosef Chaim noticed a certain man who had lived in Jerusalem, then moved abroad for several years. The man had just returned to Jerusalem, and was now clean shaven, not bearded as when R' Yosef Chaim had seen him last. R' Yosef Chaim stalked him with his eyes until he caught his attention, then signaled for him to come over. In a chiding tone, he asked, 'Where are your beard and *peyos*?' He made no such disapproving remarks to the Chevron Yeshivah boys, whose external appearance was more modern. But to those who had departed from their original path, and changed the way they looked, he was unyielding."

Another incident illustrates R' Yosef Chaim's acceptance of the Chevron Yeshivah students and staff. At a public gathering encouraging scrupulous Shabbos observance, the proceedings began with opening remarks by R' Mendel Sheinen of the Chevron Yeshivah. R' Yosef Chaim Sonnenfeld attended the gathering and listened attentively to R' Mendel's words. Afterwards, two men came over to R' Yosef Chaim and said indignantly, "Rebbe, do you see how he looks [i.e., clean-shaven]?"

R' Yosef Chaim pointed at his own ear and said firmly, "No! I don't see. I am listening to what he has to say."

The Chevron Yeshivah boys would come to see R' Yosef Chaim from time to time, to discuss the topics they were learning. Stories of these visits were told among the students with excitement and awe. As a rule, R' Yosef Chaim tried to hide his own greatness — but he was not always successful. The sharp-witted students often managed to make R' Yosef Chaim reveal some small part of his greatness in Torah.

Three yeshivah boys encountered R' Yosef Chaim on his way back from the *Kosel* one Shabbos. Being acquainted with them, he stopped and began sharing some of his thoughts connected to the day, which was Shabbos *Parashas Zachor*. One of the three related afterwards: "He spoke in the Chevron style, so that if we closed our eyes we might almost imagine that it was the Alter of Slobodka who was giving us a *mussar shmuess*. When we reached his house, there was a group of *talmidei chachamim* waiting for him, including R' Yeshayah Winograd. Immediately, R' Yosef Chaim changed his style of speech, and began to discuss Torah in his usual way. The whole group, including the three of us, then entered the house to 'talk in learning' for a while, but R' Yosef Chaim did not revert to the style he had adopted when he was alone with us."

The Meeting

R' SHOLOM ENRICHED THE JEWISH WORLD WITH GEMS HE HAD heard about R' Yosef Chaim Sonnenfeld from his rebbe, R' Leib Chasman. These stories had been told to him after a certain fateful meeting.

Jerusalem swayed back and forth in philosophical

R' Yosef Chaim Sonnenfeld (center, with cane) and R' Avraham Yitzchak Kook (to his left)

debate between Jerusalem's rabbi, R' Yosef Chaim Sonnenfeld, and R' Avraham Yitzchak Kook. R' Leib Chasman — having met Rav Kook abroad, and recognizing his giant heart and mind — wished to meet with R' Yosef Chaim in an attempt to clear the air. He arrived unexpectedly at the home of his student, R' Hirsch Kupshitz, who was married to R' Yosef Chaim's granddaughter and lived next door to R' Yosef Chaim. R' Leib sent R' Hirsch next door to ask R' Yosef Chaim if he could come in. When R' Yosef Chaim heard that R' Leib was right next door, he got up and went next door to greet him.

The meeting between the two giants was warm and moving. After a few friendly remarks and a brief foray into a Torah discussion, the two settled down to discuss the issue at hand. Their talk was part debate, part negotiation, and was conducted in a manner that could only belong to such pillars of Torah. R' Kupshitz, at a later date, expressed pain and regret that he did not write down what his ears heard during that stormy session. The words that the pair exchanged could constitute a *Shulchan Aruch* for ensuing generations.

As R' Yosef Chaim's biography (*Ish Al HaChomah*) relates, there was no difference of opinion between them with regard to Rav Kook's personality and character. But R' Yosef Chaim, for all his concern for peace and unity, was fearful of the "stamp of approval" that secularism was attaining at the hands of *mitzvah*-observant men. Though he knew that Rav Kook had chosen his particular path for the purpose of bringing Jews closer to the fold, he was certain that Rav Kook's public declarations, and his closeness to the Zionist camp, brought with them a negative influence on Orthodox Jewry and could ultimately tarnish the essential Jewish self-image. Also, he was afraid that dependence on a secular apparatus would lead to a loss of independent thinking.

It is said that R' Yosef Chaim's great-grandson, the son of R' Tzvi Hirsch Kupshitz, lay in his carriage throughout the discussion. At one point, the baby started laughing. One of the two great men smiled and said, "What shall we do? They're laughing already."

The two parted, with R' Leib finally moved to accept R' Yosef Chaim's way of thinking. Upon his return home, R' Leib told a member of his household, "Please tell Rav Kook that he has half of Chasman." He was referring to his wife, who had not participated in that meeting.

In the days that followed, R' Sholom heard a number of keen observations from his rebbe about R' Yosef Chaim Sonnenfeld. For example, "R' Yosef Chaim does

R' Aryeh Militzky, later R' Sholom's son-in-law, giving a chaburah in the Chevron Yeshivah

Chapter Ten: Chevron Yeshivah / 301

not blink an eye without some sort of *kavanah* (intention) for the sake of Heaven, because everything he does is for the sake of Heaven"; and, "Can we have any real idea of R' Yosef Chaim's *da'as Torah* [Torah-based opinions]? Here is a man who served the Torah giants of Hungary for many years — the Ksav Sofer, the *gaon* Rav Shag, and others. After that, for 20 years he was close to the Maharil Diskin, one of Lithuania's great men. And now, imagine: such talent and clear thinking combined with a keen and deep grasp, serving the Diaspora's Torah leaders for so many years ... and above it all, his *l'sheim Shamayim*, his dedication of all he is to Heaven. This is the primary ingredient in everything he does. Can any of us imagine the *da'as Torah* that forms that *gaon* and *tzaddik*'s every act?"

After R' Yosef Chaim departed this world, Jerusalem's residents hoped that R' Leib Chasman would take over his rabbinical position. R' Leib declined. He would agree to preside only over the Diskin Orphan Home.

DAVENING IN THE CHEVRON YESHIVAH WAS ALWAYS A BREATH-taking sight. A person opening the door to the *beis midrash* on Rosh

In the Chevron Furnace Hashanah night felt as though he were standing on the brink of a fiery furnace. The *Shemoneh Esrei* sounded just the way it is described in the *Shulchan Aruch*: not spoken aloud, but rather in a hum, trembling and prolonged.

The longing for spiritual elevation was everywhere, irresistibly drawing the newcomer to join: to pray with R' Chaim Aharon Tortzin, with R' Yisrael Shenker, with R' Moshe Shimon Weintraub, and so many others. Waves of emotion rippled from bench to bench, from *shtender* to *shtender*, from mouth to mouth, from heart to heart, until the entire yeshivah was aflame. Young married men surreptitiously wiped away their tears; boys clapped their hands; and the *Roshei Yeshivah* and *Rebbe'im* stood by the eastern wall, wrapped in awe, immersed in the depths of a profound intellectual experience. Suddenly, a youngster would break into sobs, his heart too full.

As the Rosh Hashanah night service ended, the worshipers

would cast a quick glance at the great figures of "Knesses Yisrael," figures such as R' Aharon Brisker and the *Rosh Yeshivah*, R' Aharon Cohen, and others who could not yet bear to be finished with their prayers. Their humble stance, beside the eastern wall, provided yet another drop of Heavenly awe for the hundreds of students filing out of the *beis midrash*.

That was the way it was scores of years ago, and the way it remains to this very day. The tears that flowed then were tears of nobility, of longing, and fear of judgment. The worshipers thirsted for elevation, and cried tears that refreshed their souls.

At the Aron Kodesh in the Chevron Yeshivah

NO ONE EVER MISSED THAT *SHMUESS* (TALK) — THE ONE THAT took place just moments before the shofar blew. The *Rosh Yeshivah*,

Before the Shofar Blew R' Yechezkel Sarna, would stand on the steps of the Holy Ark and pour out his heart in a mighty torrent. R' Tzemach Shlomovitz once remarked that the *Rosh Yeshivah* reminded him of R' Itzele Peterberger, in his time. (R' Tzemach was one of the veteran students of Gubrin and Kelm, and a student of the Alter of Kelm. He was privileged to see Rabbi Yisrael Salanter as well.)

The central point of the *shmuess* revolved around the theme, "*HaKadosh Baruch Hu* said, 'Recite the *malchuyos* before Me so that you will appoint Me King over

At the wedding of R' Chaim Sarna: among others (left to right) R' Yechezkel Sarna, R' Meir Chodosh, R' Shlomo Zimbalist (standing at the wall), R' Shabsi Yogel (standing in the foreground)

you.' " R' Yechezkel Sarna would cry continuously throughout his impassioned speech. "*HaKadosh Baruch Hu* is asking us to come and stand before Him!" When the talk was finished, there was an almost palpable wave of fear and trembling in the great hall, and the *Mussaf* service that followed led directly to the King's Throne.

THE END OF THE SILENT *MUSSAF* PRAYER FOUND THE WOR-shipers in varying frames of mind. There were those who finished

R' Sholom's Mussaf with eyes glowing and a sense of purification. There were others filled with a yearning for ele-vation. Some were joyous and others were downcast, their souls still hungry.

And then came R' Sholom's famous repetition of the *Mussaf*. His fervent prayer drew every heart after it, so that by the time it was over, each individual felt satisfied to the depths of his be-ing. R' Sholom was all melody. When he merged with the prayer, and the two merged with the Day of Judgment, and the three merged with a melody that derived directly from the heart, an incomparable symphony formed. He cried easily, with the sim-ple longing of a baby parted from its mother. In his rendition of the various *tefillos*, R' Sholom's *davening* captured the essence of supplication. He achieved a unique and unforgettable mixture of tranquility and trembling awe. It was a *Mussaf* that thousands of students carried with them into the coming year, and still carry — up to this very day!

In his praying, R' Sholom was no different than he was in his sermonizing. His innate sweetness was present throughout, punc-tuated by bouts of stormy tears. He radiated a spiritual joy in the *tefillah* that naturally transmitted itself to the other worshipers. The melodies he employed were not his own; he drew tunes from fa-mous *ba'alei tefillah*, among them R' Eliyahu Porush, R' Chaim Menachem Mendelson, R' Shlomo Zimbalist, and R' Hirsch Kupshitz. He would begin without much in the way of melody, gradually introducing the music at different points in the service. But the tears, and the special stamp that said "R' Sholom," were present from the very start.

"I'LL NEVER FORGET ONE OF R' SHOLOM'S FIRST *MUSSAF* SERvices, about 45 years ago," says R' Yehudah Shenker. "That year,

The First Time R' Shlomo Zimbalist wasn't feeling well, and it was just minutes before *Mussaf* when news of his illness became known. The yeshivah had no idea who would try to take his place.

"One of the senior students tapped me on the shoulder, pointed, and said, 'Look, I'm sure that R' Sholom will lead the *Mussaf* prayer.' I saw R' Sholom swaying back and forth, consumed with excitement, floating somewhere between Heaven and earth. He was preparing himself!

"Several minutes before the shofar was blown, the *Rosh Yeshivah*, R' Yechezkel Sarna, went over to R' Sholom to ascertain if he was ready. R' Sholom reacted with a powerful disclaimer, as if to say, 'No, no, this is not for me!' But his protests were futile. The moment had arrived. It was time for *Mussaf* to begin.

"R' Sholom stood up.

"With all the burning fervor of his preparatory moments still clear on his face, R' Sholom nevertheless took his place with his accustomed serenity. With his first syllables, his listeners were seized with trembling. And from that year on, R' Sholom's face and voice were an integral part of the Chevron Yeshivah scene on the High Holy Days, imbuing not only the yeshivah, but the entire Torah world, with a

R' Yechezkel Sarna, accompanied by R' Moshe Chodosh (left), R' Yehudah Shenker (rear) and R' Hillel Zaks (right)

special spiritual flavor that added such an intangible richness to the experience.

ON THE *YOMIM NORA'IM,* IT WAS R' SHOLOM'S HABIT TO *DAVEN Shacharis* with the *vasikin minyan* until *Shemoneh Esrei,* and then enter

Emotion
the yeshivah to recite the rest of the liturgy. He sat on the first bench behind the *ba'al tefillah* — the *mashgiach,* R' Hirsch Palei. At certain points in the service, R' Hirsch would break down in tears, whereupon R' Sholom found it impossible not to join in. His uplifted voice soared with an intensity of emotion discernible to every ear: "To He Who tests hearts on the Day of Judgment."

After *Mussaf* was over, R' Sholom was exhausted, especially on Yom Kippur. At intervals, he would nod off on his bench for a few minutes at a time, utterly spent.

"WHERE IS R' SHOLOM? WHY ISN'T HE HERE?" EVERY PAIR OF eyes watched the yeshivah doors expectantly, but R' Sholom did

Absence
not enter.
Then the word passed in sad whispers around the crowded *beis midrash:* "He's in Europe."

That summer, R' Sholom had been obliged to travel to Europe on behalf of Chinuch Atzma'i. He spent the month of Elul in England, and Rosh Hashanah and Yom Kippur in Switzerland. He found himself surrounded by scenes of breathtaking beauty, but liberally sprinkled with churches. The hundreds of students at the yeshivah were desolate without him, but the situation hit R' Sholom himself hardest of all. As Yom Kippur approached, he found himself gripped by a powerful longing for the holy city of Jerusalem, his home.

⌒⌒

The sun sank in the west as R' Sholom walked slowly through the Swiss streets in the direction of the yeshivah. It was Yom Kippur night. Jewish passersby, noting his distinctive Jerusalem-style garb and the special radiance on his face, quickly approached to wish him a humble, "Good Yom Tov" before following him to the yeshivah's entrance.

Deep in thought, the Jerusalem *Maggid* entered the *beis midrash*. Everyone there rose in a mass display of respect. Unmindful of what was happening around him, he made his way to his seat.

Ma'ariv began. Suddenly, R' Sholom remembered the Chevron Yeshivah. He had always stood up before the congregation to open the most awesome day of the year with his own special brand of trembling purity. His haunting melody at the start of each Rosh Hashanah and Yom Kippur always had the yeshivah boys swaying to his rhythm, rolling and soaring into an unstoppable force, a storm of yearning for the redemption. In his mind's eye, R' Sholom saw the Chevron *beis midrash* in faraway Jerusalem. Then, with great effort, he tore his mind away from his thoughts and began to concentrate devotedly on the *tefillah* at hand. Immediately, with total reverence, he forgot himself in the fullness of his prayer.

At *Shacharis* the next morning, R' Sholom *davened* as usual with the sunrise *minyan*, weeping softly. During *Avinu Malkeinu*, he remembered his Chevroners again. "This is another of the sufferings I took upon myself when I agreed to go into 'exile,'" he thought with a faint smile.

During the interval between *Shacharis* and *Mussaf*, the *Roshei Yeshivah* urged him repeatedly to lead them in *Mussaf*. This was the time of year when R' Sholom traditionally refrained from speech, so that his responses were confined to "Nu," "Ah," and hand motions. At last, their pleadings wore down his resistance, and he agreed.

The numerous local residents that filled the hall were deeply moved to see R' Sholom stand up before them — as were the yeshivah students themselves. His prayer touched them immeasurably, igniting a flame of spiritual fervor that grew stronger with each passing moment. The high point came at *Kedushah*, when every voice, young and old, rang out with "*Kadosh, kadosh, kadosh*," and every person present felt as though he were reaching sublime heights. When R' Sholom cried out from his heart, "*L'umasam baruch yomeiru*," the crowd responded with a veritable roar: "*Baruch kevod Hashem mimkomo!*"

The gentile cook in the building next door asked, "What's going on today?" Yom Kippur always brought its share of noisy prayer, but today the congregation was thunderous!

In a quieter vein, R' Sholom proceeded with the service. Suddenly, the liturgy was disturbed by an alien sound: the tolling of church bells wafting into the *beis midrash*. R' Sholom's heart broke. "Where am I?" he wondered in an agony of spirit. "It's not bad enough that I had to leave my home and go into exile ... but now I am an exile within an exile, church bells ringing in my ears!" A heavy sigh burst from him.

But R' Sholom was not a man to let heartbreak stop him. On the contrary, he understood that these very emotions were meant to be used as a stepping-stone to spiritual elevation. He continued the service, "as if I were in Chevron," determined to put the foreign bells of an alien faith out of his mind. Spontaneously, a new tune emerged, a melody filled with a fresh sense of peace, awe, and trembling.

In time, R' Sholom made his way back home to Jerusalem. Once again he was in his beloved room, lined with the thousands of holy books that constituted his favorite companions. Remembering the tune he had sung in Switzerland, he suited it to the verses of *"V'chol Ma'aminim,"* recited by the congregation on the High Holy Days. This became the first melody he introduced into his *Mussaf* in the Chevron Yeshivah.

"I was afraid of the yeshivah leadership, who were not accustomed to such tunes," he later confessed. *"Baruch Hashem,"* he added with a smile, "I didn't get it 'over the head.' R' Meir Chodosh even told me '*yasher ko'ach*.'"

From that point on, R' Sholom introduced other melodies into his famous *nusach*, melodies which, when taken in conjunction with his inimitable fervor and sweetness, were branded forever in the hearts of those who heard them.

≈≈

Asked about the sources of his other tunes, R' Sholom agreed to share them with his questioner.

The melody to which he sang the words *"Omnam kein yeitzer sochen banu"* on Yom Kippur night was one that he had first heard sung by a boy he had known in the Diskin Orphan Home. As the youngsters sat on their benches and learned, the boy seated opposite R' Sholom — an orphan who had been beset by many different troubles in his young life — found some measure of relief in gazing up at the ceiling, swaying back and forth, and humming a simple melody.

"That tune became etched in my brain," R' Sholom recalled. "In time, I polished it and adapted it to the words of the *piyut* [poem]." As he once remarked to his grandson, "I feel like crying every time I remember that pathetic young boy and his melodies."

"Selach na," also said on Yom Kippur night, was sung to a Lubavitcher tune, R' Sholom said. *"Ki hinei kachomer"* was composed by the famous R' Hirschel Goldstein (of Manchester), as was *"V'ye'esayu kol l'avdecha."* R' Sholom first heard this tune in England's Gateshead Yeshivah, where it was sung at *Kaddish* during the Yom Tov night service. He had long been in search of this kind of melody, and adapted it for his own use.

"U'veshofar gadol yitaka" is not a tune so much as a *nusach*, and is based on that of R' Zalman Sender Shapiro — as is also the tune to which *"Ma nomar"* was sung on Yom Kippur.

"Ya'aleh t'chinoseinu" came from a tune that R' Avraham Eliyahu Kaplan used in *davening* at the yeshivah of Slobodka in Europe. He would compose a different tune for this *tefillah* each year, and the only one that remains with us today is the one that R' Sholom instituted at the Chevron Yeshivah.

"I originated none of the melodies," R' Sholom said. "But I do have a sense of how to suit a tune to the words. And, of course, I also changed a little here and there."

THE PART OF THE LITURGY THAT PERHAPS AROUSED THE MOST emotional weeping in R' Sholom was *"V'ye'esayu kol l'avdecha."*

The Crown of Kingship What moved him so were the words themselves, with their description of the great day when each and every person will witness

Hashem's Kingship with his own eyes, and when all will rejoice in unison, from far and near. In his later years, R' Sholom found a special tune for this prayer, one well suited to the longing inherent in it. The yeshivah boys loved the melody, singing it along with R' Sholom with tremendous fervor and joy, as R' Sholom's arms swept up, down, and to every side to symbolize the era when praise for Hashem will emanate from the four corners of the world. As the prayer progressed, R' Sholom's arms would grow tired and his voice would grow hoarse with weeping. As the melody joined with the words, "*And they will hear from afar ... and they will come ... they will come ...*" he would falter and finally stop.

The worshipers would wait respectfully for the brokenhearted *ba'al tefillah* to finish sobbing and collect his strength in a final, thunderous, "*And they will give You a Crown of Kingship!*"

When he was finished, R' Sholom would lift his *tallis* over his head until his face was completely covered, then fall onto the *bimah* and cry like a baby. Anyone who was privileged to hear the *tefillah* that came afterward, "*And You alone, Hashem, will reign*," knew — from the bottom of his heart — that one day, Hashem alone *will* reign!

THIS IS A STORY THAT TRAVELED FROM PERSON TO PERSON IN the Chevron Yeshivah years ago.

For Our Sins

A certain Gerrer chassid would travel to Givat Mordechai each year to pray with the yeshivah on Rosh Hashanah. He had come when the yeshivah was still located in Geulah, but was noticed more in the new location because of its distance from the city proper.

Why, he was asked, did he travel all that distance from the city? His answer was: "About 20 years ago, the *davening* in the Gerrer *beis midrash* ended at 2:10, earlier than in other places. For some reason, I had a desire to see the 'Litvishe' *davening* in the Chevron Yeshivah. I walked down Rechov Malchei Yisrael and turned into Rechov Malachi, in the direction of Rechov Chaggi, where the yeshivah was located.

"The moment I turned left, I heard the voice ... Even in the distance, I heard the longing in it — a voice filled with Jewish tears ... I heard R' Sholom, though at the time I had no idea who it was. I hurried to the yeshivah building just as the yeshivah boys' voices came roaring forth. I was incredibly moved. Entering the building, I heard the way R' Sholom moved sweetly through the lines until he reached the words, 'And for our sins we were exiled from our land... and were distanced ... and are not able ....' I found myself shedding tears over the Beis HaMikdash along with him.

"From that day on, I had to keep coming back. When the man who had succeeded in arousing in me an appreciation for the holiness of the Mikdash moved to Givat Mordechai, I followed. I want to continue crying like a Jew."

(as told by Rabbi A.K., a student at the yeshivah)

☙☙

The Rosh Yeshivah of Yeshivas Tiferes Tzvi, R' Michel Shlapovarsky, would ask the young men in his highest shiur to make sure to daven in the Chevron Yeshivah on Rosh Hashanah, and to listen to R' Sholom's rendition of the service.

He had a special reason for making this request. There was once a student at his yeshivah, he told them, who had arrived from the southern part of Israel. At the end of Elul, he came to the Rosh Yeshivah and said that he wanted to abandon his learning and return home.

"I asked him," says R' Michel, "to wait until after Rosh Hashanah, and to daven in the Chevron Yeshivah before returning home. He agreed.

"The day after Rosh Hashanah, on the Fast of Gedaliah, that same boy asked to see me again. He informed me happily that he was sticking to his Gemara and staying in the yeshivah. Today, he is a well-known talmid chacham."

(as told by R' Nechemia Karlinsky)

AS THE SUN BEGAN SINKING TOWARD THE WEST, ITS RAYS FELL on the yeshivah buildings, where from the *beis midrash* and dormitories, the boys were emerging. It was Rosh Hashanah afternoon, and they were making their way to a local well for *Tashlich*.

Tashlich

The neighborhood's secular residents waited for this time of the year to stand on their balconies and watch the crowd pass beneath them. "Look!" they whispered, awed, "There, in the middle — the old Jerusalem rabbi." In his white coat, white socks, and white yarmulka, he was an awe-inspiring vision.

The group, hundreds strong, walked until they reached a grassy area near the well. There, they stopped to recite *Tashlich*. From time to time, R' Sholom, like many others, paused to wipe away a tear. His voice rose into the still air, articulating each word: *Shir hama'alos mi-ma'amakim kerasicha Hashem!* Everyone repeated the words after him, one by one, and then, in uplifting silence, followed him reverently back to the yeshivah and into the second day of Rosh Hashanah.

"It was a precious moment, there among the trees, in the grassy clearing," one student recalls. "The peace that emanated from R' Sholom on Rosh Hashanah was like a gift. During *Tashlich*, I tasted a tiny fraction of the ultimate Day of Judgment, when every tree will rejoice before Hashem as He comes to judge the world. *'And He will redeem Israel of all its sins.'*"

A *TALMID CHACHAM* RECALLS THE FOLLOWING INCIDENT: "I came to the Chevron Yeshivah one Yom Kippur as a person well-versed in the art of musical composition, having secular relatives who were among Israel's top musical arrangers. As a *frum* Jew, I knew that it was worth my while to hear R' Sholom. Stepping inside the yeshivah, however, I was surprised: R' Sholom was elderly then; his voice was not particularly strong and was noticeably hoarse. Was this the *ba'al tefillah* I had come all this way to hear?

Music

"The repetition of the *Mussaf* prayer began, and suddenly I heard the entire *beis midrash* — hundreds strong — chanting along with R' Sholom. As the melody wove itself between the boys, I began to feel the atmosphere of the *Yom HaDin* (Day of Judgment). The louder those hundreds of boys sang, the louder R' Sholom sang, and the sweeter his voice grew.

"And then came the hands. As he said the words, '*Avodas Kohen Gadol b'Yom HaKippurim*,' the palms of R' Sholom's hands spread outward and tears flowed onto his white beard. The crowd roared after him. I was very moved.

"I found myself swaying back and forth, my soul tremendously roused, as though I were being consumed in flames. After half an hour, I noticed that my cheeks, too, were wet with tears. I said to myself, 'Here! Here is a *ba'al tefillah*! Not a singer. Not a musician. Here is where we go down to the roots of the melody.' R' Sholom touched the inner point of the liturgy, and then the secrets of the music came to light.

"Moreover, I realized that it was precisely his hoarse voice that lent his singing its *geshmack*. R' Sholom! You gave me so much spiritual pleasure!"

⁓⁓

Another special moment was during the reading of the Torah portion on Yom Kippur. As a Kohen, R' Sholom was regularly called up first. And each year, the sight was the same:

The *ba'al korei* would begin reading the opening words, referring to the deaths of Aharon HaKohen's two sons. Immediately, R' Sholom would burst into tears. This happened each year, on every Yom Kippur — most notably in his latter years.

"I had the privilege of acting as the *ba'al korei* in the Chevron Yeshivah one year," a student of the yeshivah recalls. "I couldn't believe what was happening next to me. Suddenly, R' Sholom burst into sobs, like a small child. He cried out loud."

[The *Mishnah Berurah* (*siman* 621) says: It is brought down in the *Zohar* that anyone who feels anguish over the deaths of Aharon's sons, or sheds tears over their demise, is forgiven for his sins and will not see his children die in his lifetime. The main thing is that

Erev Yom Kippur — R' Sholom with his brother-in-law R' Shlomo Zalman Auerbach

this should cause him to repent of his sins. If mighty cedars can be consumed in flame, what will happen to the lowly hyssop that sprouts from the wall?]

ONE EVENING, A FEW DAYS BEFORE ROSH HASHANAH, R' Sholom's brother-in-law, R' Avraham Dov Auerbach, entered the

I Should Be Schwadron house.

He saw at once that R' Sholom was absorbed in

introspection, preparation of the Day of Judgment. R' Avraham Dov waited a few moments, then asked, "R' Sholom! I'd like to learn the truth about what is in the hearts of *ba'alei tefillah*, and specifically in your own heart, when you cry out emotionally: 'Here I am, impoverished of deeds, shaken and fearful.' Are you trembling only before Hashem, or is there some other fear mixed in — the apprehension of beginning *Mussaf* and knowing that the congregation is hanging on every word that comes out of your mouth?"

R' Sholom regarded him for a long moment, considering the question. Then, in sudden excitement, he seized his pen (this was the time of year when he traditionally refrained from speech) and wrote, "R' Berel! R' Berel! You speak truth! You are asking an incisive and penetrating question. But what can we do? What can we do? *Moreinu* R' Eliyahu Lopian already touched on this problem." (In the introduction to his *Lev Eliyahu*, R' Lopian indicated that he omitted the line completely. Similarly, R' Eliyahu Dessler refused to lead the *Mussaf* service out of fear of that very line.)

Two days later, from that Rosh Hashanah and for several years afterward, R' Sholom would say aloud, "Here I stand, impoverished of deeds," whisper *"tzarich lih'yos* (I should be)," then go on to say "shaken and fearful" out loud. The congregation never knew the secret of his brief pause.

Later, he changed his custom and began to chant only from the words, "Therefore, I beseech of You, G-d of Avraham, etc."

ON SIMCHAS TORAH, THE FEET ARE GUIDED AND MOTIVATED BY the heart and mind. And the heart and mind do not operate in accordance with a fleeting mood, but rather from a profound and soul-shaking connection to the essence of the day. It is this deep awareness that infuses every motion with intensity and joy. Hand clasps hand in a shared love of Torah that finds its truest expression in dance.

A Chevron Simchas Torah

Young men who labor side by side in the same *beis midrash*, working on the same bench, rise spiritually, separately and together. They know the meaning of this dance. "Blessed is our G-d,

R' Shmuel Hillel Shenker

Who created us for His glory!"

This dance has no parallel in the world. It is a dance full of content and meaning, a dance of love and joy, a dance of holiness and purity.

This was the dance that shook the rafters in the Chevron Yeshivah in those days, and continues to do so today. The yeshivah boys danced with thunderous enthusiasm, caught up in a joy that knew no bounds. It spilled out over the hundreds of Jerusalem residents who came to watch and to learn something about the meaning of Simchas Torah.

The first *hakafah* saw the *Roshei Yeshivah* dancing in the center, Torah scrolls clasped in their arms, as the yeshivah boys danced around them in a tightly packed mass, restrained by reverence from joining the inner circle. The first to burst in was R' Shmuel Hillel Shenker. That righteous man was unable to stand by while the song burned in him. "Blessed is our G-d, Who created us for His glory and separated us from those who err." He entered the inner circle holding aloft a small *sefer Torah*. With eyes closed and face ablaze, his *shtreimel* set royally on his head, he danced, and the yeshivah's leaders danced joyously around him. "And He gave us a Torah of Truth and planted eternal life in our midst!"

Second to join in the inner circle was the pious R' Shlomo Bloch, a student of the Chofetz Chaim. He leaped with tremendous fervor, clapping his hands together in time to the singing. After him came R' Moshe Menkovitz. The two twirled in dance from one end of the circle to the other.

The boys sang their hearts out, almost delirious with the joy and the excitement of the moment: "Happy is the nation whose strength resides in Him — happy is the nation whose G-d is Hashem!"

Only then, and gradually, did the younger boys dare to step into the circle.

The song repeated itself over and over, and no one was in a hurry to switch the tune. "It's true! It's true! You are the First and You are the Last."

R' Shlomo Bloch

"I remember one year after the Holocaust," one *talmid chacham* recalls, "when a number of songs reached us from abroad. That year, they sang '*Keli lamah azavtani*' during the first, second, third, fourth, fifth, and sixth *hakafos*, and only then changed to another tune. The boys were aflame with that song for the duration of all those *hakafos*. It was that kind of song, the kind that comes from the depths of the soul."

There were times when the great men of Torah continued singing even after the rest of the crowd had stopped. It was usually R' Shmuel Hillel Shenker, whose happiness radiated from him so irresistibly, and who continued to dance with all his might, never noticing that the *hakafah* had ended.

It is difficult to forget R' Yisrael Shenker, a focal point of the special atmosphere on that night. R' Yisrael shared his inner joy with everyone, drawing the crowd after him into the circle, lifting aloft on his shoulders those who needed to be higher, and leaping and twirling before the *sefer Torah* with every ounce of his strength. When they sang, "*Hashiveinu Hashem eilecha v'nashuvah, chadeish yameinu k'kedem*," R' Yisrael would shout from the depths of his heart, "*k'kedem!*" One could almost feel the walls of the *beis midrash* reverberating.

R' Hirsch Kupshitz

R' Hirsch Palei was another who danced until his strength gave out, and who required the almost constant use of a napkin to wipe away the sweat streaming down his face.

The yeshivah boys continued dancing the whole time, circle upon circle around the *Roshei Yeshivah* and the other great Torah personalities. Ecstasy danced side by side with reverence for the Torah.

R' Sholom had his own special act. Only he knew how to seize the great R' Hirsch Kupshitz's hand and draw him into the circle. When he fell to the floor in front of R' Tzemach Shlomovitz, joyous laughter spread in ripples through the layers of young revelers. This was *simchah!*

On one occasion, R' Hirsch Kupshitz and R' Yisrael Shenker felt themselves so uplifted during the *hakafos* that, in a burst of awed love for Hashem and His Torah, they spread a tablecloth on the ground and began swaying to the melody of *Aleinu*. When they reached the words *"and we bow ...,"* they prostrated themselves on the floor just like on Yom Kippur.

When the dancers tired between circuits, certain specially talented singers were honored with solo performances. They would stand in the center of the hall, by a wooden table covered with a green cloth (the *bimah* had been carried outside), and sing moving songs. Among the soloists were R' Aharon Minsker and R' Hirsch

Palei, who serves as *mashgiach* of the yeshivah today. R' Moshe Shimon Weintraub specialized in singing happy melodies, and R' Ezra Brizel would stand by the Holy Ark to sing *Ha'aderes V'ha'emunah*.

~~

As the excitement mounted in the hours before the dancing began, those who wished could acquire new insight into the meaning of love for Torah. The yeshivah boys would visit the homes of the *Roshei Yeshivah*, R' Yechezkel, R' Moshe, and R' Meir.

A description of time spent in the house of the *Mashgiach*, R' Meir Chodosh can be found in the *Siach Mordechai* on *Parashas Ki Savo*:

> As evening approached, the boys would gather together and go to the *mashgiach's* house. Crowded around his holy table, drinking and eating the cakes that the Rebbetzin served, they listened to R' Meir's *mussar* talk. Then the boys sang beautifully and with great feeling, to the point where the soul soared Heavenward ... Afterwards, old friends of the *mashgiach's* came from the benches of the Chevron and Slobodka *batei midrash*. When they were all together, the *mashgiach*, his friends and the students, would launch into a series of old melodies. The *mashgiach's* face reflected a sheen of grace, the joy of the holiday and its holiness. He himself would lead the singing, pausing now and then to speak of this tune or that, heard at a certain event in the yeshivah or at a specific time in the past ... The joy of the holy festival wafted over everyone who was present, and remains engraved in the depths of the students' hearts to this very day.

~~

When the sun turned crimson, it was time for the groups of students — including some exceptional married young men — to make their way to the Brisker Rav's house.

The throng filled the Rav's home with dance. The dancers weaved their way from room to room, one hand on the shoulder of the one in front, in fervent song. Others, who were close to the Brisker Rav came to join them as well. The Rav's face shone with pleasure.

The idea behind this concerted visit to the Brisker Rav's home had come, in a casual way, from R' Yisrael Shenker and R' Moshe Shimon Weintraub, who mentioned to the boys the custom of students going to dance in different rabbis' homes outside of the yeshivah. Hearing this, the boys at once decided to direct their footsteps toward the Brisker Rav's home. At the height of the dance, a special atmosphere of uplifted spiritual joy characterized the gathering of young *talmidei chachamim*, who came together to honor their Rav and their Torah.

IN THE MORNING, THE MEN AND BOYS JOINED VARIOUS *minyanim* and *hakafos*, meeting later, at 2 in the afternoon, for *hakafos* in the yeshivah *beis midrash*. R' Sholom attended a prestigious *minyan* in the home of Rebbetzin Kolodetzki (a woman with exceptional respect for Torah, and the mother of R' Kulitz). This special *minyan* had existed for decades. R' Yitzchak Kulitz was designated *Chasan Torah* and R' Sholom was *Chasan Bereishis*.

Intoxicated with Torah

R' Sholom was careful not to drink wine before *Mussaf*, as he did not want to become intoxicated before *Bircas Kohanim* was recited during *Mussaf*. After the *davening*, he drank. The custom in the Volozhin Yeshivah was to drink freely on Simchas Torah, and the same held true for the Telzer and Slobodka Yeshivos. The special Simchas Torah merriment of R' Yisrael Salanter and his students is famous. Those great Torah luminaries danced around the Torah scroll like young children. The *Tenu'as HaMussar* states, "He who has not witnessed this enthusiasm will hardly be able to grasp it. With the *sefer Torah* in their arms, the *geonim* danced and capered like children, and our great rabbi [R' Yisrael] with them."

The following was told by R' Yisrael Shenker, who heard it from

R' Dov Lapin, who, in turn, heard it from R' Itzele Peterberger's daughter. R' Itzele, one of R' Yisrael Salanter's students, was unique in his Simchas Torah experience. He danced until he had exhausted every ounce of his strength, and he was forced to change his clothes several times during the dancing. R' Itzele would drink wine and urge the others to do the same. Together they would go from house to house in town, singing and dancing with almost supernatural energy, tasting holiday treats in this house or that, and bursting with reverence for the Torah. In R' Itzele's old age, a doctor was brought along to keep close watch on him all through the day.

Once, when R' Itzele's wife tried to prevent him from dancing beyond his strength, R' Itzele told her, "In the same place where I cry on Rosh Hashanah and Yom Kippur, there I will rejoice on Simchas Torah. I will not give that up!"

WHEN R' SHOLOM IMBIBED WINE, HIS LOVE OF TORAH CAME pouring out. His dancing on Simchas Torah was the picture of

Vus Vet Zein Mit Mir?
joy and full-hearted devotion. Physically, he held nothing back. From the year 5711 (1951), when he grew very weak after dancing to the last of his strength and consequently required an extended period of rest, the *mashgiach*, R' Meir Chodosh, would take care to enter the circle each Simchas Torah, place a hand on R' Sholom's shoulder, and gently urge him off to the side of the *beis midrash* for a brief respite.

R' Yehudah Shenker relates the following episode, to which he was an eyewitness, and which left a deep impression on him.

"On Simchas Torah, R' Sholom made a habit of going to see R' Eliyahu Lopian. "Once," R' Shenker said, "we followed him into R' Eliyahu's room. R' Sholom and his friend, R' Hirsch Palei, entered the elderly *ba'al mussar's* home together with great respect. The visit was brief. R' Sholom stood before his rebbe and cried softly, 'What will be with me? *Vus vet zein mit mir?*'

"R' Eliyahu Lopian looked seriously at R' Sholom, listening attentively to every word. R' Sholom continued emotionally, 'What will be? I'm an object of *gashmius* from my head to the soles of my feet. *Ich bin gornisht!* I am nothing!'

"Afterwards, they sang a short song with enthusiasm. R' Eliyahu treated them warmly and parted from them with a blessing."

From there, R' Sholom and his friend proceeded to the home of R' Meir Chodosh, where the atmosphere was one of merriment. R' Sholom sang Yom Kippur melodies, and the crowd burst forth with tear-filled joy. R' Meir's son-in-law, R' Baruch Mordechai Ezrachi, spurred R' Sholom on to greater heights, along with the young students, who stood on the tables and on the windowsills. They sang, they danced, and they rejoiced with truly extraordinary happiness.

R' YEHUDAH SHENKER HAS A SECOND STORY TO TELL — ONE which, again, he witnessed personally. On Simchas Torah 5710

En Route to Brisk
(1949), R' Sholom left the Chevron Yeshivah building together with his friend, R' Yisrael Shenker. They were headed for the Brisker Rav's house. R' Yehudah and a friend decided to follow.

R' Sholom and R' Yisrael were dressed in Yerushalmi holiday garb, and both had drunk some wine.

"Fear," R' Sholom told R' Yisrael.

"Trembling and awe," answered R' Yisrael.

In unison, they said, "We're going to the Brisker Rav. Fear! Trembling!"

"'And you shall fear the L-rd, your G-d' — this includes *talmidei chachamim.*"

"*Ich hob moira!* I'm afraid, I'm afraid," R' Sholom intoned. R' Yisrael linked his arm with R' Sholom's and repeated, "*Oy,* who are we going to see? Fear and trembling, tremendous fear!"

The two walked together in intermingled joy and awe. R' Yehudah and his friend followed close behind.

"I was just a child then," R' Yehudah recalls. "I don't remember their exact words. But I did hear them discuss the laws of fear. They talked and talked, until they really did work themselves up into a state of fear. They entered the house in fear.

On the way, R' Sholom and R' Yisrael encountered an old *tzaddik* by the name of R' Yitzchak Mordechai Kahana, formerly of Minsk. They ran to him, surrounded him, and pleaded for a *"Gut Yom Tov"* from his lips. At one point, in their enthusiasm, they lifted the old man completely off the ground! R' Sholom cried, "R' Yitzchak, tell us — tell us the secret! Surely, you have merited seeing Eliyahu!"

R' Yitzchak demurred, "What do you want from me? What am I, who am I?"

Eventually, he did agree at least to bless them with a *"Gut* Yom Tov,"* and they continued on their way to the Brisker Rav's house.

They stood for a moment near the steps, then climbed them, opened the front door gently, and set foot inside. They were in the front room of the Rav's house, which was used for receiving guests. R' Yehudah and his friend crept after them into the house. The Rav was eating a Yom Tov meal with his family.

R' Yisrael Shenker, who was particularly close to the Brisker Rav, dared to cross the threshold first. He said a few words to the Rav, while R' Sholom stood ill at ease, perspiring from fear.

The Rav gestured for his visitors to be served a drink. Cups of tea were brought, which they accepted gratefully. They were seated in the outer room, in a state of gradually returning calm, talking quietly.

Suddenly, the Brisker Rav himself came out to them. He stood in the doorway of the outer room where R' Sholom and R' Yisrael sat. "Maybe," R' Yehudah speculates, "he wanted to see how two *talmidei chachamim* look when they're drunk, or maybe he just wished to honor them. In any case, the Rav himself stood in the doorway."

R' Sholom lifted his eyes, saw the Rav, and cried uncontrollably, *"Oy, oy, ich hob moira!* I'm afraid!"

"I'll never forget the sight," R' Yehudah says. "The Rav leaped back and returned at once to the inner room. His sons came out in his place. The intoxicated R' Sholom and R' Yisrael chatted with the Brisker Rav's sons. After about 20 minutes, they parted with *'Good Yom Tov'* wishes and went on their way."

IT WAS SIMCHAS TORAH, 5694 (1933). THE *ROSH YESHIVAH* OF Chevron, R' Moshe Mordechai Epstein was in his sickbed at home.

The Rosh Yeshivah's Last Dance

It would be his final illness. The spirit of rejoicing in the yeshivah touched his house, relates the wife of R' Baruch Mordechai Ezrachi. It did not succeed, however, in banishing the family's distress. His physical limitations prevented the *Rosh Yeshivah* from giving expression to the joy of Simchas Torah. He longed so much to be with his students, dancing and rejoicing in honor of the Torah, but was bound to his sickbed. It was sad to see a man whose entire essence was Torah, but whose physical weakness kept his feelings from bursting outward.

At noon on Yom Tov, before the *hakafos*, a selected group of students from the yeshivah came to their great Rebbe's house. At their appearance, the *Rosh Yeshivah*'s face lit up, and he asked them to come into his room. Subdued, the students entered, quietly wishing him a "Good Yom Tov." They sat down around the table and began singing holiday songs.

Requesting his family's support, R' Moshe Mordechai Epstein rose from his bed and feebly made his way to the table, to sit with his beloved students. From the look in his eyes, it was clear to see that his Simchas Torah was pierced through with pain and suffering. His back was bent, and every limb spoke of sickness and physical distress.

The boys sang for half an hour, from time to time casting anguished glances at their *Rosh Yeshivah*. It was hard not to compare this day with other, happier Simchas Torahs with their beloved R' Moshe Mordechai.

There was one young student present who suffered acutely from the sight of his *Rosh Yeshivah's* suffering. His feelings overpowered him, and he sighed deeply. When the singing was over and the room was silent, young Sholom Mordechai requested permission to speak.

The others stared at him in astonishment. The youth was not known in yeshivah as one who sought opportunities to speak; besides, the atmosphere was not exactly conducive to speeches.

The young student looked neither to the right nor to the left. He closed his eyes, a cold sweat shining on his face, and began.

"A story is told of a certain great rebbe who was privileged to have both Torah and greatness, spiritual and material riches together. Then, his ship sank at sea, along with most of his treasure. His pain was great.

"Conquering his grief, the rebbe stood in the doorway, lifted his brokenhearted eyes Heavenward, and quoted the Gemara in *Sanhedrin* 46, which says, 'R' Meir says: When a person is distressed, what does the *Shechinah* say? [Hashem] is distressed over the spilled blood of a wicked man, how much more so over the blood of righteous ones.' The Rebbe continued, 'This mishnah says that a person who is immersed in pain and aggravation drags, so to speak, the *Shechinah* down after him. If I am distressed, I will cause distress to the *Shechinah*. Therefore, even in this situation I will not be distressed! For the glory of *Hakadosh Baruch Hu*.'"

R' Sholom finished his speech with great emotion and immediately launched into a happy song. The boys were quick to follow suit.

The *Rosh Yeshivah* lifted his head in order to look at the young student who could not bear to see his rebbe sick and in pain. He looked at the other boys, so pained by his suffering, who sensed that the *Shechinah* was in distress on this Simchas Torah, together with all of them.

The song grew stronger. Slowly, the *Rosh Yeshivah*'s eyes filled with light. His face wore a new contentment. His back straightened. He asked two of those present to support him on either side, and with great difficulty rose to his feet, as though he wished to dance. The boys were tremendously moved by what they were witnessing, but there was no time to feel: The room was instantly overtaken by a completely different atmosphere. The elite students of the Chevron Yeshivah sang and danced to the point of exhaustion, with their leader at their head!

For several long minutes, the *Rosh Yeshivah* managed to make his beloved students happy. The dance ignited a flame that flared up to the very heart of Heaven — on this, the *Rosh Yeshivah*'s last Simchas Torah.

THE STUDY OF *MUSSAR* WAS ALWAYS ONE OF THE YESHIVAH'S founding principles. It comes as no surprise, therefore, to learn

The Voice of Mussar

that the daily *mussar* session was a tremendously inspiring sight. The *beis midrash* was filled to overflowing. The veteran "generals" sat in their places by the eastern wall, the student "troops" in their accustomed spots, as a unique blend of Slobodka-Chevron *mussar* rippled in waves through the vast hall and out the doors.

"I still feel moved when I remember the way we learned *mussar* from R' Yitzchak Meir Petziner (Ben Menachem), when he was still an older student. His sharp voice rose and broke as he sat beside the eastern wall. His intense concentration on a volume of *mussar* was reflected on his face, and poured oil onto the flames."

R' Sholom considered himself a student of R' Yitzchak Meir Petziner and clung to him in yeshivah for regular guidance. In his introduction to his first book, R' Sholom expounds at length on R' Yitzchak Meir's influence on him in Torah, *middos*, and fear of Heaven.

R' Sholom, even at the age of 40, returned to the yeshivah from time to time for the *mussar* sessions. He certainly studied *mussar* at home, but could still be found sitting and swaying in the Chevron *beis midrash* together with the young students.

From time to time, the yeshivah was privileged to host that elder statesman of *mussar*, R' Eliyahu Lopian. For periods during his tenure as *mashgiach* at Kfar Chassidim, R' Eliyahu would remain in Jerusalem at the start of the *zeman* and *daven* at the yeshivah. R' Eliyahu also learned *mussar* with the boys on a regular basis. The sight of that great man studying *mussar*, the sound of his voice roaring like a lion, was especially beautiful. He would sit by the eastern wall, as though a storm were thundering about his head. That wall was graced by other scions of Torah royalty as well: R' Yechezkel Sarna, R' Hirsch Palei, and other noble visages whose mere presence added an indefinable quality to those regular sessions, day after day.

R' Sholom Schwadron enjoyed the chance to seize a *mussar seder* with the yeshivah boys, especially when R' Eliyahu Lopian was present. He would enter the *beis midrash* and take a seat opposite his rebbe, watching him with a student's humble eyes, prepared to be ignited by his teacher's fire.

The Slobodka way of *mussar* has traditionally placed a good deal of emphasis on man's greatness. This approach has been, and will always be, nourished by the humility and the willingness to absorb every bit of *mussar*. He who bows his head to the dictates of *mussar* is indeed worthy of holding it up — twice as high.

Chapter 11

Stormy Times

R' NACHMAN WAS A MITZVAH OBSERVANT JEW whose daughter and son-in-law had unfortunately **Where Is** strayed from the path of Torah and **Yossele?** were leading the lives of secular Israelis in every respect. When the opportunity arose for the couple to travel to the faraway Soviet Union, they decided to entrust their son into his grandfather's care. They wished to live in that country for an extended period, to bask in the sun of the Communist regime.

After the boy had been living with his grandfather for a period of time, his parents had a change of heart. They regretted leaving their son behind in Israel and wanted him to join them in Russia. When R' Nachman refused to give the boy over to Communist hands, bitter words were exchanged. The controversy eventually left the private domain and made its way into the world at large. *Chareidi* and secular Israelis formed battle lines, taking sides with either the parents or the grandfather. Everyone — from the simplest citizen in the street to the most exalted army or police officer,

and even up to the highest figures in the government — had an opinion.

At first, the media expressed a certain understanding and support for the grandfather's struggle to keep the boy. Soon enough, however, the heads of state closed ranks behind the parents. They sent spies. They drafted the best military and government minds to "rescue" the boy from his "kidnapers." R' Nachman concealed Yossele, and was arrested for it. In the basement of the Israeli prison, the grandfather was interrogated. Extreme pressure was exerted to force him to reveal Yossele's whereabouts. In his characteristically staunch way, R' Nachman refused to divulge an iota of information about his grandson's hiding places among religious families. His stubborn refusal inflamed his interrogators and the government standing behind them — as well as numerous ordinary citizens who had a bone to pick with Israel's "ultra-Orthodox" population. During that difficult period, people easily identifiable as "*chareidi*" were afraid to show their faces in the secular areas of town. The taunting cry would come at them from every side: "Where is Yossele?"

Often, the mocking went beyond mere words. *Chareidim* were beaten, injured, and rained upon with stones — always to the accompaniment of that same, accusing question. *"Where is Yossele?"*

"During that period," R' Sholom related, "I was a Shabbos guest at the home of a friend in Haifa. After the Friday night meal, I headed for the shul in the Hadar neighborhood in order to learn."

It was late — nearly midnight — by the time R' Sholom left the shul. He walked slowly down Rechov HaChavatzelet, past the local high school and down a narrow lane. Suddenly, he heard a blood-curdling scream: *"Where is Yossele?"* Glancing behind him, he saw that the shout had come from a group of young adults, 18 years old and older, seated on the railing outside the school. They grinned smugly, certain that they had "caught" an old religious Jew. They waited to see him tremble with fear. He was a lone, elderly man, out late at night, facing a rowdy and menacing group of young people.

But it did not happen that way.

"I turned around to face them, crooked a finger, and motioned for them to come closer. Surprised at the sudden summons, they walked toward me without saying a word.

"While the boys crowded around me, I was pleased to see the girls hang back. Jewish *neshamos* … I could see at once that — for all the boorishness, the emptiness and the hatred — these young people still had respect and *derech eretz*."

A tense silence enveloped the group in the dark lane. The teenagers waited for R' Sholom to speak.

"You called out to me, 'Where is Yossele?'" he said at last.

"Yeah — sure!" they answered with one voice.

"Do you mean to say that I am a kidnaper and a murderer?"

"Yeah — sure!"

"*I* am a murderer? *You* are murderers! You are the true murderers," he said firmly.

One of the teenagers got mad. He balled his hand into a fist and asked angrily, "What did you say? Just say it again!"

R' Sholom's calm was unruffled. In a tranquil voice he said, "You should know that you are murderers every day."

"When I said 'every day,' the ruffian understood that I meant something other than the obvious meaning. He put down his fist. The whole group asked, 'Why do you say we're murderers every day?'

"It's simple," I told them. "Every day, you take a chicken, slaughter it, remove its feathers, cook it — and eat it. Just because that chicken is weaker than you are, does that make it permissible for you to kill it?"

The youths stood open-mouthed. They were not prepared for the question. A moment before, they had been rampaging. Suddenly, they were forced to stand quietly and answer an unexpected question.

One youngster was first to recover. "It's the law of nature," he said. "It's natural for people to eat chickens."

R' Sholom responded sharply, "You fool, what are the laws of nature to you? Are you an animal, accustomed to living only according to the laws of nature that you were born with?" Forcefully, he continued, "You asked me, 'Where is Yossele?' You said that I am a murderer. In that case, tell me, please, why *you* are not considered a murderer — killing innocent animals and chickens."

Another silence fell in the darkness. The young people began to feel embarrassed. Had they no answer? They stood confused and at a loss, grown youths unable to answer a simple question like this one.

"If we don't eat, we'll die," one of the boys finally ventured.

"What kind of answer is that? If a person has nothing to eat, does that make it permissible for him to kill? Besides, it's perfectly possible to survive on fruits, vegetables, bread, and the like. There are many people who are vegetarians, who stay away from meat and eat only vegetables. If they can survive without eating meat or chicken, so can you!"

R' Sholom spoke seriously, his manner filled with an inner compassion. When he saw them completely at a loss, R' Sholom knew his ascendancy was complete. He took advantage of the moment to throw out an additional question:

"Tell me, boys. What gave you the right to throw the Palestinian

Arabs out of the country? The Arabs lived here before you did! They lived here before you ever came to *Eretz Yisrael*. Does the fact that they have no army and no weapons give you the moral right to banish them?" [This is a question frequently asked today — by liberals. In those days, however, it was one that could easily have ended in a storm of stones hurled at the inquirer.]

Again, one of the young men raised his fists at R' Sholom. "Anti-Zionist!" he yelled.

"Don't think you're frightening me," R' Sholom returned. "Answer me to the point!" He raised his voice. "By what right did you chase the Arabs out of this country?"

"Because *Eretz Yisrael* belongs to us," they chorused.

This was what R' Sholom had been waiting for. "How do you know that *Eretz Yisrael* is yours?" he asked.

"It says so in the history books."

"If you know history, you must certainly be aware of the fact that other nations lived here before the Jews came. In that case, what gave the Jews a right to the land?"

Total silence from the group.

One youngster who had stood to one side all through these proceedings, stepped up to answer: "It says so in the *Tanach*!"

"This," R' Sholom later said, "was the answer I had been expecting. I opened my mouth again: 'If the entire proof that the land is ours is based on the *Tanach*, let us ask another question. How does it happen that what you want is written in the *Tanach*, and what you don't want is not written there? Because that same *Tanach* tells us that it is forbidden to desecrate the Shabbos, and forbidden to eat *neveilos* and *tereifos*, and many other mitzvos.'"

To R' Sholom's surprise, he sensed a yielding. The group softened with a startling suddenness, and turned to him with real respect. "Will you explain this whole subject to us, and answer all these questions?" From taunting catcalls, from 'Where is Yossele?,' they had turned around to arrive at the fine and delicate center of their Jewish souls.

Smiling emotionally, R' Sholom said, "Listen, my brothers. These kinds of questions needed to be asked by you five years ago.

You should have asked yourself these questions, or asked your parents and teachers. Here you are, 18 or older, and only now have we raised intellectual questions like these. Do you think it's possible to answer them all here, in the middle of the night, on one foot?

"In truth, the answers are essentially simple. To my mind, there's no question at all. But since you have troubled yourselves to ask, 'Where is Yossele?' right here in the middle of the street, I decided to throw a question back at you. The answers to these questions are simple. The time and the place are not suited to talking long, but I want you to ask your teachers. And now — Good Shabbos!"

R' Sholom turned away, adding again, warmly, "Good Shabbos!"

"*Shabbat Shalom*," they answered respectfully.

"We parted ways," concluded R' Sholom. "I took a few steps, then burst into tears. As I walked up the path leading to the house where I was staying, the tears flowed nonstop. They were tears of emotion in the face of these errant Jewish *neshamos* who had, in such a short span of time, moved from one extreme to the other. I cried like a baby ... And then, during that same walk, I had an idea about a wonderful *p'shat* on the Gemara in *Maseches Gittin*."

Two nights later, on Sunday, a rally was held in Bnei Brak on behalf of

Romanian *olim* (new immigrants to Israel). R' Sholom was asked to speak, and to request that each person present adopt a Romanian child into his home for an extended period, in order to save the children from spiritual devastation.

"I opened my speech," R' Sholom later recounted, "by telling the audience the *vort* that had occurred to me that Friday night, as I left that group of secular youths and walked alone through the streets of Haifa. And when I had finished, I, too, ended with the question, 'Where is Yossele?'

"Listen ..."

The Gemara brings the story of R' Yehoshua ben Chanina, who went to a large town in Rome. He had heard that there was a child in one of the prisons there, a child with beautiful eyes and a handsome face and neatly curled hair. He stood at the entrance to the prison and said, "*Who has given Yaakov over to be plundered and Israel to the looters?*" The child answered, "*It is Hashem, Whom we have sinned against, and they did not wish to walk in His ways and did not heed His Torah.*" R' Yehoshua saw in the boy a future teacher in Israel, and swore not to leave the spot until he had redeemed him for whatever sum was demanded.

Indeed, he did not leave until he had redeemed the boy for a large sum of money, and before long the boy had grown into a teacher of his people and was known as R' Yishmael ben Elisha.

"Many have spoken about this Gemara," R' Sholom said. "They speak of the hints hidden in the text concerning the boy's qualities — his beautiful eyes, handsome face, etc. and of R' Yehoshua's guarantee that the boy would become a teacher in Israel. But we are left with two powerful questions on the verse that he quoted."

R' Sholom's voice rose: "The *pasuk* begins in the singular ['*Who has given Yaakov over to be plundered*'] and continues in the plural ['*and Israel to the looters*']. Also, the verse should have said, '*and Israel to be looted,*' not '*Israel to the looters.*'

"And another question: The *pasuk* speaks of the Jewish people, who have sinned against *HaKadosh Baruch Hu*, referring to Him directly, '*It is Hashem, Whom we have sinned against*' — then continues in the third person, '*and they did not wish to walk in His ways and did not heed His Torah.'* What does this verse mean? What is the deeper meaning here?

"Rabbosai! Walking through the streets of Haifa, a different way of explaining this verse occurred to me." The *Maggid's* voice began its mellifluous, emotional chant: "We lost more than six millions Jews in the Holocaust — a tragedy greater than any we have experienced since the destruction of the Temple, and one which will, please G-d, never happen again. But instead of coming to ask the great men of our generation, *'Who has given Yaakov over to be plundered,'* they are blaming our Rabbis. Even more so, they are screaming that our Rabbis *are* the looters, that Torah leaders are stealing children [like Yossele]. *'And Israel to the looters'* — these are the nation's great men!

"Who has brought about this catastrophe? Why have we been visited with such trouble, to the point that 'Yisrael' are considered 'looters'? It was Hashem! *HaKadosh Baruch Hu* has brought this pain upon us. And why?

"Because we have sinned against Him! Because we have sinned. In what way have we sinned?

"We have mistakenly sinned and are inadvertently to blame in the very area in which they are holding us accountable. And in what area is that?

"Because *'they did not wish to walk in His ways.'* There are thousands who are on their way to spiritual destruction, who do not *'wish to walk in His ways,'* and do not *'heed His Torah.'* And we are not doing enough. We are looting them. We are causing the immigrant children to go astray, we are murdering souls. We are apathetic! We are sinning before Hashem because they do not wish to walk in His ways. We are not doing everything in our power for them."

The *Maggid's* voice was choked with tears. "Where are all the lost Yossele's in the immigrant absorption centers? Where is Yossele? Why are we not stemming the tide of this epidemic? A short conversation with these *tinokos shenishbu* is sufficient to turn their hearts from one extreme to the other. It is possible! We can do it!" Through brokenhearted sobs, R' Sholom went on to describe his Friday night encounter with the secular youths, and emphasized again the tragedy of a generation being raised to hate blindly — a tragedy it was possible to turn around.

"Where is Yossele?" R' Sholom cried aloud, and hearts trembled to hear him. *"Where is Yossele?"*

By the end of the evening, 300 Bnei Brak families had pledged to take 300 immigrant children into their homes.

"The next day," R' Sholom related, "I went to see the Brisker Rav. He wanted to hear a detailed account of what is being done to rescue these children and, *baruch Hashem*, I was able to tell him of the success we had had within the Bnei Brak community. I told him about the large number of pledges we had received from the audience. The Rav, who trembled in fear at the fate of pious immigrants being led astray, breathed a sigh of relief."

Storm Signals

WHY DID R' EZRA BRIZEL DANCE IN THE STREETS? WHAT MADE R' Chaim Shmulevitz burst into tears? What caused R' Sholom Schwadron to have a brain hemorrhage?

The following is a description of a very difficult epoch in the history of the State of Israel. It concerns the government's attempts to help new immigrants, particularly from Yemen, to assimilate into mainstream Israeli society — tossing aside their centuries-old religious heritage in the process. R' Sholom Schwadron devoted an extraordinary measure of time and energy to the "Pe'ilim" organization, which battled this trend by offering a religious education to immigrant

על אלפי עולי בריה״מ שיישלחו לקיבוצים אוכלי חמץ בפסח

על המגיעה מאלפי העולים לחוג אתם את חג הפסח

תתקיים אי״ה

עצרת מחאה

במוצש״ק פרשת מצורע אור לי״ג ניסן תשל״ג בשעה 8.30 בערב
בבית הכנסת "זכרון משה"

ינאמו:

הגה״צ ר' שלום שבדרון שליט״א
ראש ישיבת אוהלי שם

הרב אברהם רביץ
עולה מבריה״מ

children. It is a tale worth telling in all its known details. The story was put together for these pages after a visit to the home of R' Shlomo Noach Kroll, together with in-depth research by the *chareidi* author, Rabbi Yisrael Friedman.

The government of Israel, during the period in question, believed that the best way to achieve solidarity and loyalty to the fledgling state was by uprooting religion. To this end, government policy focused on the new immigrants living in state-run absorption centers. The goal, in short, was to sever the link between the children of these Oriental Jews and their Torah.

⌒⌒

Long years of yearning for the Holy Land ended for the Jews of Yemen with their flight to Israel during Operation Flying Carpet. For generations, they had dreamed of walking on the holy soil, breathing the holy air, and performing the mitzvos connected with *Eretz Yisrael*.

The Israeli government had other plans.

These Yemenite Jews had no homes of their own. They were placed first in transit camps, and later in "immigrant absorption centers." As the first step in its campaign to "modernize" its youth, the centers' administrators — implementing the military formula known as "divide and conquer" — separated the young people from their parents. They established "youth camps" for these children, camps in which the Yemenite young, for the first time in their lives, were exposed to immodest dress and mixed-gender dancing. Young people from surrounding kibbutzim were invited to participate in these dances. At first, the Yemenite youths resisted, and would not take part. Gradually, however, they were drawn in. The next things brought into the camps were indecent films. It was only after strong pressure from the Yemenite community as a whole that these showings were abolished.

The sanctity of Shabbos was not respected in the camps. Teachers and counselors smoked openly on Shabbos, oblivious to the immigrants' sensitivities. Taped music blared through loudspeakers on Shabbos. In one camp, the children were taken on a "Shabbos walk." When they reached the limit beyond which it was forbidden to walk on Shabbos (*techum Shabbos*) one boy, Shaul Sharabi, told his friends that they could not walk any farther.

"There is no Shabbos in *Eretz Yisrael*," the counselor told them, and continued to lead them onward. Arriving at an orchard, he instructed the children to pick apples from the trees. At first, the children refused.

"What are you afraid of?" the counselor asked. He led the way, picking some apples himself until the children followed suit. In time, some of the youngsters stopped *davening* and began smoking on Shabbos.

Perhaps the most glaring difference between the Yemenite newcomers and secular Israelis were the long *peyos* the immigrants wore. The administrators were determined to erase that difference. "If there's an outcry," said one leader of the campaign, "we'll say it was necessary for hygienic reasons."

Yechiah Shuker was a boy of 10 at the time. He relates: "Peninah (our counselor) gave me a note and a shilling for a haircut. The barber cut my hair and left the *peyos*. When I went back, Peninah told me that the haircut was no good. I had to go back to the barber to get it fixed. Deeply distressed, I returned to the barber and he cut off my *peyos*."

A trip organized by the Ein Shemer youth camp was open only to those children whose earlocks had been shaved off. The girls' hair was not cut. The authorities who had claimed that the removal of *peyos* was necessary to prevent head lice were at a loss to explain why those lice seemed only to strike the Yemenite boys.

The campaign was calculated to ease the immigrant youngsters into mainstream Israeli society — dropping all sign of their own heritage along the way. "*Peyos* are not necessary in *Eretz Yisrael*," the counselors would say. "Here, we are all Jews."

With tears in his eyes, R' Shlomo Noach Kroll recalled an occasion when, disguised as a secular youth, he slipped into a class of Yemenite youngsters in a transit camp at Rosh Pinah. A 16-year-old girl stood before the class, where all the boys were bareheaded. She had no suspicion that she was being observed by an outsider.

"So listen, children," she said. "In the Diaspora, far away from our holy land, it was necessary to observe the Torah meticulously. But here, in *Eretz Yisrael*, we are all Jews, and only Jews, living in our own land. There is no worry that we will become contaminated among the nations. There's no need to hold onto symbols such as *peyos*, beards, etc."

Shlomo Kroll could not hold back another second. "No! Children, no!" he called out emotionally. "We must keep the Torah and mitzvos because Hashem commanded us to do so. In *Eretz Yisrael* we must also keep the Shabbos. Our fathers devoted their lives to keeping the mitzvos and holding onto the 'symbols.' It is forbidden to cut off your *peyos*. Our fathers sacrificed for these things, everywhere."

The teacher was stupefied. Teary-eyed, she told the intruder, "I've been working slowly over a number of weeks to help the children 'progress' — to turn them into regular Israeli kids. Now you've ruined everything."

"She believed in what she was doing," R' Kroll said sadly, "and was genuinely distressed, may Hashem have mercy on her."

In a Knesset discussion on the educational conditions in the camps, a number of left-wing members attempted to broaden the law of "compulsory education" to include these immigrant absorption camps. This represented a renewed effort on the part of these left-wing parties to get the immigrants to sign their children up for the "religious track" of their own Histadrut schools. Through vigorous opposition by the religious parties, the law did not take hold. Then Prime Minister Ben-Gurion intervened personally to help forge a compromise solution under which the Ministry of Education would establish religious classes for the Yemenite children.

In practice, however, the compromise did not work. A number of such classes were indeed opened, but the teachers were not allowed to teach, and disturbances in the area of Torah studies continued.

THE SITUATION WAS ESPECIALLY GRAVE IN THE EIN SHEMER AB-
sorption camp. In accordance with an agreement with camp
Drawn Guns administrator Yaakov Trachtenberg, two
in Ein Shemer teachers were brought in by the district educational supervisor. It would be their job to
establish a religious school for the camp's Yemenite children. A
number of Yemenite students began to study in this school, and for
three weeks all went smoothly. Then Y. A. Aldema was appointed
the camp's cultural coordinator. He walked around the camp with
a large pistol dangling from his hip.

On the day after Aldema's appointment, he assembled all the
teachers of religious subjects and informed them that the teaching of
Torah in the camps was absolutely forbidden. These teachers were
then summarily fired, on the grounds that they were unfit to teach.
The regular teachers were also warned against teaching Torah. "Such
studies have not been authorized by the Department," Aldema
claimed. "We are only to teach non-controversial subjects." He was
being strictly accurate: In those stormy times, the teaching of Torah
was indeed wrapped in controversy.

Even after the religious school was closed, the teachers continued teaching Torah in the shul. But Aldema was adamant: Camp
officials were summoned to the spot to forcibly remove the children from the shul.

Shlomo Noach Knoll with a young boy in Ein Shemer, 1950

Israel's religious population was hardly aware of what was happening in the camps.

R' SHLOMO NOACH KROLL DESCRIBED THE PERIOD THAT FOLlowed. They were difficult days and nights.

A Rav's Tears

Winter of 5710 (1950):

It was Shabbos in Bnei Brak. The city's streets were swept with periodic rain and were permeated with the atmosphere of the waning Shabbos. The hour for *seudah shelishis*, the third Shabbos meal, arrived. In the Ponoviezh Yeshivah dining room, the *gaon* R' Yosef Shlomo Kahaneman was giving a Torah discourse, with the students clustered around him.

The door opened, and a tall young man stepped into the dining room. As the Rav continued speaking, the young man hurried up to the central table and — to the shocked amazement of all present — pounded on its surface. Silence descended on the room.

"Rebbe! *Men shmad'et kinder!* (They are turning children away from their faith!)" the man cried.

The Rav approached the stranger. His name was Yosef Gowitz (a student of the Nitra Yeshivah, who now resides in the U.S.), and he worked at the immigrant youth camp at Beit Lid. Gowitz proceeded to tell Rav Kahaneman and his students the dismal story of the Yemenite absorption centers, and the authorities' determined efforts to sunder the connection between these new immigrants and the Torah they cherished.

The *Rosh Yeshivah* listened attentively, his face reflecting the harsh emotional impact the words were having on him. When Gowitz finished, Rav Kahaneman thought for a few long moments.

A group of young men from Ponoviezh, Purim 1947. Right to Left: Chaim Friedlander, Shlomo Berman, Baruch Dov Povarski, unknown, Shlomo Noach Kroll, Meir Yakobovitz, Yaakov Eidelstein.

Immediately after Shabbos was over, he summoned two of his students, Sholom Ber Lifshitz (today, chairman of Yad L'Achim) and Yitzchak Yakobovitz (present rabbi of Herzliyah). That same night, the two set off for the camps. Their goal: to take a few of the immigrant children out and bring them to the yeshivah.

The wait was nerve-wracking. Rav Kahaneman remained in the yeshivah until very late, in order to see how matters developed. By devious means, the two yeshivah students slipped into the immigrant camps and smuggled several boys out under cover of the night. The children were brought to the Ponoviezh Yeshivah, where the *Rosh Yeshivah* kissed each of them on the head.

The children were warmly welcomed. They were shown to bedrooms and served a meal. When they recited the *Bircas HaMazon*, Rav Kahaneman noticed that they said, "May the Merciful One avenge us; may He punish Tzipporah." At first, he thought these words were part of Yemenite custom. It was only later that he learned Tzipporah's identity: She was the counselor who had cut off the children's *peyos*. The *Rosh Yeshivah* was shaken. Tears sprang into his eyes as he gazed upon these innocent children, who had never tasted sin, and whose *peyos* had been stolen from them by their own Jewish brethren!

R' Sholom Ber Lifshitz tells the riveting tale of that daring mission:

"After careful planning, we left in the dead of night for the Beit Lid camp. The camp gates were closed, nobody was entering or leaving. We spent a long time digging beneath the fence, and finally succeeded in creating an opening. Cautiously, we entered the camp. We passed some tents, but saw that there were no children inside. When we asked the parents where their children were, we were told that all the youngsters had been gathered together in one large building in the center of the camp.

"'Are you happy with this arrangement?' we asked.

"'They took the children against our will,' they answered. 'The female counselors dress so immodestly.'

"One parent got up suddenly and declared, 'I'm going to collect some friends and we're going to get the children out of there. You can have them — on the condition that you put them into schools where they will get a Torah education.' We waited in the tent while a few of the men went over to the building where the children were kept. The guard was dozing. The parents entered through a window, woke their children, and brought them out. The children — all of them 10 or 11 years old — were very happy to go. Together, walking slowly, we left the camp. Several hours later, at about 1 in the morning, we reached Ponoviezh."

When the yeshivah boys got wind of the Yemenite youngsters' arrival, they turned out to see them. They marveled at the long *peyos* (some had not yet been cut) and were amazed to see the burning desire to learn Torah in children so young.

The next day in the absorption center, a great outcry arose upon discovery of the missing children. Yosef Gowitz, the young man who had alerted the Ponoviezh Rav to the immigrants' plight, returned to the yeshivah in a state of great agitation. He was in danger: It had been announced throughout the camp that anyone implicated in the children's disappearance would be arrested. The *Rosh Yeshivah* ordered the children returned at once.

Yakobovitz and Lifshitz, assisted by a few yeshivah colleagues, returned each child to his parents' home, telling them, "'If you want your son to have a Torah education, you must declare it to the camp committee. Only then will it be possible to get your children out." Each of the parents made a statement to the effect that they wished to send their children with the "Jewish" young men. The camp administrators made some last-ditch attempts at persuasion, saying that the children would have no medical backup "out there," no food or clothing or social assistance. The parents stood firm.

"One of the administrators," R' Shlomo Noach Kroll recounted, "listened to a woman come in to plead that her only son be sent to learn Torah. He spoke to her about the great danger she was taking upon herself, about the tremendous difficulties she would face in terms of earning a living and getting the help she needed. The woman spoke no Hebrew. She just lifted her eyes Heavenward, and raised her hands as if to say, 'Throw your burden onto Hashem — He will help me.'

"I got very angry," R' Kroll said. "I couldn't hold myself back.

'Aren't you ashamed?' I asked the man. 'A pure woman with an only son. Listen to the way she's talking, and you're trying to turn her away?'"

The Ponoviezh students remained in Beit Lid until Sunday evening (the taking of the statements took many hours) and then returned to the yeshivah. There was general rejoicing, intertwined with pain for the others who had remained behind in the camps. A day passed, then two. On the following night, R' Sholom Schwadron told the following story:

"I walked down the street with R' Ezra Brizel," R' Sholom said. "Across the way, we saw the *gaon hatzaddik* Rav Eliyahu Dessler, who had arrived some time before from Gateshead, England. R' Ezra had never met him.

"That's Rav Dessler," I told him. "Though only a young man, he approached Rav Dessler and asked urgently for his intervention in the immigrant camps affair. R' Ezra went on to apprise him of the religious conditions there.

"Rav Dessler said decisively, 'I won't sleep tonight.' The next day, he organized a group of boys and asked them to go out to the camps. Among them were R' Shlomo Noach Kroll, rabbi of Moshav Chemed, and R' Noach Berman."

Enthusiastically, R' Sholom continued his story.

"Some time later, I was walking with R' Ezra down Rechov Ravad in Bnei Brak, and our talk turned to the Pe'ilim organization, established to rescue Jewish children for Torah. I turned to R' Ezra and said, 'It seems to me that you are one of the central factors in the founding of Pe'ilim. Merit comes about through the meritorious. It was through *you* that Rav Eliyahu Dessler entered the picture, and from then on things started moving. *You*, Ezra! You!'

"I had hardly finished speaking when R' Ezra lifted his arms and legs and right there, in the middle of Rechov Ravad, he danced in genuine joy. Waves of happiness radiated from him. And he had what to be happy about."

R' Sholom dancing with R' Ezra Brizel

Rabbi Kroll continues the tale of the plight of the Yemenite children:

"Little by little, day by day, we brought Yemenite children out of the camps. We went to R' Isaac Sher of Slobodka (the Slobodka Yeshivah housed no more than 20 students at the time) and asked for room to put up some of the rescued children.

"'Rescue more! I have room for another thirty,' R' Isaac said. We traveled to Beit Lid and received authorization to take 30 more children.

"When we had filled up the Slobodka Yeshivah, we traveled to the Novardok Yeshivah in Tel Aviv, where we met with the *Rosh Yeshivah*, R' Hillel Witkind. The *Rosh Yeshivah* was happy to participate in the *mitzvah*. 'I have room for 50 boys, but I don't have beds,' he said. We decided to approach philanthropists such as R' Ephraim Shachor and R' Avraham Bender. We also went to see the Sadegerer Rebbe — and, with Hashem's help, managed to collect the 50 beds. The children were brought to the Yeshivah."

"The work was hard, a few of us against many, with hardly any resources," R' Kroll remembered. "Mrs. Munk, from the yeshivah, prepared food; otherwise we would not have had anything to eat. At first we worked alone and there was no money for traveling. Only later, when Pe'ilim was established, did there exist the possibility of sufficient funds to handle things in the way human beings deserve.

"Rav Eliyahu Dessler emphasized," R' Kroll concluded, "that going out to fight the immigrants' battle did not constitute a halachic decision, and that nothing superseded Torah study, which is the source of everything and upon which the world rests. The order to act was given only to certain individuals on a private basis, and they were always carefully supervised to make sure they returned safely ... And after a long day of hard labor on behalf of the immigrants, these young men would return to the yeshivah and resume their regular learning schedule. It was upon these terms that consent was given. The decision was made after consideration by Jewish leaders at the time, and issued to a hand-picked group of individuals."

THE YESHIVAH BOYS CONTINUED TO PROVIDE SPIRITUAL SUPport to the new immigrants. Each visit entailed burrowing beneath a high wire fence, along whose length armed guards patrolled. The guards' presence gave the place the appearance of a concentration camp.

Journey of Fear

One day, the students were greeted by the Yemenite parents with strident criticism. Their crime? Taking their children to yeshivos where — they had been told by a gun-toting camp official — the Shabbos was routinely desecrated and unkosher meat eaten. Many of the immigrants demanded to see the yeshivos for themselves. A group of 70 of the camp's wise men went to the Ponoviezh Yeshivah. A kitchen inspection confirmed that the yeshivah did indeed serve kosher food. Aldema's plot had been foiled.

Rav Diskin, rabbi of Pardes Chanah, entered the picture to encourage and strengthen the leaders of the Yemenite community in the camps. He conducted negotiations between the *Va'ad*

HaYeshivos (Yeshivah Committee) and the Culture Committee, until it was agreed that religious classes would be instituted in the camps.

Rabbi Kroll said, "The Yeshivah Committee allotted us 10 lirot per month for each Torah teacher, and with Hashem's help the classes gradually began. It was a refreshing sight to see those children learning the way they had in Yemen. We provided men and women teachers, and the camp began to come to life again."

Meanwhile, the left-wing parties were exerting all of their considerable power to keep the enchantment of Torah from the immigrants. The few workplaces in the country were completely under their control. Parents who sent their children for a religious education lost any chance of finding jobs. Others, already employed, lived in hourly expectation of being fired under the flimsiest of pretexts. One parent who registered his children in an Agudas Yisrael school returned a short time later to withdraw the registration. "They told me that if I send my children to an Agudas Yisrael school, I won't have a job," he said sadly.

The people on the left aimed their arrows not only at the parents, but also at the children themselves. In a school in Givat Shaul Bet, they stopped serving lunch to the children who learned with a religious teacher. In Be'er Yaakov, clothing was distributed to the students — in all but the religious class. One woman had a daughter in a state school and another in a religious one. When the state-school students received clothing, she requested the same for her religious-school daughter.

She returned home empty-handed.

THE HOSTILITY WENT BEYOND THE PERSONAL, EXTENDING TO the schools and teachers themselves. When 64 parents signed a **Disruptions and Threats** petition requesting that a religious school be opened, the Agudas Yisrael party authorized the establishment of one such school in the Emka immigrant absorption center. But even after the school was given the legal green light, there were serious disruptions to its functioning. The local authority issued an explicit order not to allow teachers to approach the shul which housed the religious school.

One teacher arrived from Haifa, but the principal did not allow him to teach. R' Yitzchak Winklestein, a *Va'ad HaYeshivos* representative, was urgently summoned. He pleaded with the principal to permit religious study as mandated by the law, but his answer was a veiled threat. That evening, a group of 30 Yemenites entered the school to learn Torah. As they sat and learned, the sound of gunfire reached their ears. Suddenly, an armed man burst into the shul, ordering all present to hit the floor and douse the lights. Breathlessly, he explained that Arabs had attacked the camp.

After a brief wait in the dark, the Yemenites cautiously stepped outside. To their astonishment, the camp's lights were burning normally. Camp guards calmed the immigrants, explaining that the episode had been a ruse. Apparently, it was nothing but a fresh attempt to frighten them into putting a halt to their Torah study. The leftists were seemingly prepared to use any and all means to achieve its goals.

It grew increasingly difficult for individuals of religious appearance to enter Emka. Instructions were issued to transport workers not to bring in religious passengers. Torah teachers were forced to take alternate routes that passed through Arab villages. Coming to Emka became a matter of true self-sacrifice. In a special notice, the Yemenites were informed that "in order to prevent misunderstandings, people who do not have written permission from the Ministry will not be able to participate in the children's education."

Two teachers, R' Piltz and R' Schneerson, were sent to one center by request of the immigrant parents, and began teaching the children Torah in the local shul. Shortly after their arrival, the camp administrator informed them that there was no need to teach in the shul, as a religious school existed on the premises. The two ignored the message and continued their classes. Camp guards hurried to the spot. They thrust R' Piltz's arms behind him and dragged him to the gate. When he tried to return, he was threatened at gunpoint. Schneerson, too, was evicted, though not violently.

The head guard warned them against coming back. "If you return," he said, "the results could be ... bloodshed." The camp administrator, Yosef Bodnim, ordered the shul closed. *Sifrei kodesh* were hurled out and the doors were sealed with a secure lock. The situation was no less bleak in the Achuzah immigrant camp.

Rabbi Kroll continued. "In those days, it was necessary to visit tens of new settlements in order to sign up students. Today, because of legal and public considerations, there is no fear involved in registering students. But a great fear reigned then. Local residents were afraid to come near us. I once spent a Shabbos in Emka, together with R' Sholom Ber Lifshitz [the man responsible for that settlement was R' Yitzchak Winklestein, and we came to help him]. Before Shabbos began, a Yemenite youth approached us secretly and said with great pain, 'We are afraid to invite you into our homes. Please do not be angry; understand us. We will bring food and everything else you need for Shabbos to the shul. Don't worry.'

"In general, it was forbidden to speak out against the government. Once, I spoke in Pardes Katz, and someone in the audience called out, 'Ben-Gurion also said so-and-so ...' I replied scornfully, 'Ben-Gurion is a *rasha*, he is bringing your children to the point of spiritual destruction.' I was immediately dealt a ringing slap on the cheek."

GRADUALLY, THROUGH THE DISTRIBUTION OF LEAFLETS AND organized *Tehillim* recitations, the religious public in Israel became

A Public Outcry aware of what was transpiring in the immigrant absorption centers. The issue became a hot topic everywhere. Public feeling grew daily. There were widespread rallies and shows of public support for the immigrants. These demonstrations found their echo in the Diaspora as well.

R' Sholom Schwadron served as one of the foremost spokesmen on this burning issue. At any time and in any place, he would agree to speak. He poured every ounce of his strength into the cause — until his reserves of strength gave out. At the end of the summer of 5710 (1950), he suffered a mild brain hemorrhage.

Many prayers were organized on his behalf, particularly by his students at Yeshivas Tiferes Tzvi. Heaven heeded their pleas, and three months later R' Sholom returned to his old form.

∞∞

The public outcry was enormous. Eventually, the religious sector of the government began to interest itself in the immigrant camps. In an Education Committee meeting in the Knesset on 8 Teves 5710 (1950), MK David Tzvi Pinkus expressed himself forcefully on the subject.

Pinkus warned of the serious rift that was liable to occur, both within the government and within the reigning coalition, if the situation were not speedily rectified. "I cannot describe the situation in the immigrant camps in any other way than as intellectual coercion and an inquisition against the Jewish religion," he declared. "I cannot view what is happening in these camps as anything but cultural and religious genocide of a portion of the nation of Israel. If this thing is not stopped, it will lead to civil war and actual bloodshed."

Two weeks later, the question was brought up at a cabinet meeting. Religious representatives transmitted the immigrants' outrage, and threatened to resign if matters were not quickly adjusted. They demanded an urgent investigation into the situation. Ben-Gurion, the prime minister, declined this proposal. In protest, three religious government ministers boycotted the cabinet meetings.

Details of the stormy meeting were reported through the media, in Israel and worldwide. The cry of Yemenite children crossed the sea. American Jews joined the battle against religious persecution. The Orthodoxy of New York — comprising the Union of Orthodox Rabbis, a bloc of chassidic rebbes, the *Mo'etzes HaRabbanim*, Agudath Israel, and the Po'el HaMizrachi — sent a telegram to Jerusalem. The telegram was addressed to the Prime Minister and his cabinet, and requested that the issue of education in the immigrant camps be reviewed afresh, and that religious persecution come to a halt.

On January 23, the center of Manhattan was the site of a mass rally in which all of New York's religious Jewish organizations took part. At the same time, the winds were rising in Israel. The young men toiling on behalf of the immigrants briefed the country's Chief Rabbis on the situation, and a visit to the camps by Chief Rabbi Herzog, Rabbi Unterman of Tel Aviv, and Rabbi Diskin of Pardes Chanah was arranged. They would view the situation first hand.

On their arrival at Ein Shemer, the guards denied them entrance. Only after a fiery argument were the rabbis permitted to enter the camp grounds. Rabbi Herzog demanded to be taken to the camp administrator.

As they walked into the office, the administrator got up and fled. Taken aback by this "royal" reception, the rabbis continued on to the shul where thousands of the camp's residents awaited them. They spoke movingly, encouraging the immigrants and exhorting them to stand firm in the battle for their spiritual lives. Afterwards, they met with the camp's rabbis and heard their complaints about the educational conditions there, and the administration's wayward behavior. The trip ended with a tour of Beit Lid, Machane Yisrael, and Rosh Ha'Ayin. At each place, the harrowing tales of anti-religious coercion were the same.

But the rabbinical visit was to no avail. Nothing changed. In Israel's religious sector, the anger and the bitterness grew.

⌒⌒

As pressure increased on the government to investigate the charges against the camps' administrators, the issue became increasingly impossible to ignore. Finally, on 28 Teves 5710 (1950), the Israeli government agreed to establish a committee for this purpose.

The committee was headed by former Chief Justice Gad Fromkin. Members of the first Knesset formed the rest of the committee, including MK Yitzchak Ben-Tzvi (later to become Israel's second president), MK Rabbi Kalman Kahana, MK Avraham Elmaliach, and MK Rabbi Avraham Shag. Meeting mostly in the

Prime Minister's office in Jerusalem, the committee convened 33 times and heard from 101 witnesses. Several meetings were held in Haderah and Netanyah, in order to ease the burden of travel for witnesses from the surrounding area. Committee members visited the more populated immigration centers: Ein Shemer, Beit Lid, Rosh Ha'Ayin, and Be'er Yaakov. Included among those deposed were Education Minister S. Zalman Robashov (Shazar), as well as Ministers of the Interior, Aliyah, Health and Welfare. Tel Aviv's Rabbi Unterman testified, as well as the representative of the "working religious man," Professor Yeshayah Leibowitz. Education Ministry officials were called upon to answer questions, and so were cultural organizers, school principals, teachers, and counselors working in the immigrant camps. At the start of their operation, the committee announced that anyone wishing to testify should apply in writing, detailing the contents of his prospective testimony. Many availed themselves of this invitation. Most of the testimony, however, came from witnesses the committee summoned on its own initiative, occasionally for the purpose of clarifying or completing a previous witness' story.

Even as the committee pondered, religious coercion in the camps continued. No changes were yet apparent. Yeshivah boys still visited the camps secretly to teach Torah and encourage the immigrants. Having been humiliated by the camp administration, the Yemenites eagerly accepted whatever support a *mitzvah*-observant Jew might offer. On instructions from the *Beit Din Tzedek* (*Badatz*) of the Ein Shemer camp, the yeshivah students organized a public fast day. R' Shlomo Noach Kroll described that day:

"We fasted that day. Many yeshivah boys came to *daven* with the immigrants. Because we were not granted permission to enter the camp, the immigrants all came out to us: men, women, and children. The cries of *tefillah* reached the heart of Heaven." The Yemenites blew shofars and declared that they would not budge from the spot until they were guaranteed a religious education for their children. They also demanded a complete and immediate halt to Aldema's "Operation *Peyot*."

The event did much to strengthen the immigrants' spirits and to

A call for a fast day in the Ein Shemer camp

shore up those who had been weakened by the powerful propaganda of left-wing party representatives. They felt that they were not alone in this struggle. Others were standing beside them, to help and protect them against the inroads of apostasy. Each day, the immigrants eagerly awaited the yeshivah boys' return.

ON THE EVE OF 27 SHEVAT 5710 (1950), TWO YESHIVAH BOYS, Ponoviezh students Noach Berman and Shlomo Noach Kroll, arrived

Bullets at the camp gates at Ein Shemer, where they were detained by the custodian. After a heated debate lasting several minutes, they were brought to camp administrator Trachtenberg's office. They found the manager red-faced with fury. He demanded that they identify themselves. When they refused to answer, he locked them in his office and called the police. The pair had come, he insisted, to incite the immigrants. The yeshivah students countered this accusation, saying that they had come to inspect religious conditions in the camp and to encourage the immigrants.

They had also come, they added, to see if there were any more boys who wished to join the yeshivah in Bnei Brak. During police questioning, which took place in Trachtenberg's office, the place was liberally strewn with flyers signed by *chareidi* organizations. The flyers had been put there to lend credence to Trachtenberg's al-

Immigrants gather for the mass prayer assembly

legation that the two religious youths had been caught red-handed
while distributing them. In truth, the flyers had been distributed in
the camp about a month *before* this incident. On the same night, another yeshivah student named Yehoshua Sklar was caught in a
nearby camp.

The news of the detainment spread quickly. A large contingent
of Yemenite immigrants converged on the manager's office. "Let
the rabbis out!" they shouted. "Even if we die, we will not allow
religious Jews to be detained!"

Camp guards reacted to these demands with scorn and chose to
ignore them. The Yemenites' patience wore out. Furious, they attacked the guards and stormed the administrator's door.
Suddenly, shots rang out. The sound did not still the crowd's passion; on the contrary, it only fueled their fire.

"I asked the immigrants to take pity on themselves and leave us
where we were," R' Shlomo Noach Kroll said. "I told the
Yemenites: 'You see that you are dealing with murderers. Be care-

Chapter Eleven: Stormy Times / 355

ful.' But they would not give up, and continued to rage at the guards." An hour earlier, R' Yehoshua Sklar recalls, the immigrants had been so moved by a speech of R' Kroll's that they had lifted him onto their shoulders and carried him around in admiration. They were not about to leave him now in his time of need.

The immigrants yanked up the pegs of nearby tents and fell on the police. During the course of the struggle, men on both sides were injured, including one policeman and Trachtenberg himself.

"Magen David Adom," Israel's equivalent of the American Red Cross, was on the scene to tender first-aid to camp employees. No such assistance was offered to the Yemenites. "They only understand beating," the camp workers whispered to one another. Several normally gentle Yemenites were arrested and thrown into jail cells alongside Arab infiltrators. During the arrests, the Yemenites were cruelly beaten.

The crowd continued to rage. Apprehensive, camp officials decided to release the two yeshivah youths. They were asked to leave the grounds with great speed, in order to cool things off. The storm abated.

But in other parts of the country, public opinion began to rage. Newspapers ran vivid accounts of the incident at Ein Shemer, with reporters vying to supply the details.

THE GUNFIRE AT EIN SHEMER TURNED OUT TO BE THE PRECURsor to an episode of fatal bloodshed. It happened this way:

First Blood   A group of women was waiting in line in the camp dining room, when one of them suddenly stepped out of line. She approached a relative of hers, who worked in the kitchen. A fight broke out between the two women. One of them was hurt. The police were called in, and they interrogated the woman on camp grounds.

Detaining a woman was considered scandalous in the eyes of the Yemenite community — a breach of the modesty so precious to them. A delegation of men went to the camp guards to demand her release.

The confrontation rapidly escalated into a fistfight. Several shots were fired. "Why are you shooting?" one observer asked in trepidation.

The guard replied, "I want to get revenge on him for taking part in all the disturbances this past month."

Another volley of bullets was fired. Someone screamed. It was a Yemenite by the name of Selim ibn Selim Yaakov Giraffi, who had participated a month earlier in the demonstration against religious coercion. He was a pious Jew of good character who could fight valiantly when the cause was just.

Yaakov Giraffi fell to the ground with a bullet in his heart.

⌒⌒

The committee's deliberations dragged on, while the public waited expectantly for its published results. Meanwhile, religious persecution was continuing unabated in the immigration centers. Yeshivah students infiltrated the camps regularly, either disguised as secular Jews or by digging beneath the wire fences. Constant fear accompanied them on these visits; recognition would lead to expulsion, beatings, and arrests. But their presence gave heart to the downtrodden Yemenites, breathing new life and hope into them. The yeshivah boys would not quit the battle against the destroyers of their age-old faith. Nothing — not wire fences, nor threat of imprisonment, nor even a gun-toting Aldema — would stop them from coming.

New boys joined the fray. Some acted spontaneously, in accordance with their own consciences. There was a need for an umbrella organization to supervise and coordinate these activities, under the guidance of Torah leadership. A meeting was called. Participants included a select number of rabbis, *Roshei Yeshivah,* and businessmen.

"In order to respond to the cries of the unfortunate and the spiritually imprisoned emanating from the immigrant camps, and to guard our precious heritage, we see a need to meet together to plan rescue strategies," the letter of invitation explained.

The letter was signed by R' Isser Zalman Meltzer, R' Wiedenfeld

קטטת דמים במחנה עין שמר
עולה חדש נפצע פצעי מות

מטעם האו'צי של המשטרה מודי־
עים:

ביום השבת בשעה ! אחר הצהרים
נורה על ידי שומר במחנה עין שמר
עולה כדש בשם סאלם אבן סלאם יעקב
ג'רפי ,בן 25.

נסיבות המקרה הן כדלקמן:

אשה עולה חדשה. שהתקוטטה ליד
חדר האוכל במחנה נעצרה על ידי
אחד משומרי המחנה. קהל עולים

התפרץ למקום המעצר וניסה לשח־
רר את האשה. השומר ,משה דרוקש.
נפצע. הוא ירה מספר יריות כדי ל־
שניסה לעצור את הקהל הזתקף ו־
שפטים בשומר. המשטרה התערבה
נהרג. קהל עולים נסער ניסה לעשות
פזר את הקהל ואחד העוליים נפגע ו־
והחזירה את הסדר על כנו.

גופת ההרוג הועברה לבית החו־
לים הממשלתי בחיפה. גם השומר ה־
פציע הוּעבר לבית החיים הממשל־
תי והופקד עליו משמר.

Coverage in Hakol, a chareidi newspaper, of the killing in Ein Shemer

רצח שלא בכוונה
או רצח בכוונה תחילה ?

במערכת נתקבלה גבית עדות ו־
נמסרו פרטים על מקרה הרצח שֶבן־
צע במחנה העולים עין־שמר. בו נפל
ערבן סלים אבן סולים יעקב ג'רפי.
עולה מתימן, מכדורי **אחד** השומרים
ב**מחנה.** הפרטים שנמסרו מוכיחים
ש**הרצח** הוה לא היה מקרי שכן הנר־
צח ח.ה. היה גם קרבן למכות אכז־
ריות על ידי שומרי המחנה בקטטה
שפרצה עוד כחודש ימים לפני ה־־
מקרה ה.ה. בשעת מאסר שני הבחו־
רים מישיבת פוניבז'. שומרי המחנה
שמ׳ עיניהם על ג'רפי בגלל עמדו ב־
שער נגד כפית הדת.

בתמונה הניתנת כאן נראה ג'רפי
כשהיא מיכה וזב דם בקטטה שנזכרה
.להלן מוסרת גבית עדות זו כי בעת
הירייה הראשונות שנווו באויר. נשאל
השומר על ידי הנוכחים בחרדה. למה
אתה יורה. על כך הוא ענה. שהוא רו־
צה להתנקם בי עבור השתתפותו ב־
מהומות שלפני כן.

כמו כן נמסרה במערכה פרטים
מאלפים מפי עדים נאמנים. רובם עם
קני חינוך הנמצאים במקומית המ־
עשה במחנות שונים מהם מתקבלת
המונה מהרידה על אמצעי הכפיה ה־
נהוגיד עד היום במחנות. אחרי ההס־
כם נגד ההורים הרוצים בחינוך דתי
לבניהם.

סלים יעקב ג'ראפי הי"ד

(*Av Beis Din* of Tchebin), R' Eliezer Yehudah Finkel (the Mirrer *Rosh Yeshivah*), R' Yechezkel Sarna (the Chevron *Rosh Yeshivah*), and R' Zalman Sorotzkin (*Av Beis Din* of Lutzk). Other signatures included R' Akiva Sofer (*Av Beis Din* of Pressburg) and R' Yaakov Moshe Charlap.

THE MEETING CONVENED AT 7 P.M. ON MONDAY, 9 NISSAN 5710 (1950), in the "Sinai" auditorium of Tel Aviv's Great Synagogue.

Rescue Reports were heard on conditions in the immigrant camps and on the measures that had been taken to deal with them. Future steps were debated. The results of this meeting were far-reaching, and they left their stamp on Israeli policy for years to come.

On *Chol HaMo'ed* Pesach of that same year, another convention took place in a Jerusalem hotel. This one was attended by a large number of yeshivah men and students, and was graced by the presence of the great R' Isser Zalman Meltzer. In addition, R' Eliezer Yehudah Finkel attended, as well as R' Yechezkel Sarna, and other Torah luminaries in Israel.

Before the meeting, great attention had been paid to the question of choosing a name for the group to be established. A committee met at R' Y. Landau's home in Bnei Brak, where they debated long hours, in cooperation with Dr. Pitzipitzi. The name had to be chosen with care. They must not call themselves an "organization," but rather a *chaver*, "association." They also took care to define themselves as apolitical. The resulting name: "*Chaver Pe'ilei HaMachaneh HaTorani*," literally, "The Association of Active Workers in the Torah Sector."

The meeting raised grave concerns over the educational situation in the immigrant camps, and discussed the crucial nature of the work being done to help the Yemenites. It was decided to establish a single body whose job would be to coordinate activities in the camps.

"We will not stand at a distance and ignore the immigrants' plight, *chas v'shalom*," R' Isser Zalman Melzer announced. "We are warned

R' Sholom speaking at the Chol HaMo'ed rally

in the Torah: *'Lo sa'amod al dam rei'echa.'"* He addressed the entire yeshivah world: "It is obligatory upon each and every one of us to give of our time — at the minimum, two weeks per year — for this holy work of saving Jewish souls, as was decided at the convention of *Roshei Yeshivah* from all parts of the country some time ago."

R' Isser Zalman went on to assure his listeners that anyone who gave of his time in this way would not find his learning negatively

R' Isser Zalman Meltzer addresses the rally

affected, because it was inconceivable that rescue would come from those who did not know how to learn.

R' Yaakov Landau spoke as well, forcefully urging his listeners to be unafraid to go out and do whatever was necessary. Then young R' Sholom Schwadron, not yet 40, rose to speak. As it turned out, his speech became the pivotal point of the evening.

R' Yaakov Landau addressing the rally

"I'll never forget," says one outstanding Torah scholar who was present at the meeting, "the way the *gaon* R' Eliezer Yehudah Finkel sat and cried during R' Sholom Schwadron's speech."

Rabbi Kroll summarized that memorable talk. "R' Sholom spoke in his chanting voice, with many brokenhearted sighs. His words [about the spiritual destruction in the immigrant camps] were electrifying."

This was the founding meeting of the Pe'ilim organization, later to be known as "Yad L'Achim." The original body was comprised of 130 members, of whom 30 were women, from every part of Eretz Yisrael. They wasted little time on formalities; the primary focus of the group was practical action. They were determined to fight a holy battle without thought of reward or political consideration. Areas of activity included the struggle in the

immigrant camps, the establishment of schools, arranging dormitory facilities for children, adult care, and night classes and lectures in the settlements. The yeshivah boys returned to the fray with a renewed sense of commitment.

THE GOVERNMENT INVESTIGATORY COMMITTEE PUBLISHED ITS results on Tuesday, 22 Iyar, 5710 (1950). Its unanimous decision: it

Government Crisis had been a mistake to place the immigrant children's education in the hands of the "Department of Culture," whose bureaucrats were not suited to dealing with children raised with religious values — children to whom any desecration of the Torah or its mitzvos caused genuine trauma. With respect to assigning blame for specific events, the committee ruled as follows:

1) The cutting of the Yemenite boys *peyos* had been a policy decision rather than a group of isolated episodes. Those responsible misled the Minister of Education by stating that there had been only twelve cases.

2) Similarly, the disruptions to Torah classes had also been a systematic policy. The shortage of religious teachers did not constitute sufficient cause for this, as most of those responsible for education in the camps also lacked pedagogic training.

3) Camp authorities had not been respectful of Sabbath observance and prayer, and there had been incidents where prayer services was disrupted.

The committee laid the blame at the government's door. "The entire government bears a collective responsibility for every activity of the State, including immigrant education," the report read. Despite its relatively mild conclusions, the report represented an important achievement for Torah Jewry. It proved that new immigrants were not the left-wing parties' exclusive property — and that a gun dangling from the hip is not the decisive factor in forming policy for them.

Ben-Gurion's government rejected the report out of hand. "This assessment is unacceptable," the Prime Minister declared. Interior Minister M. Shapiro came out forcefully against this reaction:

"How can we educate our public to respect our government's judgments even when they dislike them?" he asked at a cabinet meeting. "If the committee's report had come against the religious parties, saying that there had never been any religious coercion — would you *then* have insisted that the results were doubtful? You would have embraced them wholeheartedly!"

The left-wing press, inevitably, came out strongly against the committee's findings. They called for the formation of a new committee, one that would do a better job at investigating conditions in the camps. Despite the report, no changes were made in Education Ministry policy in the immigrant absorption camps.

In October, 5710 (1949), a food rationing plan was presented to the government. Prime Minister Ben-Gurion asked the Knesset for a confidence vote. As a condition for supporting him in this vote, the religious bloc demanded an immediate investigation into the educational problems in the transit and absorption camps. This demand was denied. Without the support of the religious block, the minority government did not survive the confidence vote. Ben-Gurion was forced to resign.

After frenzied negotiations, Ben-Gurion returned as the head of a 13-member coalition, this time including the religious bloc. The new coalition agreement promised the religious parties that the status quo in religious affairs would be respected. In addition, a committee of cabinet ministers was established to look into problems in the religious domain. But as early as the first month of the agreement's existence, it became clear that it would not enjoy a long life. Another impending government crisis could be seen on the horizon.

⌒⌒

"During that period," R' Kroll said, "we went persistently from person to person, from rabbi to rabbi, to spread word of the spiritual tragedy and to rouse them to action. One night, I went to see R' Chaim Shmulevitz. I spoke and spoke, and R' Chaim didn't stop

A gathering at Yeshivah Tiferes Tzvi, Chol HaMo'ed Pesach 1951. At the head table, right to left: R' Sholom, R' Eliyahu Dessler, R' Zalman Sorotzkin (speaking), R' Yaakov Landau.

crying! Afterwards, he began thinking about the *halachah l'ma'aseh*, that is, the practical question of whether he was obligated to close his Gemara in order to help us. Suddenly, he burst into bitter tears and cried aloud, *'Ich vill lernen!'* ('I want to learn!') Who knows how much he accomplished through those tears. For my part, I learned that night how much one should cry. His tears are a part of me even today."

R' Kroll continued:

"I was honored by R' Sholom Schwadron's asking me to come and talk about the situation to a group of great men, with R' Eliyahu Lopian at their head. Present in R' Lopian's room in Meah Shearim were R' Sholom, R' Benzion Bruk, R' Hillel Palei, R' Yisrael Dworetz, R' Moshe Yemini, R' Moshe Sofer, and others. I entered the room in awe, a young man facing such an august and elderly gathering. R' Sholom urged me to speak in great detail. I said what I thought needed to be said, and left.

In the middle of the summer, Rav Dessler told me that it would be a good idea to collect a group of exceptional *kollel* men and ex-

R' Sholom at Yeshivas Beer Sheva

plain the situation to them. I invited R' Sholom Schwadron, R' Shlomo Wolbe, R' Tzvi Markowitz, R' Eliyahu Mishkovsky, R' Rephael Shapiro, R' Avraham Farbstein, and R' Avraham Yaakov Zeleznik to make up this group. The meeting took place at Rav Dessler's home in Bnei Brak. It was decided that, in light of the situation, a committee of *Roshei Yeshivah* should be established to concern themselves with children and students from various immigrant groups. This committee remained in existence for a number of years. The *Roshei Yeshivah* traveled to test students and were extremely helpful in assuring their success."

R' Sholom was very active in the cause of Torah learning. "I remember when the yeshivah at Be'er Sheva opened," R' Kroll said, "they lacked a *maggid shiur* and needed one urgently. R' Sholom went to R' Betzalel Kamenetzky's store in Sha'arei Chesed and pleaded with him to close up shop *that very day* in order to serve as a *maggid shiur* until the yeshivah could find a replacement."

It is very difficult to name every person who joined in this holy work. R' Ezra Brizel, *maggid shiur* in Yeshivah Tiferes Tzvi, was an active member in this struggle. R' Baruch Yadler was one of the central players in the formation of Pe'ilim, and served as the acting arm of the *Va'ad HaYeshivos*. There were many, many Jews who sacrificed on behalf of this worthy cause, and who we hope will forgive the fact that we have not mentioned their names — because we do not know them! They worked *l'shem Shamayim*, with no thought of fame. May they be rewarded!

There were those — including Rav Dessler and the philanthropist Mr. Reichman — who donated money to Pe'ilim on a regular basis. Others contributed hours of learning and teaching in Jewish settlements.

"I asked the Chazon Ish whether it was permissible to send young *bnei Torah* out to teach *Chumash* to uneducated Jews," R' Kroll said. "He answered: 'That is the meaning of *lilmod ul'lamed* (to learn and to teach).' We organized a small group of *talmidei chachamim* who traveled devotedly to help simple Jews with *Chumash* and *Mishnah*. The group included R' Binyamin Karlinstein, R' Weiner, R' Tuvia Shechter, R' Yechiel Benedict, and others. They crossed the wire fences to teach Torah, bringing new life to scores of Jews in these settlements."

∽∽

With the coming of Winter 5711 (1951), Pe'ilim faced new challenges. It was a hard winter. Peilim arranged for the immigrants' most urgent seasonal needs to be met, and settled children in private homes. "Operation Winter" was launched in the transit and absorption camps. R' Kroll continued. "Personal gear and blankets were distributed to the immigrants. We made holes in the wire fence and passed the warm clothing through. We were afraid of Aldema, who always walked around armed.

"The immigrants were living in tents, and the cold was numbing. We collected clothing and made tens of trips to deliver it. At the same time, our activities in the camps themselves intensified. The bond between the immigrants and Pe'ilim grew. New schools were opened and parents registered their children. More children were saved from spiritual destruction."

R' Sholom Ber Lifshitz recently published his personal account of "Operation Winter." In his words:

Pe'ilim volunteers collect winter clothes for the immigrants

"The big challenges came in the winter, when heavy snow fell in the area and freezing cold penetrated the Yemenite children's bones. The Jewish Agency made it known that they would not provide warm clothing to those children who were studying Torah with Yemenite teachers. Word spread quickly to Bnei Brak. A number of young men and Ponoviezh Yeshivah students organized themselves to collect warm clothing for the children.

"It was a surrealistic sight to see scores of Ponoviezh Yeshivah boys walking through the streets of Bnei Brak, sacks over their shoulders, going from house to house asking for donations of clothes for these innocent children."

"I remember," R' Lifshitz continues, "going to see the *gaon* Rav Eliyahu Dessler, who gave us all the warm clothing in the house — a large load. He donated everything he had brought with him from Gateshead. When Rebbetzin Dessler returned home, she was astonished to find her clothes cupboards bare … By the end of the operation, we had collected 80 bags of clothing.

"A day or so later, R' Simchah Brand, R' Yitzchak Yakobovitz, and I rented two trucks and loaded all the sacks onto them. We drove out to Rosh Ha'Ayin in the dead of night. For fear the armed guards would confiscate the clothing, we did not drive the trucks right up to the gate. Instead, we drove about three miles around the camp's perimeter. For two long hours, in freezing weather, we unloaded the sacks. We managed to gain entry into the camp by forcing a small hole in the fence. The sacks of clothes were passed immediately over to the Yemenite teachers. Each tent received a bag of warm clothing for its inhabitants. When the project was completed, we danced jubilantly over the success of our secret operation.

"Afterwards, we drove through the night, back to Bnei Brak. In the morning we spread the news throughout the Torah world: The bags of clothing had reached their destination."

During the course of this work, the young men were treated warmly by the Torah leadership. Rav Dessler himself made sure to prepare an evening meal for them in his home when they returned late at night from their exhausting labor on behalf of the Yemenite children.

The Government Falls

MEANWHILE, THE POLITICAL SITUATION RETAINED AN UNEASY stability. Religious Affairs Minister Maimon tendered his resignation and left the country with the situation still unresolved. Members on both sides of the political fence were working to bridge their differences, when Education Minister David Remez made a fateful announcement: Parents living in the transit camps who wished their children to have a religious education had two options to choose from: the state-religious track, or the religious sub-track of the Histadrut (labor-run) school system. In practical terms, this meant that the left-wing government bureaucrats would continue their policy of religious oppression.

The religious bloc objected strenuously. But Ben-Gurion declared, "This is the limit of our concessions."

In the wake of its economic policies, the government had already lost credibility in the public eye. The feeling on the street was that Remez's proposal was nothing more than a sly attempt to gain official recognition for the Histadrut's religious sub-track, one which the law of compulsory education did not cover. In addition,

Press coverage of the government's collapse

the religious bloc accused the government of not honoring its promises. A crisis was inevitable.

On February 14, 1951, Ben-Gurion's government asked the Knesset for a show of confidence. A positive vote would serve to endorse Remez's proposal. The majority opposition parties, including the religious bloc and the Sephardic members, voted against the government, with the progressive parties abstaining. The government could not survive.

Ben-Gurion handed the President his resignation. Israel's first government became a transitional government.

The end of Ben-Gurion's reign marked a break in the left's overwhelming control of the fledgling state. Those who had chafed under its policies breathed a sigh of relief. A new era had begun.

Though the religious bloc had forced the formation of the investigatory committee, the first real change had come about through the zeal and devotion of yeshivah boys who had tunneled beneath the wire fences to penetrate the immigrant camps. It had been

Torah Jewry who courageously confronted Aldema and his dangling gun. They were the ones who exposed the lies being fed to impressionable young Yemenite children: the lies that said there was no need for a Shabbos in the Holy Land, and that *peyos* were a relic of the past.

Now there was an organized Pe'ilim to take up the battle cry whenever and wherever it might be needed.

THE TIRELESS LABORERS ON BEHALF OF THIS VITAL CAUSE RE-quired a man of stature, gifted with the power of oratory, to
Spokesman articulate their position. R' Sholom was the natural choice. With Torah leadership behind him, R' Sholom dedicated his resonant voice to the cause for tens of years. The immigrants who streamed into Israel by the thousands had a spokesman.

"They called R' Sholom and R' Ezra Brizel 'the Chazon Ish's soldiers,'" R' Yehoshua Sklar recalls.

Apart from his trips abroad to raise funds for Pe'ilim, R' Sholom traveled extensively around the country itself, visiting settlement after settlement to bring hope and faith to new immigrants whose age-old customs were under siege. Many tales are told of his dedication to this task, and of the remarkable success he enjoyed. His

R' Sholom visiting Pe'ilim volunteers at "Beis Yosef-Yardena"

smile, his *joie de vivre*, and the frank pleasure he took in practical action — all these inspired hundreds of Pe'ilim volunteers to give their fullest. During those periods when he regularly visited the Pe'ilim offices in Tel Aviv, he "radiated dedication and responsibility. No one every saw him sitting idly," says R' Menachem Cohen. "When he walked into the office, his habit was to introduce a challenging Talmudic question, and to thus ignite a spark of Torah that flew amongst those seated in the room. In general, these were original Torah thoughts from the Maharsham's works, which R' Sholom labored over most of the day.

Walking into the office, you were likely to find R' Sholom poring over his Gemara or *mussar sefer* while he waited for a report. But the best moments came when the news from the "front" was good. Every time he heard about the rescue of more children or the opening of a new Torah center, R' Sholom would jump up as though electrified, sometimes breaking into a spontaneous little dance, and always speaking rousing words that charged those present with the will and the energy to go out and save some more lives."

R' Menachem Cohen relates an interesting episode from one of these visits. Once, R' Sholom entered the Pe'ilim office, where he encountered R' Dov (Berel) Schwartzman. Greeting him in his usual friendly manner, R' Sholom immediately launched into some thought from the Maharsham. He mentioned that he had been excited that morning by the Maharsham's question on the *Tosafos* in the tractate *Temurah, daf* 6. R' Berel listened to the question, then said decisively, "There is no such *Tosafos* in *Temurah, daf* 6."

A battle-light sprang into R' Sholom's eyes. "What are you talking about?"

"There is no such *Tosafos!*" R' Berel insisted.

"This morning, just a few hours ago, I opened my Gemara, saw the *Tosafos*, and wrote down the Maharsham's question!" R' Sholom cried. The two faced off in stormy debate, each flinging quotes and questions from the tractate at the other. The raised voices attracted attention from the old-age home facing the office, and its residents came out onto their balconies to see what the shouting was all about. Both men were insistent on their positions.

Menachem Cohen continues, "I went to a nearby shul — or, more accurately, I ran to a nearby shul — and brought a Gemara *Temurah* back in order to subdue the storm. 'Let's open a *sefer* and take a look!' I called as I passed through the doorway. The voices stilled. R' Sholom took the Gemara and opened it. He began reading the *Tosafos* aloud ... and stopped. Silence fell.

A long moment passed, and then R' Sholom sat down and said, "The language is not precisely the way I said. You're right, R' Berel. The difference in the language of the *Tosafos* makes it possible to say that the Maharsham's question is not the deciding factor. It's true." R' Sholom appeared drained but content, sitting in the quiet after the storm.

Some three minutes had passed when R' Sholom suddenly roused himself, "But the Maharsham! The Maharsham asks the question! How can this be? What's going on here? We have to understand this!"

Smiling soothingly, R' Dov Schwartzman said, "I'll tell you a secret. The Maharsham is right — but not in light of the language of this particular *Tosafos*. In the version brought down in the *gilyon* (margin of the Gemara) by one of the *Rishonim*, the *Tosafos* is quoted differently."

R' Sholom with R' Dov Schwartzman

R' Sholom clutched his head in both his hands. "*Oy, oy*, you're right! The Maharsham adds two words, according to *Tosafos* in *Temurah, daf 6, 'gilyon* version' … Amazing!" Sheer excitement raised R' Sholom from his seat. He seized his walking stick, waved it aloft, and broke into a crow of jubilation as his feet danced in the abundance of his joy."

"WE TRAVELED TO THE SETTLEMENTS TOGETHER," R' SHOLOM related. "R' Avraham Yaakov Zeleznik, R' Baruch Yadler, R' Ezra

The Chazon Ish and Pe'ilim

Brizel, and me, the least among them. This was during the period of *'yaldei Teiman'* (the Yemenite children).

"Together we traveled to Rechovot (where we met the *gaon*, R' Eliezer Shach) and then went on to other settlements, with the goal of rousing the local rabbis in our rescue work for the immigrants in the camps. We fasted that day; it was the 17th of Tammuz.

"By nightfall, before we broke our fast, we reached Bnei Brak and went to see the Chazon Ish to report on our activities. The Chazon Ish was aware of the situation and of the work we were doing.

"We found the Chazon Ish resting, due to his weakness, on the porch of his house. We told him about our day's work. In the middle of the conversation, I noticed how weak R' Yaakov Zeleznik looked. I whispered, 'You'd better go eat something. The fast has been over an hour and a half already.'

R' Sholom arriving to speak at a settlement in the north

R' Sholom at work in America, at the home of R' Avraham Zelig Krohn

"The Chazon Ish overheard. 'At once! Come right now!' Overcoming his own weakness, he rose and announced quietly, 'You are eating here.' He walked quickly into an inner room and we followed him. Two minutes later, he reappeared, a loaf of bread in his hand. Then he went back inside and returned with fish and salt. A third trip brought a cup of water and a large bowl; a towel was slung over one shoulder. *Hachnasas orchim!* He placed everything on the table and left the room, leaving us to eat alone (as is suggested in the *Rambam*).

"We ate quickly, *bentched*, and returned to the porch, where we found the Chazon Ish absorbed in his learning. He greeted us warmly and the discussion was resumed about our activities, past and future. We sought his advice about whether and how to call for a mass rally to inform the wider public of the plight of the immigrants. The Chazon Ish reacted positively to the idea of a rally and went on to make a suggestion about the best way to summon the public to attend it: 'There is surely a need for specific language in addressing each group individually. One version for Bnei Brak and another for Yerushalayim,' he said.

"On his advice, we decided to hold the rally in Bnei Brak on the following day, at 7 p.m. in the evening. At once, he took a large sheet of paper and began writing down the announcement for Bnei Brak. When we asked him where to hold the rally, he said 'You can have it here, in my house.'

"R' Ezra Brizel ventured, 'And perhaps the Rav will sign the announcement?'

"The Chazon Ish answered simply, 'It's already late, 11 at night, but for such a matter as we are dealing with here I would walk, even now, on foot, to Tel Aviv. But signing is harder for me.'

"Respectfully, we took our departure.

"The next day, we visited all the Torah institutions in the central part of the country, to announce that the Chazon Ish was calling for a rally at his house. When we entered the Heichal HaTalmud in Tel Aviv to make the announcement, R' Shlomo Shimshon Karelitz was there. He turned to me and asked, 'Are you sure that the Chazon Ish is behind this? I know that he isn't in the habit of calling for rallies.' Confidently, I explained that we had been with the Chazon Ish until nearly midnight the previous evening, that he had written the text for us, encouraged us, and agreed to have the rally at his home. The only thing to which he had not agreed, I said, was to sign the announcement.

"We went from yeshivah to yeshivah and from *kollel* to *kollel*, until we saw that it was nearly time for the rally to begin. Flagging down a taxi, we traveled back to Bnei Brak and came up to the house at 1 minute to 7.

"Outside the Chazon Ish's home were scores of young yeshivah men and Torah scholars. But what was very strange was the fact that the house was completely dark. Everything was locked and shuttered.

"My heart and eyes grew dark.

"What had happened? I walked around the house on every side, seeking a ray of light — but all was shrouded in darkness. Why, I wondered in confusion, had the Chazon Ish darkened his home?

"Suddenly, a man whispered in my ear, 'R' Sholom, I heard that the Chazon Ish said, "Am I one who calls people to rallies?"'

"I was astonished — and shaken. In deep pain, I wondered what I had done. If I had made a mistake and caused the Chazon Ish dis-

R' Sholom at a Pe'ilim meeting with R' Moshe Feinstein

tress, I would be obligated to beg for forgiveness from that great Torah leader! I trembled ...

"'Everything's locked up. You have to help me,' I whispered to someone whom I recognized as being close to the Chazon Ish. He consented to lead me around to the back of the house, near some trees, and help me find my way into the house.

"I entered hesitantly. The Chazon Ish was lying in bed, with R' Beinish Finkel and another young man standing nearby. There were no electric lights shining in the room, just a small oil lamp that cast a weak illumination over the trio. I stood face-to-face with the Chazon Ish, and he recognized me. He looked at me ...

"Immediately, I launched into my apology. The Chazon Ish waited a minute, then sat up in bed, raised his voice, and said, 'I think that it's a chutzpah!' I thought I was going to faint.

"Then he elaborated, 'I think it's a chutzpah for me to call a rally. What am I doing calling rallies?'

"Noting my trepidation, he hastened to calm me. Then, smiling, he said, 'Nu, turn on the lights and let the people in.' And the rally took place as planned.

"The Chazon Ish had told us, 'Signing is harder for me.' But we hadn't understood."

Chapter 12

Summary of a Life

HIS NAME WAS RENOWNED, NEAR AND FAR: Rabbeinu Sholom Mordechai HaKohen Schwadron, **Beloved Above and Below** who departed this world on the bitter day of 22 Kislev, 5758 (1997).

How can we weigh or calculate even a fraction of his praise? Who can delve into the depths of his ways? He wanted to learn and to teach, with all his heart, in every place that his hand reached. From the four walls of halachah, with monumental devotion, he merited becoming a paragon for others, beloved above and below. He was 85 years old. For 85 years pearls of wisdom flowed from his mouth.

His very essence was in *Torah tavlin*, the spice of Torah, — *bekius* and *charifus* — and day and night, always, he was immersed in his love of Torah! He raised soldiers of Torah, established congregations and heaped merit on the masses. He stood with arms outstretched to honor the Torah, and unsheathed the sword of his tongue in the *beis midrash*, to praise and honor and elevate

A strongly worded letter to a friend — written in 1935 — regarding Torah and mussar.

those who study the Torah, those who stand sentinel over the glowing coals of toil in Torah. He raised his voice like a shofar, to spread the word: This is Torah, and this is its reward! He succeeded in bringing merit to great numbers of people, both in our Holy Land and abroad, everywhere he went. From the previous generation to our own, he formed a passage filled with the waters of life, the light of life, a way of life studded with the jewels of *mussar*, a living Torah, and love of *chesed*.

In the very place where his greatness is to be found, there you will find his humility. He did not lay the smallest matter to rest without soliciting the opinions of the elders of his generation; his feet did not take a step until he had heard from his teachers. He never left himself without a rebbe from whom to ask and from whom to humbly learn. R' Sholom was a true student, and in this he was unique in his time. Even in the years of his wisdom, even in his 70's and later, he always found another great man of Torah and piety to nourish him with knowledge and wisdom.

R' Sholom was a leading light because he had a : "listening ear." With all his might, he tried to hear more and more from every person, and whatever he heard he thirstily absorbed.

And his humility was greater than anything else. When he sat at home learning Torah or stood bowed in prayer, he humbled himself like a servant before a king, without any sense of self. His approach to all people was with tremendous humility ... And when he went out in his strength to rebuke people for a lack of respect for Heaven's honor, he girded his loins like a warrior, his lips spewing deadly arrows against those who broke the covenant and led others into evil. His heart was like a torch, aflame with might ... For such a man, for R' Sholom Mordechai, heaven and earth are weeping.

Our rebbe had a special countenance, famous in our time for its joy in life. Everyone who came near him found peace and tranquility. This, too, derived from his greatness in *bein adam lachavero* (interpersonal relations). His pure heart wished to improve the lot of his fellow man, to help him walk in Hashem's ways. Receiving every person pleasantly was a high priority with him, and the Name of Heaven was sanctified through him. "See!" all would say. "See! That *gaon* and *tzaddik* — how pleasant is his manner, how correct all his behavior."

(from a speech by R' Avraham Yosef Leizerson)

The following are some precious vignettes from the life of this *tzaddik*, a man impossible to replace.

R' SHOLOM'S FATHER, THE BRILLIANT *GAON*, R' YITZCHAK HaKohen Schwadron, was widowed in the year 5658 (1898), when **Strong Roots** his rebbetzin, Chayah Leah, departed this world, leaving behind nine orphans. In the year 5663 (1903), before the passing of his father, the Maharsham of Berzan, R' Yitzchak moved to *Eretz Yisrael*, where he remarried Rebbetzin Frayda, with whom he had more children. His children were: Esther Toba, later to become the wife of R' Leib Lieberman;

Nechamah, who later married R' Eliyahu Segal; R' Yaakov Schwadron; Yehudis, later the wife of R' Shimon Klein; R' Chaim Schwadron, who had many students and passed away in the year 5757 (1997); R' Eliyahu Schwadron; Chaya Rochel, R' Sholom Mordechai, and Sarah.

It was on the 25th day of Sivan, 5672 (1912), a year and a half after the Maharsham's passing, that Rebbetzin Frayda first embraced the son that would be named after his illustrious grandfather, Sholom Mordechai. These were strong roots. As a boy, Sholom Mordechai suffered much and faced many challenges until he found his way onto the correct path in life. He never reveled in material pleasure, never rejoiced in the flavors of this world. It was not his way to complain, even in the most difficult years. It is quite possible that R' Sholom, known for his joy in life, derived his contentment precisely from those difficult times — times that laid the foundation for his spiritual life.

R' Yitzchak Schwadron, son of the Maharsham, passed away in the year 5680 (1920). He left behind his broken-hearted widow and six small children (the youngest was a girl, just six months old). One of them was R' Sholom, then a 7-year-old, learning in the Talmud Torah of Meah Shearim. The widow, the righteous Rebbetzin Frayda, embarked on a terribly arduous period in her life.

In those days, after years of world war, Jerusalem was neglected and downtrodden, afflicted by famine and other sufferings. The Rebbetzin was forced to sustain her family through her own efforts, as well as raise her children to be observant of Torah and mitzvos. Earning a livelihood proved nearly impossible. One man came along and promised to help. He got Jerusalem's rabbis to sign a plea on behalf of this *talmid chacham's* widow and orphans — but ended up taking the money he collected and keeping it for himself. Rebbetzin Frayda and her children were left destitute. These conditions formed the early years of R' Sholom's life.

In an effort to transmit their father's precepts to the children, the Rebbetzin would relate Torah thoughts she had heard from her husband, R' Yitzchak. In later days, R' Sholom published some of them in the introductions to his work, *Oholei Shem* and *Da'as Torah*,

Part Two. In his preface to the first volume, R' Sholom wrote, "I possess several wonderful stories of my father's chassidus and purity, as told to me by my mother, the Rebbetzin, may she live and be well."

The young R' Sholom was a boy with a happy attitude towards life, filled with youthful energy and endless possibility, a strong ambition coupled with strong roots. He was taken to the Diskin Orphan Home, which he left on his own, finding his way back to the Talmud Torah of Meah Shearim.

Even before his bar mitzvah, Sholom Mordechai was known as a boy of sensitivity and fine *middos*, possessor of a sharp and brilliant mind — a boy who displayed the kind of outstanding diligence in his learning that befit the son of R' Yitzchak and the grandson of the great Maharsham.

WHEN HE WAS 12, SHOLOM MORDECHAI BEGAN SHOWING UP at the *beis midrash* on a regular basis. This ran parallel with his en-

Early Influences try into a yeshivah for young boys called Yeshivas Tzion. The *Rosh Yeshivah*, R' Yaakov Katzenelenbogen, saw special strengths in the boy, and began learning certain works with him. A love of learning blossomed immediately in R' Sholom: "R' Yaakov gave me a *geshmack* for learning," he would relate many years later. He also formed an attachment to R' Aharon Katzenelenbogen, whose talks, parables, and stories became etched into R' Sholom's soul. R' Aharon stood devotedly at Rebbetzin Frayda's side during her widowhood, helping her financially and supporting her in marrying off her orphaned children.

FROM JERUSALEM, R' SHOLOM MADE HIS WAY, THREE YEARS later, to the Lomzhe Yeshivah in Petach Tikvah. Here, too, ob-

Petach Tikvah servers witnessed the inner struggles of this teenager who had no father, and whose mother was far away. They saw him persevere, deriving genuine pleasure from learning Torah. R' Eliyahu Dushnitzer's personal example pointed all the yeshivah's students, including R' Sholom,

R' Eliyahu Dushnitzer

in the right direction. R' Eliyahu gathered a small *chaburah* (group) of select students around him, teaching and guiding them in a very personal way. Young Sholom Mordechai was included in this group. R' Eliyahu's image remained with him throughout his life. It was in the Lomzhe Yeshivah that the boy from Jerusalem developed and honed his abilities in learning Gemara.

We were privileged to hear a few tidbits about this era in R' Sholom's life from an old friend of his, R' Shmuel Aharon Isaacov:

In the Lomzhe Yeshivah, R' Eliyahu Dushnitzer conducted a *va'ad*, in which he chose a few outstanding *bachurim* and instructed them on a regular basis. During one of these sessions, for example, he talked to us about *chesed*. He explained that a person is obligated to perform *chesed* every day, in some way: to help an elderly person in the street, to help a fellow student find the *sefer* he needs. And that's what we did. We were careful to observe the mitzvah of *gemilus chasadim* every day.

There was a *va'ad* that emphasized the importance of having the proper intentions in reciting the first *berachah* in the *Shemoneh Esrei*. In another, R' Eliyahu asked us never to go out into the street "empty-handed": We should always leave with something in our heads, such as a few *mishnayos* we had memorized, or something similar to review, and to be absorbed in this [in order not to waste time in the street, and to remain focused on matters of Torah and piety]. R' Sholom Schwadron was one of the good boys selected to join this group, which met in the *mashgiach's* home.

I'll never forget the first Rosh Hashanah in the yeshivah — especially the *davening*. The *ba'al tefillah* prayed in an emotional voice, lips burning and heart in flames. I did not know who he was, until someone told me that he was the *maggid shiur,* R' Schachna [Kolodetsky]. Apart from his greatness in Torah, his *davening* was awesome! On Yom Kippur we *davened* with R' Eliyahu Dushnitzer.

We came to Petach Tikvah in the year 5687 (1927), simply because there were hardly any yeshivos in Jerusalem. And if you will ask why we left Petach Tikvah afterwards and returned to Jerusalem ... there was great fear of the Arabs in all parts of the country. Petach Tikvah residents and those from the surrounding area armed themselves with knives whenever possible, and organized patrols among the orchards and trees, while we yeshivah boys said *Tehillim.* There were incidents in Chevron in the year 5689 (1929). The larger settlement in Yerushalayim was less fearful at that time, and if there existed a good and famous yeshivah there — Yeshivas Chevron — why not go?

THE CHEVRON YESHIVAH RELOCATED FROM CHEVRON TO Jerusalem in mid-Elul 5689 (1929). The great R' Yosef Chaim **On to** Sonnenfeld, who served as the generation's Torah **Chevron** leader in *Eretz Yisrael,* encouraged the yeshivah and sent his own grandsons to study there, paving the way for native-born Yerushalmi youths to join the Lithuanian and German immigrants who made up the original student body.

About this group of Yerushalmi boys, and the *kollel* they later established, R' Yisrael Zissel Dworetz wrote in his monthly *Tevunah,* in the year 5701 (1941): "These students, while still in the yeshivah, constituted a special group and were extremely involved in the yeshivah's experiences. From a desire to preserve their independence and their links with the yeshivah, they deemed it appropriate to found a Torah institution for themselves. Without resources, they devoted themselves with sacrifice for Torah, and the Torah's teachings ... Their success and their spiritual elevation roused a certain amount of *kinas sofrim* (professional envy). In this *kollel,* the Chevron Yeshivah's administration saw a future for their top students. This close relationship led the *kollel* to flourish, actualizing the Alter of Slobdoka's dream."

The first group of young men included R' Shmuel Aharon Isaacov, R' Yisrael Shenker, R' Chaim Aharon Turzin, R' Hillel Cohen, and R' Mordechai Ofel.

R' Sholom Schwadron was among the first to join the yeshivah at the start of the winter of 5690 (1930).

"The first time I walked into the Chevron Yeshivah *beis midrash*," R' Sholom related, "was during the *mussar seder*. The voices moved me, and tears stood in my eyes."

The *mashgiach* who took over after the Alter of Slobodka was R' Leib Chasman, with R' Meir Chodosh also serving as an additional *mashgiach*. R' Leib had a special preference for students who were extremely diligent and talented, and he extended his affection to several such boys — among them young Sholom Schwadron. R' Leib recognized R' Sholom's "listening ear" and sensitive heart; R' Sholom, on his part, reverently took this *mussar* giant as his rebbe. Among the younger yeshivah boys, R' Sholom was closest to R' Leib.

R' Sholom never missed one of his rebbe's *mussar* talks in

"Der Rebbbe," R' Leib Chasman

yeshivah. When his very good friend, R' Avraham Roth, was married in Jerusalem's Old City, R' Sholom walked the long distance to the yeshivah to hear his rebbe's talk, and then returned to the wedding.

R' Leib guided and taught R' Sholom as only he knew how. And R' Sholom referred to him as "the Rebbe" to the end of his days.

☞☜

Though just a young student during R' Moshe

Mordechai Epstein's lifetime, R' Sholom managed to win the *Rosh Yeshivah's* approving notice. One of R' Moshe Mordechai's sons-in-law, a fine Torah scholar in his own right, wore a frock coat. With his discerning eye, young R' Sholom noted that the garment, being four-cornered and mostly open, required *tzitzis*. Unwilling to tell him so face to face, and yet equally loathe to refrain from bringing this possibility of a Biblical infraction to his notice, R' Sholom wrote the *Rosh Yeshivah's* son-in-law an unsigned letter.

The son-in-law made every effort to ascertain the letter-writer's identity. It was R' Moshe Mordechai himself who said, "It seems to me that the Schwadron boy is the one who sent the letter." As the story has it, the *Rosh Yeshivah* investigated R' Sholom's character and found no intention of disrespect in his sending the letter, but rather a genuine desire to serve *l'sheim Shamayim* — for the sake of Heaven.

"The boys were saying the *berachah* over the *Rosh Yeshivah's es-rog*," said R' Sholom. "A special honor was accorded the one who transferred the *esrog* from boy to boy. Usually, this honor was given to one of the older yeshivah boys. That year, after I had written the letter, the *Rosh Yeshivah* put me in charge of the *esrog*."

After the incident, R' Sholom became close to the *Rosh Yeshivah's* son-in-law, R' Aharon Cohen. There are those who still remember R' Aharon's first *shiur*, which the *mashgiach*, R' Leib Chasman, attended. They remember, too, the way young Sholom Schwadron argued heatedly about a question that the *mashgiach* had whispered in his ear during the *shiur*.

"There was a group in the yeshivah," says R' Shmuel Aharon Isaacov, "that was known among the other boys as the '*tzaddikim*.' They took many stringencies upon themselves, including numerous all-nighters of learning (e.g., Hoshana Rabbah night, the first night in which *Selichos* is said, etc.), and periods of speech-fasts. R' Sholom was a member of this group. They did not draw attention to themselves or their own righteousness — but the yeshivah knew that they had organized certain practices among themselves.

"R' Sholom himself was involved with people to an extraordinary degree," R' Isaacov recalls. "Everybody loved him. As in all yeshivos, the younger boys were afraid to approach the older ones; but they approached R' Sholom."

Friends from that period of his life likened R' Sholom to a burning flame. "I remember him being like a storm when it came to learning. As a student of R' Leib Chasman, the walls of the *beis midrash* shook when he delivered a *mussar* session. But even during the rest of the day, you could see his 'fire' in learning *Shas* and the commentaries," relates R' Alter Gelerenter.

"I still remember the way he learned *Maseches Sotah* together with a partner — like a burning flame!" tells R' Shimshon Harari. Picture the intensity that can lead others to remember, decades later, which tractate R' Sholom was learning at the time!

For a time, R' Sholom was deeply immersed in learning the *Sha'agas Aryeh*. As he himself recalled, during that period when he asked questions on the material the yeshivah was learning, his friends remarked that his questions were reminiscent of those of the *Sha'agas Aryeh*. He had a sharp mind, and an all-absorbent one.

The *mashgiach*, R' Meir Chodosh, told us, "When R' Sholom was a young *bachur* in the yeshivah, during the years 5691-93 (1931-1933), I worked with him and a group of others to set a goal of

Left to Right: R' Ezra Brizel, R' Meir Chodosh, R' Sholom, R' Nachum Sheinelson (R' Sholom's son-in-law), R' Shlomo Zalman Auerbach

learning all of *Shas* [at a serious pace]. The boys accepted the challenge. We guided them in how to learn and how to review all they had learned. With Heaven's help, within a short space of time they were very successful."

R' Sholom used to show his grandsons the notebooks he kept from that period. "Look in here and see how much ground we covered! How much we learned! In quantity and quality, in depth and in sheer volume!"

R' Meir Chodosh not only encouraged young R' Sholom to learn tremendous quantities on his own, but also enjoyed "playing" with him in Torah study. The two would regularly pace the *beis midrash* together, debating questions on the material being learned — until R' Leib Chasman once chided R' Meir: "Do you want to turn him into a *ba'al ga'avah* (a prideful person)?"

Even after he was married, R' Sholom continued his program of studies as set down by R' Meir Chodosh. Then, he added long hours of the *Shulchan Aruch* and the *Tur* to the program.

Marriage AFTER HIS WEDDING, THE "YOUNG MAHARSHAM" (AS HE WAS fondly called by his teacher, R' Yitzchak Meir Petziner, as well as by the Steipler) moved in with his father-in-law, R' Chaim Leib Auerbach. He was R' Chaim Leib's first son-in-law. The wedding took place on *erev Shabbos, Parashas Miketz*, during Chanukah 5696 (1936).

The Auerbachs lived in the Nachalas Tzadok neighborhood, adjoining Sha'arei Chesed. For three years, R' Sholom lived under their modest roof. Then he moved into an apartment in Sha'arei Chesed, near the Gra Shul, where he could learn uninterrupted. He would live there the rest of his life.

R' Chaim Leib was very pleased with his new son-in-law. For his part, R' Sholom absorbed the atmosphere of the home, where material poverty went hand-in-hand with a joyous love of Torah. In his first book, *Oholei Shem*, R' Sholom writes a few words of appreciation: "I must give thanks and blessings to my father-in-law, the *gaon* R' Chaim Yehudah Leib, *Rosh Yeshivah* of Sha'ar HaShamayim, who gave me the vision to approach this holy work; and to my mother-in-law, the righteous Rebbetzin Tzivia, who supported me at their table for several years and loved me like a son."

From the early days of his marriage, R' Sholom fasted every Monday and Thursday, spending the day learning in his room wrapped in his *tallis* and *tefillin*. He continued this practice until his strength failed him, in the year 5710 (1950). Apart from this, he instituted a speech-fast every Monday and Thursday, every *Rosh Chodesh* eve, on most Shabbosos, and during the forty days between *Rosh Chodesh* Elul and *Motza'ei* Yom Kippur. This famous regimen led other Torah scholars to attempt to follow in his footsteps and refrain from speech at specified times.

His Rebbetzin, Leah Schwadron, was able to transfer from her parents' home to her own the concept of being content with little in the way of material riches. She expanded R' Sholom's four cubits of halachah with a boundless joy. Her wisdom and nobility built a spiritual palace within their modest abode.

Anyone who set foot in R' Sholom's home saw a small, plain residence. "Even when we already had three children, I still slept on a mattress on the floor," R' Sholom related. And yet, R' Sholom was known far and wide for the joy in life that is reserved for the great men in Israel. He attributed it all to his good wife's merit. It is of women like Rebbetzin Leah that it says, "And it will be good for them in the World to Come!"

Learning and Teaching

IMMEDIATELY AFTER HIS WEEK OF *SHEVA BERACHOS*, R' SHOLOM joined the famous "Ohel Torah" *kollel*, under the leadership of R' Aharon (Brisker) Biyalistoki. There he became acquainted with such future lights of Torah as R' Shmuel HaLevi Wosner, R' Eliezer Waldenberg, author of the *Tzitz Eliezer*, and others. Some years later, R' Yosef Sholom Elyashiv joined the *kollel*, and R' Sholom soon grew attached to him, sharing with him a bond of their mutual love for Torah. In the introduction to his first written work, R' Sholom expresses his gratitude to R' Elyashiv for his help in composing the *sefer*, and heaps great praise on him as an outstanding *talmid chacham* and profound thinker.

R' Sholom dancing beside R' Yosef Sholom Elyashiv

During those years, R' Sholom taught an early-evening Gemara class to local residents of Sha'arei Chesed, after which he regularly learned with his illustrious brother-in-law, R' Shlomo Zalman Auerbach. These sessions lasted until the small hours of the night, and were instrumental in forging a powerful bond between the two. R' Sholom considered himself a student of his brother-in-law, and did not make a halachic decision without consulting with him. R' Shlomo Zalman, on his part, felt a deep friendship for R' Sholom, a friendship based on their boundless love for Torah.

R' Sholom left the *kollel* in the year 5708 (1948). From that period onward, he would travel to consult with the Chazon Ish on all matters that gave him doubt.

"Always, when we parted, the Chazon Ish would bless me, *'V'ha'amidu talmidim harbei* — May you establish many students,'" R' Sholom related.

In the year 5697 (1937), R' Chanoch Henoch Tovoleski started an evening class for Sha'arei Chesed householders, and appointed R' Sholom to deliver the Gemara *shiur* each evening.

He would continue to deliver it for the next quarter century.

THE YEAR 5703 (1943) SAW R' SHOLOM JOIN THE STAFF OF Yeshivah Tiferes Tzvi as the *mashgiach ruchani* (spiritual supervi-

A New Role sor). The position gave him an important influence over numerous young souls. This was where R' Sholom began to "establish many students."

He had the look of a *mashgiach*, former students of the yeshivah remember. He would stroll up and down the *beis midrash*, passing among the students while deeply immersed in his own learning. The mere sight of him had a powerful impact on the boys. Another lasting impression came from his talks, which remained etched in their hearts and their memories.

"Whenever we entered the *beis midrash*," one such student recalls, "what did we see? R' Schwadron was either learning with his friend, R' Ezra Brizel, a *maggid shiur* at the yeshivah, or writing down his own original Torah thoughts. From time to time, when it became necessary, he would lift his eyes to look at someone — and that boy quickly improved."

These were the days when R' Sholom was also involved in the difficult task of preparing the fiery talks of R' Leib Chasman for publication. R' Sholom wrote them down during his rebbe's lifetime, and received R' Leib's approval to print them. In the year 5711 (1951), he completed the first section of the *Ohr Yahel*.

R' SHOLOM INVESTED AN ENORMOUS AMOUNT OF LABOR IN preparing the works of his grandfather, the Maharsham, for publi-

A Special Desire cation. The great *Oholei Shem* was published in the year 5706 (1946), and comprised two sections. The first was made up of the Maharsham's responsa and his commentary on the *Shulchan Aruch*, which had never before appeared in print; the second section consisted of R' Sholom's thoughts and explanations on these responsa. He had asked the Chazon Ish, "I have a special desire to work on my grandfather's manuscript. Am I worthy of doing this?" The Chazon Ish encouraged him to satisfy this craving.

Subsequently, R' Sholom toiled long years and sleepless nights over the *Shulchan Aruch*, gearing his study to the Maharsham's

Giving a shiur at Yeshivas Oholei Shem — a yeshivah for Sefardic young men

manuscript, stage by stage. After R' Sholom departed this world, the *Oholei Shem* was reprinted, together with many of his own additional writings.

IN THE YEAR 5710 (1950), R' SHOLOM WAS ASKED TO SERVE AS *Rosh Yeshivah* for Yeshivah Mekor Chaim, a large *beis midrash* tar-

The Rosh Yeshivah geted specifically for boys of Sephardic background. The student body was made up of the sons of immigrants from such countries as Morocco, Iraq, India, Libya, etc. Mekor Chaim was opened through the Chazon Ish's initiative and with the support of the Brisker Rav. R' Sholom would serve there for 10 tears.

R' Sholom taught the highest *shiur.* The yeshivah attained a fine reputation, attracting boys from older and more well-established yeshivos. Each student maintained a personal bond with R' Sholom, a bond that often lasted 30 or 40 years. It was a moving sight to see former Mekor Chaim students grieving over their former *Rosh Yeshivah's* passing. One well-known Torah scholar, and former student, who serves in an important rabbinical post today, came to comfort R' Sholom's daughters as they sat *shivah* for their father. The man did not say much. He just stood in the doorway and cried.

In his succah, with talmidim from Yeshivah Mekor Chaim

In Yeshivah Mekor Chaim, and later as *mashgiach* of Yeshivah Tiferes Tzvi, R' Sholom's impact on the impressionable students was a powerful and lasting one. Once, he entered the *beis midrash* in the middle of the morning learning session, in time to see a certain student drop his head onto his Gemara, struggle to lift it, and continue learning. A few minutes later, the same thing happened all over again. R' Sholom approached him.

"What's the matter?" he asked. "Don't you feel well?"

R' Sholom with R' Moshe Shimon Weintraub at the wedding of R' Yosef Ber Sholom, a talmid of Yeshivah Mekor Chaim

"Yes, yes, I'm fine, *baruch Hashem*," the student answered quickly. "Everything's all right."

"In that case, why do you keep falling asleep on your *shtender*?"

The student explained. "Last night, the *mashgiach* [R'

Sholom] gave us a talk about how precious the Torah is, painting such a vivid picture that, afterwards, I just couldn't help staying up all night to learn. That's why I am falling asleep now."

R' Sholom sent the boy to bed at once.

Another Tiferes Tzvi student, R' Yisrael Aharon Kupshitz, tells this tale:

It was dusk, and Shabbos was nearly over. R' Sholom walked to the yeshivah from his home in Sha'arei Chesed to deliver a *mussar* shmuess to the students. The month was Elul.

The electric lights had not yet been turned on, and R' Sholom spoke in the dark about the great light of Elul. *HaKadosh Baruch Hu*, he declaimed, does not spend his time watching the thousands of angels, stars, and heavenly hosts. He turns His eyes on the poor man, the downtrodden, the individual who trembles at His word. R' Sholom went on to expand on this theme as his students sat spellbound, touched to the core. Then came the moment when the *mashgiach* asked them all to recite with him the verse upon which his speech had been constructed. The boys responded with such fervent shouts that a couple of neighbors came running in to see what had happened. "We thought maybe a fire had broken out!" one of them gasped.

R' Sholom possessed the "magical" key that unlocked his students' hearts and ignited in them a burning aspiration to walk the road that his eloquence painted for them.

"The Chofetz Chaim said that a yeshivah needs three things in order to succeed," R' Avraham Toker says. "A proper location (i.e., far from the bustling city center), good nourishing food, and a *Rosh Yeshivah* to serve as a personal example outside of the framework of the learning itself. (The Alter of Slobodka disagreed with the Chofetz Chaim on the necessity of the first condition.)

"R' Sholom, who taught us in Tiferes Tzvi, served as an example with unusual influence. It was a difficult time, with young men

R' Sholom speaking at a simchah. At right are R' Elyah Lopian and R' Chaim Chaikel Militzki

joining groups to fight for Israel's defense, then the establishment of the State and all that came afterwards. How many of us remained in 'Talmud Torah?' Even without his sermons ... R' Sholom Schwadron was a magnet that drew one into the edifice of Torah."

The year 5710 (1950) saw the illustrious R' Eliyahu Lopian come to live in *Eretz Yisrael.* With alacrity, R' Sholom formed a bond of Torah and *mussar* with that great figure, meeting with him hundreds of times and traveling to Kfar Chassidim to consult with him on matters of Torah and piety. R' Eliyahu had a special appreciation for R' Sholom, and when he moved to Zichron Yaakov he took R' Sholom's son, Yitzchak, as a student in his yeshivah. R' Sholom was privileged to disseminate R' Eliyahu's teachings throughout the world by publishing his *Lev Eliyahu,* a work on which R' Sholom labored for many years.

THE BRISKER RAV URGED R' SHOLOM TO INVOLVE HIMSELF IN the spiritual rescue of Jewish children who had immigrated to

Extracurricular Activities Israel; R' Sholom subsequently became a vocal figure in Pe'ilim. His day was long and difficult, filled with meaning: In the mornings he taught Torah to his students at Yeshivah Mekor Chaim; in the afternoons he guided his boys as *mashgiach* of Yeshivah Tiferes Tzvi; any spare minute was used to toil over the manuscripts by R' Leib Chasman and the Maharsham, along with R' Sholom's own original thoughts; and then, above and beyond all this, he exerted his energies crying aloud for the masses of children from Yemen and Morocco who had come to *Eretz Yisrael.* Day and night he labored without cease, and this was after he had already taken ill, at the start of the year 5710 (1949), and required an enforced, three-month rest. Despite all this, in the year 5712 (1952), he inaugurated a regular lecture at the Zichron Moshe Shul, for the public's benefit.

These were the years in which he began to *daven* his famous *Mussaf* in the Chevron *beis midrash.* The Days of Awe received a new character; the yeshivah had always been aflame during these days, but now it burned even more brightly. R' Sholom's *davening* captured the hearts of a generation of young men. His voice resonated through the hearts of thousands of yeshivah students for tens of years, and continues to accompany them to this day. The tears he shed were absorbed by his listeners, providing a fertile soil from which piety and fear of Heaven might sprout.

His personal prayer was a source of inspiration as well. He once told a son-in-law, "With each child born to me, I never skipped a day praying for his success, and I never missed a day praying that he, too, would have children." R' Avraham Yosef Leizerson remembers R' Sholom's beautiful rendition of *Nishmas* at the Pesach Seder, as they all sat together at the table of his father-in-law, R' Chaim Leib Auerbach. The melody, the voice, and the devotion in the *tefillah* deeply moved all those who were present.

∽∽

It was the regular, Friday-night speech at the Zichron Moshe Shul that made R' Sholom the famous personality he became throughout Jerusalem. The talks always started with halachah and wound up with fiery, elevating *mussar* that touched the hearts of

R' Sholom with his brother-in-law, R' Shlomo Zalman Auerbach

the thousands who came to hear him over the years. R' Sholom became a beloved figure in Jerusalem, known as the *"Maggid* of Yerushalayim," or "Rebbe Sholom." His people loved him for stiffening their backbones, and for burnishing the image of those who devoted their lives to Torah.

For 25 years, as we have mentioned, R' Sholom delivered a *shiur* in Gemara. These classes were very popular, threaded through with the inevitable strands of *mussar*. Many, many families changed as a result of listening faithfully to what R' Sholom had to say. Their lives became monuments to Torah as they, their sons, their brothers and brothers-in-law, pored faithfully over the pages of the Gemara. R' Sholom made sure that the precepts of his beloved Torah were never far from their lips and never strayed from their hearts.

ONE OF R' SHOLOM'S CHIEF PLEASURES WAS SUBMITTING HIS character to painstaking scrutiny, subjugating the physical to the

Bending to His Will intellect, "breaking" his desires in favor of a higher purpose. There were periods when he jotted down his self-evaluations in notebooks: his current personal state, his lapses and how to repair them. As these notebooks testify, R' Sholom was the master of the *cheshbon hanefesh*. As he would often say, "Everyone — chassidim, *misnagdim,* those of a philosophical bent — agrees that man's purpose in this world is to subjugate his nature and rise above it."

There was one story he enjoyed relating:

> During the half-year that I stayed with R' Eliyahu Lopian in Kamenitz, there was an occasion when I cried over my spiritual state. As was his custom, R' Eliyahu was quiet as I spoke and did not interrupt. When I stopped talking, he asked, "Are you finished?" I answered in the affirmative, whereupon he stood up, took hold of my beard, and said, "R' Sholom! R' Sholom! If I only had a black beard like yours … If I had your black beard!" And he sat down.

"From these few words, I derived subject matter for many *shmuessen* [sermons]. I could still work to change whatever needed to be changed!

"I say this to young men to this day: 'Remember! Time is ahead of you! Remember your Creator in the days of your youth.'"

R' Sholom once said, in the name of R' Yitzchak Blazer: "When a man is young he is able, but unwilling. Then, when he grows old, he is willing, but unable."

He would also say, in the name of R' Eliyahu, "A person who does not crush his desires at a young age will find that they surround him in old age, even when his body would not naturally seek them out any longer. Even then, they run after him. [But one who accustoms himself to struggle and overcomes his nature, and educates himself — when he ages he will not leave this habit, but will continue to learn and grow.]"

Similarly, R' Sholom frequently quoted the Vilna Gaon on the verse, "*You raise the poor man from the dust and the destitute from the trash-heap.*" Hashem takes someone who is destitute of mitzvos and raises him from the dust of his own material nature, lighting up his eyes with Torah and mitzvos. The "trash-heap" refers to one who

defiles himself with sins and desires, then abandons them and weeps with remorse. Hashem will raise this individual, too, and seat him among the great men of our nation — our forefathers and prophets.

"To sit among the great!" R' Sholom would exclaim in excitement, when quoting this thought. "It *is* possible!"

R' Shlomo Noach Kroll relates:

I once met R' Sholom on a Bnei Brak street. He embraced me, then suddenly burst into tears. As he walked along the street, he had been absorbed in the *sugya* that deals with conquering the evil inclination, his emotions storming in response to his reflections. Upon meeting me, he burst out, "R' Shlomo Noach! I've already dealt with every *yetzer hara, baruch Hashem*. There's just one area where I haven't had luck yet [he went on to specify]." His own words brought fresh tears with them, and he cried there in the middle of Rechov Dessler in Bnei Brak.

Numerous times, R' Sholom would repeat, "The *mashgiach*, R' Nosson Wachtfogel, had the custom of saying, 'There is a difference between improving in spirituality and changing. It is possible to find people who elevate themselves, who improve and become better, greater, loftier, and more pleasant individuals. But to find a person who has *changed* — that is the truly precious thing.'"

The following is an excerpt from a talk delivered to Torah students:

R' Sholom pounded on his *shtender*. Man! Man is born into this world in order to break his nature. That is what chassidim say, what *misnagdim* say, what philosophical researchers say. This is man's purpose, all his life.

This reminds me of a story. It was related to me by one of the older boys at the Chevron Yeshivah — a true story.

A group of older yeshivah boys were sitting around a table, with R' Leib Chasman at its head. R' Leib asked, "Who has *shteiged* (worked diligently and elevated himself) most in the yeshivah?"

The young men offered their answers. One mentioned

this name, another mentioned that. At each student's name, the *mashgiach* shook his head. "No, no, no!" Finally, he smiled. "You know who has *shteiged* more than anyone else? The yeshivah's *shammas*, R' Yisrael!" (The name has been changed.)

"When R' Yisrael originally arrived at the yeshivah, he was held tightly in the grip of his character traits. It was difficult to have a normal conversation with him because he was so rigorous and stern. But slowly, slowly, he threw away these traits — and changed! Whoever has known R' Yisrael in recent years knows that he is pleasant, obliging, eager to perform a kindness in every area. His piety is also beyond question; every morning he recites the *Bircas HaShachar* with devotion beside the *bimah* and the students answer *Amen*. A *tzaddik*. He performs many good deeds in secret, and returns his salary checks to the yeshivah's coffers."

Incidentally, R' Sholom, knowing that the *shammas* would not take money from the yeshivah, would send his daughters every *Rosh Chodesh* to smuggle money into R' Yisrael's house.

An American resident wrote the following in a letter:

I will always remember what happened to me on my first visit to *Eretz Yisrael*, on my first morning with R' Sholom. He told his daughter that they had a guest and asked her to run to the grocery store to buy him some wafers. He stressed that the wafers should be chocolate ones. Upon her return, he served me a cup of coffee along with a plate full of wafers. I ate the wafers and drank the coffee. R' Sholom also drank coffee, while sitting beside me.

Suddenly, he turned to me and asked, "Do you like wafers?" I answered in the affirmative. He said, "I also like them." Then, after a brief pause, he went on to add, "So I don't eat them!"

This revelation both astonished and bewildered me. The wafers were strictly kosher, bearing a very good *hash-*

gachah. Why, then, wouldn't he eat them if he liked them? What could be wrong?

I expressed my wonder. Then he explained the approach of the *mussar* masters, especially in Kelm, who taught the importance of breaking one's desires even in the realm of the permissible, because it is vital to limit our pleasures in this world and because a man should train himself to be his own master so that he will not come to transgress. "If I won't eat something that is kosher *lemehadrin*, I certainly won't eat something that is questionable or forbidden."

～～

In summary, let us quote R' Sholom's thoughts on the person who struggles to gain a foothold in Torah and mitzvos. In our prayers on the High Holy Days, we say, "May it be Your Will that I do not sin any more, and that which I have already sinned, erase in Your great mercy, but not through bad suffering and sickness."

R' Sholom asked, "Is there such a thing as *good* suffering and *good* sickness?"

And the answer is — "Yes!" For example, suppose a person desires to learn Torah but keeps falling asleep. He struggles to stay awake and continues learning, as well as *davening* and performing the other mitzvos. This is suffering — but it is good suffering. From this kind of suffering we accomplish both in this world and for the next. Similarly, there are "good" illnesses: "I am sick with love for You." This kind of sickness is sweet.

While "good" suffering may be difficult to bear, it holds all manner of wonderful rewards. Step by step, it fills the individual with happiness and true spiritual wealth.

"I DON'T REMEMBER MUCH OF WHAT HE SPOKE ABOUT," ONE young yeshivah man relates. "Rabbi Schwadron would come once **Person to** each year to speak at a party in Yeshivah Ohr Torah. **Person** Other students would join us from nearby Yeshivah Tiferes Moshe. Exactly what he said I don't recall —

Visiting R' Yehudah Zev Segal in Manchester

but I can't forget what he always did at the end of the party. Every year, he would go to the kitchen doorway, look for the cooks, and thank them warmly for their efforts."

⤙⤚

On the infrequent occasions when R' Sholom was ill or had to attend a family *simchah*, he would appoint a Torah scholar to speak in his place at the Zichron Moshe Shul on Friday night. On one occasion, when the audience saw a stranger standing in R' Sholom's usual place, most of them got up and left the shul. This distressed R' Sholom deeply. On the following Shabbos, he railed at his listeners. "Where is respect for a *talmid chacham*? Where is *derech eretz* and good manners — to look a man in the face and immediately turn your backs on him? And only because he doesn't happen to be 'Sholom Schwadron'?!"

(as told by R' Avraham Tovoleski)

⤙⤚

One Rosh Hashanah, as R' Sholom prepared to lead the congregation gathered in the Chevron *beis midrash*, he felt ill and decided to ask someone to take his place. The decision was made just minutes before *Mussaf* was due to begin. His daughter, who was there with him, had already taken her place in the women's section. (This was Rebbetzin Segal, who, from the time of her mother's passing, ran her father's home and cared devotedly for all his needs.) R' Sholom was afraid that when she heard a strange voice leading the service, she would be consumed with worry for the several moments it would take her to ascertain her father's condition. Accordingly, R' Sholom sent his grandson to find his daughter before the start of *Mussaf*, to let her know that there was nothing to worry about: He wasn't leading the *davening* because he felt only *slightly* unwell.

He was a person who thought of others — usually, more than himself. One of the most wonderful characteristics of R' Sholom was the way he would walk long distances to hear young Torah scholars speak, in order to gladden and encourage them.

(as told by R' Yitzchak Ezrachi)

His daughter once told him that she had purchased a new baby carriage, and asked if he knew of anyone who needed the old one.

"I want to get the mitzvah of passing it on to someone in need."

R' Sholom asked, "Why not give some poor person the *new* one?"

Typical R' Sholom!

"He was a complete palace," R' Baruch Mordechai Ezrachi says. "Imagine a fool who enters a multi-storied palace, and on his way out points at one handsome marble stone in the hallway, saying, 'Here! Look at this!' What was R' Sholom? A *tzaddik*? A *gaon*? Or something else? R' Sholom was a complete palace, great in wisdom, in Torah, in *yirah*, and in *mussar*. They dubbed him 'the Jerusalem *Maggid*,' but that was not the whole man. R' Sholom — a complete and beautiful palace! Among his other vast treasures, he was also a '*maggid*.'"

A Word to the Wise

WHEN STILL A YOUTH, R' SHOLOM ONCE ASKED R' LEIB Chasman whether he should busy himself with communal service. The *mashgiach* did not answer his question directly. All he said was, "Why did R' Meir Shapiro of Lublin succeed in communal service? Because he was a great man."

R' Sholom Asks a Question

DECADES AGO, WHILE STILL A STUDENT IN THE CHEVRON Yeshivah, R' Sholom came across a fellow student who was strolling along the dormitory corridor, whistling. R' Sholom chided him.

"Where does it say that I can't whistle?" the student demanded. Then, mockingly, he added, "If you have a problem with my whistling, go ask the Chazon Ish!" (The Chazon Ish had already immigrated to *Eretz Yisrael* by that time and was living in Bnei Brak.)

"I did it!" R' Sholom later related. "I got permission, and traveled to Bnei Brak. I asked the Chazon Ish — is whistling permitted or forbidden? [Author's Note: It is unclear whether he was inquiring about whistling in general, or specifically on Shabbos.]

The Chazon Ish answered. "There are some things that can't be labeled "permissible" or "prohibited." You have to sense them."

R' SHOLOM USED TO QUOTE THE VERSE, "*AND YOU SHALL NOT stray after your hearts and after your eyes.*" It does not say, "Stray *in* your hearts or *with* your eyes." He repeated the following explanation, which he had heard from R' Dushinsky: "If a person mistakenly strays — if he thinks impure thoughts in his heart or sees what he ought not see — then, the Torah instructs him, he should take care not to *continue* thinking those thoughts or seeing those things *afterwards*.

After the Fact

"I ONCE SPOKE WITH R' LEIB CHASMAN," R' SHOLOM RELATED, "about taking on a specific goal before the *Yom HaDin*. R' Leib instructed me to think and search for some small area in which I might improve and strengthen myself — an area that was very clear and that carried along with it a good opportunity for success.

A Steadfast Goal

"When he finished talking, he suggested that I take some time to think about it carefully, and then return and tell him when I had selected a clear goal.

"The next day, I went back to him and said: 'I have thought about it and I have found something that I'm sure of.'

"R' Leib said, 'Now take off *half* of that, and take the remainder upon yourself. The goal must be rock-steady. Whoever undertakes a goal and does not stick to it — alas for him.'"

◦◦

R' Shlomo Noach Kroll once related:

R' Sholom was in the confidence of great masters of *mussar* such as R' Eliyahu Lopian and others, though he generally revealed no more than a drop from those encounters. R' Sholom was the epitome of modesty, and scrupulously avoided talking much about himself.

On one occasion, R' Sholom yielded to my pleas and brought me to R' Eliyahu Lopian's room. I stayed for an hour, and we discussed a number of things. In the middle of my visit there came a knock on the door. A man came in with a *sefer* that he offered to sell to R' Eliyahu Lopian.

Turning to the newcomer, R' Eliyahu said, "Reb Yid, look at the *sefarim* in my bookcases. There aren't that many of them, and yet I have not yet gone through them all. I probably won't have time to look into this one, either. I'm old. This *sefer* would end up as an inheritance. I won't buy the book," he ended, on a note of apology. R' Sholom, listening to this exchange, was visibly moved.

Our conversation resumed. During its course, R' Eliyahu told a story: "When the Maharam of Padua was still a youth, in the city of Brisk, he was already known as an *iluy*. One of the city's prosperous men wished to take him as a husband for his daughter. The Maharam came to the man's house to meet the girl.

"In those days," R' Eliyahu continued, "the custom was not as it is today, to serve a cup of tea with the tea and sugar already inside. They just brought a cup of hot water to the table, a spoon, tea leaves, and sugar. The poor young man marveled at the sight. He did not know what to do with so many ingredients. He thought about it, made up his mind, and acted in accordance with his understanding: He drank the water, then ate the sugar separately. Not knowing what the spoon was for, he assumed it was for eating the tea leaves, and proceeded to do so.

"The girl was amazed. 'I saw that he was going to be a great *talmid chacham*,' she said. 'But he is not what I would call a man. I won't marry him.'

Years later, her father learned that that same rejected suitor was none other than the Maharam of Padua, one of the foremost Torah luminaries of the time. His heart broke in anguish."

R' Eliyahu concluded: "How great was their love of Torah then! Even though the father thought the young man uncivilized, because he knew that he was a great *talmid chacham*, his distress over the loss broke his heart."

R' Sholom used to tell of the time he went out with R' Eliyahu Lopian to collect money for a certain charitable cause. "We were walking in the Geulah neighborhood when R' Eliyahu suddenly stopped, leaned on his cane, and said, "R' Sholom, do you know what the difference is between a person who gives *tzedakah* and a person who gets others to give *tzedakah*? The one who gives is doing something for himself as well, while the collector does it only for others. The one who gives is heaped with praise, while the collector is heaped with scorn. The first gives money, while the second gives time — and time is life."

R' SHOLOM RELATED THE FOLLOWING:

Fear of Falling The women in Jerusalem used to wear wooden slippers, known as *kalatehs*. The local bathhouse / *mikveh* in Sha'arei Chesed purchased tens of such pairs of slippers to prevent bathers from slipping on the wet floors.

On one occasion, an American Jew entered the *mikveh* and noticed that the Tchebiner Rav was not wearing slippers. "Why aren't you wearing *kalatehs*?" he asked repeatedly. Finally, the Rav answered: "I'm afraid of slipping."

When the Rav left the bathhouse, R' Sholom followed

R' Sholom at a pidyon haben

him into the street." Was the Rav afraid of 'slipping' — on the prohibition against wearing women's clothing?'

"Yes, yes," the *gaon* answered.

R' Sholom derived great satisfaction from his success in plumbing the depths of that great man's pithy answer.

THE FOLLOWING IS A LITTLE-KNOWN STORY OF R' SHOLOM'S, which he heard from R' Yaakov Teitelbaum, who heard it from the

Until the Last Minute

Butshasher Rebbe's son:

"My father," said the Butshasher Rebbe's son," "was extremely careful with regard to wine, going to extremes in his stringencies regarding its preparation and storage. He used to make his own wine, tending to the grapes in a closed room without windows so that no non-Jew should even see the wine. If he had to travel anywhere with his jugs of wine, he would cover them with several layers so that no gentile would touch them. He would take extraordinary degrees of caution.

"I once asked him, 'Father, why are you so careful about wine?' And he answered, 'It has been revealed to me that the purpose of my *tikkun* (correction) in this world is in the matter of *yayin nesech*. I was already in the world, and have been returned here for this purpose.' Apparently, in a previous *gilgul*, he had a defect in this area.

"When my father lay on his sickbed, in his last hours his condition deteriorated rapidly, and a doctor was urgently summoned. Seeing his patient's condition, the doctor gave instructions to run to the nearest pharmacy and bring a certain medicine. Someone did so at once, returning with the drug in hand.

"The medicine was poured into a spoon and introduced into the patient's mouth. Suddenly, my father spat it out. Raising his voice, with his last remaining strength he cried out, '*Oy! Yayin nesech!*' — and his soul left his body.

"Afterwards, someone was sent back to the pharmacy, where the pharmacist divulged that 20 percent of that medicine had been wine."

To this extent, don't trust yourself to your dying day! It says in the *Midrash Tanchuma* that one chassid used the version, "Do not trust yourself until your old age," but Heaven showed him his mistake....

"ONCE, WHEN I WENT TO CONSULT WITH THE BRISKER RAV," R' Sholom related, "the Rav pointed at a nearby chair and instructed

Mein Benkel

me to sit down. I discerned at once that it was the Rav's chair, the one on which he himself was accustomed to sit.

"I was at a loss. To sit on the chair — how was that possible? And yet, how was it possible to take another one? The Rav had ordered me to sit, and one does not refuse a *gadol*! With no choice, and filled with the awe of reverence, I sat in his chair. The Rav spoke with me at length, and then I left the house. As I walked down the street, I was gnawed with doubt: Had I done the right thing? Pangs of conscience stayed with me all that day. I decided to ask a 'great man' what the correct behavior would be.

"But whom should I ask? I considered, and then made my decision: Tomorrow I would go to ask the Brisker Rav.

"In the meantime, I had a message to pass on from the Brisker Rav to the Tchebiner Rav. I went to the Tchebiner Rav's house, and later, before we parted, I posed my question about the Brisker Rav's chair. Was this a case of 'one does not refuse a *gadol*'?

"Citing a *Tosafos*, the Tchebiner Rav replied to the effect that the rule of not refusing a *gadol* did not apply to the case of sitting in his personal chair."

(Incidentally, R' Sholom remarked on a habit of the Tchebiner Rav: Whenever R' Sholom returned from delivering a message from the Rav to some other Torah leader, the Rav would ask, "What did you see there?" He was most interested in the personal behavior of the *gedolim*. Always, when R' Sholom mentioned a specific behavior, the Rav would immediately comment, "That's from this Gemara, or that *Tosafos*, or they learned it from this specific halachah in the *Shulchan Aruch*, etc.")

"The next day," R' Sholom continued, "I went back to see the Brisker Rav and began to discuss with him what had happened [the day before]. As soon as he understood what I was referring to, the Rav raised his voice dismissively. *'Ah, mein benkel? Mein benkel?'* (My chair?) He continued in this vein, with disdain and amazing humility — his voice implying both a question and an answer — as he repeated the same self-abnegating words 13 times: Ah! *Mein Benkel?'"*

It is worthwhile to note here that, according to those closest to the Brisker Rav, it was almost unheard of for a visitor to be accorded the honor of being invited to sit in his personal chair. R' Sholom had earned an extraordinary place in the Rav's esteem.

IN ONE OF HIS SERMONS, R' SHOLOM QUOTED THE WORDS, "IF A Rav resembles an angel of G-d, seek to learn Torah from him. And

No Change

if not, do not seek." What is the meaning of the term *malach Hashem* — an Angel of G-d?

The world gives this interpretation: In the same way that we have no concept of what an angel is, if you lack the same concept of what your rabbi is, then you may seek to learn Torah from him.

R' Zevulun Graz had a different explanation. "An angel," he said, "is forever unchanging. There is no time when it is not an angel. That, too, is a Rav: one without change!

"The words *'b'chol beisi ne'eman hu* — Of all My house, he is faithful' — refer to Moshe *Rabbeinu*. The *Ibn Ezra* translates the word *ne'eman*, faithful, as 'unchanging.' To be faithful is not to change. This was the level that Moshe reached in his service of Hashem.

"And, to a certain extent, we have been privileged to witness this same trait in the Torah leaders of our own time. On weekdays, on Shabbos, on Yom Kippur, on Purim — their behavior has been the same. The same fear of Heaven, diligence in Torah, and scrupulous behavior has characterized these luminaries."

The following is an excerpt from a letter that was found among R' Sholom's possessions. Written by R' Aryeh Zev Gurwitz, it contains a number of facts about his father-in-law, R' Eliyahu Lopian. R' Gurwitz yielded to R' Sholom's pleas and mailed him the letter from Gateshead, England.

I MUST CONFESS IN SHAME THAT, TO OUR SORROW, WE KNEW little of his *middos* and his stature. He [R' Eliyahu] tried always to

Know Him from Afar
conceal his ways, and in this he was successful, even with the members of his own household. The time he spent inside his house was very minimal. When here in London, he would spend the majority of his time, until late at night, at the yeshivah. Upon his return home, he would generally absorb himself in a *sefer*, speaking to the household only when addressed. Even at the Shabbos or Yom Tov table he did not speak much, just listened to the others' conversation and inserted a comment from time to time. From what I've heard, this was his way in Kelm as well: to remain a steady presence in the *beis midrash* or yeshivah, to the point that his family knew him only from a distance. They were in such awe of him that they did not dare converse with him much.

He was like a ladder resting on the ground with its head touching the sky. And because of this, those who did not lift their eyes to look upward, to his full height, saw only the part that rested on the ground.

Part of his greatness lay in the way he spoke to others on their own level, until he seemed like a simple person when speaking with them. Only men of stature themselves saw and understood that their thoughts were not his thoughts, and their ways were not his ways.

About his family history and childhood there is not much to say. His forebears were simple people but, apparently, very G-d-fearing. His father was forced to move to America but my father-in-law, then a youth, did not want to go with the family. He remained alone, bereft of his forebears.

His father remained in America for close to 50 years, and for all

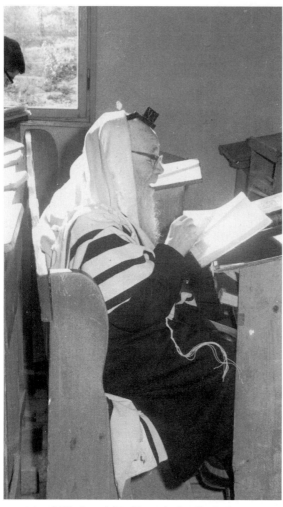

R' Elyah studying Chumash after Shacharis

those years he never tasted meat, because he did not rely on the *kashrus* in America.

I heard a story about [R' Eliyahu's] mother: Once, when traveling from a city to her home in the village, the skies suddenly darkened and a heavy rain began to fall. She got off the road to take shelter beneath a tree, but while she stood there a gentile man came along, wishing to hide from the rain under the same tree. Immediately suspecting a possible problem of *yichud*, she ran back to the road in the downpour.

After she left the tree, there was a boom of thunder and a flash of lightning — which hit the tree, killing the gentile who still stood beneath it.

⁓⁓

R' Eliyah Lopian's son-in-law continued: The family does not have many of [his] writings, as it seems to me he did not spend much of his time writing. His service took the form of labor of the heart — "And you shall inscribe it on the tablet of your heart." Everyone who knew him knew that all the great concepts and words of *mussar* that he would deliver did not emanate just from his mind and his memory, but came directly from the heart, buried so deep as to have become a part of him.

R' Elyah on Motza'ei Yom Kippur

I remember when he would deliver a sermon to masses of people in London during the *Yamin Nora'im*, and people would call him a *"malach Hashem,"* lamenting about whether it is possible for words emerging from such a pure heart to enter their own.

I heard something amazing about the time he was in the city. He established a yeshivah for young boys there, and some of the men with whom he dealt in this matter did not recognize his greatness, believing him to be like them. They thought he was concerned with running after honor and money. When he tried, with great effort, to open a dining room for the students, so that they might come to yeshivah on time for *davening* in the morning and then eat breakfast without the trouble of going back home, the *gabba'im* suspected him of self-interest. They thought that he wanted his own sons, who learned in the yeshivah, to enjoy a free breakfast. Their suspicions reached the extent that, although he assured them that his sons would not eat there, but only in their own home, there were several men who came to see for themselves, to check whether his sons were among those eating [in the communal dining room]. It was truly astonishing to see how blind people can be, to the point that they were unable to recognize his stature — even those who were near him.

⌒⌒

I heard from my wife that when the *gaon,* R' Aharon Baksht [who taught at the yeshivah in Kelm] found it necessary to return home for a short time, he asked my father-in-law to teach in his place while he was gone. R' Bakst left, and did not return; he was offered a rabbinical post which he accepted. My father-in-law was bound to the yeshivah ... and his family did not come to live with him in Kelm until much later. In the meantime, he lived at a friend's house, a pious man who served as one of the yeshivah's *gabba'im.*

When his family arrived, among them his daughter (my wife), she stayed in the same house where [her father] had been staying. She saw that the woman of the house, one of the righteous women who helped in supporting the yeshivah, did not cover her hair when in her own home. The girl asked her father why he did not rebuke [the woman] for this; and he, in his innocence, grew angry with her for suspecting the worst, saying that the woman was surely wearing a wig. The daughter took it upon herself to investigate the matter, and learned that it was no wig. When she informed her father of this, he said simply, "Believe me, I would not know what her face looks like."

Then, for the first time, she saw his greatness. It was unbelievable! He had lived in that house over the course of several months, speaking often to all the people there. Was it possible that he had never seen the woman's face? There are *tzaddikim* who don't look into women's faces, like the *gaon,* R' Baruch Ber Leibowitz, who turns his head to the side when talking to women, in order not to look at them. But he [R' Eliyahu] would stand and talk to them face-to-face, and despite this, his strength was so great that he did not see what he did not wish to see.

This helps us to understand what our Sages meant when they said that when *HaKadosh Baruch Hu* told Avraham, "Walk before Me and be complete," He was giving Avraham dominion over five parts of the body over which he had not reigned before. One of those parts was the eyes. In other words, not only can [a person] turn his head when he encounters something he should not see — in the manner of closing one's eyes — but he will not see it even when he is forced to stand right before it with his eyes open.

Because of this, I understood what I had heard about his great *talmid*, the *gaon* R' Mordechai Pogromansky, who was in Switzerland after the war working to rescue people from the camps. He worked together with several individuals, among them the great woman famous for the souls she rescued — Mrs. Recha Sternbuch. Once, as they talked about recognizing people's faces, he said that he possessed the ability to read people's deeds in their faces. The woman turned to him and asked, "And what do you see in my face?" Whereupon he answered, "Believe me, I have never seen your face all this time." Amazing! Apparently, he learned this skill from his great rebbe.

It is no wonder, as we mentioned earlier, that there were people surrounding him who did not recognize [R' Eliyahu] or his deeds. In everything, he acted like a simple man, without displaying any extraordinary behavior. He was involved with people, visiting homeowners who supported the yeshivah and chatting with members of their families, and they never knew that he was gazing at them from the heavens.

R' Elyah entering a dormitory room to awaken the talmidim

Such was not the case in Kelm. There, yeshivah leaders recognized his greatness and the level of his righteousness. I heard from his sons here that the yeshivah heads urged him always to be the *ba'al toke'a* on Rosh Hashanah, despite the fact that he was generally unsuccessful at blowing the shofar. Perhaps it was because of his fear of judgment [on that day], but most of the time after just a few blows he would have to be replaced. Still, they wanted him to begin the shofar-blowing every year, saying," A few *tekiyos* from R' Eliyahu is enough to sweeten our *Yom HaDin*."

The following is a letter written by R' Sholom, discussing his approach to learning.

Erev Shabbos Kodesh, Parashas Ha'azinu

I am approaching you in writing … because I have great reservations as to whether what I want to say to you is correct. Perhaps I am wrong. And even if you will find that I am right, you may be embarrassed, *chas v'shalom*. After all, I do not yet know your character that well. For these reasons, I have decided not to speak to you face to face, but rather to write to you. I will phrase myself in the form of a question, since I do not know — perhaps everything I wish to say is unnecessary.

That was my introduction!

Now, to the heart of the matter. I, for my part, am not happy with your learning according to the Brisker *derech*. Not that I am offering a general opinion on that approach to learning, because, as you know, I am

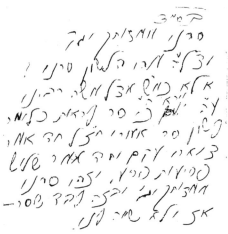

R' Sholom's last written mussar thought

well-versed in it, *baruch Hashem*. I am coming to you from an entirely different angle, however.

My mother told me, in my father's name, that *Chazal* say that *HaKadosh Baruch Hu* weeps over three types of people. Among them are: One who is capable of involving himself in Torah but does not involve himself, and one who is not able to involve himself in Torah but does so anyway. My father used to say that it is not difficult to understand why Hashem would cry over the first type, who is capable of learning Torah but does not. But in the case of a person who is not capable of learning but does so anyway, should there not be universal rejoicing? Why the weeping?

He offered a deep, and not awesome response, one that entails the absolute truth: We know that just as people's faces are not the same, so, too, are their opinions different. This is also true of their talents, their natures, etc.

Therefore, you have a man who has a good memory but poor understanding, so he is incapable of originating new Torah thoughts. Clearly, his portion in Torah should be to learn a great deal in order to be conversant with all of *Shas* — *Bavli, Yerushalmi, Rishonim, Acharonim*, etc. But if this person were to sit and learn one tractate every year or two, doing this by *"kvetching"* over each page, without being a man of deep understanding or original thought, what does he have left? Neither breadth of knowledge nor mental acuity. He will be left empty!

And there is the talented individual whose memory is not especially good but who possesses a sound understanding and the capacity for original thinking. His portion in Torah is to learn slowly, in order to take note of details, to plumb the depths and to come up with new ideas. This is what is known as being *involved* with Torah, because this is its essence: to understand and to intuit. The first approach was called *limud Torah*, the study of Torah. And this is the meaning of *"v'sein chelkeinu b'sorasecha* — and give us *our* portion in Torah"*: Each person has his own portion.

But what does the Satan, the *yetzer hara*, do? It switches our inclinations. It convinces one who is capable of involving himself in Torah, of understanding and originating, that he must hurry and "grab" 50 pages of Gemara a day, whether he grasps them or not. *HaKadosh Baruch Hu* weeps over such a person, who is capable of *involving* himself in Torah but only *learns* it. On the other hand, there is a person who should be "learning" Torah but chooses instead to "involve himself" in it, despite his limited abilities in this approach. For such a person, understanding follows on the heels of absorbing a breadth of knowledge, but the Satan comes and tells him, "What are you doing? Rushing to grab pages and swallowing them without understanding? This way, you will remain ignorant! It's better for you to 'kvetch' over each line — then you will become a great *talmid chacham!*" *HaKadosh Baruch Hu* weeps over this individual because he cannot become *involved* in Torah (he should rather learn it, as noted) and he does so anyway! It is truly amazing! All this, in short, I heard from my mother, in my father's name.

And now, I would like to add a few words for our own generation about our approach to learning. It is clear that for us, specifically, there is a need for [both approaches]. Every boy and young married yeshivah man, almost without exception, needs two sessions: one *seder* for learning *bekius* [that is, covering ground], and another for *iyun* [in-depth study].

This seems incontrovertible. We must discuss, however, the definition of *iyun* — what it is and how it should be learned — for here, too, abilities and natures differ among *bnei yeshivah*.

And now, my dear, to you! When I spoke to you in learning, I saw that you have made a change in your learning style. The first time we spoke, your approach was to embrace a broad approach, to learn and understand "around" a subject until you arrived at the point of the *sugya*. This approach, coupled with your diligence, led to your success. But now you have abandoned your "portion." You keep asking "What is this?" and answering "This is ..." In other words, *kvetching* ... and this is not suited to your abilities.

You know, very simply, that I want what is best for you — that you rise higher and higher in the study of our holy Torah. That is why I want to ask you one general question, which you should respond to and contemplate on your own:

a) How many tractates have you learned this year? And how

many times did you review them? Did you study them with the *Rishonim*? Which ones? And with the *Acharonim*? Which ones?

b) Have you come up with original Torah thoughts (*chiddushim*) this year? How many? Long ones, or short? And how many notebooks have you filled?

I will respond, in place of receiving an answer: a) If you learned at least five tractates this year, with the *Rishonim*, such as the *Rif*, the *Ran*, *Nimukei Yosef*, and *Rosh*, and with the main *Acharonim*, and b) if you originated at least five complex pieces of broad scope [original thoughts, not mere reviews of the *sugya* or the positions of *Rishonim* and *Acharonim*] as was your style then, each one filling at least two or three medium-sized notebooks of the kind you used previously...

If you have done that, then everything I have written here has no validity, and that's it! But if this is not the case, then it is a sign that you have abandoned *your* Torah portion. You have begun to stand in one place and to dig deep! As a parable, you have taken an airplane and made a tractor out of it! And that is not suited to your nature.

The suggestion is simple; abandon the way you are currently studying. Take a partner and learn in the manner appropriate for you, for your nature and your abilities — with breadth, with scope, originating *chiddushim*, to learn, and to understand from all sides until you arrive at the point of the *sugya* in all its aspects. And if you write down original thoughts, don't agonize over whether or not they are 100 percent correct, etc. Then you will call and Hashem will answer, and you will merit rising ever higher in Torah and in *yirah*, as you wish to do — and as your devoted one, who wants what's best for you, wishes for you.

(Signed)
Sholom Mordechai HaCohen

The funeral

Credits

We would like to present a list of the nearly 60 people from whom we heard facts and stories that added much to this attempt to paint an accurate picture of R' Sholom's life. There were some who provided rare photographs, and others who gave of their time to review the material, to comment and to edit.

Among them are Torah leaders, some of them friends of R' Sholom's youth, may Hashem bless them with long life! All are Torah scholars and men of G-d who had a specific connection to R' Sholom. Unfortunately, it is not possible for us to provide titles appropriate to their lofty qualities. We have listed the names in the order in which we interviewed them:

R' Meir Soloveitchik, R' Avraham Erlanger, R' Alter Gelernter, R' Yitzchak Peretz, R'Shlomo Zalman Reichman, R' Shimshon Harari, R' Avraham Tucker, R' Yisrael Grossman, R' Mordechai Auerbach, R' Aharon Dovid Dinar, R' Yaakov Auerback, R' Avraham Horowitz, R' Yehuda Shapiro, R' Moshe Mordechai Shulzinger, R' Shlomo Noach Kroll, R' Yehudah Edes, R' Avraham Dov Auerbach, R' Avraham Tobolsky, R' Shmuel Aharon Isaacov, R' Dovid Klein, R' Yeshaya Lapin, R' Baruch Mordechai Ezrachi, R' Menachem Tzvi Berlin, R' Reuven Karlenstein, R' Avraham Tzvi Taub, R' Sholom Ber Lifshitz, R' Meir Gruzman, R' Dovid Mor, R' Menachem Cohen, R' Avraham Kahn, R' Yom Tov Lipa Rakow, R' Tzvi Zelzenik, R' Chaim Rosner, R' Ezra Novak, R' Shraga Plonchik, R' Yechezkel Schlaff, R' Aharon Breish, R' Chaim Brim, R' Yehuda Shenker, R' Yisrael Aharon Kupshitz, R' Moshe Kupshitz, R' Chaim Dovid Ackerman, R' Zev Edelman, R' Yisrael Druck, R' Meir Stern (whose assistance was invaluable), R'

Kalman Krohn, R' Aryeh Krohn, R' Pesach Krohn, R' Gedalia Sheinen, R' Yehuda Landi, R' Tzvi Tauber, R' Naftali Levi, R' Avraham Yeshaya Wolfe, R' Yeshaya Horowitz, R' Dov Cohen, R' Moshe Segal, R' Nechemya Karlinsky, R' Avraham Yosef Leizerson, R' Shlomo Stensel.

We discussed some details with the *Gaon* R' Chaim Kanievsky. R' Chaim Shenker, R' Yaakov Meir Cohen, R' Moshe Dessler, R' Tzidkiyahu Cohen, and R' Yisrael Gliss (who donated his wonderful treasury of photos and anecdotes).